3<u>00</u>

P9-DNA-211

About Island Press

Island Press is the only nonprofit organization in the United States whose principal purpose is the publication of books on environmental issues and natural resource management. We provide solutions-oriented information to professionals, public officials, business and community leaders, and concerned citizens who are shaping responses to environmental problems.

In 2000, Island Press celebrates its sixteenth anniversary as the leading provider of timely and practical books that take a multidisciplinary approach to critical environmental concerns. Our growing list of titles reflects our commitment to bringing the best of an expanding body of literature to the environmental community throughout North America and the world.

Support for Island Press is provided by The Jenifer Altman Foundation, The Bullitt Foundation, The Mary Flagler Cary Charitable Trust, The Nathan Cummings Foundation, The Geraldine R. Dodge Foundation, The Charles Engelhard Foundation, The Ford Foundation, The Vira I. Heinz Endowment, The William and Flora Hewlett Foundation, The W. Alton Jones Foundation, The John D. and Catherine T. MacArthur Foundation, The Andrew W. Mellon Foundation, The Charles Stewart Mott Foundation, The Curtis and Edith Munson Foundation, The National Fish and Wildlife Foundation, The National Science Foundation, The New-Land Foundation, The David and Lucile Packard Foundation, The Pew Charitable Trusts, The Rockefeller Brothers Fund, Rockefeller Financial Services, The Surdna Foundation, The Winslow Foundation, and individual donors.

Confronting
Suburban
Decline

Confronting Suburban Decline

Strategic Planning for Metropolitan Renewal

William H. Lucy
David L. Phillips

ISLAND PRESS
Washington, D.C. • Covelo, California

Copyright © 2000 by Island Press

All rights reserved under International and Pan-American Copyright Conventions. No part of this book may be reproduced in any form or by any means without permission in writing from the publisher: Island Press, 1718 Connecticut Avenue, N.W., Suite 300, Washington, DC 20009.

ISLAND PRESS is a trademark of The Center for Resource Economics.

Library of Congress Cataloging-in-Publication Data
Lucy, William H.
    Confronting suburban decline : strategic planning for metropolitan renewal / William H. Lucy and David L. Phillips.
        p. cm.
Includes bibliographical references (p.) and index.
    ISBN 1-55963-770-6 (pbk. : alk. paper)
    1. Suburbs—United States. 2. Suburbs—United States—Case studies.
3. Urban policy—United States. 4. Metropolitan areas—United States.
5. United States—Social conditions—1960– I. Phillips, David L. II.
Title.
    HT352.U6 L83 2000
    307.1'216'0973—dc21

                                                    99-050952

Printed on recycled, acid-free paper

Manufactured in the United States of America
10 9 8 7 6 5 4 3 2 1

Contents

List of Figures, Tables, and Maps

Figures

Tables

Maps

Preface

Alan Campbell, when he was dean of the Maxwell School of Syracuse University, told colleagues and students that if academics want to be listened to by public officials, they need to count things. If they come up with some useful numbers, public officials also might tolerate hearing some theory and policy proposals, he counseled.

Here we offer some numbers, because we would like to be listened to. Which numbers matter is illuminated by theories and concepts—theories and concepts here about strategic planning and the evolution of metropolitan areas. We bring three public policy themes to the table for discussion—sprawl, reinvestment, and disparities. Each theme is important in its own right. Each theme also illuminates the others. The reasons for too much sprawl in outer suburbia and exurbia are illuminated by the reasons for too little reinvestment in cities and older suburbs and for the large income disparities among local governments. Conversely, disparities are large and reinvestments are scarce because sprawl is excessive. These problems and explanations are intertwined.

Another goal here is to frame issues that matter to environmentalists, urbanists, economic developers, and politicians so that they may see more common interests and engage in more collaborative actions. In 1994, at an organizing meeting of the Partnership for Urban Virginia, we put a coalition-building proposition to the organizers, who included city managers, mayors, regional business leaders, and a few leaders of the Virginia Chamber of Commerce. Perhaps it would be useful, we suggested, to bring environmental groups into the organizing effort. Being committed to the Virginia version of politeness, the assembled organizers greeted this thought with dead silence—rather than ridicule. This alliance was committed, they said, to reducing income and resource disparities that disadvantage central cities and thereby encouraging regional economic growth by strengthening cities. They could not imagine, as we interpreted their silence, that environmentalists would be interested either in reducing disparities or in economic development. The city managers and mayors believed they needed business allies, because state legislators and the governor might listen to business. The local elected officials did not believe they would get a meaningful hearing at the state level on their own. Nor did they believe, we inferred, that environmentalists would get a hearing, or that business would be willing to negotiate with environmentalists. We believed those attitudes were shortsighted. Indeed, in the final negotiations with the governor two years later, business's priorities prevailed and the cities' goals fell to the side.

The numbers presented here have emerged in analyses conducted since 1988. The theories began to emerge in the early 1970s and first appeared in a journal in 1975 (Lucy 1975), which was ignored, appropriately perhaps, because it emphasized theories and concepts and contained no numbers. In 1988, we began analyzing city and suburban income trends for 1960, 1970, and 1980. We tried to explain as well as describe. It was a national study of 147 metropolitan areas, in which the overwhelming presence of cities declining in income relative to their suburbs was confirmed.

In 1992 we decided to examine within-state trends, looking at governance indicators: mainly fiscal, but also social. We discovered growing city-suburb income and poverty disparities in Virginia. When we examined a social indicator—the location of welfare and food stamp recipients—we found major increases in suburban recipients. These large increases were curious: they were inconsistent with income and population, and employment trends, and therefore, were inconsistent also with theories of spatial transitions.

We repeated the national city-suburb income ratio analysis in 1993, adding 1990 data, which yielded three decades of trends. We found more of the same: cities continued to decline relative to suburbs. There were a few puzzles; for instance, why was Newark, the worst-off city, seemingly doing better in 1990 than in 1980? And why had the city decline rate slowed rather than accelerated in the 1980s? If cities' social and economic problems were increasing, the exodus of the middle class from cities also should be increasing.

The Reagan-era devolution of many domestic policy responsibilities to the states had made more evident the key role of state policies affecting local governments, policies concerning land use regulation, finance, boundary adjustments, transportation, and elementary and secondary education. Nearly every commentary on cities included the critique that federal policies, especially interstate highways and deductions of property taxes and mortgage interest from federal income taxes, had subsidized suburbanization and, hence, the decline of cities. But this universal critique failed to discuss whether city problems varied and whether these federal policies, which allegedly affected every city, could account for variations in disparities. We extended the city-suburb income disparity analysis to all 320 metropolitan areas in 50 states. By studying 1990 data for all metropolitan areas, we obtained a sample large enough to provide clues about whether state policy might have a discernible impact on city-suburb income disparities. We discovered that in some states, cities were as well off as suburbs; in other states, cities were nearly as well off as suburbs. State policies, therefore, seemed more important than previously suspected.

In 1994, Katherine Imhoff, executive director of the Virginia Commission on Population Growth and Development, asked us to analyze metropolitan population and economic trends. We discovered high rates of farmland loss. These studies overlapped with a presentation by Myron Orfield in Washington, D.C. about the potential for mapping income, social, tax, and spending disparities among local government jurisdictions as part of a coalition-building process, similar to what had occurred in the Minneapolis–St. Paul region.

We thought the approach of comparing suburban jurisdictions would not work adequately in Virginia and Maryland, because counties are large and few other local governments exist, limiting potential to gather data and map conditions and trends. We thought a census tract analysis of income and other changes was needed. By doing that, we would discover whether some parts of suburbia were experiencing problems of population and income decline that for years had been familiar in central cities. We began these analyses in central cities and suburbs in Richmond, Hampton Roads, and Northern Virginia near Washington, D.C. Subsequently these analyses were extended for the Partnership for Urban Virginia.

Michael Pratt, director of the Center for Urban Development at Virginia Commonwealth University, supported research for this fledgling coalition of cities and businesses. He agreed to support our research showing how Virginia compared with metropolitan areas in other states. Such research could buttress our belief that suburban decline had become a national phenomenon. As such, similarities between problems in cities and suburbs would constitute a new basis for coalitions to support mutually beneficial public policy changes. This concept led to our study of income, population, poverty, racial, and housing transitions in 554 suburbs in 24 metropolitan areas across the United States, in which we confirmed widespread suburban decline, often faster than central city decline, as well as substantial income disparity polarization among suburbs.

In addition, the Partnership for Urban Virginia wanted to compare metropolitan economic development in Virginia with metropolitan areas in North Carolina and other states. The city officials and business leaders had been stimulated by David Rusk's ideas about elastic cities, which included the argument that strong regions required strong cities. Our study of economic trends in 59 metropolitan areas in the South confronted this question and led to somewhat different results.

Interspersed with these studies was consultation and then action on a strategic plan for Charlottesville. The Charlottesville City Council had been urged by city manager Cole Hendrix to prepare a strategic plan, but the council could not come to agreement about its goals or methods. During this process, the city manager suggested to us that Charlottesville's excess supply of small houses was an important reason why the city was in danger of losing much of its middle class. This suggestion led to development on our own of strategic planning analyses for Charlottesville, with special attention to the small dwelling problem and to the increase in free lunch–eligible students in the public schools. These discoveries became clues that led to generic interpretations of city and suburban decline.

A variety of projects followed, including a study for Fannie Mae about under-investment in neighborhoods whose pattern and design characteristics seemed to make them sustainable, analyses of sprawl in the Washington, D.C. region (for the Chesapeake Bay Foundation) and in the Piedmont of Virginia (funded by the Sacharuna Foundation), and a project for the City of Lynchburg about connections between middle-income housing purchases and perceptions of school conditions. These studies sharpened our awareness about connections between sprawl on the fringe and underinvestment in cities and middle-aged suburbs. In addition, we were influenced by transportation and development planner EM Risse's argument that metropolitan fringe development is typically much denser at subdivision scale than low-density detached housing, and by his discovery that sequential 10-mile radii contained similar housing with as much as a $100,000 difference in sales prices per unit, with prices falling with increases in distance from the center of the Washington, D.C. region. Discussions about these findings and other ideas led to our concept about the tyranny of easy development decisions explaining much about excessive sprawl and too little reinvestment.

By then it had become clear that income disparities, which we had started analyzing 10 years earlier, while important, should not obscure closely related problems. Other spatial elements—sprawl on the edge and reinvestment in the center and inner suburbs—also need distinct attention. This triumvirate of problems and policy goals contributed focus and glue that tied the analytic elements together.

Planners, policy analysts, and social and environmental scientists need a research agenda focusing on links among these elements—sprawl, disparities, and reinvestment. We have scratched the surface of links among these important subjects. They are useful scratches supported by numbers. We have been counting some useful things. More counting is needed—but also more theorizing, and more conversion of numbers and theories into viable public policies. A beginning has been made here, for which we have many people to thank for discussions, suggestions, reactions to drafts, financial support, and answers to specific questions, including Carolyn Adams, James Babcock, James Bacon, Roy Bahl, Neal Barber, Timothy Beatley, Robert Beauregard, Guthrie Birkhead, Warren Boeschenstein, David Bowers, Jay Brodie, John Bryson, Frank Buck, Alan Campbell, Jean Clary, Richard Collins, Errol Cowan, Warner Dallhouse, Bruce Dotson, James Eason, John Epling, Anton Gardner, Thomas Guterbock, John Hager, Cole Hendrix, Robert Herbert, Satyendra Huja, Katherine Imhoff, Joseph Julian, Patrick Kane, Hugh Keogh, Sylvia Lewis, Russell Linden, Louis Masotti, William McDonough, Robert McNergney, Tayloe Murphy, Eugene Nickerson, Garland Okerlund, James Oliver, Robert O'Neill, Ayse Pamuk,

K. C. Parsons, Kristin Pauley, Sandy Peaslee, Douglas Porter, Michael Pratt, Roger Richman, EM Risse, Jaquelin Robertson, Peter Salins, Joseph Schilling, Marshall Segall, James Self, Lloyd Smith, Daphne Spain, Carl Stenberg, Israel Stollman, David Varady, Jackson Walter, Elizabeth Waters, John Wheeler, Orion White, and Robert Yaro. In addition, we would like to thank the Chesapeake Bay Foundation, City of Lynchburg, Fannie Mae, Partnership for Urban Virginia, Sacharuna Foundation, University of Virginia School of Architecture, Virginia Commission on Population Growth and Development, and Virginia Commonwealth University Center for Urban Development.

We also acknowledge the assistance of Heather Boyer, editor at Island Press, the advice of peer reviewers, editorial assistant Joelle Herr, and production editorial supervisor Christine McGowan. The manuscript has been improved greatly due to their suggestions. In working on the numerous studies, we have been aided by many talented graduate students in the Master of Planning Program in the School of Architecture at the University of Virginia, including Thomas Brockenbrough, Matthew Dalbey, Michael Fenner, Jana Lynott, Kristin Mitchell, Michelle O'Hare, Christine Piwonka, Lori Savron, Douglas Stanford, and Steven Tredennick. Assistance in typing tables was provided skillfully by Bettie Hall.

Parts of several chapters were included in reports to sponsoring agencies, as referred to above. Much of the material in Chapter 3 was published in the *Journal of Landscape and Urban Planning* 1997, 36: 259–275 under the title "The Post-Suburban Era Comes to Richmond: City Decline, Suburban Transition, and Exurban Growth." Major variations on other material appeared in the *Journal of the American Planning Association,* 1994, under the title "If Planning Includes Too Much, Maybe It Should Include More"; in *Planning,* 1992, as "Recognizing Reality Is the First Step Toward a Solution"; in *Planning,* 1995, as "Why Some Suburbs Thrive"; and in *Colonnade,* 1996, as "The Post-Suburban Era: Declining Suburbs and Exurban Sprawl."

We would like to acknowledge the tolerance, and assistance, of our families—Sherry, Rachel, Zachary, Cybele, and Michael; Carole, Elizabeth, Andrew, and Cathleen—in dealing with disrupted schedules and our being less available than we would have liked.

Pictures are from the photography storehouse of settlement patterns by EM Risse, Synergy/Photography, Fairfax, Virginia, except for photographs of Alexandria, Charlottesville, Chesterfield County, Fairfax County, and Henrico County by David Phillips.

Confronting Suburban Decline

C h a p t e r   1

Strategic Planning and the Postsuburban Era

In the wake of the 1992 Los Angeles riots, political leaders trotted out the usual culprits to explain why the disturbances occurred. The Bush Administration initially blamed social programs of the 1960s and 1970s for destroying the family. Bill Clinton pointed to 12 years of neglect under Presidents Reagan and Bush. Neither claim illuminated causes or solutions. If family destruction was the problem, why weren't there thousands of riots across the country? If presidential neglect was the problem, what type of attention would have made a difference?

Riots in some respects are inexplicable, and generally include a spark, such as a controversial act by police, that strikes flammable material. One theory about why the situation was flammable is because poverty was so concentrated. Some areas have higher concentrations of problems than others do. While family conditions and presidential leadership are worth analysis, spatial decline involving demographic transitions and diminishing income relative to other areas will be our focus here. The most unrelenting, deepest, and least recognized problem manifested in the Los Angeles riots was how decisions by individuals and practices by private businesses, interacting with federal, state, regional, and local public policies, have guaranteed the creation of hundreds of crisis poverty ghettoes in metropolitan regions across the nation (Lucy 1992). Los Angeles's upheaval was a class and racial explosion grounded partially in the demise of thousands of industrial jobs in and near south-central Los Angeles. Impacts of those problems were exaggerated by large concentrations of poor individuals and families (Wilson 1987).

If poverty concentrations were confined within central cities, that would focus analytic efforts on conditions in cities. But by the 1990s, poverty concentrations no longer were limited to sections of central cities and remote rural areas; substantial suburban income decline also was widespread. To understand severe poverty concentrations, income decline in suburbs also should be analyzed.

Suburban Poverty

In the 1980s and 1990s, income decline, crime increases, and tax base erosion affected many suburbs to an extent previously associated with old industrial cities. According to an account in the *Chicago Tribune* (McCarron 1998), the poverty- and crime-ridden suburb of Harvey, south of Chicago, had a tax base so depleted that the owners of a house worth $100,000 were forced to pay about $5,500 a year in taxes, or three times what they would pay in the wealthy suburb of Barrington Hills. In nearby working-class Posen, real household income fell in the 1980s, as its traditional industries moved or closed and the rising "edge cities," with their office buildings in parklike settings and festive enclosed shopping malls, attracted middle- and upper-income residents to nearby, but distinctly separate, neighborhoods (Glastris 1992). Even in Evanston, "well known," according to an article in *USA Today* (Nasser 1999), "for its stately brick and stone homes, lakefront mansions and the lovely Northwestern University campus . . . more than a third of Evanston's elementary and middle school students qualify for free or reduced lunches—an all-time high. At the Second Baptist Church downtown, lines for free lunches are so long that the soup kitchen has moved from the 48-seat dining room to the 150-seat fellowship hall." In parts of suburban Prince George's County, Maryland, news articles revealed that the murder frequency in the late 1990s rivaled that of adjacent Washington, D.C. Economic problems also were common. One news article (Spinner 1999) began this way: "For more than a decade, the little town of Capitol Heights, whose 4,000 residents are some of the poorest in Prince George's County, has been able to offer business investors big-money incentives . . . But despite status as a state enterprise zone . . . Capitol Heights has not attracted a single, substantial project. . . ."

Suburban decline commonly involves post–World War II suburbs of small, modest single-family houses sinking into disrepair amid expanses of similar deteriorating dwellings. They are in areas with little sense of place, not much nearby employment, and few alternatives to auto transportation, where public and private institutions are insufficiently committed to reinvestment in private dwellings and public infrastructure. We identify the period since 1980 as the era of suburban decline because of this widespread deterioration. We found, for example, that 20 percent of 554 suburbs declined faster in income from 1960 to 1990 relative to the central cities in 24 large metropolitan areas from the Atlantic to the Pacific. Between 1980 and 1990, more than 32 percent of these suburbs declined in income faster than their central cities relative to metropolitan income norms.

While we often refer to suburban decline as income decline in certain local government jurisdictions and in census tracts relative to metropolitan norms, decline has many dimensions. By emphasizing suburban decline, we are not claiming uniform trends in all of suburbia. Rather, we are calling attention to the diversity that now characterizes suburbia—continued expansion in some areas, stability in many, widespread gradual decline also in many, and crisis poverty conditions in some where social, health, crime, and unemployment problems are concentrated. This diversity distinguishes the post-1980 period from the 1945 to 1980 period, during which growth and expansion in the suburbs was so common that many people mistakenly assumed expansion and prosperity would last indefinitely. Confidence in suburban prosperity was being trumpeted in the 1990s in the popular press (*Louisville Courier Journal* in Savitch et al. 1993) and by some futurists (Drucker 1992) as signs that suburbs no longer needed cities. But findings presented here suggest that this image of suburban dominance became outmoded almost as soon as it became common.

Some important questions we explore throughout the book include: Why do crisis city and suburban poverty ghettoes, such as south-central Los Angeles, Harvey, and parts of Prince George's County, exist? Why are so many suburban neighborhoods sliding into decline where post–World War II single-family housing units are prominent? What conditions and trends have emerged in the era of suburban decline? What is bringing about these trends? What are some concepts that help explain the trends and how they vary from place to place? What do these trends imply for strategic planning?

By strategic planning, we mean analysis of organizations' and territories' (here local governments' and regions') strengths, weaknesses, dangers, and opportunities in competitive contexts. Strategic planning also involves selecting priority goals, devising means of achieving them, and implementing those means, bearing in mind competitive contexts during each process. In this book, we emphasize analyzing dangers and, to a lesser extent, devising means for coping with them by identifying opportunities. Analyzing the era of suburban decline reveals many of those dangers to local governments, regions, residents, and businesses.

Metropolitan Evolution in the United States

Since the 1920s, increases in affluence, automobile use, highway expansion, and plentiful land have established opportunities for metropolitan sprawl. Population expansion in the 1920s created pressures for invasion by commercial enterprises, apartments, and other rental units into lower-density residential areas in cities (Burgess 1925). Concerns about in-migrants, crime, and schools added "push" factors from older neighborhoods to the "pulls" associated with new neighborhoods. The leading edge of outward relocation often was led by the affluent into scenic areas before, as well as after, World War II (Hoyt 1939). Individual preferences provided the motivation, and development institutions and policies (lenders, developers, secondary mortgage market firms, FHA and VHA federally insured mortgages, and local real property taxes deducted from federal income taxes) provided the means, especially after World War II, for suburban sprawl to occur. Rising affluence increased the proportion of the population that could afford single-family detached dwellings. As private and public institutions created new housing opportunities for middle- and upper-income people in sectors outside cities, city populations diminished and relative income decline by city residents occurred in comparison with suburban residents (Bradbury, Downs, and Small 1982). Poorer households gravitated to the older housing left behind (Downs 1981; Lowry 1960). Older housing also was located where distances to private services were shorter, and where public transportation and social services were nearby. Close proximity added the lure of convenience to cities and older suburbs for low-income people. In some older neighborhoods, concentrations of poor people grew, so that unemployment, poverty, crime, and inadequate preparation for school sometimes led to persistent social crises (Wilson 1987).

After World War II, settlements were developed at lower densities because of the prevalence of automobiles, the increasing use of trucks for heavy transport, and the development of immense highway capacity to serve low-density configurations. Some new suburbs grew up around older industrial villages. Most suburbs in the 1950s and 1960s were developed as subdivisions or gradual accumulations of single units where the residents usually commuted to central cities (Jackson 1985). During the 1960s, two-thirds of suburban development occurred in a sprawl, rather than in a compact, pattern (Lamb 1983, 42).

Manufacturing steadily decentralized after World War II, extending a trend that began earlier. Between 1958 and 1963, manufacturing employment fell by 6 percent in central cities while it expanded by 16 percent in suburbs (Douglass Commission 1969, 413). During the 1960s, the suburban labor force grew by 40 percent, while employment in suburbs rose by 48 percent (Logan 1976, 335). Retailing followed the outward-moving population, needing to locate close to customers. Expressways were constructed around and outside many central cities, with spokes connecting to the central city. Population and manufacturing on lower-cost suburban land accumulated a critical mass for commerce to serve. The beltways and their radial spokes created settings where entrepreneurs built massive enclosed shopping malls, prestige office buildings and hotels, and industrial parks (Hartshorn and Muller 1989). A common feature in early and later post–World War II suburbanization was the separation of specialized land uses in low-density patterns. As the decades passed, the scale of commercial development increased, as did the probability that commuters would drive from suburban residences to suburban workplaces rather than driving from suburbs to central cities.

The Postsuburban Era

In this and later chapters, "cities" refers to central cities as identified by the U.S. Bureau of the Census. "Suburbs" is a loose category corresponding generally to the Census's definitions of urbanized areas and the other urban areas outside central cities. For definitions used by the Census, see Note 1.1. We use the term "exurban" informally, following Nelson (1992, 356): "The rising occupancy of rural territory beyond the suburbs but within long-distance commuting range of urban employment opportunities justifies distinguishing exurban areas as a separate category." More precisely, Nelson (1992, 361) suggested, "[E]xurban counties are those within 50 miles of the boundary of the central city of an MA [a metropolitan area] with a population of between 500,000 and less than 2 million, or within 70 miles of the boundary of the central city of an MA with a population of more than 2 million, but not otherwise classified as a central county or traditional suburban county."

From our perspective, the period of mature suburbs blends with the post-suburban era. The postsuburban era is characterized by many suburbs losing population, many suburbs declining in income of residents relative to regional income, and exurban rural areas, growing rapidly in population at extremely low densities and, for the first time, matching or exceeding the median income of families in the metropolitan region.

Nelson (1992, 350) has calculated exurban population as already "home to nearly sixty million people" by 1990. In his view (1992, 350–351): "Four factors explain exurbanization. They include the continued deconcentration of employment and the rise of exurban industrialization, the latent antiurban and rural location preferences of U.S. households, improving technology that makes exurban living possible, and the apparent bias of policy favoring exurban development over compact development."

Other analysts have emphasized the multicentered character of postindustrial suburbia. Gottdiener (1985) called it a multinucleated, deconcentrated spatial form. Kling, Olin, and Poster (1991, 3) claimed to coin the term "postsuburban" to describe "this new postsuburban spatial form." Garreau (1991) referred to the largest commercial and office concentrations as edge cities. Knox (1994, 135) labeled these agglomerations "stealth cities," because they typically lacked a local government and even lacked a distinctive postal address despite their huge size, frequently having more office and retail space than traditional downtowns in cities.

A Time Period That Includes Decline

Our use of the term "postsuburban" is different, however, from its use by Kling, Olin, and Poster. They used it to refer to a spatial form. We use it to refer to a time period that is succeeding the era of suburban dominance. It includes several spatial forms, including a sprawling exurban rural pattern that is much lower in density than most suburbs. From a time perspective, we think of the edge city, stealth city, multinucleated deconcentrated spatial form as characteristic of the era in which the suburbs matured. Maturity includes adding enough jobs in suburbia to substantially reduce commuting from suburbs to central cities. Adding jobs also buttresses suburban property tax bases, thereby leading many suburban public officials to believe that suburbs have succeeded in taking advantage of regional development dynamics.

This time period also includes uneven suburban decline. By suburban decline we mean primarily the decline in suburban income relative to metropolitan income. This income indicator reveals that many suburbs are not as attractive to middle- and upper-income residents as they were previously. In some instances, suburban decline has been severe. In many instances, suburban decline has been more rapid than central city decline. As suburbs age, they are vulnerable to decline similar to the decline previously experienced by central cities. As employment decentralizes, the territory from which workplaces are accessible increases proportionately. Suburbanization threatened central cities. Exurbanization constitutes a similar, perhaps greater, danger to suburbs.

Why Suburbs Decline Rapidly

Why should some suburban jurisdictions and neighborhoods decline rapidly in median family income relative to the metropolitan median, even faster than central cities? There are several reasons why this may occur. Sometimes substantial segments of suburban housing were developed to modest standards within a short time frame. The housing in these areas ages in unison (Kling, Olin, and Poster 1991, 6), creating special pressures on people considering whether to reinvest in maintaining and upgrading their property.

Owners have the following choices. They can reinvest, and if neighbors follow and also reinvest, the neighborhood will be stable or revive; or, if neighbors do not follow their lead, then the neighborhood will decline and the original reinvestors may lose money when they sell. If owners stay and do not reinvest, then decline may ensue. If owners move without reinvesting, then their replacements will tend to be lower-income households, if the region's population has expanded and the number of low- and moderate-income households has increased. This outcome is more likely if the previous owners rent rather than sell to newcomers. This occupancy transition process may escalate, because a similarity of housing in age and quality amplifies to reinvestors the risks in rehabilitation and upgrading. If owners of other dwellings, which are similar in age and whose components are wearing out, do not follow their lead, many houses may lose value. An image of low attractiveness and dim prospects in the neighborhood in general may spread rapidly, because the decision time is compressed when undesirable effects of low reinvestment become visible.

Fickle Housing Markets

Many suburbs, especially post-1945 suburbs, are vulnerable, because they are almost wholly creatures of private housing markets in which demand accelerated due to federal mortgage guarantees and tax incentives. Being on the leading edge of middle- and upper-income housing market preferences has been an economic advantage for growing suburbs. What happens when the leading edges of housing preferences turn elsewhere? And what happens to fringe areas initially developed at modest quality standards?

Some metropolitan neighborhoods are vulnerable because an average of 50 percent of their residents move in any five-year period, with high–home ownership neighborhoods having less mobility and high-rental neighborhoods experiencing more. During their first two decades, new neighborhoods may decline slightly in population, if most owners stay in place and their family size diminishes as children grow up and leave home. As outmoving occurs to be closer to new jobs or to occupy more expensive homes, and some couples divorce or incomes fall for other reasons, the characteristics of inmovers become crucial. If outmovers are not replaced by inmovers of similar or greater resources, deterioration of housing can occur quickly, especially as housing enters its third, fourth, and fifth decades. Which decade is crucial for reinvestment depends on the quality of initial construction and characteristics of neighborhoods, school districts, and jurisdictions.

Housing markets are dynamic and fickle. Housing structures deteriorate but are long-lasting. If housing as it ages does not earn reinvestment from loyal owners or their eager replacements, neighborhoods may deteriorate quickly. Eventually, the resilience of a suburb, like any neighborhood, depends on lasting qualities of "place" to renew middle- and upper-income movers' demand for it.

Economic Assets

Cities were created around important economic assets. Nonmarket organizations such as government centers, major universities, and a multitude of churches and cultural institutions also nurtured them. Most post-1945 suburbs, and many earlier ones, have few of these assets. The suburban decline process may accelerate if an insufficient number of public and private nonprofit institutions are nearby. Some people associated with public and private nonprofit institutions, as well as the leaders of the institutions themselves, have reasons to reinvest in their own aging neighborhoods, even when such expenditures may not seem the best investments based on housing resale profit criteria alone. Institutions such as government centers, universities, hospitals, and cultural facilities, as well as aesthetic characteristics such as interesting architecture or convenient and walkable mixed-use environments, help attract replacement neighbors. Most of these conditions may entice significant numbers of people to reinvest in housing and other aging structures.

Economic transitions also may induce population changes. Suburbs may decline in some instances after employers move out. In other suburbs, new job centers may have been created, bringing more traffic, noise, and pollution and disrupting the privacy and isolation that had encouraged previous residents to move there. The success of suburbs in attracting employment contains a threat to suburban residential stability. As Nelson (1992, 351) has observed, where jobs are concentrated in the central business district, a five-mile commute can take 30 minutes in large metropolitan areas. Commuters from exurban rural areas to suburban jobs may be able to travel 20 miles in 30 minutes. The territory for settlement from which commuting is relatively convenient expands in mathematical proportions (area = pi times radius squared) with the suburbanization of employment. Thus, some inner suburban residential areas may not have the same ease-of-commuting advantages as before. The attractiveness of exurban rural locations will be enhanced, in particular, if commuting thresholds constitute a substantial zone of commuting indifference, as Clark and Burt (1980, 60) suggest. Up to some reasonable time limit, commuters may be indifferent to the time spent, rather than calculating costs in something more akin to a ratio scale, as theorists of commuting time tradeoffs with housing space acquisition (Alonso 1964) may believe.

Old Neighborhoods' Advantages

Compared with inner suburbs, many central city neighborhoods are likely to have the advantages of more nonprofit institutions, interesting architecture, walkable neighborhoods, and access to mass transit. For people in the housing market who value these qualities, few suburbs will offer attractive alternatives to such central city locations. Thus, portions of central cities may increase their attractiveness to middle- and upper-income people even as other, usually larger, areas of these cities decline, while some suburbs built to modest standards decline also.

When relative or absolute income decline occurs in suburbs, the impulse by some middle- and upper-income people to avoid such areas will strengthen. Since central cities already will have been experiencing this avoidance phenomenon, when substantial suburban avoidance contributes to location decisions, the potential for more relocation to outer suburbs and exurban rural areas increases. Escalation in overall metropolitan sprawl is the likely result. This expectation is consistent with residential location preferences discovered in a 1989 survey in Florida. In that survey, the residents who were most interested in relocating lived in the suburbs of major cities. They most often preferred farming and semirural areas or the downtowns of major cities. Most residents also said they would commute longer to move to their preferred location (Audirac, Shermyen, and Smith 1990, 475). People acting on such preferences will contribute to exurban sprawl into agricultural areas, as well as to revival of some central city neighborhoods.

Isolation, Maturity, and Deterioration

Local jurisdictions in the United States cope with enormous population movements. Between 1985 and 1990, 52 percent of metropolitan residents moved. Stable cities and suburbs require a steady supply of replacement residents. Inmovers need to replace outmovers similar to them in status in order to maintain socioeconomically stable places. Unless limitations on intrusions into rural areas are combined with greater attractiveness and greater density in developed areas, metropolitan sprawl will continue for the foreseeable future. Some planners and urban designers, such as Peter Calthorpe (1993), argue that greater density can attract more residents in inner suburbs when placed in mixed-use configurations in close proximity to mass transit. This proposal is consistent with land values that reflect demand, and it has been used in Alexandria and Arlington, Virginia, adjacent to Washington, D.C.; in Portland, Oregon; and in some other places. But it has not been widely tested, partly because infill projects amid established settlements are usually resisted by current residents. The prospect of delays and sometimes rejections of infill projects discourages some developers from proposing them. The conclusion that continuing sprawl is more likely than reconcentration or stability in older jurisdictions, in addition to reflecting development experience, is consistent with survey research that confirms that low-density exurban sprawl is what many people prefer, given current residential alternatives (Davis, Nelson, and Deuker 1994, 52; Zuiches 1981, 83–84).

Suburban decline increases the scale of urban problems. It adds one more incentive for residents to escape from urban problems by moving farther out from city centers, potentially increasing the pace and scope of outer suburban and exurban sprawl. Development pressure on farmland will increase as a result of selective suburban decline. At the same time, some city neighborhoods will revive because they seem like better location options than some declining suburban neighborhoods.

In most of the United States, suburbia developed in small government jurisdictions with average populations of less than 20,000 residents. These small suburbs generally do not attract the interest, and certainly not the allegiance, of regional elites such as business, higher education, and hospital executives; state officials; special district board members; and elected officials of large local governments. When any of these small suburbs declines substantially, there is little reason why the county or city political elites, or the regional economic elites, should muster a rescue operation. Indeed, from a regional perspective, declining suburbs may seem like a routine transition, adding useful suburban diversity. Regional elites may worry about regional economic development involving large infrastructure projects like airports, bridges, highways, tunnels, sewage treatment plants, and water supply facilities. They also may worry about the security of downtown investments. But why should regional elites be concerned about individual small aging suburban jurisdictions where they may never have set foot and where they may have no acquaintances or investments? They may have interests in some suburbs, but probably not the "at risk" suburbs.

The Postsuburban Era and Metropolitan Renewal

Strategic planning for neighborhoods or government jurisdictions in a metropolitan region, and for the region itself, requires interpreting their positions in the regional context. A new metropolitan mosaic emerged in the 1980s and 1990s. The trends with the broadest implications for the quality of life and future prospects that have emerged, from our perspective, are excessive sprawl on the metropolitan fringe, insufficient reinvestment in and near established neighborhoods, and large and growing income disparities among local government jurisdictions. Renewal and balance within the new metropolitan mosaic depend on grappling with these trends. The main outlines of recent metropolitan conditions and trends are summarized in this section, and some of their policy implications are explained.

The tyranny of easy development decisions, which will be diagnosed in Chapter 2, helps explain suburban decline and exurban sprawl as well as decline of central cities. The tyranny of easy development decisions means that development does not follow the path of buyer preferences as much as it goes where risk is limited and profits are satisfactory. The tyranny of easy development decisions is a land development version of the "satisficing" decisions in governments and businesses described by Herbert Simon (1997). Land development involves risks related to financing, construction speed, and timing of sales, as well as demand sufficient to make some profit. Development conditions should be satisfactory, although they need not be optimum. Settings where lending institutions will finance development readily, and where opposition to development will be low to modest and will not delay construction or escalate costs, meet these satisfactory, or "satisficing," conditions. Conditions meeting "satisficing" criteria are more prevalent in fringe locations than in central city, inner suburb, or even midrange suburban settings. Opposition by neighbors to infill development, and insufficient motivation for developers, lenders, and public officials to overcome opposition and higher acquisition costs compared to green space, leads development actors to avoid most major infill projects. The residential building sector of the economy operates according to satisficing principles, rather than seeking to maximize profits in high-risk settings.

High rates of residential mobility create dangers and opportunities for neighborhoods and jurisdictions. When 50 percent or more of all residents move in five years, and 50 percent of homeowners move in eight years, the condition of dwellings, street blocks, neighborhoods, and small jurisdictions can change rapidly, especially in high-rental areas. Some neighborhoods and jurisdictions will prosper. If new neighborhoods on the metropolitan fringe and some well-positioned old neighborhoods continue to attract most of the better-off residents, and middle-aged neighborhoods are not adapted to fit contemporary preferences, then more neighborhoods will decline than will prosper. Houses and neighborhoods should be renewed and recycled, but premature discarding often occurs instead. Healthy transitions are not the norm; excessive fringe development discourages reinvestment in established neighborhoods.

The amount and location of reinvestment in housing will determine whether neighborhoods and jurisdictions will be stable, decline, or improve. Reinvestment is the means by which aging structures and their functioning systems are renewed and adapted to new technologies and emergent preferences. Insufficient reinvestment and infill are the most common result of the sum of legislation, voter dynamics, and prevalence of risks. Reinvestment in public infrastructure, public buildings, parks, and street aesthetics also is a necessary companion of, and inducement to, private reinvestment. Such public reinvestment often competes against investment in new infrastructure and amenities for developing settlements on the metropolitan fringe. Even where reinvestment in deteriorating public facilities is adequate, reinvestment in private housing often lags. In sum, strategies of maintenance and transition are needed. Since neighborhood reinvestment is influenced by the ease of fringe development, federal and state policies that encourage fringe development diminish prospects for neighborhood reinvestment.

Public reinvestment can encourage private reinvestment by increasing private owners' confidence in the future of their neighborhoods. Places can be nurtured by improving access to pedestrian paths and public transportation. Strong regional transit systems can help sustain and revive some jurisdictions. Heavy-rail transit, in particular, can have major development impacts. Suburban communities as well as central cities can be strengthened. Older suburban communities can be enhanced as employment destinations, as well as be reinforced as residential centers that are close to local employment and intermediate central city and new edge city employment concentrations. Alexandria and Arlington, Virginia (see Chapter 5), illustrate the renaissance potential of old dwellings, convenient neighborhoods, attractive architecture, and multimodal transportation options including heavy-rail transit.

State policies may influence conditions in cities and suburbs more than do federal policies. Federal policies, especially the interstate highway program and deduction of local property taxes and mortgage interest from federal income taxes, often are blamed for suburbanization and the related decline of cities. But federal policies, some of which are nearly uniform nationwide, cannot account for all of the substantial income disparities among states and between cities and suburbs in metropolitan areas. In 1990, cities in 25 states were doing equally or nearly as well as suburbs in relative income, while in other states, most cities were devastated or declining rapidly. To explain these differences, causes other than federal policies must be explored. State policies are one possibility. Annexation of suburbs by cities, fiscal arrangements between state and local governments concerning revenue and expenditure responsibilities, and land development and infrastructure policies are plausible state policy influences on the size of city-suburb income disparities. We will focus on interstate variations in metropolitan conditions to show effects of state policies on metropolitan conditions.

Development on the metropolitan fringe often has led to incorporation of distinct suburban governments. Early development outside city limits stimulated political pressure on state legislatures to insulate suburbanites from annexation (Teaford 1979). David Rusk (1993) and others have argued that strong regions depend on strong cities or, at least, that regions are stronger if central cities are strong; but the economic relationships are not actually that clear. Growing cities are sometimes associated with regional economic advances, but some strong regions have cities that suffer large income disparities and high poverty, such as Atlanta. Where suburbanization occurred early in the 20th century without extensive annexation, central cities often declined as suburbanization, and then exurbanization, continued, such as in the Boston, Cleveland, Philadelphia, and St. Louis areas. The advantages of large metropolitan size, which often are associated with early suburbanization, provided economic assets in some regions that have attracted businesses in the postindustrial, high-technology, information era. Thus, some large, high-disparity regions have prospered, especially in the South and West, such as Atlanta, San Francisco, and Washington, D.C. Intuition suggests that struggling or strangled cities diminish regional economic potential, but this argument, while probably valid, is not easily demonstrated with economic data alone.

Regional approaches to economics, environment, and politics can help achieve better metropolitan results by focusing on how metropolitan dynamics undermine or nourish quality of life. In some respects, contemporary economic conditions encourage integrated economic development policy and environmental conservation measures supported by effective local public finance and service delivery. Footloose businesses with highly skilled, mobile employees locate and stay where the quality of life is high. Regions are best able to provide satisfactory public infrastructure and effective public services where disparities among jurisdictions are limited. High quality of life can persist, if environmental conservation is treated as a fundamental value. The freshness of a new subdivision may stimulate exaggerated confidence by residents that their housing investments have been prudent, but a settlement with no "soul" is fragile. If residents feel no attachment to it beyond shelter and finance, then it will wither in the first drought that occurs from shifts in buyer preferences.

Opportunities to build regional coalitions will increase, because cities' and suburbs' fates increasingly will be interpreted as being linked. Coalitions between city and suburban legislators in state policy arenas will become more likely. City and suburban coalitions may claim prominent places on policy agendas, as in Minnesota (Orfield 1997). This linkage between city and suburban trends will be subject to varying interpretations. Decline in cities, for example, may have occurred in neighborhoods with grid street networks, while in suburbs, decline may be most evident in neighborhoods with cul-de-sac streets. Analysis of causes of decline will need to go beyond street patterns and engage other dimensions: housing size and quality, proximity, convenience, access, social problems, and aesthetics, as well as how fringe development policies are linked to reinvestment in established neighborhoods.

Mobility and Strategy

Residential mobility is the most important behavior to interpret when conducting planning and policymaking for metropolitan areas (Lucy 1975; Varady and Raffel 1995). By residential mobility, we mean choosing residential locations that vary according to preferences, supply, ability to pay, and discriminatory practices. The fate of neighborhoods, government jurisdictions, and regions depends on how residential mobility is manifested over time (Carmon 1997). Mobility rates in metropolitan areas average about 50 percent in five years. Although owners move much less than renters, the median stay of homeowners is only eight years (U.S. Bureau of the Census 1997). One-half of homeowners move in eight years or less. In 10 years, the time that elapses between national censuses of the population, more than 50 percent of homeowners in many neighborhoods have moved. High mobility rates mean that residents' income in neighborhoods that fail to attract replacement movers of similar or higher incomes will decline, sometimes rapidly. As their housing goals and capacities evolve, households have the option of reinvesting where they are. More often, they use mobility to enhance their housing quality, leaving their dwellings and neighborhoods behind (Varady and Raffel 1995, 100). Markets, regulations, and incentives contribute to these outcomes.

Different eras have been influenced, of course, by transportation technologies that have had diverse spatial consequences. When walking predominated, high densities and short travel distances were common. Train and streetcar technologies spread settlement farther out, with concentrated nodes of development near train stations and streetcar routes. Auto transport spread cities into suburbs and then into exurbs beyond. Spatial consequences using the same technology within eras, however, have not been identical. Some metropolitan areas sprawl more than others with greater income disparities among jurisdictions and less reinvestment in older neighborhoods. What patterns—in regions, cities, and suburbs—have these spatial consequences taken? What are some conditions—

income distribution, housing age, job locations, racial patterns, local government boundaries—that influence, and result from, residential mobility?

Income and Stability

Income of residents is the variable that reveals the most useful information to
policy strategists about movers and stayers. Tracking residents' income in jurisdictions and neighborhoods over time identifies the results of moving behavior.
It indirectly reveals preferences and opportunities as well as judgments about
quality of life in neighborhoods and local governments. It is a richer and more
accessible source of such information than wage rates and housing value, which
have been suggested by others as indicators of quality of life (Burnell and Galster
1992; Luger 1996; Rosen 1979; Stover and Leven 1992). Income of residents in
neighborhoods and jurisdictions demonstrates ability to pay taxes. Lower
income leads to greater reliance on public services. A wide range of incomes in
distinct government jurisdictions within metropolitan regions indicates a separation of need, and usually demand, for public services from the resources to pay
for them. Income also indicates ability to pay for housing and to maintain and
improve it. Consequently, income is used here most often to explain the significance of residential patterns, because it provides the richest trend data with
which to analyze recent and current conditions and to anticipate the future of
neighborhoods and jurisdictions.

Decline, therefore, can be measured by income change in one neighborhood
or jurisdiction relative to income change in other neighborhoods and jurisdictions within a metropolitan area. Income per family or household is a superior
indicator of decline compared with population loss or racial change; income
measures capacity to reinvest and pay taxes better than these other factors.
Population can drop while income rises, or population can rise while income
falls. Racial change in neighborhoods, which increasingly has included black-to-
white as well as white-to-black transitions (Nyden et al. 1998; Spain 1980), can
increase as well as decrease income.

One key task for strategic planning is to predict how public policies may
affect the viability of neighborhoods and jurisdictions over time by analyzing the
relationships of the policies to residential mobility. Analysis of income, housing,
and mobility also can illuminate the cumulative results of physical planning
processes—growth management, transportation planning, urban design, comprehensive planning, capital improvement investments, citizen participation,
zoning, business incentives, and environmental regulation. Are the results of
these and other public policies stable and viable neighborhoods and jurisdictions? Do they retain current residents and attract new ones so that they are vital
and renewable through recurring investments? In regulated market economies,
as in the United States, stability depends on consumer choices among the locations available. As David Varady (1986, 144) has noted, "Over time, stability is

dependent upon attracting new middle-income families to replace those relocating as a result of normal turnover." For settlements to be meaningful communities, a significant amount of market success is needed. Market indicators, such as the income of residents and the value of housing, help to show the vitality of neighborhoods and jurisdictions. Residents' income and housing values, therefore, are useful indicators of stability and decline.

Housing and Development Policies

Aging cities and suburbs will continue to have poor neighborhoods as long as poor people are housed almost entirely in old and middle-aged dwellings. In most regions housing rehabilitation receives modest or little attention, and large tracts of single-use housing are developed in fringe locations. This combination of public policies, decisions by private lenders and developers, and personal behavior by residents is not conducive to creating and sustaining attractive communities.

In the United States, more than 98 percent of the population is housed in private market housing based on ability to pay. That system has the virtue of efficiency for the middle class, matching willing buyers and sellers in decentralized markets. While creating serviceable individualized structures, the system of housing markets, regulations, and incentives generally has failed to create attractive places. Much aging housing usually ends up being occupied by poor people. Large concentrations of poor people in poverty ghettoes have been one result (Downs 1994; Jargowsky 1997). Another result has been a less perceptible slide of middle-aged housing into disinvestment, which shortens the life span of houses, neighborhood schools, and strip shopping structures and diminishes the quality of life in entire neighborhoods and government jurisdictions. These trends are dangers to neighborhoods, local governments, and even regions.

Strategic Planning and Competition

Strategic planning emphasizes analyzing strengths, weaknesses, dangers, and opportunities in competitive contexts. Typical features of strategic planning are participatory processes that engage key stakeholders, environmental scans of external conditions and organizational capacities, and the choice of several, rather than many, top priorities on which to focus implementation efforts. Competition includes struggle by local government officials to retain and attract residents of sufficient means to pay taxes, invest in housing, purchase goods and services, populate public schools, and enforce norms of public conduct. Successful neighborhoods and jurisdictions then can be stable or rising in quality rather than declining into an array of problematic conditions, including crisis poverty ghettoes with their extreme social, economic, and political problems.

Effective strategic planning for local governments depends on the nature of the competition. Residents, business investors and managers, nonprofit organizations and other governments (local, state, and federal) determine the competitive environment for local governments. Some residents, businesses, and nonprofit organizations are more attractive constituents than others because they have more resources (such as jobs, property value, income, education, skills, participation, civic virtue, and family support). Strengths of local governments are determined by whether they help attract and retain the residents, businesses, and nonprofits that are valued more highly than others or that are valued more highly than those currently within a local government's boundary. In contrast with most games and war, in local governments strategic planners are not trying to vanquish their opponents. Instead, they want to attract a reasonable share of a metropolitan area's valued actors and their assets.

Movers and Security

The essence of strategic situations is that the best decision for one player is influenced by actions of other players (Schelling 1963). The best actions for local governments, therefore, depend on the actions that other governments, residents, businesses, and nonprofit organizations have taken and are likely to take. In this case, the moves that occur are the migrations of residents, businesses, and nonprofits into and out of local jurisdictions. Money is moving about too, through investments, shopping, tourism, and commuting. The movement of money also inflicts costs and bestows benefits on local governments and their constituents through changes in taxpaying capacity and social problems.

Mobility also influences the dangers faced by households. Most people are risk-averse; they seek safety of person and secure investments in housing. The search for safety has contributed to moves to suburbs and exurbs. For most residents, a housing purchase may be their largest single investment. Secure housing investments, therefore, are prominent values in home buyers' calculations of dangers and opportunities (Lucy 1975; Varady and Raffel 1995). If people anticipate being mobile, secure housing investments become more important because if housing investments "pay off," the homeowners will be able to move to more secure settings.

For most households, housing characteristics, interacting with evolving stage-of-life preferences for various sizes, styles, cost, and quality of housing, are the dominant reasons for moving. Housing characteristics, therefore, also influence whether current and future residents will choose to reinvest in existing dwellings or purchase new ones. The small size of dwellings built in the 25 years after World War II may be a major obstacle to effecting enough housing reinvestment to achieve neighborhood stability, a possibility analyzed in Chapters 3 and 8.

Local government jurisdictions may win or lose in attempting to attract desirable residents who are calculating how housing investments may increase their quality of life. One certain condition, however, is that government jurisdictions' lifetimes will be longer than the duration of the average resident's stay at a particular location. Renters move about four times more frequently than owners do. Ten percent of owners moved in 1976 (Downs 1981, 27). Eight percent of owners and 36 percent of renters moved in 1995 (U.S. Bureau of the Census 1997, 64). The typical adult in the United States makes 13 moves in his or her lifetime (Long and Boertlein 1976). As a consequence, the well-being of local government jurisdictions and metropolitan regions has a different time frame and a more varied constituency than the interests of any current set of residents and voters.

The lives of most residential structures, while they vary greatly, also are much longer than the stay of specific occupants. Housing materials and equipment wear at varying rates. Every dwelling needs reinvestment to avoid being discarded when the first vital system (roof, walls, heating, water, sewer, electricity) no longer functions adequately (National Association of Home Builders 1997). The well-being of neighborhoods, local governments, and regions is linked to reinvestment in structures. If the reinvestment motivation and capacity of too many current owners is insufficient, neighborhoods, local governments, and regions will suffer.

The duration of most residents' stays in specific structures and the longevity of dwellings and local government jurisdictions are highly varied. Current and potential residents, reinvestors, and local public officials, therefore, are apt to have widely differing time frames and decision perspectives, leading to decisions that do not necessarily act to create and maintain a healthy, prosperous, and sustainable region. The disconnect between these actors' decision time frames augments traditional efficiency and effectiveness arguments for regional planning. Efficient and effective public infrastructure that serves the average of 90 local governments per metropolitan region, many thousands of reinvestors, and sometimes millions of residents clearly requires some long-range planning and implementation. The potential also is apparent for inequitable spatial patterns to emerge and inadequate representation of some individuals to occur. These dangers constitute additional reasons for regional planning. Any notion that regional planning is a panacea for inefficiency, ineffectiveness, inequity, or unrepresentativeness should be avoided, however. More planning, even if implemented, is not a cure-all. Planning to achieve different outcomes should be an element in a complicated network of governance, however, because the interplay of decisions by residents, businesses, and government officials has led to excessive suburban and exurban sprawl, too little reinvestment in private and public structures and infrastructure, and excessively large income disparities among local government jurisdictions. In this book we explore why these outcomes are common. We explain how strategic planning can help identify opportunities to achieve more satisfying regional results, and we set the stage for richer discussions among readers about other opportunities to create and maintain healthy and sustainable regional communities.

Plan of the Book

For the broad policy-making process known as strategic planning to be meaningfully applied to spaces and places, territorial indicators such as income transitions are required. The discovery of dangers, and of weaknesses, strengths, and opportunities, must include the competitive spatial context. In the following chapters we describe that context among residents, businesses, and local governments by analyzing conditions and trends in cities and suburbs from 1960 into the 1990s. We also make some general predictions about the future of cities and suburbs. Policy alternatives for coping with the undesirable results of competition among residents, businesses, and local governments are emphasized in Chapters 6, 9, and 10. The analyses are conducted with the implications of numerous policies in mind. This book is mainly about the conditions that reflect the impacts of public policies and that dictate the challenges public policies should address. Except for Chapter 9, policies and plans are described conceptually and generally rather than specifically. This book analyzes the foundation around which policies and plans can be built and makes recommendations for how to structure their elements and interactions.

Our discussion of strategic planning is informed by analysis of postsuburban era characteristics. Chapter 2 discusses the tension between strategic planning for individual jurisdictions and regions, including the effects of the tyranny of easy development decisions. We explain how such tyranny leads to decline in both cities and suburbs, especially if local jurisdictions emphasize achieving fast growth more than pursuing quality of life. Chapter 3 explains how strategic planning can help assess dangers. We explore the potential use of leading indicators of neighborhood and jurisdiction change to identify dangers, and examine the scarcity of leading indicators in several strategic plans.

Chapter 4 describes postsuburban era characteristics. The reasons that suburban decline has become widespread are explained through a case study of the Richmond, Virginia, metropolitan area. Chapter 5 explains how some suburbs have stabilized or revived in the face of dramatic suburban and exurban sprawl, using the Washington, D.C. metropolitan area as an example. These examples provide clues about how other suburbs, and central cities as well, can improve their prospects for resisting decline.

Chapter 6 describes how central cities in some states have maintained income levels as high as incomes in their suburbs. We explain how state policies can help some cities succeed and may in fact have more influence than federal policies on suburban sprawl and cities' vitality. Focusing on relationships between regional and central city economic trends in 59 southern metropolitan areas, we discover that regional prosperity may lead to central cities' decline if suburban sprawl runs too far ahead of city annexation. Cities with growing populations, however, have helped their regions prosper.

Chapter 7 reports on income, population, and, to a lesser extent, racial transitions in 554 suburbs in the 24 largest metropolitan areas, describing faster decline by many suburbs than by central cities from 1960 to 1990. Thirty-year trends reveal that suburban decline is widespread, substantial in degree, and increasing. Chapter 8 discusses findings and speculations about how the age, size, and location of housing can help policy makers anticipate dangers and opportunities facing neighborhoods and jurisdictions in the postsuburban era, explaining why middle-aged neighborhoods and suburbs are in more danger than some older neighborhoods and central cities. These findings challenge conventional wisdom that the oldest housing is occupied by lower-income people; the highest-valued housing in a metropolitan area occasionally is the oldest housing.

In Chapter 9, policy innovations for coping with postsuburban regions are examined for Minneapolis–St. Paul, Portland (Oregon), Maryland, Virginia, Tennessee, New York, the New Urbanism, and public transit. Some policies recognize that regions' environmental and economic success depends on effective interactions of local jurisdictions and regions. We offer a proposal for a new Sustainable Region Incentive Fund to leverage incipient policy intentions into effective multigovernment decisions. Chapter 10 suggests six policies with federal, state, regional, and local dimensions that can achieve healthier communities and regions than the containment policies traditionally followed in the United States.

Given the scope of these chapters, one might ask which fields or disciplines this study represents. Aspects of sociology, economics, politics, and geography are present. Planning, policy analysis, and public administration are represented. Is it social science, or is it planning and public policy? Clearly it is both. Strategic planning and public policy designs depend on social science understandings. And the social sciences yield more useful perspectives if questions are asked and answered with strategic planning and public policy design in mind.

Note

1.1. In this chapter and elsewhere in this book, central cities and metropolitan areas are referred to as defined by the U.S. Bureau of the Census. The outside central city area, which is the area within the metropolitan area and outside the central city, is referred to here as suburban, outer suburban, metropolitan fringe, and exurban territory. Outer suburban, metropolitan fringe, and exurban areas are less likely to be contiguous to urban settlements, whereas suburban areas are generally contiguous. The suburban area corresponds to the urban fringe in the census definition of an urbanized area (see below). Outer suburban, metropolitan fringe, and exurban areas also are less densely populated than suburban and central city areas. These terms are used loosely here, however, rather than precisely.

The U.S. Bureau of the Census (1992, A-8 to A-12) definition of a metropolitan area follows:

> The general concept of a metropolitan area (MA) is one of a large population nucleus, together with adjacent communities that have a high degree of economic and social integration with that nucleus. Some MA's are defined around two or more nuclei.
>
> Each MA must contain either a place with a minimum population of 50,000 or a Census Bureau–defined urbanized area and a total MA population of at least 100,000 (75,000 in New England). An MA comprises one or more central counties. An MA also may include one or more outlying counties that have close economic and social relationships with the central county. An outlying county must have a specified level of commuting to the central counties and also must meet certain standards regarding metropolitan character, such as population density, urban population, and population growth. In New England, MA's are composed of cities and towns rather than whole counties.

The Census Bureau delineates urbanized areas (UAs) to provide a better separation of urban and rural territory, population, and housing in the vicinity of large places. A UA comprises one or more places ("central place") and the adjacent densely settled surrounding territory ("urban fringe") that together have a minimum of 50,000 persons. The urban fringe generally consists of contiguous territory having a density of at least 1,000 persons per square mile. The urban fringe also includes outlying territory of such density if it is connected to the core of the contiguous area by road and is within one road mile of that core or within five road miles of the core but separated by water or other undeveloped territory.

Sprawl and the Tyranny of Easy Development Decisions

Business managers attempt to calculate which activities and locations will be satisfactorily profitable among the available options (Simon 1997). These calculations are imprecise, as indicated by numerous business failures. Markets involve assessments of experience, current practices, and predictions of future events. In land development, business calculations may lead to options that are relatively easy to accomplish, such as commercial buildings in freestanding strip developments and greenfield residential subdivisions with curvilinear street and cul-de-sac layouts and a narrow range of dwelling types. They receive extra weight compared with options that are difficult to implement, such as mixed-use residential and commercial developments on infill sites, even if the more difficult options hold potential for higher profits. Lenders, developers, and builders generally favor what we call easy development decisions—decisions to develop where risks are predictable and manageable. The result of motivations of participants in land markets, and influences by governments on land market processes, is the tyranny of easy development decisions.

Limiting Private Risk and Public Influence

Several problems with metropolitan markets contribute to the tyranny of easy development decisions. The notion of a tyranny of easy development decisions is intended to be ironic. One meaning of "tyranny" is strong, even complete, control leading to unjust results. In metropolitan markets, lax influence over development on the metropolitan fringe leads to unintended consequences over which central city and suburban public officials have little influence. Cities and suburbs are subjected to a tyranny of remote decisions. These decentralized decisions have unjust consequences over which city and inner suburban influence is minuscule. The ironic consequence is that freedom for some is equated with tyranny by others.

Tom Daniels (1999, 55) describes such decision situations in *When City and Country Collide:* "Developers, like any businesspeople, prefer to have as much predictability and certainty as possible for their projects. Real estate development runs on borrowed money. Developers bear the risk of building a project that can't be sold, losing money if their projects are denied or delayed, or selling a project at a loss if the economy turns sour. In short, the sooner a development is built and sold, the sooner the developer can pay off real estate loans and turn a profit."

In some instances, low risk for developers in developing the fringe, by which we mean the countryside beyond the suburbs (Daniels 1999, 2) may correspond with low influence by public-sector regulators. Daniels has identified eight obstacles (1999, 45) to "coordinated, long-term, and effective growth management in the metro fringe: 1) Fragmented and overlapping governments, authorities, and special districts. 2) The large size of fringe areas. 3) Lack of a community, county, or regional vision. 4) Lack of a sense of place and identity. 5) Newcomers, social conflicts, and rapid population growth. 6) The spread of scattered new development. 7) Too few planning resources. 8) Outdated planning and zoning techniques." The net effect of these obstacles usually is limited public-sector influence on development patterns due to confusion about goals or insufficient means to accomplish them in those relatively rare instances when goals are clear.

In other words, land development outcomes can be a product of what is easy

"Farmettes" in western Loudoun County, Virginia, carve up the rural landscape but are still within the commute range of the westward expansion of employment centers in the Washington, D.C. region. (Synergy/Photography)

Mansion-size homes on large lots with adjoining golf course on land previously planned for agriculture in western Loudoun County, Virginia. (Synergy/Photography)

to accomplish rather than a product of what consumers prefer. Businesses interpret market opportunities through three lenses: 1) new inventions, products, and services, 2) changes in regulations and incentives, and 3) modulation of supply to demand based on trial-and-error explorations, including trying to shape preferences. Uncertain relationships between new opportunities, ease of action, and consumer preferences yield ambiguous messages from markets. Whether producers respond to consumers or consumers respond to producers whose products are determined by multiple influences is obscure and, one suspects, in flux. Ambiguous messages from markets also complicate calculations about relationships between quantity and quality in strategic planning and between goals for jurisdictions and regions.

Regional Strategic Planning

Greater regional planning, policy, development, and management capacity is needed to cope with the tyranny of easy development decisions and its accompanying conditions—excessive income disparities among local government jurisdictions and too little reinvestment in middle-aged and older housing and neighborhoods. With what kinds of goals should regional strategic planning be concerned? Both quantity and quality goals are important. Quantity issues involve how a region can attract more jobs and how a region can grow faster. The bias in quantity planning is usually that more is better. Quantity planning interacts with quality planning through concern about being competitive. Quality of life has a vast impact on attracting and retaining highly skilled, mobile employees in the contemporary era of footloose businesses that are not tied to natural resources, rail and water transportation, or the hometown of the founder (Blakely 1994). A region's most important asset is its people (Yaro and Hiss 1996). Highly skilled employees, even more than businesses, are footloose, able to live wherever they choose. The quality of life that a region offers, comprising such factors as environmental conditions, education, safety, culture, and recreation, significantly affects the quantity of business activity and its pace of expansion. Moreover, rapid growth often is difficult to absorb effectively. A rapid growth rate may embody the seeds of deterioration by damaging the quality of life through expanding population faster than schools are built, overextending water supply systems, and relying on highways that become increasingly congested rather than designing multimodal transportation systems and walkable neighborhoods.

Interregional and intraregional strategic planning also interact through quality-of-life issues. Because regions are composed of many jurisdictions, some of which overlap and many of which are geographically distinct, complex patterns of interjurisdictional competition and cooperation occur. Jurisdictions compete with other jurisdictions within the region to attract a larger quantity of businesses with certain characteristics—high property values, high salaries, low pollution, and not too much traffic. They may compete by offering tax incentives or other direct benefits to specific businesses, but they also compete by trying to provide a good quality of life. Each jurisdiction to some extent faces variations on the potential conflict between more quantity and quality.

Governance Within but Not by Regions

The term "regional strategic planning" may seem internally contradictory. Strategic planning should aim at priorities, action steps, implementation, and coping with opposition, as well as environmental scans of strengths, weaknesses, dangers, and opportunities in competitive contexts. But setting priorities, taking actions, and implementing plans requires governments willing to perform according to plans and to modulate their plans in reaction to changing circumstances. Regions, however, are notoriously lacking in regional government systems that lead directly to action and implementation. Regions do not have unitary governments, although a few, like Minneapolis–St. Paul and Portland, Oregon, have regional governments that perform several important functions. Large regions have many general governments and many special districts. The average number of governments for all 320 metropolitan areas in the United States is about 90. Usually no major government unit has the interactive success of the region and its constituent elements significantly in mind when making decisions from day to day.

Still, it is undeniable that governance *within* regions, if not *by* regions, does occur. Local governments blanket metropolitan areas in complex quilt patterns. Multijurisdiction special districts are numerous, each performing one or a few government functions. State and federal governments perform diverse governance functions. Governance outcomes occur, sometimes with and more often without formal coordination or unified action required by legislation. The notion of mutual adjustments among local governments, interacting with federal and state governments and with private and nonprofit organizations, helps considerably with understanding how governance evolves within regions.

Mutual Adjustments

Charles Lindblom (1965, 3), in *The Intelligence of Democracy*, said his purpose was to explain that "people can coordinate with each other without anyone's coordinating them, without a dominant common purpose, and without rules that fully prescribe their relations to each other." Adaptive and manipulated adjustments are the two modes in which mutual adjustments occur, Lindblom (1965, 33–34) said. In adaptive adjustments, decision makers adapt to decisions without regard to consequences or to avoid adverse consequences. In manipulated adjustments, decision makers adapt by bargaining, discussion, compensation, reciprocity, and authority. Both sorts of adjustments are means of altering the decision-making environment. Decentralized public and private decision makers in metropolitan areas use them to achieve governance outcomes, such as shared provision of education, health, and social services; locate landfills and negotiate trash disposal costs; coordinate heavy-rail line and highway locations; share costs in staffing emergency services; and communicate across government lines during some police investigations.

Another useful image is Norton Long's (1959) concept of the local (or metropolitan) community as an ecology of games among private and public actors pursuing personal and organizational goals. Decisions and actions emerge from a variety of cooperative and conflictual circumstances. They result in a more cohesive society than seems warranted by their uncoordinated characteristics. Planners and public administrators have assigned similar labels to planning contexts involving complex decision situations. They have used various images, such as planning occurring in a "shared power world" (Bryson and Crosby 1992), "through debate" (Healey 1996), by "consensual group process" (Innes 1992; Ozawa 1991), with uneasy relations between professionals (practical realists), citizen participators (realistic idealists), and the citizens (naïve skeptics) they supposedly represent (Beatley, Brower, and Lucy 1994).

Mutual adjustments in an ecology of games and planning context affect the design and implementation of strategic planning. In an ecology of games, individuals in businesses, governments, households, and nonprofit organizations are pursuing personal and organizational goals simultaneously, as well as sometimes discussing with each other how to achieve some public purpose. Strategy involves anticipating the moves of other government, business, individual, and nonprofit organizational actors. Prospects of achieving goals that differ from routine outcomes are not high. Any proposal that would shift who would pay or increase the amounts paid, or that would increase housing density, decentralize affordable housing, or expand locations for servicing the homeless or drug dependent, will meet opposition. Paths by which outcomes occur are numerous, decentralized, and convoluted. Achieving unusual results requires considerable skill in fitting policy options to emergent opportunities. Obtaining agreements among several local governments, for example, for fixed-rail mass transit routes requires overcoming fractious opposition from businesses and citizens adversely affected by proposed locations. Voluntary cooperation among local governments is the most benign mutual adjustment, but difficult issues, such as distributing and redistributing resources and siting major infrastructure, require concentrated authority (Nunn and Rosentraub 1997).

Regional Governance

In light of the modest role for regional authority—rather than persuasion and negotiation—in directing decisions, can it be said that governance *for* regions, as well as *within* regions, occurs? Governance with regions as the primary concern occurs mainly through states, the federal government, and regional special districts. States determine how transportation will be planned and managed, what the powers of local government will be, who will exercise land use controls, how state and local governments will be financed, how local governments can collaborate, and how public education policy will be formulated, implemented, and financed. More specifically, states determine whether transportation modes and locations will aim at moving people and goods or be balanced with community development and stability goals. States determine whether cities can expand their boundaries as urbanization spreads and whether consolidation of governments will occur by referendum, by votes of local governing bodies, or incrementally in response to state incentives or directives. States decide whether land use controls will be exercised by counties or by townships and villages within counties, and whether local land use decisions must take into account state goals and regulations. States determine whether local governments can levy sales taxes or share sales taxes levied at the regional scale, as well as authorizing other tax options. States decide whether local governments can share services by contract or by forming special districts to provide transportation, water, sewer, and solid waste services. States determine whether elementary and secondary public education will be financed mainly by local property taxes or mainly by state taxes distributed by formula to localities. The federal government has some influence over these subjects, especially highway funding, and has an additional large role in environmental policy that affects state and local land use and transportation policies, but state authority is much greater than federal power in most instances. For this reason, this book addresses state policies in more depth than federal policies, especially in Chapters 6 and 9.

Special districts have been the primary direct mechanism by which governance for regions has occurred. They are authorized by state legislation, which establishes means for creating, governing, and raising funds for them. Regional special districts commonly have power to collect revenues, levy taxes, construct and manage facilities, and make policies for water supply, sewage disposal, solid waste disposal, airports, seaports, bridges, tunnels, and public transportation. Sometimes these functions are bundled. Transportation special districts may deal with two or more transportation functions. Often water supply and sewage disposal are managed by one special district. Having transportation, water, and solid waste administered by a single special district is rare. Usually governmental concern for regions is expressed disjointedly, function by function—education, health, jails, highways—rather than with serious attention to cumulative effects on sprawl, disparities, settlement patterns, and reinvestment. Occasionally regional governments with limited, multifunction powers exist, as in the areas of Minneapolis–St. Paul and Portland, Oregon.

Actors' Decisions and Metropolitan Housing Markets

Three types of actors make uncoordinated decisions that produce the tyranny of easy development decisions, which leads to suburban and exurban sprawl. First, government decision makers, especially in local government, consider pursuing quantitative economic growth and qualitative improvements, reacting to interest groups, citizens, and their own beliefs. Second, developers and lenders are "satisficers" who limit risk while seeking satisfactory profits. In producing residential, commercial, and industrial buildings, they prefer easy development decisions with satisfactory profits to high-risk projects with the possibility of maximum profits but significant potential for losses. Third, consumers make housing location choices in neighborhoods and jurisdictions in "distorted markets." Decisions by government officials, developers, consumers, and citizens are influenced by jurisdictions' geographic settings within metropolitan areas. Interactions among these actors also shape prospects for reinvestment in established neighborhoods and trends in income disparities among local jurisdictions. The interplay between these actors occurs on the stage for regional strategic planning.

Strategic planning for regions should take into account the roles of individuals, businesses, and governments. Some of these roles can be generalized, and some will be specific to each region. Here we will deal mainly with general approaches to strategic planning for regions by discussing the circumstances of private-sector development decisions and residential location decisions that take market complexity into account. We will examine how jurisdictions' settings within metropolitan regions influence their policies, including contributing to the tyranny of easy development decisions.

Every market is structured; one purpose of structure is to reduce risks. Standard devices like incorporation, insurance, and bankruptcy laws serve this risk-reduction purpose, but risks cannot be eliminated. Market structures bias outcomes in one direction or another, depending on how their structures, processes, and incentives encourage certain investments due to reducing some risks and increasing others. In that sense, markets are distorted through structures, incentives, rules, and biases.

Metropolitan housing market problems include the following:

- markets that are distorted by democracy
- markets that lack a full range of institutions to arrive at better outcomes
- markets that are multiple and involve dimensions beyond the usual producing and selling of commodities and quasi-commodities, including government, neighborhood, and school dimensions
- markets with uncertain outcomes

Strengths, weaknesses, dangers, and opportunities in competitive contexts in specific settings, the essence of strategic planning analyses, can be traced to these general market circumstances that affect every setting.

Participatory Democracy

Markets are distorted by local participatory democracy. The supply of housing does not react sufficiently to demand for more development between the center and fringe, partly because current residents often oppose any substantial change in their settings. Whether the change is adding condominiums on single-family dwelling sites or replacing 50-year-old, 800-square-foot houses with new 2,000-square-foot single-family dwellings, neighbors are more likely to fight than welcome the proposed changes. David Varady and Jeffrey Raffel (1995, 174–175) believe "it has become increasingly difficult for cities to promote the construction of market-rate housing in established lower-income areas. . . . Owners fight such developments fearing that their homes will be taken through eminent domain. . . . Renters resist, citing fears that area improvement will lead to higher rents. . . ." From residents' vantage point, this "market distortion" is the means by which they try to protect the quality of their neighborhoods. Using threats of votes and campaign contributions, current residents often intimidate elected officials and their appointees to maintain the status quo. In most instances the social gains are too uncertain, and the gratitude of future residents too unlikely, to persuade elected officials to oppose the preferences of intense minorities who have votes to cast and money to dispense.

Some social theorists interpret infill as mere densification promoted by landlords who treat housing as a commodity. Commodification is typically resisted by renters trying to protect place aspects of their neighborhood (Molotch and

Logan 1987). Increased population density in cities, however, has been rare. Since 1960, nearly all sizable cities and many suburbs have become less rather than more densely populated. Many jurisdictions have declined in population, unless they have annexed adjacent territory. Home ownership rates, rather than succumbing to commodification by landlords, have been stable. In some neighborhoods, home ownership has increased because of more condominiums. Furthermore, more density often can create more livable, less auto-dependent neighborhoods through mixed-use redevelopment and greater access to transportation alternatives.

As seen by John Colvin (Gurwitt 1999, 23), a developer who is a member of the Maryland planning commission, compact development sometimes "works if government has the backbone to stand up with a developer against communities that say, 'If I have to spend one more cycle at the light, then I'm against that field behind my house being developed.' I don't think local government has figured out that the key component of Smart Growth is supporting appropriate development against local opposition. . . ." Voter anger over infill development in suburban Fairfax County outside Washington, D.C. was acknowledged by elected Supervisor Gerald Connolly (Eggan and O'Hanlon 1999): "In some ways, it's more controversial than any other kind of development. It's in people's neighborhoods, right next door. That can get a lot more attention than 1,000 new houses out on farmland somewhere." To some residents (including some who may see their property values by development nearby), any added inconvenience, such as a minor traffic delay, may be sufficient to stir their opposition to an infill project. Greater density is not always appropriate. Deciding where, when, and at what political cost to support greater density is one of the challenges of strategic planning.

Reinvestment Incentives and Institutions

Markets lack the full range of lending, redeveloping, planning, and implementing institutions needed to arrive at better reinvestment results. The problem of democratic distortions of markets is compounded by institutions that are deficient in "patient money"—money that waits for profits. Therefore, holders of money need to be especially motivated to achieve satisfactory reinvestment. Those with sufficient motivation may be current owners; local institutions such as universities, hospitals, and churches; federal, state, or local governments; or public-spirited entrepreneurs.

Time delays are costly. Local governments can be organized to reduce delays, or they may be lackadaisical or intimidated by citizen opposition, with delay a consequence of either posture. Uncertainty about whether delays will be lengthy increases risk and decreases willingness to wait. In established neighborhoods, development delays are likely. As opportunities to move money rapidly among capital markets nationally and internationally have increased, the supply of patient money may have decreased. Since renewal and reinvestment in housing and neighborhoods has not been a major goal in the United States, institutions and incentives for reinvestment are inadequate. Incentives for money to be patient need to increase, therefore, and institutions committed to using patient money in pursuit of better spatial patterns should be supported where they exist and created where they do not. Action by federal and state governments will be needed to augment tax incentives, create sources of infrastructure spending, acquire properties under certain conditions, or make funds available directly or indirectly for first or second mortgages, construction loans, and mortgage and construction insurance.

Most reinvestment in housing, however, is made in modest amounts from savings or windfalls (such as bonuses) by owner-occupants, including recent purchasers. Institutions need to serve these potential reinvestors, and incentives should be sufficient for more of them to reinvest. The combination of institutions and incentives has not been adequate, as data about remodeling activity attest. According to Harvard University's Joint Center for Housing Studies (1999), residential remodeling has been increasing, with a 15 percent increase from 1996 to 1998 leading to an annual reinvestment rate of $150 billion. In this context, "remodeling" includes maintenance and repair as well as replacement of structural, mechanical, and electrical systems, upgrades, expansions, improvements to grounds, and repair of damage from natural disasters. Yet the sum of remodeling activity amounts to less annually than the cost of new housing construction. New construction, however, adds less than 2 percent annually to the nation's housing stock. Remodeling reinvestment on more than 98 percent of the housing stock is less than new investment in 1 to 2 percent of housing. The median age of housing has reached 30 years—a notable threshold, the Harvard study noted, "because many major systems need replacement every 25 to 30 years. . . ." Despite the rising median age of housing, which increased by five years between 1985 and 1995, and the rising median age of the population, which now includes more households in the peak earning ages of the 40s and 50s, "the absolute number of home improvement projects is not expected to show much of an increase over the next decade." These projections, which assume no major change in institutional capacity or reinvestment incentives, have grim implications for established neighborhoods and local government jurisdictions, since without additional reinvestment their downward trajectory will accelerate.

Complex Housing Markets

Market conditions make real estate commodities unusually complex. The real estate maxim that property values are a function of "location, location, and location" reveals additional complexity. Features of land and dwelling are far from irrelevant, but dwellings are sought as investments as well as for shelter, complicating the purchase of housing compared with most purchases of goods and services. Many other considerations enter location decisions. Limiting attention to land and structures leaves out too much and obscures complex real markets (Galster 1987). Real housing markets include characteristics of governments, neighborhoods, and schools within commuting-to-work zones. Commuters vary in their tolerance for travel distance, time, cost, stress, and danger. Rarely is there only one jurisdiction, neighborhood, and school within a tolerable commuting territory. Sometimes more than one state is included within commuting zones, adding considerable policy and tax variety to location choices. Moreover, locations also have negative characteristics, such as the social behavior and personal characteristics of neighbors. Moving decisions and destination choices include pushes away from negative characteristics as well as pulls toward positive ones.

Housing Market Uncertainties

Uncertain outcomes from housing markets are to be expected. For the majority of lenders, developers, and buyers, limiting uncertainty is a goal. A common strategy to limit uncertainty is to make conventional choices, hoping that "following the crowd" into the suburbs or exurbs will limit risk.

Market uncertainties have many dimensions. Concerning a residence, it is one thing to assess its physical soundness, consider its match with potential occupants' stylistic preferences, and imagine whether living in it would equal its appeal on a 20-minute walk-through visit. But what about transportation options—after a job change? What about school conditions—after redistricting? What about neighborhood safety—after the income status of neighbors falls? What about time for house and children—after one parent falls ill or departs permanently? What happens to the jurisdiction if the major employer moves out, the state government cuts state aid by 25 percent in a financial crisis, and the police chief pleads guilty to collusion with drug dealers? What happens if a supposedly safe destination is chosen, perhaps in a gated subdivision, and then the school bus is hit broadside while turning from the subdivision onto a high speed road, the developer goes bankrupt before the park is built, and the commuting distance disrupts family life on late worknights?

These possibilities are difficult for individuals to calculate or even approximate, as well as being difficult for any two members of a single household to evaluate identically. As a consequence, many people make cautious location decisions in which personal safety and investment security figure prominently.

Discussion of these four conditions—participatory democracy, reinvestment incentives, housing market uncertainties and complexities—reveals numerous obstacles to housing market participants' ability to make fully informed decisions. The potential risks to producers and buyers are substantial. Most real estate producers and consumers cope with these risks by aiming for what they consider relatively safe and secure investments—that is, they are risk averse. Rapid change adds to the difficulty of being adequately informed as well as contributes to greater risks. We argue that the net effect of these conditions falls short of meeting the social or societal aspirations of market participants. The exercise of preferences in the current market structure leads to imbalance, disequilibrium, substantial risk, and questionable satisfaction. This disequilibrium is a challenge for strategic planning. Changing the incentive and risk structure may lead to better results by increasing reinvestment.

Jurisdictions' Policy Goals

Some political theorists have interpreted how elected officials react to their jurisdictions' locations in establishing and pursuing goals. Paul Peterson (1981, 20), for example, argued that "policies and programs can be said to be in the interest of cities whenever the policies maintain or enhance the economic position, social prestige, or political power of the city. . . ." This concept, even if it were generally sound, provides no guidance as to how different settings may alter the policies that will promote economic and social strength. It also leaves out of the accounting those settings that are so disadvantaged due to economic deterioration, poverty, and social problems that no policies or programs available to local officials are likely to meet that test.

Charles Tiebout (1956) and some successors (Ostrom, Tiebout, and Warren 1961) argued that local elected officials pursue optimum jurisdiction size for efficient delivery of services. As a practical matter, this goal is unworkable, since most jurisdictions lack meaningful annexation power. It also provides no basis for assessing whether suburbs and exurbs have the same optimum size as central cities in light of their different positions and functions. Nor do such approaches take into account how states assign service responsibilities and financial authority to cities, towns, villages, counties, and special districts, all of which would influence optimum efficient size. In fact, efficient size analyses have produced inconsistent results concerning specific services and comparisons among services. Moreover, elected officials pursue diverse goals, including ones other than promoting their jurisdiction's economic power and social prestige. These include short-range goals such as getting reelected, dispensing favors, providing services effectively, responding to citizen concerns, and obtaining favorable media coverage.

In addition, the location of jurisdictions influences which goals seem rational, reasonable, useful, achievable, and even necessary. Elected officials will be especially concerned, for instance, about large differences in tax rates between their area and adjacent areas. Their degree of concern will be influenced by their jurisdiction's share of metropolitan population and territory, their economic strength and tax base relative to those of neighboring governments, and local revenue options provided by state government. Their opinions also will be influenced by their location relative to employment and nonresidential property development and retail sales trends. In turn, these opinions will influence attempts to shape development, with consequences for sprawl patterns.

Commuting Influences Decisions

Local governments can be categorized as "destination" jurisdictions or as "pass-through," "balanced," or "feeder" jurisdictions relative to current employment locations and development trends. These categories influence how local public officials and citizens evaluate alternative development patterns. Destination jurisdictions have many commuters as well as local residents employed within their boundaries. Feeder jurisdictions have more residents employed and looking for work than jobs available within their boundaries. Pass-through jurisdictions are between destination and feeder jurisdictions. Balanced jurisdictions are also between destination and feeder jurisdictions but are substantial employment subcenters and may have more jobs than residents employed and seeking work (Figure 2.1). Balanced jurisdictions may be old suburbs or new edge cities (Garreau 1991).

Central cities are often destinations. The extent to which they continue to be destinations depends on whether they have lost jobs during the postindustrial era. Some inner suburbs are in the balanced category, while others are pass-through jurisdictions. Outer suburbs and exurbs, and many other suburbs in large metropolitan areas, are usually feeder jurisdictions, although there are occasional edge city exceptions to this generalization. These categories are not stagnant. Positioning evolves with changes in metropolitan scale, national and international employment trends, and the success and failure of local enterprises. Policies of local elected officials will be influenced by perceptions of where their jurisdiction is positioned, but also by where they believe it has been positioned and where they think it is headed. Often these policies concern whether their jurisdiction has enough local revenue sources, and the prospect of future resources, to meet anticipated public service costs.

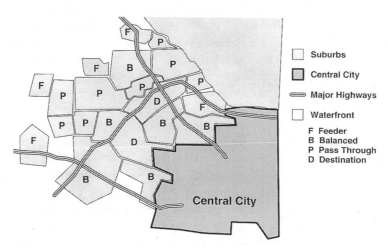

Figure 2.1. Suburbs in a Housing and Workplace Mosaic

Costs of Growth

Typical patterns of metropolitan evolution also influence policies of elected officials. Elected officials of feeder jurisdictions are confronted with the short-run and long-run conflicts between quantity and quality. Residential development in fringe jurisdictions typically moves ahead of attracting employment and retail sales, so these jurisdictions become feeders. Local jurisdictions usually rely mainly on real property taxes to pay for local public services, especially for public education. If each new residence contained even a single school-age child, the value of each structure often would need to be $250,000 (Daniels 1999, 141), or $400,000 in the case of Loudoun County, Virginia (Brookings Institution 1998), to pay for the local share of education and other public service costs. Such residential structures get built in fringe jurisdictions, but the average value usually is less. Consequently, real property tax rates in some fringe jurisdictions, such as Loudoun and Prince William County on the fringe of the Washington, D.C. metropolitan area, may be high or rising rapidly relative to rates in inner and middle suburbs that have more business properties.

Elected officials react to these high real property tax rates, and the conflicting demands for more schools and lower taxes, by trying to increase business properties within their jurisdiction. This desire by elected officials contributes to the tyranny of easy development decisions. Loudoun County, Virginia, provides an example of a jurisdiction where, until the end of the 1990s, public officials had faith that business growth would produce tax benefits. Loudoun, which is west of Washington, D.C. and Fairfax County, was the eighth-fastest-growing county in the United States from 1990 through 1997 and the third fastest in 1998.

The belief that business properties would constitute a net gain to the public fisc was so ingrained in the assumptions of Loudoun County supervisors that until 1998 the county had never conducted an analysis of revenue and expenditure effects of new businesses. In that year, the prospect that World Com Inc. would locate its headquarters and 30,000 jobs in Loudoun led to a revenue-expenditure analysis. The analysis assumed that one-third of the employees would live in Loudoun, many of them with children in public schools (Blum 1998). Little if any net revenue gain was expected after taking account of new public expenditures, especially for schools. Local officials estimated that houses would need to sell for $400,000, instead of the typical $200,000, to pay for school, infrastructure, and other service costs. While this analysis reframed the local debate about how much to encourage or resist growth, the counterargument in this unresolved controversy was stated by the chair of the Loudoun Economic Development Commission: "Let's say we slow down the economic engine. That, in my opinion, is setting the framework in motion for the residential growth to keep on growing without the commercial development." Implicit in this argument was the belief that residential growth cannot or will not be limited. It implicitly acknowledged that the tyranny of easy development decisions was in control in Loudoun County. The Loudoun Board of

Supervisors was split in 1999 over how to deal with this dilemma. It united, however, in turning to the Virginia General Assembly for relief, arguing that some means of tapping residents' income growth was needed since it was so far outstripping increases in real property values.

Boundary Locations

Attracting more employment has several spatial effects. Within suburban and exurban jurisdictions, local government officials often encourage employment growth near their boundaries. Boundary locations maximize tax base gains while minimizing traffic within the jurisdiction, or so it seems initially. In suburban and exurban jurisdictions, the most attractive boundary for business development often will be the boundary closest to the central city (Map 2.1). This ten-

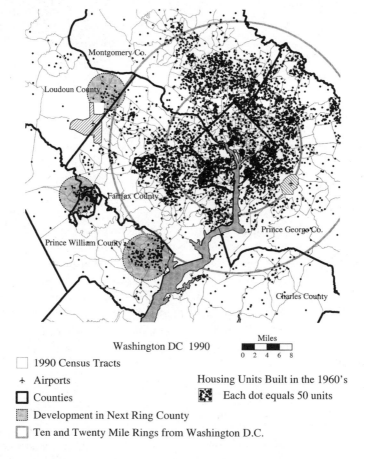

Washington DC 1990

1990 Census Tracts

+ Airports

Counties

Development in Next Ring County

Ten and Twenty Mile Rings from Washington D.C.

Miles
0 2 4 6 8

Housing Units Built in the 1960's
Each dot equals 50 units

Map 2.1. Residential Development Spillover across County Boundaries: Washington, D.C. Region, 1990 Housing Units Built in the 1960s.

Loudoun County developments Sugarland Run and Lowes Island are just over the Fairfax County line (just to the right of the development). (Synergy/Photography)

dency has two effects on adjacent jurisdictions. Elected officials and residents of the next inner jurisdiction resent it. It is close to the outer boundary of the next inner jurisdiction, which often has been reserved for residences, based on a goal of separating residences from nuisances such as traffic. Thus, residents' initial security from congestion and cut-through traffic is threatened. Planning director Robert Marriott of Montgomery County, Maryland, adjacent to Washington, D.C., has observed that many traffic problems are caused by through traffic from fringe counties, so that braking development within Montgomery County "is the equivalent of 'shooting yourself in the foot.'" Sometimes, as in Baltimore County, surrounding Baltimore, Maryland, a growth boundary has been established with a rural zone beyond it. But in an adjacent county, Carroll, the area immediately across the county line has been targeted for local growth near its existing towns (Gurwitt 1999, 22). As a result, Douglas Porter (1997, 42) noted: "Only a more rational, workable regional planning process, highly unlikely in the Washington, D.C. area, would begin to overcome this problem."

Effects on Transportation

A second spatial effect is that the commuting shed extends another 20 miles or so beyond each new area of major job creation. Employment opportunities in the fringe jurisdiction create commuting opportunities 20 miles farther out in other jurisdictions. These more remote commuters then drive through the juris-

diction that has received the business enhancement, either to work in that jurisdiction or to travel beyond it to other jurisdictions. By this sequence, each residential area toward the central city receives more traffic congestion and may be
a potential cut-through traffic neighborhood. Avoidance of cut-through traffic
is reinforced as a local neighborhood and political goal.

Each of these settlements takes on a unimodal transportation pattern. Only private automobiles can cope effectively with this arrangement of land uses. Thus, the
tyranny of easy development decisions passes through more turns of the screw,
leading toward a widening territory of mediocre development that threatens the
cumulative quality of life within each jurisdiction and for the region as a whole.

Contending Political Goals

In each category of jurisdictions (destination, feeder, pass-through, and balanced), contending forces are inspired by different interests and goals. Some
groups are interested in expansion, because they gain from it. Other groups are
opposed to expansion, because they fear uncertainties that come with it. Some
elected officials believe their duty is to represent constituents and their jurisdiction to enhance their position. Other elected officials are more apt to accept a
larger sense of regional merit, believing that the concerns of residents and
elected officials from other jurisdictions deserve consideration.

*Looking east along U.S. Route 50 toward Dulles Airport (left horizon), the extension of
four lanes of highway into the lower-density portion of Loudoun County, Virginia, previously
planned for agricultural use, signals the expanding commute shed as employment centers grow
in the outer suburban jurisdictions. (Synergy/Photography)*

Some elected officials believe their role is to cope with projections of population and employment as though the projections are immutable forces of nature. Other officials try to imagine a better quality of life and figure out how to move toward it. Each of these attitudes, values, and interests will be in play. Their frequency and distribution at a given time and space will influence the pattern and density that occur as structural imperatives unfold, based partially on jurisdictions' metropolitan locations.

Distance, Prices, and Developers

When planning commissioners, elected officials, citizens, and professionals discuss prospects for guiding the location of land development or reining in its pace in suburban and exurban areas, this idea is usually expressed: "It is not feasible to try to force compact development, because people don't want it and the market won't support it." In nearly the same breath, a curious companion idea may be mentioned: "Housing is too expensive closer to the center of the metropolitan area. Fringe development is where affordable housing can be found" (Goodman 1998).

Inconsistencies between these ideas are likely to be missed. If housing closer to the center, where development is more compact, is more expensive, that indicates demand is high relative to supply. Conversely, if affordable housing is found on the fringe, that may mean that demand is low relative to supply. Therefore, if more people want to live closer to the center in more compact settlements than the available supply permits, they will be willing to pay more to do so. If more housing were available between the fringe and the center, then housing prices there would fall. Much land for new development exists there, and more property exists for redevelopment closer to the center. But where demand for central sites is high, obstacles to development often frustrate it. Housing markets are segmented. One can say accurately that some people do not want to live near the center—and, in practice, some central sites have no effective demand, perhaps because of such factors as hazardous waste pollution or adverse neighborhood social conditions.

In some metropolitan housing markets, such as Washington, D.C., prices for essentially the same dwelling may vary by $100,000 or more between middle-distance suburban housing and fringe dwellings. EM Risse (1998a, 26–32) compared identical newly constructed dwellings offered for sale by the same builders in two radii around Washington, D.C. Prices in the ring 10 to 20 miles from the metropolitan core averaged about $100,000 more than the same houses in the ring 20 to 30 miles from the center. Risse attributed most of this price difference to demand variation rather than to varying costs to the builders. Furthermore, builders, like all entrepreneurs, prefer more profits to less. If they do not always try to maximize profits, at least they seek satisfactory profits. For these reasons, more development should be occurring where demand is high,

New 1990s infill housing in Fairfax County, Virginia, sells for $100,000 more than identical housing on the metropolitan fringe in Loudoun County.

with a consequent rise in developers' profits and a decline in prices due to increasing supply.

Why more housing is not built closer to the center compared with the amount that is built on the fringe, therefore, is a puzzle. In some instances, the obstacle does not seem to be a shortage of land free of brownfield contamination for development. EM Risse (1998b) estimated that in Northern Virginia land is "planned and zoned for over 20 times the expected 20-year demand for employment/tax base land uses." Furthermore, Risse (1998b, 3) estimated: "There is enough vacant and severely underutilized land within one-half mile of these [101 METRO rail transit] stations, if developed at Rosslyn/Ballston Corridor densities, to serve all the future development needs projected by MWCOG [Metropolitan Washington Council of Governments] . . . 900,000+/- jobs and 550,000+/- households between now and the year 2000." In addition, "approximately 1,500,000 [acres in Northern Virginia] is currently planned, zoned or held by current owners for intensive urban uses," Risse wrote. "If this land were all developed at minimum viable densities, this amount of land would accommodate a population of 15,000,000."

In 1999, despite a brisk real estate market in the Washington, D.C. region, about 25 percent of sellers, mostly in outlying areas, were discovering they had negative equity in their dwellings. Sellers were bringing money to closings to deal with settlement costs, because either sales prices were below their purchase prices, or their property had not appreciated enough to cover closing costs on top of the purchase price, constituting what Realtors call negative equity. As one Realtor said: "In close-in areas, negative equity is pretty much gone. In outlying areas, you're seeing more of it" (Deane 1999). On the other hand, most metropolitan regions have a sector in which expensive new residences are constructed in fringe locations. Many local jurisdictions use zoning regulations to encourage construction of expensive homes and to discourage construction of lesser dwellings. Myron Orfield (1998), analyzing "metropolitics" in the Chicago area, blamed requirements for "huge lot sizes" for locking "the region into low-density sprawling development patterns that are costly to sustain" and that "needlessly destroy tens of thousands of acres of rich farmland."

Sprawl, Regulations, and Risk

The key to development locations lies in the concept of the tyranny of easy development decisions. The automobile, affluence, personal preferences, infrastructure investments, and metropolitan spatial form created conditions in which vast territories can be developed. Numerous local governments with the power to control land use govern these vast territories. Typically they adopt zoning codes that require separating residences from locations of work, commerce, and even schools. Isolated pods of automobile-dependent development

Cul-de-sac developments in Ashburn Farm (foreground) and Ashburn Village (background) in Loudoun County, Virginia, share a "green space" between them. These miscellaneous parcels are also zoned for residential development, however. Even easy development decisions at the fringe may become contested as these neighbors protest the loss of green space. (Synergy/Photography)

inevitably result (Norquist and Schundler 1999). State governments limit local governments' powers. Landowners retain powerful rights to development. Land developers, once they have launched development processes, also gain development rights. The jurisdictions and subareas where they can exercise these rights are numerous. Local governments' growth management successes, therefore, may have unintended spillover effects in nearby jurisdictions. As Douglas Porter (1997, 41) has observed: "It is generally believed by Washington, D.C. real estate watchers that [Montgomery] County's rigorous development reviews, restrictive agricultural zoning, and developer exactions have driven small developers, in particular, to other less demanding jurisdictions. . . ."

The net effect is that numerous development opportunities exist, which lending institutions have been ready to finance, and other institutions have been willing to insure against some risks. A large proportion of these relatively low development-risk situations have been in fringe locations. In this decentralized decision-making system, effectively plugging the plentiful leaks in the proverbial dike is very difficult. The tyranny of easy development decisions follows from too many development opportunities and leads to excessive sprawl, insufficient reinvestment, and increasing income disparities among local jurisdictions.

Chapter 3

Strategic Planning: Assessing Dangers in a Postsuburban Era

In this chapter we explore how an understanding of trends can be used in strategic planning to identify and avert dangers. We will discuss characteristics of strategic planning, emphasizing the role of dangers. We will examine some analytic concepts useful in illuminating dangers, explore the potential usefulness of leading indicators of dangers, and consider how dangers have been conceived in a few strategic plans for cities and suburbs.

The tyranny of easy development decisions intersects with disinvestment in neighborhoods and income disparities among local jurisdictions. The postsuburban era unfolds under these influences, as will be seen in Chapter 4 for the Richmond, Virginia, area. Many suburbs may follow the path of decline trod previously by central cities. In the Washington, D.C. area, some suburbs have declined faster than the city, but others have been stable while adapting to postsuburban trends, as will be discussed in Chapter 5.

The Role of Dangers in Strategic Planning

In the postsuburban era, income and population decline have become normal in many suburbs, as occurred earlier in central cities, resulting in larger income disparities among local jurisdictions. When income disparities are large, developers have greater incentives to supply housing where potential residents believe they will be protected from undesirable neighborhood effects on housing values and social conditions. The tyranny of easy development decisions on the metropolitan fringe nourishes these tendencies by developers and potential residents. Reinvestment is inadequate, partly due to political obstacles from nearby residents. The most pervasive danger facing metropolitan regions, and many local governments within regions, is imbalance or disequilibrium that leads to polarizing extremes of spatial concentrations of wealth and poverty. Sprawl, disinvestment, and income disparities are manifestations of pervasive imbalance and disequilibrium.

Strategic planning for regions is more difficult than for jurisdictions for three reasons: 1) regions' decentralized authority structure, 2) policy biases that reflect local jurisdictions' positions within the metropolitan mosaic, and 3) markets' inability to allocate investments effectively to reduce sprawl, increase reinvestment, and limit income disparities. Several concepts have special utility in planning for regions, although they also are useful within jurisdictions. Applying the four paired concepts—area and power, pattern and density, population and neighborhood, space and place—to metropolitan conditions helps reveal why sprawl, disinvestment, and disparities emerge, and what can be done about them. Discussion of using these four paired concepts to illuminate dangers and opportunities will be expanded later in this chapter.

Strengths, weaknesses, dangers, and opportunities are strategic planning concepts that require attention to questions such as: What is a strength in relation to some type of goal or current condition? Dangers in particular call for an answer to this contextual question. Organizations' strengths and weaknesses include internal characteristics, but outward evaluation of organizations within their environment also is implied by these concepts. When assessing dangers, however, the paramount focus is on external conditions and trends that threaten the organization. Opportunities also depend on interactions between an organization and its environment (Bryson 1995, 83). Opportunities will be examined preliminarily in Chapters 6 and 8 and more extensively in Chapters 9 and 10. Here the focus is on dangers.

Averting Dangers

Averting dangers implies long-term viability, which, in many instances, requires surmounting the difficult challenge of altering economic and population trends. Rarely can one municipality acting alone alter them, unless that jurisdiction is well positioned. Strategic planning, whether for municipalities or regions, should take jurisdictions' metropolitan context into account. But advocates for a metropolitan public interest should not expect balanced metropolitan outcomes from decisions by and for individual municipalities. Strategic planning, especially by well-off local jurisdictions, may exacerbate rather than reduce interjurisdictional income and tax base inequalities within metropolitan areas. If well-off jurisdictions try to enhance their advantages, their decisions may increase inequalities among jurisdictions.

From the perspective of achieving and retaining reasonable socioeconomic and fiscal balance among municipalities, strategic planning by poor jurisdictions should aim at strengthening their economic and fiscal foundations and attracting middle-income residents (Varady and Raffel 1995). Strategic planning by well-off municipalities and most counties should provide more low-income housing and contribute to income redistribution, as politically unpopular as that may seem. With these goals, crisis poverty conditions become less likely, greater balance and long-term equilibrium can be achieved, and sustainable communities become possible.

The improbability of this combination of policies by poor and well-off jurisdictions indicates that strategic planning should not be left solely to municipalities and counties, even though they should practice it. Routine decisions by developers, investors, and residential movers also tend to increase spatial inequalities among neighborhoods and jurisdictions. More effective governance by regions, states, and the nation should correct some of the intrametropolitan imbalances that flow from local self-serving action (Downs 1994; Rusk 1993).

Strategic Planning Claims

Public officials in most municipalities of more than 25,000 residents claim to have a strategic plan. These plans have several common elements (Streib and Poister 1990), including assessing dangers. How dangers are assessed is not apparent in surveys and other summary descriptions (Kemp 1992) of strategic planning practice. Nor is it evident how dangers should be assessed. One could infer from the sparse treatment of this subject, however, that writers about strategic planning assume public officials will be competent, even adept, at such analyses. These discussions rarely have probed how to describe and predict dangers (for useful articles and books about strategic planning, see Note 3.1). The notion that dangers should be avoided and perhaps overcome implies that dangers can be revealed through leading indicators of trends. A conceptual gap between strategic planning and analyzing dangers exists because strategic planning, policy analyses, and urban theories rarely are combined. Our intent here is to establish links among them.

Closing the divide between technocratic and political planning is an idea embedded explicitly in some discussions about the utility of strategic planning. John Bryson (1995, 10), for example, stated that "the strategic planning process presented here builds on the nature of political decision making. So many other management techniques fail because they ignore, try to circumvent, or even try to counter the political nature of life in private, public, and nonprofit organizations." Bryson (1995, 89–90) went on to observe: "In my experience, members of a public or nonprofit organization's governing board, particularly if they are elected, are generally better at identifying and assessing external threats and opportunities than are the organization's employees." Although strategic planning emphasizes coping with competition, it also may facilitate internal cooperation among elected officials, as Gerald Gabris (1992, 77) wrote: "In working with many city councils as a strategic planning facilitator, . . . a major side benefit, . . . has been the cultivation of cooperative decision-making norms between elected and appointed officials." In addition, consensus may emerge for a surprising reason, according to Gabris (1992, 80): "Elected officials learn . . . that many hold the same views but never knew it."

Reclaiming the Public Interest

While broad agreement sometimes may emerge through strategic planning, the norms, and therefore the strategies, of elected officials often are in tension with some jurisdiction values. Peterson (1981) has argued that cities, like other organizations, have an interest in enhancing their power and prestige. "Because cities have limits," Peterson (1981, 4) wrote, "one explains urban public policy by looking at the place of the city in the larger socioeconomic and political context. The position of the city within the larger political economy of the nation fundamentally affects the policy choices that cities make. In making these decisions, cities select those policies which are in the interests of the city, taken as a whole."

This passage, and Peterson's theme, can be interpreted as an attempt to reclaim the concept of "the public interest" from the oblivion into which it had been cast by interpreters of American politics as "interest group politics" (Banfield 1961; Bentley 1908; Lowi 1979; McConnell 1966; Schattschneider 1960; Schubert 1960; Truman 1951). In the approach of "realist" critics of the public interest concept, the public interest is a mirage, unknown and probably unknowable. Private interests expressed through interest groups become known because they are articulated and advocated. These interest group opinions, collectively, come as close to constituting a public interest as can be known, in this realist critique. On the other hand, one can infer that the public interest of cities, in Peterson's view, involves cities sustaining themselves through their own action in the competitive context of intrametropolitan competition among jurisdictions and intermetropolitan competition for investments and residents.

The identity of Peterson's decision-making "city" or metropolitan area is not evident. Who are the actors who personify the city or metropolitan area? Nor is it evident how one would determine that elected and appointed officials are making decisions based on "the interests of the city, taken as a whole." In addition, Peterson (1981, 20) argued that policies are "in the interest of cities whenever the policies maintain or enhance the economic position, social prestige, or political power of the city, taken as a whole." Perhaps the notion of power and prestige incorporates the idea that jurisdictions should renew their capacities and compete effectively for investment, employment, tax base, and a representative population mix. Enhancing power and prestige seems to imply long-range planning and implementation to deal with broad and deep forces impinging on distinct jurisdictions within multijurisdictional metropolitan contexts.

Many constituents, however, may want their immediate needs and wants satisfied. Rather than confronting issues of power and prestige that require long-range planning and implementation, they may want to be left alone with local taxes kept modest. As Bryson and Roering (1988, 1002) noted: "governmental strategic planning is probably most needed where it is least likely to work."

Elected Officials' Goals

When analyzing local strategic planning, it is important to distinguish between the goals of elected officials and the well-being of jurisdictions. Elected officials typically have some version of the well-being of their jurisdiction in mind, but many such images are possible, including self-serving ones. Elected officials are likely to interpret their own well-being as obtaining enough votes to be reelected. The type of political strategic planning in which elected officials engage usually includes calculations about how constituents' votes will be influenced by the officials' policy decisions.

In democratic systems, voters get some say about which inducements will be offered to current constituents and potential in- and outmovers. Local governments are not independent of their constituents. Elected and appointed officials interact with constituents within a political culture. One constant in democratic systems is that some recurring, often regular, means of confirming or overturning the power of particular authorities occurs through elections. Practitioners of strategic planning, therefore, cope with competition for power by elected officials and constituents within local jurisdictions as well as with multijurisdictional competition.

Coping well with complex metropolitan settings requires long-range planning, steady and coordinated implementation, and integration of population settlement patterns with employment opportunities, environmental goals, and adequate fiscal capacities. Actions by elected officials who are competing for votes from current residents often are not consistent either with long-range planning or steady implementation. They may be cultivating favor with interest groups and angling for favorable treatment in the next day's news coverage. One of the challenges in planning strategically is to reconcile preferences for short-term rewards by many elected officials and their constituents with more fundamental actions that may stabilize or enhance local jurisdictions' viability.

Can Indicators Help Predict Dangers?

Economic indicators have been used since 1949 to describe national economic conditions and predict the immediate future performance of the U.S. economy (President's Council of Economic Advisors 1996). The Federal Reserve Board decides when to change the interest rates it charges banks to borrow from the federal banking system. This decision is informed by trend data, including the Index of Economic Indicators, which contribute to judgments about whether the quantity of economic activity should be stimulated, slowed, or maintained. The Federal Reserve Board attempts to influence an open system, the national economy, by manipulating significant policy levers—interest rates and the money supply.

In urban affairs, the tool that perhaps most resembles national economic indicators is the revenue and expenditure projections used by local financial officials to design operating and capital budgets. The intent is quite different, however, as is the implied scope of understanding. Local financial administrators are predicting flows of money into and out of public coffers, rather than describing and predicting the ebb and flow of the regional economy. Nor are local financial managers trying to modulate the month-to-month functioning of their region's economy through their operating and capital budget recommendations.

Leading Indicators

Based on examining strategic plans, it appears that leading indicators rarely are used to predict dangers. In their account of strategic planning practices in eight jurisdictions in the Minneapolis area, Bryson and Roering (1988) do not cite the ability to assess dangers as an important element that should be available in initiating a strategic planning process. Gerald L. Gordon, in his handbook *Strategic Planning for Local Government* (1993, 71), observed: "The process of formal strategic planning has emerged relatively recently, and forecasting is an even more recent addition to the process." Gordon noted that forecasts are most reliable when there has been constancy in historical trends, but he did not suggest any data for forecasts for the future viability of local government jurisdictions. Nor are examples of forecasting dangers contained in a handbook published in 1993 by the most prominent organization of professionals, the International City/County Management Association. From these omissions, one can infer that such practices have rarely been followed.

Neighborhood Change

In a literature review about neighborhood indicators, Sawicki and Flynn (1996) described how neighborhood conditions have been assessed. Their article was related to the Urban Institute's National Neighborhood Indicators Project, whose overall objective, they wrote, "is to help local institutions develop a comprehensive and technically sound set of indicators of neighborhood conditions, so that community residents, public officials, and civic leaders can better plan appropriate strategies to improve their communities" (1996, 165). But they did not find or propose methods for predicting neighborhood, jurisdiction, or institutional (e.g., public school) futures based on neighborhood trends, including housing. Instead, they examined obstacles to useful predictions, concluding: "Unraveling the factors that cause change either in neighborhoods or in their residents' well-being is difficult for many reasons. . . . [T]he causes of change emanate from the physical, social, and economic environments, as well as from the inhabitants themselves. . . . Finally, cause and effect are often difficult to distinguish. . . . Also critical to understanding cause and effect will be research on geographic mobility and its role in neighborhood and resident change" (1996, 177–178).

In another analysis, Kenneth Temkin and William Rohe (1996, 159) suggested that ". . . neighborhoods within a single city can follow one of three trajectories: stability, decline, or upgrading. We argue that a neighborhood's trajectory results from its ability to position itself favorably with external sources of financial, political, and social resources and that this ability is largely dependent on the physical, social, and locational characteristics of the community." They constructed what they believe is a synthesis of three perspectives—ecological, subcultural, and political economy. They suggested that the ecological perspective is more deterministic, which is its weakness; it needs to be complemented by a subcultural perspective that evokes potential for effective action by residents in some neighborhoods on behalf of stability. Institutions in a neighborhood's political economy also can sometimes act to resist change. Unfortunately, the authors did not suggest how public officials or citizens might interpret data to anticipate dangers, except to suggest that a neighborhood's resiliency in resisting change is influenced significantly by its "social fabric." Temkin and Rohe (1996, 168–169) advised: "Policymakers must have information regarding the social fabric of neighborhoods and the perceptions outsiders have of the community in order to predict neighborhood trajectories and design stabilization or improvement efforts. Unfortunately, census data does not have information on level of attachment felt by residents, the use of local commercial facilities and the pattern of social interactions within a neighborhood. . . . [C]ities must supplement census information with a social census in order to determine the strength of each neighborhood's social fabric." Social fabric data could be useful, but it would be quickly out of date as well as expensive to gather for the many neighborhoods and jurisdictions that should be included in such analyses. Alternatives to this approach, therefore, are essential.

Urban sustainability analysis is a recent approach which uses indicators to assess conditions and trends that also could emphasize attempts to predict future trends. Virginia Maclaren (1996), in a review and evaluation of sustainability analyses, found only modest efforts to predict future results based on recent trends. In addition, she cautioned (1996, 187) that "predictive sustainability indicators rely on mathematical models . . . which are inherently disputable." She suggested use of the "conditional indicator" as a more promising approach. Conditional indicators, according to Maclaren, "depend on a form of scenario development; they answer the question: 'If a given indicator achieves or is set at a certain level, what will the level of an associated indicator be in the future?'"

Excessive Inequalities

On the dimension of inequalities, David Rusk (1993) has argued that when central cities have declined so much that their per capita income is 70 percent or less of that in their suburbs, they have "passed the 'point of no return.'" Rusk (1993, 75–76) added: "At this point city-suburb economic disparities become so severe that the city, in a broad sense, is no longer a place to invest or create jobs (except in some fortress-type downtowns)." Rusk did not explain what the leading indicators of this point of no return are, other than per capita income relationships that are discovered each decade. Rusk believes that inelastic cities are headed in the direction of the "point of no return." Inelastic cities are those that cannot expand their boundaries through annexation or consolidation. By that interpretation, more than 90 percent of sizable cities are headed toward the "point of no return," but their trajectory is not predicted by Rusk in terms of rate, timing, or duration, or how those trend characteristics will be influenced by conditions other than inelasticity. Consequently, Rusk's formulation helps identify dangers only in the broadest sense.

Aging Housing and Poverty Concentrations

Decline by inelastic cities is a consequence of neighborhood changes. Neighborhood changes commonly are attributed to the interaction between aging of housing stock and a mobile population. Anthony Downs (1981, 3), for example, has suggested: "A life cycle is evident in many neighborhoods. They evolve from births as new subdivisions occupied by relatively affluent households, through middle age, when they shelter relatively less affluent households but remain in good condition, to their deaths through decay and abandonment by the poor households that finally occupy them."

Even Downs does not provide clear guidance for how analysts might use data to anticipate the trajectory of their local jurisdiction. Downs is well positioned to provide such advice because connections among conditions, trends, neighborhoods, cities, suburbs, metropolitan areas, and public policies have been prominent in his work (1973, 1982, 1994). Downs may believe such advice would fall on deaf ears. He also has argued (1981, 7) that public officials generally fail to acknowledge that the United States' system of allocating housing requires that poverty concentrations be located somewhere: ". . . [P]ublic officials almost never confront or even discuss the important issue of where the [housing] deterioration needed to cope with poverty ought to be located for the good of the entire community. If they did, many residents of the areas selected would become outraged. They would feel their neighborhoods were being relegated to a state of permanent deterioration. Consequently, all 'comprehensive plans' use platitudes to avoid dealing with the vital issue of where poor people will live. This situation makes it almost impossible for anyone to formulate realistic overall strategies for coping with neighborhood deterioration in a metropolitan area as a whole, or even in a single large city as a whole."

Downs (1981, 18–19) also has observed that neighborhoods are too varied to permit general predictions about their income trajectory. In addition, Downs said that "crucial to every neighborhood are prevailing expectations there about future property maintenance and other conditions. These expectations are mutually reinforcing and thus self-fulfilling." That also makes predictions based on neighborhood characteristics and their surroundings difficult.

Plausible Predictions

We share Downs's perspective about the inevitability that some neighborhoods will deteriorate, but some predictions are reasonable, even though they should be subject to correction based on periodic evaluation of new data. Only modest predictions are plausible. Modest predictions are statements such as "recent trends are expected to continue, and trends are likely to accelerate [or decrease or level off or reverse direction]." The rates of change and the endpoints of change processes are much more difficult to predict. Furthermore, nearly all social science predictions are about probabilities; they are based on empirical findings which indicate that some result occurred more frequently than chance, rather than always or nearly always. Thus, conclusions are predicted tentatively by saying that a trend probably will continue or that it will change.

Trends can be evaluated as being a serious problem or a problem of little consequence. Plausible reactions depend on interpreting the trends, policy traditions, and political consequences of adopting potential policies. Economic development reactions to employment and tax base problems, and financial/budget policy reactions to fiscal problems, are traditional and politically viable in many instances. Environmental policy reactions are more problematic, partly because they may conflict with economic development and financial goals. Reactions to socioeconomic population problems are most problematic, because they are less traditional, the means of achieving success are more difficult to discern, and political conflicts are likely to emerge when policy reactions are proposed. Socioeconomic conditions, trends, and interpretations of them will be emphasized here, because they are the most difficult problems and the ones that are least likely to be confronted effectively.

Metropolitan Evolution

In strategic planning, economic characteristics (such as employment, tax base, and fiscal trends) are most likely to be included routinely in assessments of strengths, weaknesses, and dangers. But assessing economic characteristics is only one of several fundamental subjects to explore in discerning dangers; environmental conditions also are crucial, for instance. Water supply limits development in many parts of the United States, despite Herculean and often misguided efforts to overcome these limits. Manmade damage, such as the land pollution at Love Canal near Buffalo and the brownfield decimation of specific sites in scores of cities, is also widespread. Despite these serious environmental constraints on sustainable communities, environment is less likely than economics to be included in strategic planning.

Our attention here, however, is addressed mainly to another fundamental condition that Anthony Downs (1981, 7) has said public officials almost never confront. This sometimes more difficult subject concerns the socioeconomic composition of municipalities' population. Certain cases of economic strength demonstrate the importance of this subject. The case of Richmond, Virginia, illustrates how surplus employment per resident (more jobs than residents in the labor force) can fail to revive a city's median income standing in its metropolitan area. In addition, outcommuting to suburban jobs increased even though employment in the central city continued to expand (Lucy and Phillips 1997). Because so many workers tolerate long commutes in exchange for residential location choices, employment increases in a jurisdiction may not enhance or even maintain the socioeconomic standing of its population relative to the region's population characteristics. Examples like Richmond indicate that economic development planning is part, but not the entirety, of strategic planning.

Age and Mobility

Most municipalities in metropolitan areas are susceptible to diminished capacities as they age (Bradbury, Downs, and Small 1982; Guest and Nelson 1978; Rusk 1993). Regional economic trends and subregional socioeconomic population differentiation unfold in ways that may render many municipalities vulnerable to rapid, sometimes undesirable, changes (Leven 1979). Shifts in national and international economic activity, deterioration of housing as it ages, modifications in individuals' housing preferences and housing supply opportunities, variations in interregional and international migration by racial and ethnic minorities, and changes in regional transportation and other public infrastructure interact with high residential mobility rates and fickle business attachments to places. These interactions create uncertain prospects for population stability and financial vitality for many jurisdictions. Evolutionary trends should be described to help assess whether conditions constitute dangers.

Among the metropolitan phenomena that influence the evolution of dangers are these: On average, about 50 percent of metropolitan residents move every five years. Residential mobility in individual metropolitan areas ranges from 35 to 65 percent in five years. Commuting distances have increased (Cervero 1989). Fewer people live in the jurisdiction where they work, suburbanization has continued (Leinberger 1995), exurbanization has flourished (Nelson 1992), many suburbs have declined rapidly in population and relative income standing (Orfield 1997; Phillips and Lucy 1996), poverty concentrations have increased among enclaves of African-Americans, Hispanics, and whites (Galster and Mincy 1993), and central cities generally have declined in income standing whether or not employment increased.

Connections among Dangers: Four Paired Concepts

Elected officials rarely publicly associate problems with population characteristics. They worry that someone will take offense at suggestions that some people are problems. They do not want to project themselves as social engineers of population composition. They probably believe they cannot influence population composition during their terms of office anyway. Thus, public officials often are tongue-tied about some of the most fundamental indicators of community well-being. They may be much more comfortable pursuing economic gains, whether that means bringing in outside industry and nurturing local businesses' expansion (Blakely 1994), constructing sports arenas (Baade 1996), or serving as general community boosters (Lucy 1988). Bragging about economic gains, most elected officials calculate, will do more for their re-election prospects than bemoaning the problem characteristics of some constituents who are potential voters.

Public officials will be more likely to confront population issues if they are able to apply concepts that relate population characteristics to physical settings. The danger to local jurisdictions that we have been describing can be summed up as imbalances between population and neighborhood. The analysis above also includes references to three related dangers. These are the dangers of imbalances between area and power, metropolitan pattern and density relationships that may be ineffective and distort prospects for viability in some jurisdictions, and spaces that do not function well as places (Lucy 1994a). Conditions illuminated by these concepts, such as sprawl, disinvestment, and disparities, should be considered over time and within large commuting territories. Each of these paired concepts illuminates the spatial context in which strategic planning occurs. They also represent how people and places are linked. Each paired concept raises qualitative questions that lead to assessing opportunities and dangers.

Area and Power

Area and power refer to how political power is structured territorially and how that structuring matches natural processes and society's activities. Area refers to inhabited territory in which environmental, economic, social, political, and cultural activities occur. Some activities, especially public service utilities, draw on watersheds, groundwater regimes, and air sheds. Area also refers to the functional extent of activities. It can refer to the region an activity draws upon for resources; each activity may draw resources from, or provide services to, a different area. In aggregate, area refers to the territorial extent of all related activities.

Each business firm has a local market area for customers, which typically differs from its labor market area and from its area for raw materials and intermediate products. Each household has areas, which often differ, for commuting to work, as well as for shopping, recreating, learning, and worshiping. They obtain information about the economy and government from the principal modes of communication (newspapers, television, and radio), which probably serve the largest area and therefore cannot serve small parts of the region adequately (Giddens 1979). For this reason, as well as because of insufficient attentiveness, firms and households rarely have all the information they need to make decisions.

Power refers to government authority. Area and power together address problems stemming from the geographic span of government influence. How does governmental power, expressed through taxes, regulations, and public services, correspond to the area of activities in the region? From the perspective of business firms and interest groups, questions also include: How many governments influence, control, or tax business activities? How easily can access and influence be gained relative to pertinent government authorities? What will be gained or lost by moving to or from, or expanding in, a location in one or another set of local governments?

Area and power relationships raise issues about how regions of resources match regions of need. If governance is spatially fragmented, then location options are available, and firms and households can see advantages in "voting with their feet" (Tiebout 1956). More opportunities for moving to enhance firms' and households' advantages, however, lead to more separation of needs and resources, of which income disparities are one important indicator. With an average of 90 local governments per metropolitan region in the United States, adaptive adjustments by firms, households, and governments to each other's activities constitute the daily, monthly, and yearly decisions that cumulatively shape much of the quality of life in each government jurisdiction.

Pattern and Density

Pattern refers to arrangements of physical facilities in space, and density refers to concentrations of people. Pattern focuses attention on the size, mix, and proximity of buildings and spaces. Are housing units isolated from shopping, leisure, recreation, employment, health care, schools, and work? Are complementary activities concentrated, allowing multipurpose trips? How much distance separates activities, and which transportation modes link them?

Density focuses on population concentration. Density and overcrowding are sometimes confused with each other. Overcrowding stems from too many persons per dwelling unit, especially too little space per person within the dwelling unit. Density refers to concentration of dwelling units occupied by people. Low density leads to automobile dependency, because either other transport modes are absent or their use requires excessive time. Relevant questions, therefore, include: Is density sufficient to support mass transportation? Are walking and bicycling feasible and encouraged? Are transportation and land use relationships relatively safe or dangerous?

Crossroads hamlet in western Loudoun County, Virginia, with surrounding "farmettes." (Synergy/Photography)

Rural hamlet in Wurttemberg, Germany, clusters residential and commercial uses while maintaining productive agriculture. (Synergy/Photography)

Suburban townhouse development in Ashburn Village in eastern Loudoun County, Virginia. (Synergy/Photography)

Broadlands townhouse development backs up to neither shopping nor services nor green park, but to the toll road in Loudoun County, Virginia. (Synergy/Photography)

Pattern and density are paired, because answers to questions about density and transportation necessarily depend on the pattern in which physical facilities and activities are arranged spatially. Conversely, patterns of physical arrangements reveal little about practical effects without information on settlements' population density as well. On a regional scale, these issues can be engaged through growth management, regional transportation planning, and sustainability analyses. On a small scale, pattern and density issues concern how attractive a setting is as a place to live, work, and engage in other activities, and how attractive and renewable it may remain in the future. These issues lead to infill, redevelopment, and urban design planning.

Population and Neighborhood

Population refers to people described variously, such as by income, age, family status, race, ethnicity, and religion. Neighborhood refers to subjurisdictional settlements where residents feel attachments, assign a place name, conduct activities outside the residence, or merely treat dwellings as financial investments.

   The population concept elicits categories of meaningful similarities and differences among people. These characteristics may be meaningful to outsiders such as political candidates or marketers of products. Or they may be meaningful to insiders, as with different political or religious opinions or behavioral propensities (which may be real or imagined, and perhaps related to characteristics of race, ethnicity, age, or income). These characteristics, behaviors, and opinions may contribute to cohesion or dissension within the neighborhood. Hence, they help define what the notion of neighborhood means in a particular setting.

   Neighborhood refers to a settlement in a subjurisdictional territory, which may be clearly or haphazardly bounded. In pre-automobile and pre–motorized mass transportation settlements, neighborhoods typically encompassed numerous daily activities outside each residence. By the late 20th century,

Modest single-story 1950 tract housing on lots with small backyards and long street blocks is typical of some "declining" suburban neighborhoods in Fairfax County, Virginia.

Modest story-and-a-half or two-story 1950 tract housing on lots with backyards large enough to allow expansion or garden development, short street blocks, and proximity to school and shopping typifies some "improving" suburban neighborhoods in Fairfax County, Virginia. These homes are within one mile of those in the previous photo.

many—perhaps most—residents did not conduct any daily activities outside their residences and within their neighborhoods, except passing through them on the way to and from work. First mass transportation technology and then automobiles widened daily activity territories. In consequence, the meaning of neighborhood became thinner for more residents. Due to frequent residential moves (13 in an average lifetime in the United States), many people's attachments to any neighborhood have diminished. For a given neighborhood and resident, neighborhood may retain much of its pre–motorized transportation meaning, but for others, neighborhood may mean little except a place to sleep or to recoup a housing investment before moving to the next dwelling.

Pairing population and neighborhood leads to the question of whether population concentrations should be homogeneous or heterogeneous (Lucy 1994a). Some political economy theorists argue that homogeneity at jurisdictional scale allows government to achieve the best fit between supply of services and constituent desires (Advisory Commission on Intergovernmental Relations 1987; Bish 1971). Others have argued that in most metropolitan regions, the existence of numerous local governments permits enormous disparities among jurisdictions that shortchange those most in need of services (Campbell and Sacks 1967; Lowi 1979).

Population heterogeneity at the scale of neighborhoods, streets, and blocks makes some buyers and lenders reluctant to invest in housing in view of substantial differences in quality in close proximity (Angwin 1993). Moreover, some analysts inquire whether social interaction is likely to be positive or confrontational in heterogeneous settings (e.g., Gans 1961, 1982). Organic planning theorists such as Lewis Mumford and Kevin Lynch have argued that ethnic, racial, age, and income diversity in communities enriches the human spirit and that homogeneity diminishes human potential (Hill 1992). While homogeneity may foster cooperation in relatively prosperous communities, the companion piece to that social pattern is homogeneity in poor communities (Harvey 1989). Poverty concentrations eliminate positive peer examples for young people, thereby diminishing the rising generation's aspirations (Wilson 1987). The danger then is that very large concentrations of poverty, isolation, and alienation will undermine democratic legitimacy (Banfield 1974).

Healthy people need healthy places in which to be nurtured, and healthy people are necessary for healthy places (Lucy 1994a). Hence, a satisfactory people-place connection is necessary for neighborhood renewal. Naomi Carmon (1997, 135) noted this in arguing that some neighborhoods need population transitions in order to be regenerated: "We should have learned by now that the status of a residential area is determined mainly by the socioeconomic status of its residents, which is a much more powerful determinant than housing conditions and the level of local services . . . the image of a neighborhood is mainly dependent not on its instrumental qualities, but rather on its being perceived as an appropriate place of living for respectable people."

Space and Place

Space refers to territories. Place refers to the inhabited spaces to which people feel attachments. "Placeness" can be achieved for any scale of territory and may not be limited to a residence and its environs. Place also refers to a space to which one is sufficiently attached that he or she is committed to defending it against outside threats. Where a stronger sense of place is present, more intense resistance to threats is likely. Various spaces may take on the attributes of place, including a street, development or subdivision, neighborhood, school attendance zone, area near a park, shopping district, political jurisdiction, city, region, state, nation, or planet.

At the smallest level, the dwelling space becomes a place when it becomes "home." The meanings attached to home involve physical safety, privacy, family, support, and even spirituality. Dwellings also have become significant in their contribution to financial security. To a person contemplating moving, a house becomes a "futures commodity," prompting predictions about future value compared with other potential investments. More meaning may adhere to the abstract "futures" residence than the "placeness" of the current home.

Is this place worth preserving? That is both a policy question in historic preservation and a personal question in considering investment and reinvest-

Typical pedestrian setting in Old Town Alexandria, Virginia.

ment alternatives. From either vantage point, a given structure, and also the physical fabric of buildings and streets, may be worth preserving. Suburban decline occurs partially because place attachments are inadequate. Declarations in public hearings that proposed public and private actions will "decrease my property values" embody genuine beliefs. They also indicate anticipation that other people in attendance will identify with and support an individualized anxiety that is expressed publicly. Public opposition to development is typically justified in terms of personal impacts rather than defense of place values.

A neighborhood may be mainly an accumulation of investments in structures. Modest changes in such investment neighborhoods are threatening, injecting strong elements of incivility into public statements. When residents consider reinvesting, market tests predominate. Will an investment be recouped within a short time, say two years, if the investor moves? If a national or regional recession occurs, will housing investments be at risk? If resale risks are high, why reinvest at all? Why not move soon? Weak attachments impact reinvestment, politics, and civility. When the meaning of neighborhood is shallow, the importance of politics also diminishes. What is the meaning of local citizenship when too many separations between neighborhood and activities suck meaning from space?

Equilibrium

Equilibrium implies renewal capacity. Both living organisms and social systems require external resources for renewal. For organisms, the most important resources are sun energy, the earth, air, and water. In humans, the term "homeostasis" refers to a range of variation within which healthy functioning can continue. If the limits of variation are exceeded, illness results. Excessive illness leads to breakdown of the organism. But resistance and recovery are possible. In fact, in humans they are normal, especially with timely application of medical remedies.

Equilibrium does not imply static, unvarying conditions. It implies variation within limits. It also implies survival, persistence, and periodic renewal. The instruments by which renewal can be achieved, from within and without social systems such as neighborhoods and jurisdictions, are little studied and not well understood. References to old neighborhoods in the United States and to much older settlements and societies on other continents inform us that renewal often occurs. We infer that where internal resources are scarce and social commitment to the well-being of neighborhoods is weak, renewal capacity (hence equilibrium) is inadequate.

These concepts—area and power, pattern and density, population and neighborhood, space and place—can help reveal strengths, weaknesses, dangers, and opportunities in competitive contexts. They can provide clues about indicators of conditions and trends that may illuminate renewal capacity in neighborhoods, jurisdictions, and regions. Each of these concepts, and the interactions among them, yields potential subjects for indicators. Attention to income, poverty, population, race and ethnicity, housing age, housing size, mobility rates, housing locations, employment locations, commuting times, tax rates, revenue effort, housing and other building footprints, remodeling permits, street networks, traffic deaths, violent crime, social service recipients, free lunch eligibility, standard school test scores, and other related subjects have considerable potential for describing conditions and trends, predicting (in a modest sense) future trends (see Chapter 8), and stimulating policy alternatives with potential for coping with the conditions and trends. Our intention here is to deal mainly with concepts, results, and interpretations rather than with specific indicators (these are discussed in Appendix 8.1 to Chapter 8). From a scattered review of strategic plans, it appears that more attention to each of these—concepts, results, interpretations, and indicators—may prove valuable.

Housing Comes First

Housing concerns, interacting with changing family characteristics and preferences, have generally been found to be the main pushes and pulls that influence residential mobility (Goodman 1978; Spain 1989; Varady and Raffel 1995). As families enlarge or diminish in numbers, and as heads of household increase or decrease in financial resources, status aspirations, and stage of life preferences, the housing characteristics they will pay for often change. Mickey Lauria (1998, 399) has observed that ". . . neighborhood change is based on the characteristics of inmovers and outmovers. Where there is contention in the literature it is over why people move in or move out."

Housing preferences and housing purchase capacities are revealed in the size of new housing that is built, as well as in its tenure and infrastructure features. Housing preferences do not explain some residential patterns due to discrimination and redlining, as David Harvey (1989, 123) has argued. But preferences must be relevant in many instances; otherwise the dominant tendency would be for people who can afford choices to purchase what they dislike, while they pass up what they prefer and can afford. This is an unlikely explanation of middle-income housing patterns.

The median size of new single-family detached housing units increased from about 1,100 square feet in 1950 to more than 1,900 square feet by 1995 (National Association of Home Builders 1997). Greater purchasing capacity, changes in preferences, and changes in housing supply processes led to this increase. The typical 1995 buyer of a new 1,900-square-foot dwelling was not likely to be attracted to a median 1,100-square-foot dwelling built in 1950. To the extent that neighborhoods and jurisdictions in 1995 were heavily populated by 1,100-square-foot dwellings built around 1950, they were not particularly

Newer developments in Old Town Alexandria, Virginia, include attention to needs of pedestrians and bicyclists.

attractive to the typical above-median-income buyers of new 1,900-square-foot houses, unless location factors were strong.

Consequently, jurisdictions with large concentrations of 40- to 50-year-old, 1,100-square-foot housing units are vulnerable to substantial reductions in median family (and per capita and per household) income from their relative income standing in previous decades. The abundance of small, middle-aged housing units in some suburbs probably caused them to decline faster in relative income than their central cities. It follows from this speculation that indicators of housing age and size should be used in assessments of dangers in strategic planning.

Findings from metropolitan analyses in Virginia are consistent with the interpretation that housing's age and, by inference, its size help describe and explain trends, including suburban decline. Where sizable proportions of housing units were constructed in the 1950s and 1960s, median family income declined in a substantial majority of census tracts (Lucy and Phillips 1997). Conversely, where 40 percent or more of housing units were constructed before 1940, median family income increased in about 60 percent of the census tracts. One should remember the danger of misinterpretation by committing the ecological fallacy, however; spatial tendencies for incomes to increase or decrease do not demonstrate that the cause was the housing's age rather than other conditions (Robinson 1950). Characteristics associated with old housing may not have been the only influences on recovery; the housing's settings, as well as nonhousing factors, may have played important roles in neighborhood attractiveness.

Metropolitan Dynamics

Interactions among housing, neighborhoods, schools, jurisdictions, developers, and mobile residents may occur as follows.

Most new housing is constructed on open land, usually in suburban and exurban settings. Poorer people occupy the housing that is left over after people with more resources choose preferred housing and locations (Downs 1981). Some of the housing is avoided by middle- and upper-income people because it is too small, deteriorated, or inadequately outfitted and detailed. In addition, housing choices are influenced by a variety of neighborhood and access conditions (Varady and Raffel 1995). Poverty increases in some neighborhoods in older jurisdictions; when this happens, the nearest elementary school is usually affected. Lower-income children tend to be less prepared than more affluent children to cope with classroom settings and reading and calculating skills (Argetsinger 1999). Discipline issues increase. More often, issues concern student attentiveness and how teachers can provide enough help to slower learners while meeting the needs and expectations of the parents of faster learners. Educational opportunities available to low-income children are limited in these settings (Galster and Killen 1995; Rosenbaum 1995). Opportunities to improve one's quality of life are at lowest ebb where poverty concentrations are most intense. In these settings, teenage pregnancies, school dropouts, violent crime, drug abuse, and unemployment rates are high (Hogan and Kitigawa 1985; Kasarda 1993b; Massey and Denton 1993; Mayer 1991). The Gautreaux project in the Chicago area provides some evidence that when poor families move into middle-class settings in the city or suburbs, the performance of both parents in jobs and children in school improves (Popkin, Rosenbaum, and Meaden 1993; Rosenbaum, Kulieke, and Rubinowitz 1988).

The quality of education shifts in various residential locations, affecting location decisions of some parents (Galster and Killen 1995). Elementary schools serve larger areas than the blocks where poor families are increasing. Some middle-income families become concerned about the elementary school and move away, while other middle-income families decide not to move in for the same reason. Better-quality housing in such neighborhoods then loses some attractiveness to families with children, since parents can afford to live in other areas that they perceive as having better schools (Guterbock, Lucy, and Cohoon 1996). As the number of prospective middle-income buyers and stayers diminishes, housing values in school attendance zones with more problem children may stagnate.

If elementary schools with small attendance zones have been adversely affected, middle schools with larger attendance zones will be next. Housing market effects will occur in their attendance zone. Discipline and behavior issues become more significant in middle schools. Potential impacts on middle-income buyers and stayers with children increase beyond the number of children involved. Housing markets are affected by these changes, so that fiscal resources do not grow as fast as in some parts of the metropolitan area. Restraint on housing prices helps attract some buyers, but fewer of them tend to be families with children as these trends continue over the years. Some middle-income families choose outer suburban locations to have more influence over schools or to have less anxiety about their children's friends (Dionne 1999).

A minority of households include children. Impressions of public schools, therefore, have little direct influence on location decisions of many households. But neighborhoods with many low-income families with children in schools may have other characteristics—high crime and deteriorating housing—that many middle-income households without children try to avoid. Hence, school enrollments may reveal dangers of neighborhood transitions whose negative effects will influence households without children.

The interaction among housing characteristics, school conditions, and location preferences is embedded in the dynamic social behavior by which neighborhoods and jurisdictions evolve. Other transitions in manufacturing and office building locations also may tip more investment toward suburbs (Garreau 1991; Leven 1979). Such circumstances often lead to imbalances between financial resources and demands and needs for public services. Local jurisdictions' services compare less favorably with services in more prosperous jurisdictions. This sequence has occurred in many central cities; it also has become common in suburbs.

Outcomes akin to these were predicted by Kerry Vandell (1995, 103), who argued that "natural market forces (demand, supply, and equilibrium price adjustments) . . . create spatial clustering of households." He concluded that "there is a tendency for housing market equilibrium to result in a spatial bias toward concentration of like residents and housing units because of household preferences for homogeneity . . ." (1995, 129). Taking a microeconomic approach, he then offered "two basic justifications for intervention in the degree of segregation in urban neighborhoods . . . (1) to overcome the significant negative externalities imposed on certain classes of households as a result of segregation and (2) to provide a 'decent home and suitable living environment' for every American family, which has been articulated as an entitlement not requiring justification on efficiency grounds" (1995, 130).

Important Conditions and Leading Indicators of Trends

Income measures of central tendency (median family, median household, per capita) have multiple meanings. They indicate taxpaying potential but, more importantly, they summarize housing market opportunities and results. How? Housing is allocated overwhelmingly in private markets. Income conditions and trends embody the results of decisions people have made about remaining in place or moving to more desirable settings. With about 50 percent of metropolitan residents moving within five years, income trends reveal a great deal about the preferences that people with resources have expressed in housing markets. Census indicators will reveal which jurisdictions are becoming more, and which less, successful in retaining and attracting residents whose resources give them location choices.

Poverty indicators are crucial also. They describe where varying proportions of a region's poor population is living. Poor people generally live in neighborhoods and dwellings where people who can afford choices do not want to live. Poverty indicates where taxpaying capacity is low; it also indicates where the need for public services is high and where social ills usually accumulate. Family poverty and poor families with children are clearer indicators than total poverty of need for public services and of the challenges faced by providers of public services, especially public education (Orfield 1997).

Income and poverty indicators from the U.S. census are available only at 10-year intervals. With high residential mobility rates within each five-year period, dangerous changes evolve rapidly. Clues from intermittent—preferably annual—indicators are needed; social service indicators, and especially public school indicators, can help. Comparative data compiled across local jurisdictions about trends in the number of people receiving food stamps or Aid to Dependent Children can provide information about shifts in locations of dependent populations. But these indicators provide little information about local burdens because they are related to federally funded programs that, in most jurisdictions, do not commit a significant amount of funds locally.

Free-Lunch Eligibles

A better source of clues about local burdens is data on free (and reduced-price) lunch eligibility of children in the public schools. Free-lunch eligibility is fundamental for three reasons. First, public education is the most expensive public service and is financed heavily with local tax revenues. Second, success in public education is the main avenue by which low-income and other individuals acquire the skills and capacities to lead productive lives and to avoid personal and social calamities. Third, performance in public education is strongly related to family conditions, such as free-lunch eligibility (Orfield and Eaton 1996). Data about free-lunch eligibility are relevant, in particular, because of their potential interaction with residential location decisions.

Are Predictive Concepts and Leading Indicators Used in Strategic Plans?

Gerald L. Gordon (1993, 29), in his handbook *Strategic Planning for Local Government,* emphasizes the importance of external (local, regional, state, and national) environmental scans, saying: "The environmental scan is the basis for better understanding the future." He does not focus extensively on means of detecting emerging and growing dangers. Nor does he address how trends can interact, and how some data discernible between national censuses can be combined with each decade's census data to provide substantial impressions of emerging and growing dangers. The trend data types referred to here concerning poverty, free-lunch eligibility, and housing age and size are not mentioned (Gordon 1993, 30–37). Nor is there any discussion of influences on residential mobility and how changes in the population mix are related to jurisdictions' housing stock, education, crime, neighborhood conditions, and public service and tax packages. Perhaps such connections and specificity should not be expected from a handbook. But if not there, then where can they be found?

Strategic plans are possible sources. Sampling local governments' strategic plans reveals that they vary in scope and purpose. Some of the strategic plans we perused made general efforts at predictions based on concepts of metropolitan evolution and tracking of trends. Some strategic plans dealt only with departmental or local government priorities and did not examine at all the changing character and prospects of the local jurisdiction's population, economy, natural features, and infrastructure (e.g., Santa Barbara Board of Supervisors 1996). Strategic plans dealing with local economies necessarily question the role of the local and regional economies in larger settings and calculate at least loosely in what circumstances the locality and region may be competitively attractive for expansion and attraction. But these strategic plans may not analyze local and regional prospects in competitive contexts. Instead, they may analyze the parts of the locality that are and might become more attractive for certain types of economic activity and therefore should be targets of local energy, investment, and action (e.g., Charlottesville Office of Economic Development 1994).

Milwaukee, Wisconsin

Some strategic plans describe trends for the jurisdiction in its metropolitan context. Milwaukee's 1996 strategic plan took this approach, comparing trends and conditions in the city with those in the metropolitan area, state, and nation— for population, minorities, middle-income households, income, poverty, and segregation. It emphasized the dangers of the increasing poverty and diminishing share of middle-income households in the total city population, as well as relative to the region's share. The plan then dealt with economic activity, health, safety, and education. Each is relevant, but the plan did not discuss connections among these subjects and problems. Although the plan emphasized poverty and education issues, it did not describe free-lunch eligibility or test scores. Nor did this 1996 plan discuss how housing conditions are related to poverty or education, even though Milwaukee has been a leader in connecting housing and social policy.

Milwaukee's strategic plan did not consider any types of data to be leading indicators that predict some aspect of the future. The closest the plan (1996, 14) came to connecting housing, poverty, and education conditions was in recommending "development of new housing or renovation of existing housing that is uniquely urban in design and that will appeal to middle-income buyers." Recognizing the importance of leading indicators, the strategic plan advised: "Develop an 'early warning' system that will monitor neighborhoods for signs of decline." The development of this early warning system was a proposal, however, rather than an analysis on which the strategic plan was based.

Duarte, California

Some strategic plans are focused on the policy proposals that come out of deliberative processes and reveal little of the conditions and trends that may have led to the proposals. One such strategic plan is *Duarte Resurgence: Concept to Reality* (Duarte City Council 1988), adopted by a rapidly growing Southern California city. The Duarte strategic plan included the problem of deteriorating middle-aged housing and socioeconomic population change related to housing characteristics. It was not prominent in Duarte's plan, however, being issue 22 out of 33, nor were proposed actions very substantial. Issue 22 is described as follows:

> Many homes built in the San Gabriel Valley during the 1940's and 1950's were built on minimum size lots with minimum housing square footages. These homes have deteriorated due to economic decline brought on by the economic cycles. Upward spiraling interest rates have caused many homes to remain in their current condition. The other extreme is the sharp downturn in interest rates which caused homeowners to upgrade to better areas. Replacement buyers are generally first-time buyers and typically cannot afford to upgrade the property. An increase in absentee landlords is also a result of lower interest rates. This tends to further perpetuate a decline in the neighborhood through a lack of pride of ownership. Twenty-five percent of the housing stock in the City of Duarte falls within this declining category. These areas have all of the problems perpetuated by the economy and the migration of people out of the area.

The Duarte strategic plan proposed stricter code enforcement, better information dissemination about choosing contractors, and, more appropriately, expansion of a "Home Rebate Program" whose characteristics were not identified. These proposed policies in the Duarte plan were mild and probably not well connected to the diagnosis of the problem.

West Hartford, Connecticut

The West Hartford, Connecticut, strategic plan began by focusing on "future trends," noting that in strategic planning the "real questions" include "how will the community change" and "how will it be economically, politically, socially or demographically different in the future. . . ." (West Hartford Town Council 1994, 3). The plan then stated that "West Hartford will be shaped by the following trends," including these: "The first ring suburbs, which includes West Hartford, are attractive areas to which Hartford residents, who are interested in moving, will move. This will occur because real estate prices, particularly in East Hartford and Bloomfield, will remain affordable, but given the change in property values in general, particularly in certain West Hartford neighborhoods, West Hartford will become home to an increasing number of residents from Hartford" (1994, 4).

The plan did not identify the characteristics of these future inmovers, but the prevalence of low-income residents in Hartford would be consistent with anticipating a lower-income population moving into West Hartford. The plan then listed "six major public policies for the future," including policies concerning safety, schools, and physical appearance (1994, 8). The plan did not discuss housing policies in relation to anticipated demographic, social, or economic change, however, nor did it explain how policies on safety, schools, and physical appearance are expected to influence or alter the characteristics of future trends.

Hennepin County, Minnesota

Sometimes procedures for preparing strategic plans include explanations of useful treatment of data and imply that leading indicators of change should be used. One such is the *Strategic Planning Manual* of Hennepin County, Minnesota, where Minneapolis is located (Hennepin County Office of Planning and Development 1983). The first item under the heading "Strategic Planning Assumptions" stated: "Many major issues resulting from demographic, economic and other changes can be foreseen and, with advance planning and preparation, can be controlled, influenced, or appropriately responded to." City government department officials were provided with "county profiles and projections" to assist them in identifying issues and proposing alternatives, "because County services need to respond to . . . changing social, economic and geographic characteristics of . . . its population. . . ." "A strategic issue arises," the manual continued, "when events beyond the control of County government (externally-caused) have occurred or are projected to occur that will make it very difficult or impossible to accomplish basic County service delivery objectives at affordable costs . . . [such as] changes in the size, composition or distribution of the County population. . . ." When the *Strategic Planning Manual* described county policy objectives, however, it cited objectives for service delivery, finance, and management; it did not cite any population mix or distribution objectives or suggest that there was any relationship between population objectives and the county's ability to meet its other objectives.

Hennepin County's manual provided a diverse profile of the county, with some projections and many trends, including comparisons with other counties in the metropolitan area and with Minneapolis. It reported that the county had experienced its first population decline, 1.9 percent, between 1970 and 1980. In addition to Minneapolis's losing 14.6 percent of its population, 19 suburbs declined in population from 1970 to 1980, compared with only one very small suburb that lost population between 1960 and 1970. Twenty-seven suburbs increased in population between 1970 and 1980. The manual explained how various age categories were changing absolutely and relative to other age groups in Hennepin County, hinting at the policy implications of these changes.

The manual discussed residential growth trends and noted that "a population shift can be expected from the first and second ring suburbs to the new development areas as households continue to move outward." But it did not include any data on housing age or size, nor much income or poverty data, and it did not relate housing conditions to poverty or income trends. Nor did it include data related to the public schools, such as free-lunch eligibility and test scores.

School data may have been omitted because county government does not administer or finance public schools; hence, to include school data without a purpose may have seemed inappropriate, perhaps even unnecessarily intrusive. Housing age seemed to implicitly have some bearing on population and other trends, given the expectation stated in the manual that outward movement from the inner-ring suburbs would continue. Poverty concentrations in 1980 were not identified, and the potential effects of housing characteristics and school conditions on poverty concentrations were not mentioned.

Leading indicators were used in the sense of relating population age distribution, household characteristics, land conversion, and population movement to township boundaries within the county through mapped comparisons. These indicators were related loosely to service and finance implications, and county departments were invited to elaborate on the policy implications of these trends for their departmental functions. Leading indicators about future population characteristic trends, such as housing age and size and free-lunch eligibility, could have been helpful, especially because the manual emphasized that population changes were causing needs for and demands on county services. Population characteristics apparently were treated as controlled by influences outside county government influence, or perhaps it was considered inappropriate for county officials to try to influence population characteristics and their distribution.

Policy Implications

The strategic plans we reviewed are consistent with Anthony Downs's view that public officials rarely emphasize population characteristics or how concentrations of poor people in modest housing (or worse) inevitably emerge in metropolitan areas. Some plans did mention this tendency, and they treated some parts of their jurisdiction as threatened. But they did not explain, diagnose, trace, anticipate, or predict it, or discuss how to alter or overcome it.

Every scholarly analysis of local moving decisions has emphasized the central importance of housing characteristics interacting with evolving household characteristics and preferences. Common sense affirms that since people live in dwellings, location choices by people with substantial resources depend on the availability of satisfactory dwellings. Yet rarely are housing policies proposed to help redress socioeconomic and fiscal imbalances among local jurisdictions within metropolitan areas (see Varady and Raffel 1995 for an exception). Instead, even Anthony Downs, an analyst with a broad perspective, has favored priorities such as "reduce personal insecurity," "improve the care of poor children," and "improve job opportunities" (Downs 1994, 119–120). Why?

Perhaps analysts believe housing problems are too resistant to public action, or that effective public action is unlikely because of political opposition. Engaging the public sector in attracting middle- and upper-income people to live in poorer jurisdictions may seem quixotic or inappropriate. Indeed, such policies seem to bestow more benefits—in the form of more choices, and perhaps direct or indirect subsidies—on middle- and upper-income people, who already enjoy favored status in society. A variation on this theme was expressed in a 1998 debate between the Clinton administration and some members of Congress over legislation to expand the income distribution in federally funded public housing. Both Andrew Cuomo, Secretary of Housing and Urban Development, and Representative Rick Lazio (R-New York) agreed that mixed-income housing projects are better than poverty level–only projects. But faced with the proposed combination of an increase in the eligibility limit (to $35,000) and zero production of new public housing, Cuomo opposed the legislation because "you are losing that unit for somebody who needs it desperately" (Havemann 1998). This debate happened to concern the low-income end of the housing spectrum—poverty-level versus moderate-income tenants—but it involved the same issue of fairness raised by any public subsidy for housing.

From the perspective of sustaining neighborhoods and jurisdictions, however, if jurisdictions cannot provide a satisfactory supply of housing, then they will fade with age, especially if they were developed in an era when small houses were in vogue. The social and individual calamities that go along with impoverished jurisdictions will accompany physical decay. Consequently, ignoring characteristics of the housing stock is a recipe for severe decline. Indeed, decay has been the fate of hundreds of neighborhoods and scores of jurisdictions. More will follow unless a clearer strategic sense about the interaction between the well-being of jurisdictions and people emerges and is embedded in local, regional, state, and federal strategic thinking and perhaps in formal strategic planning. The essence of the competitive context in metropolitan areas is that each jurisdiction is vulnerable to the interactions that occur between a highly mobile population and private housing-supply institutions, for whom protection of jurisdiction viability tends to be either absent from consideration or at most an afterthought.

Sawicki and Flynn (1996, 179) concluded their review and analysis of neighborhood indicators as follows: ". . . [T]he geographic indicators movement, especially on the neighborhood scale, is in its infancy. Though such indicators are useful for consciousness-raising, they are just beginning to be used to make and evaluate policy, and to search for the causes of change in neighborhoods and in the lives of their residents." Their critique suggests that assessment of weaknesses of, and dangers to, local government jurisdictions is also in its infancy. Greater attention by strategic planners and scholars to obstacles to meaningful analysis is warranted.

Next Steps

In the preceding chapters, we described the evolution of the postsuburban era, including its aspects of suburban decline. We explained why the fate of cities and suburbs is bound up with the tyranny of easy development decisions, which tolerates or encourages sprawl on the metropolitan fringe. Addressing these conditions requires action on many fronts—national and state policies, regional structures and processes, and local government attention to dangers inherent in neighborhood transitions. If local governments control major policy decisions, regional outcomes will be diminished by tendencies for many local governments to seek gains at other government jurisdictions' expense. Maximizing gains for some local jurisdictions leads to greater disparities, less reinvestment, and more sprawl. The goal of federal, state, and regional strategic planning should be better regional results, defined as less sprawl, more reinvestment, and smaller disparities.

The four paired concepts (area and power, pattern and density, population and neighborhood, and space and place) focus attention on how success for people, especially less advantaged people, depends on whether they live in a successful place. Planning with these concepts in mind can improve interjurisdictional balance and enhance the quality of life for a majority of people and places. In the following chapters, we analyze conditions in larger groups of cities and suburbs in metropolitan areas, and examine how housing and neighborhood indicators can illuminate the need for public policy action, including action that is beyond the control of any single local government. Then we describe several approaches to regional governance. We conclude by proposing six policies that should be implemented by combinations of national, state, regional, and local governments. The potential usefulness of these policies will be suggested by how they have worked in western Europe and Canada.

Note

3.1. The References list a number of particularly useful articles and books about strate-
     gic planning by the following writers: John M. Bryson and Robert C. Einsweiler;
     Ian Caulfield and John Schultz; William R. Dodge and Kim Montgomery; D. C.
     Eadie; Michael Fladeland; Joseph E. Garcia, David E. Merrifield, and Stephen V.
     Senge; Michael Garrah; Arie Halachmi; Jerome Kaufman and Harvey Jacobs; Kurt
     Jenne; Mary L. McLean and Kenneth P. Voytek; and Patricia Plugge.

Chapter 4

The Postsuburban Era
Comes to Richmond

The political success of suburbs has been based on preventing annexation by cities. Suburbia's economic success derives from attracting employment and commercial property tax base, which before 1970 was concentrated in central cities. Ironically, the decline of many suburbs in population and relative income of residents in the 1970s and 1980s accompanied the economic success of suburbia during this same period.

From the perspective of suburbs, attracting employment was a victory. It enriched their taxable resources, which had been stressed by rapid growth and overreliance on residential property taxes. For many residents, it shortened commuting distances. It raised the prospect of ending suburbs' dependence on central cities for employment and culture (Garreau 1991). In any organization or organism, however, maturity embodies both strength and vulnerability. And the maturing suburbs of Richmond, Virginia, contained the seeds of deterioration.

The Richmond metropolitan area exhibits decline in middle-aged suburbs, sprawl in outer suburbia and exurbia, and revival in several old city neighborhoods amid general city decline (see Note 1.1). It is an example of the postsuburban conditions that evolved in metropolitan areas in the 1980s. Postsuburban Richmond is also a test of a common policy prescription for what ails U.S. cities. As suburbs have gained employment, some cities have lost employment. A prescription for saving cities sometimes is offered, claiming that revitalizing cities' economies will enhance their tax capacity and bring back the middle class to live closer to work. Richmond demonstrates the limitations of this hope. Employment increased in Richmond during the 1980s and 1990s, yet the city continued to lose population, income declined relative to its region, and family poverty increased. Business gains in the city did not translate immediately into social stability.

Richmond also illustrates an opportunity. The Richmond region experienced increasing sprawl, inadequate reinvestment, and growing disparities between the central city and its suburbs. In these respects, Richmond reflected trends we hypothesize as typical of this recent era. While the city declined in population and relative income, some neighborhoods thrived in the 1980s. Often these were old neighborhoods; in fact, a majority of Richmond's old neighborhoods increased in income relative to typical city, suburban, and exurban areas, indicating that the flaws of aging structures can sometimes be countered effectively. Plausible explanations for this significant exception to the dominant trends will be examined here.

Recent Evolution of the Richmond-Petersburg Metropolitan Area

Since 1960, the Richmond-Petersburg metropolitan area has evolved in ways that epitomize the city-suburban-exurban evolution of most metropolitan areas in the United States (Map 4.1). In 1960, employment was concentrated in Richmond and regional poverty was highest in the outlying agricultural coun-

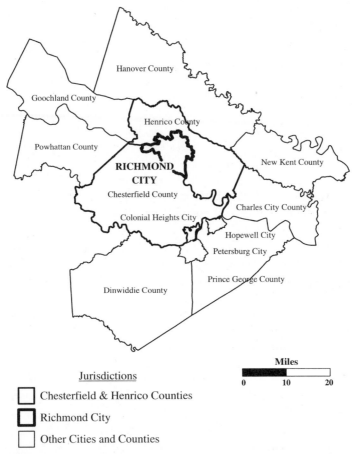

Map 4.1. Political Jurisdictions of the 1990 Richmond-Petersburg MA.

ties. By 1990 there were more private-sector jobs outside than inside Richmond, and family poverty rates had more than doubled. City crime rates were much higher and school test scores were much lower than in the suburbs. Substantial portions of the African-American middle class had moved to the suburbs. Many agricultural areas had turned into exurbs dominated by commuters, and in a majority of the exurban-rural counties, family income was equal to or higher than the region's median income (Lucy 1994c).

Richmond contained 38 percent of metropolitan population in 1970 but only 23 percent by 1990, decreasing by 46,276 residents. The city's African-American population had increased for decades, but even it declined by 235 residents between 1980 and 1990. In 1990, African-Americans constituted 55 percent of Richmond's total population. The African-American population of adjacent Chesterfield and Henrico Counties grew by more than 50,000 between 1970 and 1990. Most of the suburban population increase was in these two counties, each of which by 1990 slightly exceeded Richmond in population (Richmond 203,056; Chesterfield 209,274; Henrico 217,881). By 1995, their populations were Richmond 198,273, Chesterfield 239,659, and Henrico 232,799.

More Employment Is Not Enough

Richmond remained a major employment center, retaining 46 percent of the region's private-sector jobs in 1990, a particularly impressive share when the city contained only 23 percent of the region's population. Moreover, Richmond added nearly 30,000 jobs during the 1980s (Table 4.1). The lure of more employment in Richmond was not sufficient, however, to prevent the city's population from shrinking. Employment gains in Richmond also were insufficient to prevent relative income decline in the city. Median family income in Richmond was 78 percent of the metropolitan median income in 1980; it fell to 72 percent in 1990. A trickle of private employment growth continued in Richmond from 1990 to 1995, while population declined by nearly 5,000. Richmond's economy was so strong that the city contained 10 private jobs (not including public-sector employees) for each 11 residents, many of whom were too young, old, or infirm to be in the labor market.

Most of the job growth in the Richmond region from 1970 to 1995 was in the suburbs. Henrico and Chesterfield Counties added more than three times the employment increase in Richmond from 1970 to 1990. Suburban employment increases between 1980 and 1995 were mainly in services, finance, insurance, real estate, and retailing (Table 4.2). These employment sectors lent themselves to development configurations in shopping malls, office parks, and strings of structures along highways and intersections.

Employment shifts were accompanied by major changes in commuting patterns. In 1990, Richmond residents were commuting to other jurisdictions to

Table 4.1. Number of Employees and Percentage of Richmond-Petersburg MA: Total Reported Employment

	1970		1980		1989		1990	
	Number	*% of MA*	*Number*	*% of MA*	*Number*	*% of MA*	*Number*	*% of MA*
Charles City County	215	0	87	0	276	0	264	0
Chesterfield County	17,106	8	29,042	10	59,759	16	64,086	16
Dinwiddie County	1,125	1	1,076	0	1,454	0	1,464	0
Goochland County	611	0	793	0	2,102	1	2,269	1
Hanover County	3,703	2	14,238	5	22,809	6	24,324	6
Henrico County	22,640	10	62,701	22	83,536	22	84,790	22
New Kent County	453	0	996	0	1,469	0	1,414	0
Powhatan County	544	0	930	0	1,332	0	1,466	0
Prince George's County	1,163	1	1,403	0	3,741	1	4,370	1
Colonial Heights	1,431	1	2,434	1	5,856	2	6,725	2
Hopewell	7,268	3	8,409	3	7,012	2	7,110	2
Petersburg	15,716	7	15,746	5	13,281	3	13,396	3
Richmond	145,526	67	148,520	52	178,148	47	177,666	46
Richmond-Petersburg MA[1]	217,501		286,375		380,775		389,344	

Source: U.S. Bureau of the Census, *County Business Patterns—Virginia*
[1] Equivalent region to 1990 MA

Table 4.2. Distribution of Employment by Industry in Chesterfield, Hanover, and Henrico Counties: Number of Employees and Percentage of Jurisdiction's Total Employment, 1980 and 1995

	Chesterfield		Hanover		Henrico	
	1980 (%)	1995 (%)	1980 (%)	1995 (%)	1980 (%)	1995 (%)
Agriculture, Forestry, and Fishing	210 (1)	440 (1)	69 (0)	337 (1)	174 (0)	681 (1)
Mining	100–249 (1)	283 (0)	119 (1)	156 (1)	35 (0)	256 (0)
Construction	3,610 (12)	6,789 (10)	2,526 (18)	4,622 (16)	5,343 (9)	5,595 (5)
Manufacturing	7,549 (26)	8,033 (12)	1,512 (11)	3,977 (14)	11,301 (18)	11,191 (11)
Transportation and Public Utilities	2,584 (9)	7,394 (11)	482 (3)	1,261 (4)	4,790 (8)	4,627 (5)
Wholesale Trade	1,023 (4)	2,699 (4)	2,597 (18)	4,738 (17)	5,813 (9)	7,868 (8)
Retail Trade	7,865 (27)	20,466 (30)	4,082 (29)	5,809 (21)	15,232 (24)	23,401 (23)
Finance, Insurance, and Real Estate	1,263 (4)	4,433 (6)	340 (2)	1,100 (4)	5,798 (9)	17,868 (17)
Services (including business, personal, health, education, hotels, social, and legal)	4,652 (16)	18,251 (26)	2,393 (17)	6,200 (22)	13,979 (22)	30,979 (30)
Unclassified Establishments	100–249 (1)	87 (0)	118 (1)	34 (0)	236 (0)	39 (0)
TOTAL	29,042	68,875	14,238	28,234	62,701	102,505

Source: U.S. Bureau of the Census, County Business Patterns—Virginia

Table 4.3. Percentage of Workers of the Richmond-Petersburg MA
Employed Outside City or County of Residence

	1960	1970	1980	1990	1960–90
Charles City County	62%	65%	80%	80%	29%
Chesterfield County	62	66	71	55	−11
Dinwiddie County	49	68	73	69	61
Goochland County	43	56	67	70	67
Hanover County	56	66	67	62	11
Henrico County	77	69	66	51	−34
New Kent County	48	58	80	80	46
Powhatan County	35	55	70	75	114
Prince George's County	22	25	43	50	127
Colonial Heights	81	81	75	77	−5
Hopewell	27	41	44	54	100
Petersburg	32	30	44	46	44
Richmond	8	17	20	32	300

Source: U.S. Bureau of the Census, *Census of Population and Housing*

work at four times (32 percent) the Richmond outcommuting rate in 1960 (8 percent). Outcommuting declined in Henrico and Chesterfield as employment there increased. As the agricultural character of the outlying counties eroded, outcommuting from them to Richmond, Henrico, and Chesterfield increased. An average of 70 percent of all outlying county residents in the workforce in 1990 commuted outside their county of residence (Table 4.3).

Stable Commuting Times

Despite the increase in commuting among jurisdictions between 1980 and 1990, commuting times did not increase. Suburbanization of employment reduced some commuting distances for suburban and exurban workers, but more people also were commuting from the suburbs into Richmond. Stable commuting times indicate that the highway system expanded sufficiently to maintain the same level of commuting convenience. A tollway was added from the suburbs to Richmond, and an interstate bypass connected western and eastern exurban areas north of the city. Mean commuting times were approximately 20 minutes in the cities and inner suburbs and 30 minutes in the exurban-rural counties in 1980 and 1990. Consequently, commuting is not likely to be more of a deterrent to metropolitan residential sprawl in this region in the near future. Instead, another planned extension of an interstate beltway outside the inner suburbs and the impending addition of a computer chip manufacturing factory employing several thousand on the western fringe of the metropolitan area will expand exurbanization still farther into rural areas.

Farm employment data confirm the intrusion of exurbia into the agricultural hinterland. In 1960, seven counties had 10 percent or more of employed residents working in farming, and in two counties, farm employment exceeded 20 percent. By 1990, Goochland County was highest with 5 percent of its employed workforce in farming, Dinwiddie had 4 percent, New Kent and Charles City had 3 percent, and the other counties had 1 or 2 percent (U.S. Bureau of the Census 1962 and 1992).

City and Suburban Population Loss and Relative Income Decline

More old housing, lower home ownership, and higher mobility rates have made cities vulnerable to income decline relative to their suburbs. Rapid residential mobility makes all aging neighborhoods and jurisdictions vulnerable to population and income decline relative to newer settlements. In the Richmond region, 53 percent of metropolitan residents moved (54 percent in Richmond and 53 percent in the balance of the region) between 1985 and 1990, according to the U.S. Bureau of the Census. The median year when Richmond housing was built was 1953, compared with 1970 in Henrico and 1978 in Chesterfield. The home ownership rate in Richmond was 42 percent in 1990, compared with 60 percent in Henrico and 76 percent in Chesterfield. The national home ownership rate has fluctuated near 65 percent. Home ownership is a key indicator that has explained some of the difference between city and suburban incomes. With so much old housing and high rental rates, Richmond was particularly inviting as a location choice for the growing number of low- and moderate-income people who were attracted to the region as private employment increased by 36 percent between 1980 and 1990.

Most states contain many small suburbs with government responsibilities. In Virginia, there are few suburban municipalities; counties provide most suburban services. Virginia's counties are large and diverse. To discern income decline in areas of neighborhood size, census tract data were analyzed. In Richmond's most populous suburban counties, substantial relative income decline and population loss occurred between 1980 and 1990. The amount of decline was striking given the young age of the housing stock and the relatively high rates of home ownership.

Most Suburban Census Tracts Declined

In Henrico, relative median family income status declined by more than 20 percent between 1979 and 1989 in three census tracts, and in 18 of 49 census tracts (37 percent), it declined by more than 10 percent. In Chesterfield, three out of its 40 census tracts declined by 20 percent or more, while 11 declined by at least 10 percent between 1980 and 1990. In both Henrico and Chesterfield Counties, more census tracts declined than improved in relative median family income; 35 declined while 14 improved in Henrico, and 25 declined while 15 improved in Chesterfield (Map 4.2). Nearly all the census tracts in Henrico

County, and most of those in Chesterfield, that bordered Richmond declined in relative income, except those adjacent to the wealthiest parts of Richmond. This is the location pattern one would expect if income decline is related to aging housing. We will see later, however, that age of housing alone is not an accurate predictor of income decline, sometimes being associated with income increases.

In Richmond, more census tracts declined in median family income status by more than 20 percent (18 tracts) than in Henrico (3) and Chesterfield (3). But more census tracts improved in Richmond (26, or 39 percent) than in Henrico (14, or 29 percent) and Chesterfield (15, or 38 percent). A slightly higher percentage of tracts in Richmond (10 percent) than in Henrico and Chesterfield combined (9 percent) improved in relative median family income by more than 20 percent (Lucy and Phillips 1994b).

Social service data indicate that suburban decline continued after 1990 in Henrico and Chesterfield Counties. Persons receiving Aid to Families with

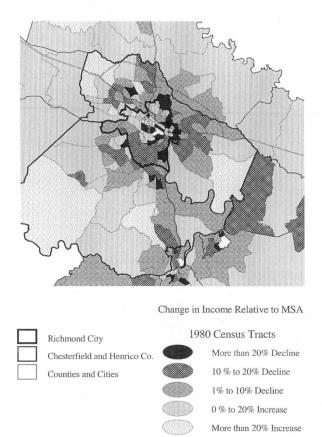

Change in Income Relative to MSA

☐ Richmond City

☐ Chesterfield and Henrico Co.

☐ Counties and Cities

1980 Census Tracts

⬤ More than 20% Decline

⬤ 10 % to 20% Decline

⬤ 1% to 10% Decline

⬤ 0 % to 20% Increase

⬤ More than 20% Increase

Map 4.2. Change in Median Family Income Relative to Metropolitan Income 1979–1989 in the Richmond-Petersburg MA.

Modest one-story late 1950s and early 1960s homes in Henrico County, Virginia, are part of a "declining" suburban neighborhood.

Dependent Children (ADC) and food stamps increased in Henrico and Chesterfield after 1988, as expected, due to effects of the national recession. But as the recession was ending nationally and in the Richmond region, ADC and food stamp recipients continued to increase in Henrico and Chesterfield. By 1994, the caseloads in both counties were at least double their number in 1988 (Virginia Department of Social Services 1994). In addition, the percentage of children in Chesterfield elementary schools eligible for free or reduced-price school lunches increased by more than 50 percent from 1990 to 1994. In 10 of Chesterfield's 33 elementary schools, at least 20 percent, and as many as 72 percent, of the children were eligible for these subsidized lunches because of the low incomes of their families (Chesterfield County Planning Department 1995).

Suburban-Exurban Sprawl

Land development outside Richmond has been sprawling at low densities, converting farmland as it moved outward. In the process, agricultural areas have been rapidly turning into exurbs where 70 percent or more of the workers commute out of their county of residence to their jobs.

The term "suburban-exurban sprawl" lacks precise meaning, partly because of widespread vague, pejorative use of the term (Audirac, Shermyen, and Smith 1990, 475) and partly because it is better understood as a portion of a continuum rather than as an absolute condition. Suburban-exurban sprawl can be measured. In this analysis, we measure it by seven factors. Six are discussed below: changes in population density, population gains in outer census tracts, population losses in inner suburban census tracts, farmland conversion, farm coverage of rural counties, and locations of new housing built in the 1950s and in the 1980s. The seventh factor, outcommuting, has been described above. Evaluating the results discovered by these methods may be controversial.

Population Density

We measured population density in two ways—first, a ratio of population density in Richmond to each of the main suburban counties, and second, the number of persons per acre by jurisdiction. In 1960, the gross number of persons per square mile in Richmond was 12 times greater than in Henrico, 38 times greater than in Chesterfield, and 101 times greater in Hanover. These ratios narrowed steadily as Richmond lost population and the suburbs grew. By 1990, Richmond was four times denser than Henrico, 7 times denser than Chesterfield, and 25 times denser than Hanover (Table 4.4).

Growth in Henrico, Chesterfield, and Hanover did not lead, however, to significant residential densities. By 1990, the gross population densities were 1.4 persons per acre in Henrico, 0.8 persons per acre in Chesterfield, and 0.2 persons per acre in Hanover. After deducting the amount of county land covered by farms, the resulting population densities were Henrico 1.7 persons per acre, Chesterfield 0.8, and Hanover 0.3 (Table 4.5). With an average household size between two and three persons, the average housing density was about one

Table 4.4. Density Comparisons: Richmond to the Largest Counties in the Richmond-Petersburg Metropolitan Area

	Ratio of Persons per Square Mile				
	1960	*1970*	*1980*	*1990*	*1995*
Richmond/Henrico	12/1	6/1	5/1	4/1	3.4/1
Richmond/Chesterfield	38/1	24/1	11/1	7/1	5.9/1
Richmond/Hanover	101/1	51/1	34/1	25/1	21/1

Source: U.S. Bureau of the Census, Census of Population and Housing

Table 4.5. Population Density in the Richmond Area and Its Suburbs

	Population Density: Persons per Acre					
	1960	*1970*	*1980*	*1990*	*1995*	*% Change 1960–1995*
Richmond	9.3	6.5	5.7	5.3	5.2	–44%
Chesterfield County	0.2	0.3	0.5	0.8	0.9	350%
Hanover County	0.1	0.1	0.2	0.2	0.2	100%
Henrico County	0.8	1.0	1.2	1.4	1.5	87%

household for each one and one-half acres in Henrico, one household per three acres in Chesterfield, and less than one household per seven acres in Hanover.

The Richmond region's population increased by 14 percent between 1980 and 1990. Much of that growth was in the most populous counties. Henrico increased by 21 percent, Chesterfield by 48 percent, and Hanover by 26 percent. Thirty-four census tracts in these three counties increased by more than 25 percent during that decade. Thirty-one of these rapidly growing census tracts were in Henrico and Chesterfield; most of them were in the outer parts of these counties separated from Richmond by other census tracts.

Inner Suburban Population Loss

Many of the inner suburban census tracts actually lost population between 1980 and 1990. In Henrico County, 45 percent of the census tracts declined in population, as did 25 percent of the census tracts in Chesterfield County. Nearly all of these census tracts either were adjacent to Richmond or were bordered by other population-losing tracts that were adjacent to or near Richmond. This location pattern is consistent with our interpretation that it is areas of middle-aged hous-

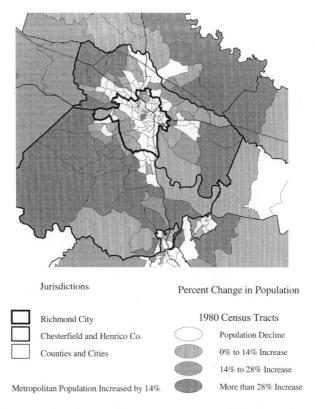

Jurisdictions

☐ Richmond City
☐ Chesterfield and Henrico Co.
☐ Counties and Cities

Metropolitan Population Increased by 14%

Percent Change in Population

1980 Census Tracts

◯ Population Decline
◯ 0% to 14% Increase
◯ 14% to 28% Increase
⬤ More than 28% Increase

Map 4.3. Percentage Population Change 1980–1990 in the Richmond-Petersburg MA.

ing that have tended to lose population and to decline in income relative to the metropolitan area's median income. Richmond's population declined by 7 percent in the 1980s, but just as parts of Richmond increased in relative income, 22 percent of its census tracts also increased in population (Map 4.3).

Farmland Loss and Coverage

In the Richmond metropolitan area, 47 percent of the farmland was converted to other uses between 1959 and 1992. If the amount of farmland loss between these years is projected to the year 2020, the loss would reach 86 percent of all the 1959 farmland in the Richmond area. In addition, 100 percent of the 1959 farmland would be lost in Chesterfield and Henrico Counties by 2020.

Another important perspective on the role of farmland in Virginia's metropolitan areas is gained by comparing farm acreage to the total land area in each county. In the Richmond region, for example, farms covered substantial portions of nearby counties in 1959—Chesterfield 26 percent, Hanover 51 percent,

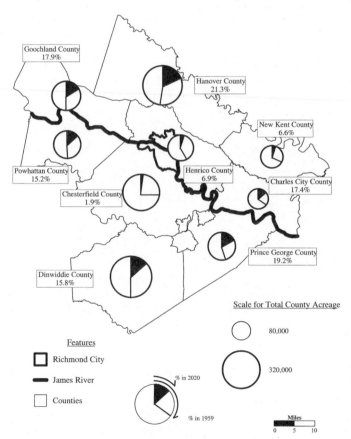

Map 4.4. Farmland Loss in the Richmond Region, 1959–2020.

and Henrico 42 percent. Projecting to the year 2020, based on the rate of farmland loss from 1959 to 1992 (Map 4.4), and applying the equivalent annual rate of farmland change to the declining amount of farmland remaining each year (a more conservative projection method than the one used above), the following land coverage by farms would exist in those counties—Chesterfield 2 percent, Hanover 24 percent, and Henrico 6 percent.

These projections of farmland loss are not predictions. Actual rates will vary from historic trends. Nothing in the recent history of farmland loss, however, provides reasons to expect that trends in farmland loss will be reduced significantly in most counties.

Location of New Housing

Figures representing new housing construction by decade also reveal how suburban sprawl in the 1950s in the Richmond region evolved into exurban rural sprawl in the 1980s. Between 1950 and 1960 in Chesterfield County, 11 dots representing 550 houses appear on Map 4.5 in 10 census tracts in the south,

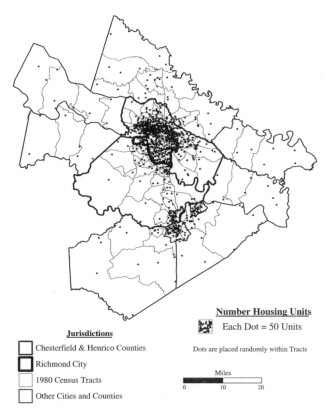

Number Housing Units

Each Dot = 50 Units

Dots are placed randomly within Tracts

Jurisdictions

Chesterfield & Henrico Counties

Richmond City

1980 Census Tracts

Other Cities and Counties

Miles

0   10   20

Map 4.5. Distribution of 1990 Housing Units Built in the 1950s in the Richmond-Petersburg MA.

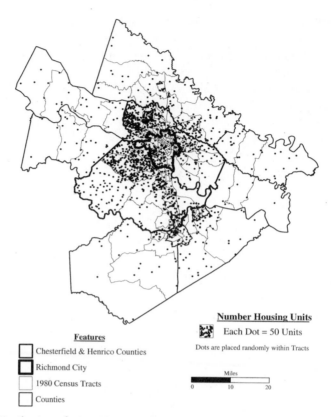

Number Housing Units

Each Dot = 50 Units

Dots are placed randomly within Tracts

Features

☐ Chesterfield & Henrico Counties

◼ Richmond City

☐ 1980 Census Tracts

☐ Counties

Miles

0   10   20

Map 4.6. Distribution of 1990 Housing Units Built in the 1980s in the Richmond-Petersburg MA.

central, and western portions of the county. More than 150 dots representing 7,500 houses appear in those same census tracts for the 1980s (Map 4.6).

By each measure of suburban-exurban sprawl (exurban outcommuting, population density, population gains and losses in census tracts, farmland loss, farm coverage, and new housing locations in the 1950s and 1980s), the Richmond region has been evolving in an extremely low density pattern.

The Postsuburban Era: Detailed Definition

In the era of suburban dominance, the population of most suburbs increased, most suburbs held their status positions relative to other established suburbs, most suburbs increased in income relative to the metropolitan median income, income in rural areas within metropolitan areas was lower than the metropolitan median income, and most suburbanites commuted to work in central cities.

The notion of suburban dominance refers to a period of increase in income and population that resulted in higher suburban than city income and more population and voters in suburbs than in central cities.

The postsuburban era exhibits a more complicated pattern. During this era, many suburbs decline in population and income status, many suburbanites remain in the suburbs to work, farmland loss is prevalent in counties outside traditional suburbs, income in many exurban rural areas exceeds the metropolitan median, and outcommuting from low-density exurban counties to cities and older suburbs increases greatly.

Four Conditions

We suggest that the term "postsuburban era" be used when the following conditions prevail, indicating that suburban counties have matured Each of these conditions can be measured on a continuum; we offer the following as plausible levels that indicate a threshold has been crossed, recognizing that any threshold is a social construct subject to revision.

1. Outside the central cities, a majority of the census tracts or jurisdictions (above 2,500 residents in 1960) in one or more counties have lost population or declined in income relative to the metropolitan median income during the most recent decade, or the county overall has lost population during the most recent decade. This criterion indicates whether suburban persistence or relative suburban decline has been dominant.
2. Farm coverage of county territory is less than 20 percent, or the county had lost more than 50 percent of its 1959 farmland by 1992. This criterion helps indicate how rapidly land for low-density development has been consumed and how much remains. Timber coverage of county land also is relevant, but data about it are difficult to acquire.
3. County employment increased by 20 percent or more during the most recent decade, or the percentage of employed workers who commuted to work locations outside the county decreased by 10 percent or more during the most recent decade, and outcommuting was less than 60 percent of the employed workforce in 1990. This criterion indicates emergence of a polycentric metropolis, with several employment centers, geographic adjustment of retailing to population dispersal, and adjustment of the labor force's residential locations to be more accessible to suburban employment.
4. A majority of exurban rural jurisdictions have median family incomes equal to or greater than the metropolitan area's median family income. Suburban areas, on average, have had residents with higher median family income than their metropolitan median at least since 1960, while rural areas within metropolitan regions have had lower-income residents than the metropolitan median. In 1960, median family income in rural nonfarm parts of

all metropolitan areas in the United States was 92.2 percent of the metropolitan median, while income in the rural farm portion was 71.8 percent of the metropolitan median. By 1990, when the incomes of residents of rural nonfarm and rural farm parts of metropolitan areas were combined, they were 99.1 percent of the metropolitan median.

The Richmond Region Meets Criteria

The Richmond region meets these criteria. In Henrico, 71 percent of the census tracts declined in relative income (surpassing the 50 percent criterion) while nearly meeting the alternative population decline criteria, as 45 percent of its census tracts lost population. Only 16 percent of Henrico's territory was covered by farms in 1992 (less than the 20 percent criterion), and 63 percent of its 1959 farmland had been converted to other uses by 1992 (exceeding the 50 percent criterion). In addition, employment grew by 35 percent (exceeding the 20 percent increase criterion), and outcommuting decreased by 23 percent (exceeding the 10 percent reduction criterion), dropping to a 51 percent rate. Thus, Henrico met each criterion of a mature county by 1990, ushering in the postsuburban era.

In Chesterfield, 63 percent of the census tracts declined in relative income (surpassing the 50 percent criterion), while 25 percent lost population (falling short of the population decline criterion). Barely 6 percent of Chesterfield's territory was covered with farms in 1992 (less than the 20 percent criterion), and 75 percent of its 1959 farmland had been converted to other uses by 1992 (exceeding the 50 percent criterion). Employment increased by 121 percent (exceeding the 20 percent increase criterion), and outcommuting fell by 23 percent (exceeding the 10 percent reduction criterion), dropping to a 55 percent rate. Therefore, by 1990 Chesterfield also met each criterion of a mature county in the postsuburban era.

In the seven exurban rural counties in the Richmond region, four counties (Goochland, Hanover, New Kent, and Powhatan) had median family incomes equal to or greater than the metropolitan median in 1990. In 1980, only one exurban rural county had median family income higher than the metropolitan median. The unweighted average of median family incomes in these seven counties rose from 65 percent of the metropolitan median in 1960 to 78 percent in 1970, 92 percent in 1980, and 96 percent in 1990.

Maturing Suburbs

These trends and conditions reflect the maturing of the suburban territory and sprawl settlement of exurban rural territory. Maturity involves a closer balance between residences and workplaces, but it also leaves less territory for expansion in a low-density, sprawl pattern; hence, little territory remains covered by farms. Maturity also means that some housing has been aging, reducing its attractiveness to middle- and upper-income people. Some residents have been aging in place, reducing the area's population as children leave home. Most suburban population and income increases have occurred in the middle and outer suburbs, while many middle-aged suburbs have declined. These were conditions and trends that became dominant in Henrico County and Chesterfield County between 1980 and 1990.

Several urban theories are consistent with our contention that these findings for the Richmond region have, or will, become common in metropolitan areas throughout the United States. It is generally held that neighborhood life cycles tend to lead to decline in neighborhoods' relative income (Downs 1981; Lowry 1960). It is generally held that outer parts (Burgess 1925) or substantial sectors (Hoyt 1939) of metropolitan areas will tend to become the residence of most middle- and upper-income people, who will trade more space and housing size and quality for less convenience (Alonso 1964; Choldin, Hanson, and Bohrer 1980; Schnore 1972;). Given these theories, inner suburban decline would be expected. We will discover in subsequent chapters, however, that suburban decline is neither limited to, nor necessarily concentrated within, inner and older suburbs.

The postsuburban era involves the maturing of more suburbs. Maturing suburbs usually increase employment within their borders, so the necessity for suburbanites to commute to central cities declines. But even as maturity brings greater capacities in employment and tax base, it is associated with diminished

Farmland in Henrico County, Virginia, is still being converted to urban use. (See adjacent development in the next photo.)

Suburban apartments (one bedroom at $610 in 1999) are now being developed near the outer interstate loop in Henrico County, Virginia. (See previous photo for adjacent farm lot for sale.)

capacities and elements of decline in some respects. In organisms, decline becomes deterioration, ending in death. In metropolitan development, maturity will lead to substantial areas of severe deterioration and still larger areas of stagnation. Planning and design will play an important role in determining which territories decline and persist and which territories may even augment the strengths that accompany maturity. The role of planning and design includes creating and adapting physical characteristics that help turn territories into places and communities or enhance the place status that has previously been achieved. If suburban territories evolve into places toward which people feel community attachments, then suburban decline is less likely to lead to severe deterioration.

Chapter 5

Planning Strategies and Market Results for Old Suburbs: The Washington, D.C. Region

Each local government jurisdiction is subject to market tests because of fragmented governance of metropolitan areas. Persons in the moderate to high income range have sufficient financial means to live in more than one neighborhood and local government jurisdiction within metropolitan areas, which contain on average 90 local governments. Therefore, local jurisdictions are constantly subject to housing market competition that determines how viable they will remain.

The tendency for metropolitan areas to sprawl at low densities into exurban rural territories, consuming farmland at a rapid pace, is well documented (Nelson 1992). Survey evidence indicates that low-density, even rural, environments are preferred by a majority of Americans as residential settings (Audirac, Shermyen, and Smith 1990; Davis, Nelson, and Dueker 1994; Levin and Mark 1977). Some of these same surveys (Audirac, Shermyen, and Smith 1990) reveal preferences for downtown locations over suburban areas. These findings, together with high land and housing values per square foot in some denser settings, suggest that sufficient demand exists for many compact neighborhoods and jurisdictions to be stable or renewed.

Planning and Competition

Achieving goals like balance, equilibrium, and sustainable communities must occur in competitive residential markets in which older neighborhoods and jurisdictions capture significant reinvestment and attract a portion of the population that approximates the socioeconomic population distribution of its region. Several jurisdictions in the Washington, D.C. region have achieved that goal. The reasons for their success include walkable neighborhoods, convenience, transportation alternatives to automobiles, taking advantage of regional mass transit investments, and long-term commitments to consensus planning and implementation.

The Washington, D.C. region as a whole has exhibited many of the standard post-suburban symptoms of suburban decline, exurban sprawl, and edge city prominence. Many older suburbs, primarily in Prince George's County, Maryland, have declined faster in relative income of residents than Washington, D.C. itself. Some of the region's jurisdictions have tried to withstand sprawl tendencies and even to increase their density. Here we will describe some results achieved in the city of Alexandria, Virginia; in Arlington, Fairfax, and Prince William Counties, Virginia; and in Prince George's County, Maryland.

The main measure of market success used in this analysis is the median family income of residents of jurisdictions and census tracts compared with the income of the region's residents. We refer to jurisdictions or census tracts as declining if the income of their residents has decreased relative to the region's income, and as improved if their residents' income has increased relative to the region's median family or per capita income. This relative income indicator measures jurisdictions' market performance in competition with other jurisdictions. We will supplement this income test with data about median housing value changes. From the perspective of lenders and developers, housing value may be a more persuasive indicator of market success than income of residents.

The Washington, D.C. Region

Population in the metropolitan region of Washington, D.C. nearly doubled from 1960 to 1990. Its 1990 population of 3,923,574 made it the eighth most populous metropolitan area in the United States. Much of that population growth occurred in a low-density, sprawl pattern. The central city lost 21 percent of its population during that 30 years, dropping from 763,956 to 606,900. By 1995, Washington, D.C.'s population had fallen to an estimated 554,256 (U.S. Bureau of the Census 1996). Most of the region's population growth from 1960 to 1990 had occurred in Fairfax County, Virginia; Montgomery County, Maryland; and Prince George's County, Maryland—each of which contained more residents than the District of Columbia (Table 5.1 and Map 5.1).

By 1990, the metropolitan area included such low-density Virginia jurisdictions as Loudoun, Stafford, and Prince William Counties, with population densities of 166, 227, and 637 persons per square mile, respectively (0.3 to 1 person per acre). During the 1990s, Loudoun was among the 10 fastest-growing counties in the United States. In Maryland, the metropolitan area included Calvert, Charles, and Frederick Counties, each having population densities of approximately 0.4 persons per acre. Sprawl of the metropolitan population into these low-density counties was facilitated by highway expansion (Gordon, Richardson, and Jun 1991, 417). Employment relocation, housing location adjustments, and highway capacity increases were sufficient so that "average trip times have remained stable or declined in this period [1968 to 1988] for all trip purposes and all modes of travel, despite increased trip distances" (Levinson and

Table 5.1. Population and Race in the Washington, D.C. Metropolitan Area, 1960–1995

	1960	1970		1980		1990		1995
	Total Population	Black Population Number (%)	Total Population	Black Population Number (%)	Total Population	Black Population Number (%)	Total Population	Total Population
Washington, D.C.	763,956	537,570 (71)	756,510	448,906 (70)	638,333	399,604 (66)	606,900	554,256
Virginia Counties								
Arlington	163,401	10,076 (6)	174,284	14,028 (9)	152,599	17,940 (10)	170,936	172,660
Fairfax	275,002	15,859 (3)	455,021	34,994 (6)	596,901	63,325 (8)	818,584	887,205
Loudoun	24,549	4,648 (13)	37,150	5,018 (9)	57,427	6,168 (7)	86,129	115,870
Prince William	50,164	5,925 (5)	111,102	11,918 (8)	144,703	25,078 (12)	215,686	245,184
Stafford	16,876	2,284 (9)	24,587	2,905 (7)	40,470	4,304 (7)	61,236	80,107
Virginia Cities								
Alexandria	91,023	15,644 (14)	110,938	23,006 (22)	103,217	24,339 (22)	111,183	115,609
Fairfax	13,585	370 (2)	21,970	585 (3)	19,390	966 (5)	19,622	20,637
Falls Church	10,192	152 (1)	10,772	223 (2)	9,515	298 (3)	9,578	9,617
Manassas	3,555	950 (10)	9,164	1,403 (9)	15,438	2,889 (10)	27,957	32,657
Virginia Non-MA Counties								
Spotsylvania	13,819	3,578 (18)	16,424	5,082 (15)	34,435	6,178 (11)	57,403	71,981
Fauquier	24,066	5,858 (22)	26,375	5,635 (16)	35,889	5,462 (11)	48,741	51,473
Clarke	7,942	1,193 (15)	8,102	1,144 (11)	9,965	1,054 (9)	12,101	12,390
Frederick	21,941	454 (2)	28,893	484 (1)	34,150	832 (2)	45,723	51,549
Virginia Total	716,115	57,991 (6)	1,034,782	106,425 (8)	1,254,099	158,853 (9)	1,684,879	1,866,939

(continues)

Table 5.1. Continued

	1960	1970		1980		1990		1995
	Total Population	Total Population	Black Population Number (%)	Total Population	Black Population Number (%)	Total Population	Black Population Number (%)	Total Population
Maryland Counties								
Montgomery	340,928	522,809	21,551 (4)	579,053	50,756 (9)	757,027	89,184 (12)	809,569
Prince George's	357,395	660,567	91,808 (14)	665,071	247,860 (37)	729,268	369,791 (51)	767,413
Calvert	15,826	20,682	7,760 (38)	34,638	7,689 (22)	51,372	8,046 (16)	64,598
Charles	32,572	47,678	13,295 (28)	72,751	14,736 (20)	101,154	18,419 (18)	111,633
Frederick	71,930	84,927	5,852 (7)	114,792	6,344 (6)	150,208	8,010 (5)	175,399
MARYLAND TOTAL	818,651	1,336,663	140,266 (10)	1,466,305	327,385 (22)	1,789,029	493,450 (28)	1,928,612
METROPOLITAN TOTAL	2,001,897	2,861,123	702,329 (25)	3,060,922	853,719 (28)	3,923,574	1,041,934 (27)	4,349,807

Source: U.S. Bureau of the Census, *Census of Population,* 1960, 1970, 1980, 1990; U.S. Bureau of the Census, 1995

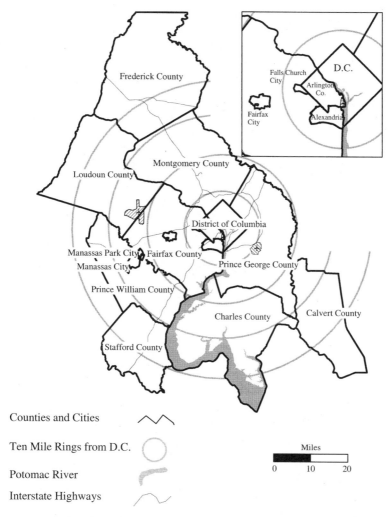

Map 5.1. Political Jurisdictions of the 1990 Washington, D.C. MA with Concentric 10-Mile Rings.

Kumar 1994, 320). During the 1990s, employment and housing shifts outward continued. Employment declined in the central city but increased in the inner suburbs. Subway use increased. Carpooling was stable. Auto traffic increases occurred almost entirely outside the I-495 Beltway (Sipress 1999).

Employment also was deconcentrating, with Fairfax County, Virginia, leading the pace of suburban job growth. In 1970, Fairfax County contained only 49,292 private-sector jobs for a resident population of 455,021. Population growth continued, but the central city to suburb gap in the ratio of population to employment closed rapidly, dropping from 9.2 residents to 2.5 residents per job as private-sector employment shot to 326,458 jobs by 1990 and 372,035 by 1995. The forces of employment dispersion, however, were significantly weaker than those of population dispersal. While Washington, D.C.'s population was declining by 150,000 from 1970 to 1990, its private-sector employment increased from 326,584 to 426,959 (Table 5.2). In 1995, Washington, D.C. still had a much higher ratio of jobs to residents than did Fairfax County: 134 residents per 100 private-sector jobs in D.C. to 238 residents per 100 private-sector jobs in Fairfax. These data do not include government employment, which was more concentrated in the District of Columbia than private-sector employment.

Farmland had been rapidly converted to other uses. In Virginia, farmland conversions from 1959 to 1992 occurred as follows: Fairfax County, 75 percent;

Table 5.2. Private Employment in the Washington, D.C. Metropolitan Area[1]

	1970	1980	1990	1995	% Change 1990–1995
Washington, D.C.	326,584	342,906	426,959	413,757	3.0%
Virginia Counties					
Arlington	55,075	61,842	102,275	111,363	8.9%
Fairfax	49,292	150,485	326,458	372,035	14.0%
Loudoun	4,816	11,184	34,167	39,966	17.0%
Prince William	11,104	19,069	44,876	50,056	11.5%
Stafford	1,210	2,244	10,997	19,666	78.8%
Virginia Cities					
Alexandria	33,160	44,336	71,518	69,906	−2.3%
Fairfax	7,513	17,282	31,910	28,287	−11.4%
Falls Church	12,005	7,121	12,845	12,904	0.5%
Manassass	—	7,608	18,371	17,961	−2.2%
VIRGINIA TOTAL	174,175	321,171	653,417	722,144	10.5%
Maryland Counties					
Montgomery	114,703	216,687	351,499	342,624	−2.5%
Prince George's	96,669	160,609	250,372	233,595	−6.7%
Calvert	2,659	4,256	9,645	12,682	31.5%
Charles	7,028	10,395	22,495	26,833	19.3%
Frederick	19,485	28,488	49,531	57,817	16.7%
MARYLAND TOTAL	240,544	420,435	683,542	683,551	0.0%
METROPOLITAN TOTAL	741,303	1,084,512	1,763,918	1,819,452	3.1%

Source: U.S. Bureau of the Census, *County Business Patterns*
[1] Private employment the week of March 12

Loudoun County, 23 percent; Prince William County, 63 percent; and Stafford County, 65 percent. Similar rates of decline occurred in Maryland: Calvert County, 56 percent; Charles County, 59 percent; Frederick County, 29 percent; Montgomery County, 51 percent; and Prince George's County, 56 percent.

The overall trend in the Washington, D.C. region has been a combination of rapid population growth, employment deconcentration, and low-density sprawl. There have been exceptions, however—and the implications of these exceptions are intriguing.

Inner Suburban Revival in Northern Virginia

Alexandria and Arlington are older, inner suburbs bordering Washington, D.C. One can question whether Alexandria and Arlington are suburbs. They are subordinate in size and economic function to neighboring Washington, D.C., but their densities of 7,267 and 6,600 persons per square mile in 1990 were higher than the densities in any of Virginia's larger cities, and their home ownership and median age of housing were similar to the older central cities elsewhere in Virginia. In the context of the general decline of cities in the United States, the ambiguity of their city or suburban status makes their revival in the 1980s all the more surprising.

In 1990, 282,119 people lived in Alexandria and Arlington. That was slightly less than in 1970, but it was 10 percent more than in 1980. The population of Northern Virginia was racing outward during the 1970s: while Northern Virginia's population grew by 21 percent in the 1970s, the inner suburbs of Arlington and Alexandria declined by 10 percent.

Because of the large size of most Northern Virginia jurisdictions, we analyzed income change by census tracts to identify small-scale changes that would be more analogous to changes in small suburban jurisdictions in metropolitan areas in most states. Using 1980 census tract boundaries, we analyzed median family income changes between 1979 and 1989 in each of the Northern Virginia jurisdictions. The average population of these census tracts in 1990 ranged from 3,474 in Alexandria to 6,958 in Prince William.

Between 1980 and 1990, the transitions in Arlington and Alexandria at census tract scale were dramatic. Population increased in 20 of Alexandria's 32 census tracts and in 33 of Arlington's 39 tracts. The income transitions also were impressive: 66 percent of the census tracts in Alexandria increased in relative median family income, and 54 percent of the tracts in Arlington increased. Even more impressive was the range of neighborhoods where income increases occurred. In Alexandria and Arlington, one-half or more of low-, moderate-, and middle-income census tracts increased in relative income. Moreover, 28 percent of Alexandria's tracts and 13 percent of Arlington's went up by more than 20 percent in income relative to the region's median. Median family income in Arlington rose by $6,205 (in 1990 constant dollars) in the 1980s, compared with a $2,703 increase in the 1970s. In Alexandria, median family income increased by $7,265 in the 1980s. What events led to these results?

Arlington

Decisions were made in the 1960s to construct the METRO heavy-rail mass transit system in Washington, D.C. and its Virginia and Maryland suburbs. In a 1968 referendum, voters supported investing the local share of capital construction costs. Local governments in the path of the suburban rail lines had to make decisions in the 1960s and 1970s about how to adapt to the future arrival of METRO service.

In Arlington, two crucial decisions were made. One decision brought METRO rail service to places with substantial commercial density in the Wilson Boulevard corridor. The second decision used METRO stations to concentrate redevelopment nearby (Parker 1995). By 1979 the five stations in the Rosslyn-Ballston (Wilson Boulevard) corridor had opened. In 1980 residential and office construction took off, especially in METRO station areas, where more than 6,000 housing units (Figure 5.1) and more than 16 million square feet of office space (Figure 5.2) were constructed by 1991. That was 95 percent of all the new office space in Arlington (Tables 5.3 and 5.4). Because many of the new residences near METRO stations were rental units, median family income declined in some areas where they were developed. But in nearly all of the older residential tracts nearby, median family income rose, increasing by more than 10 percent relative to the region in 29 percent of the tracts from 1980 to 1990.

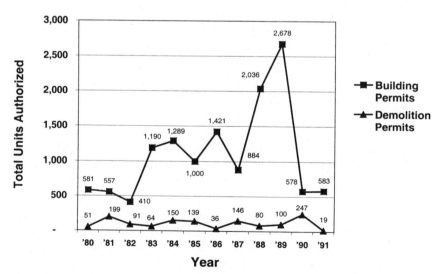

Figure 5.1. Residential Units Authorized by Building and Demolition Permits: 1980–1991, Arlington County, Virginia.

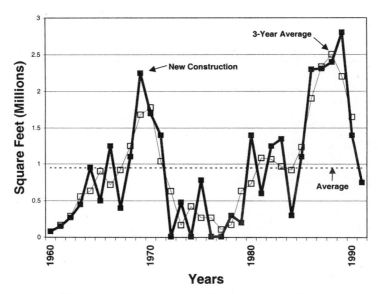

Figure 5.2. Office Space Construction: 1960–1991, Arlington County, Virginia.

Table 5.3. Summary of Residential Development in the Rosslyn-Ballston Metro Corridor Station Areas

	Total Units	Rosslyn Number (%)	Court House Number (%)	Clarendon Number (%)	Virginia Square Number (%)	Ballston Number (%)
1960–69	1,865	891 (48)	470 (25)	30 (2)	62 (3)	412 (22)
1970–79	700	94 (13)	0 (0)	23 (3)	252 (36)	331 (47)
1980–89	5,042	1,532 (30)	1,193 (24)	0 (0)	42 (1)	2,275 (45)
1990–91	1,367	46 (3)	850 (62)	0 (0)	350 (26)	121 (9)
1960–91	8,974	2,563 (29)	2,513 (28)	53 (1)	706 (8)	3,139 (35)

Source: Department of Economic Development, Arlington County, Virginia

Table 5.4. Square Feet of Office/Commercial Gross Floor Area by Location, Arlington County, Virginia

	Rosslyn-Ballston Corridor	% of Decade	Jefferson Davis Corridor	% of Decade	Outside Metro	% of Decade
1960–69	4,443,382	59.2%	2,851,292	38%	211,032	2.8%
1970–79	1,646,216	32.5%	2,870,382	56.8%	540,974	10.7%
1980–89	8,823,859	55.4%	6,466,396	40.6%	645,411	4.1%
1990–91	1,192,901	61.3%	608,851	31.3%	144,967	7.4%
TOTAL	16,106,358	52.9%	12,796,921	42.0%	1,542,384	5.1%

Source: Department of Economic Development, Arlington County, Virginia

Higher-density mixed-use development around the Ballston-MU Metrorail station in Arlington, Virginia, provided employment and retail services in a pedestrian environment. Concentrating development around Metro stops also helped preserve older suburban residential neighborhoods within four to eight blocks of the stop. (Synergy/Photography)

Although some local governments have not perceived transit-based housing positively (Boarnet and Crane 1997), Arlington has demonstrated that transit-related housing, commerce, and offices are compatible.

Arlington competed successfully against one of the East's most imposing edge cities served by expressways but not by heavy-rail transit. Robert Cervero (1994, 89) found that "from 1978 to 1989, . . . Ballston averaged an annual office rent premium of over three dollars per square foot . . . over Tysons Corner, a massive 'suburban downtown' that lies six miles to the southwest." Another METRO station area, Clarendon, redeveloped old buildings as a restaurant and entertainment center. Alan Ehrenhalt (1998) interpreted METRO as necessary but insufficient: "Once the infrastructure [subway] is in place, established businesses suddenly find themselves willing to take a chance on an older neighborhood, confident that its future is based on something more permanent than speeches and architectural drawings. . . . County zoning was flexible enough to allow for sidewalk cafes and other small-scale experiments, and to permit businesses located near the subway stop to dispense with parking-space requirements they would have been hard-pressed to meet."

The period from 1980 to 1990 was the optimum time for this development effort because the office construction boom in the Washington, D.C. region provided the raw material for success. Arlington's reinvention was also attributable to the unified commitment of its board of supervisors, political parties, neighborhood associations, and citizens to the vision of concentrating mixed-use development around METRO stations. Both political parties embraced the land use plan that evolved in the 1960s, and neighborhood associations have

Tysons Corner in Fairfax County, Virginia, is a typical "edge city" of concentrated suburban employment in the sea of single-family subdivisions. (Synergy/Photography)

sustained the vision contained in the plan. When a growth–no growth debate occurred in the 1970s, the issue was the pace at which the land use plan should be implemented, not whether to implement it (Gardner 1995). Arlington demonstrates Robert Cervero's (1998, 83) assertion, based on studies of Atlanta, Philadelphia, San Francisco, and Washington, D.C., that "rail investments can induce meaningful changes in urban landscapes, though only when the public sector is committed to closely working with the private sector to bring this about."

Private employment growth continued in Arlington between 1990 and 1995, increasing 8.9 percent to 111,363 jobs, while the number of jobs declined slightly in Alexandria (2.3 percent), Montgomery County (2.5 percent), Prince George's County (6.7 percent), and Washington, D.C. (3 percent). Arlington then contained 155 residents for each 100 private jobs. Many residents were not in the labor market because of age, infirmity, or choice, so more private jobs than residents looking for work were located in Arlington.

By 1998, more than 30 million square feet of office and other employment space had been built in the Rosslyn-Ballston METRO corridor. Arlington's goal was to construct a total of 80 million square feet of employment space in this corridor. Development successes had increased usage of the Rosslyn-Ballston segment of METRO. The number of trains was limited by the fact that the east-west Rosslyn-Ballston Orange Line shared track near Washington, D.C. with the north-south Blue Line. Investing in expansions of METRO toward the outer reaches of suburbia, rather than reinvesting in inner areas to separate the Orange and Blue Lines, could reduce Arlington's potential to fully implement its development plans in the Rosslyn-Ballston corridor, according to some analysts (Risse 1999).

Alexandria

Alexandria was once part of the District of Columbia, reverting to Virginia's control in 1823. Alexandria's housing density was higher than Arlington's in 1990: 7,267 persons per square mile (11.4 persons per acre) compared with 6,600 (10.3 persons per acre). Although the median age year in which Alexandria's housing was constructed is more recent than in Arlington, 1963 compared with 1956, in important respects Alexandria is much older.

The Old Town neighborhood, nestled adjacent to the downtown commercial core, is one of the largest areas of preserved 18th- and 19th-century residential districts in the United States (138 square blocks). It is a magnet for hotels and restaurants. An increase in two-worker households and single adults in Alexandria spurred a burst of new restaurant activity there in the 1970s and 1980s, providing a vibrant commercial use for some of the city's old buildings. The neighborhood's appeal is so strong that $400,000 townhouses attract buyers even though they are across from public housing, grocery stores, and warehouses.

Waterfront redevelopment, another of Alexandria's major planning successes, also has been age driven. For many years, ambiguity about the city's waterfront boundary line blocked renewal of the waterfront adjacent to downtown and Old Town. Starting about 1983, the city government worked with the National Park Service to reach agreements for disposition of property, based on agreeing to property boundaries. That led to revitalization of many properties, and it added to the ambiance of nearby Old Town (Lynn 1995).

Transportation also has played a key role in Alexandria's revival. Commercial development has been influenced by Alexandria's proximity to downtown Washington, D.C., the opening of METRO stations in Alexandria starting in 1983, and the city's high-quality bus service (Lynn 1995). The King Street and Braddock Street METRO stations became areas of high-density mixed-use redevelopment in the late 1980s and 1990s. More than seven million square feet of retail, commercial, and residential uses were developed near the King Street station (McQuilken 1998). METRO-linked expansion was not as strong in Alexandria as in Arlington, perhaps because Alexandria had fewer METRO stations in commercial areas. By 1995, Alexandria's employment-to-population ratio remained strong at 165 residents per 100 private jobs, having slipped from 155 residents per 100 private jobs in 1990, but still well ahead of Fairfax County's ratio of 238 residents per 100 private jobs.

Alexandria's high-quality bus service has probably contributed to the city's success. In fiscal 1985, its first full year of city operation, city buses carried

King Street in Alexandria, Virginia, connects the Metrorail station and the Amtrak and commuter rail station in the foreground with the Old Town waterfront on the Potomac River in the background. Commercial, mixed-use, and higher-density residential development between the two have been well served by an efficient bus system. Older neighborhoods in the lower left have also been "rapid improvers" among suburban neighborhoods.

923,000 passengers; by 1994, they carried about 2,200,000 passengers. The bus system is configured to serve METRO stations, with about one-half of the bus riders transferring to METRO (Hurd 1995).

Despite income increases in many Alexandria neighborhoods, low-income people were not forced out of the jurisdiction. The number of recipients of Aid

Attention to pedestrian circulation, maintenance of the small stores along King Street, and good bus service has kept Alexandria, Virginia, an attractive and vital community. Newer commercial, residential, and hotel developments have occurred without overpowering the pedestrian experience.

to Dependent Children (ADC) declined throughout Northern Virginia during the economic expansion of the 1980s. From a low point of 1,752 in 1988, however, the number of ADC recipients in Alexandria increased to 4,093 in 1994. In Arlington, a low of 1,448 ADC recipients occurred in 1989, followed by a rise to 3,369 in 1994.

Fairfax County

Fairfax County constitutes the next tier of suburban development, south and west of Alexandria and Arlington. It is served by Interstate 95 going south from Washington, D.C., Interstate 66 going west, and Interstate 495 looping around Alexandria and Arlington; in addition, Dulles International Airport, and the highways leading to it, constitute a fringe office development magnet at the county's western edge. While Fairfax contains the planned community of Reston, most of the county was developed at low densities in single-unit detached houses. Development in the 1980s and 1990s included considerable condominium and townhouse construction. The overall county density was 2,069 persons per square mile (3.2 persons per acre) in 1990.

Fairfax Chooses Low Density

Fairfax County government officials faced the same type of decisions concerning METRO as did Arlington and Alexandria officials. In the 1960s and 1970s, the county's land use plans for METRO station areas emphasized high-density and mixed-use development. The plan for one station area called for 15 to 20 million square feet of office and commercial space.

The proposed Virginia Center project of the Hazel-Peterson Corporation, for example, called for four million square feet of office and retail space and 2,000 dwelling units. The county's plan was amended, however, so that when the Vienna METRO station opened in 1986, the development that occurred involved no mixed use, no offices and retail, and perhaps 1,500 townhouses (Risse 1995). Fairfax's experience was the opposite of Boarnet and Crane's (1997) observations about Los Angeles, where residences were rejected in most instances and offices and commerce were favored.

As a consequence, Fairfax missed an opportunity of major scale to develop communities with a balance of jobs, housing, retail services, and amenities. According to planner EM Risse (1995), "The Washington, D.C. region has about 275 million square feet of office space currently [1995]. Since 1975, 200 million square feet of that has been developed. The most optimistic forecast is that in the next 20 years, the region will need only 10 million more square feet of office space. Arlington and Alexandria seized the opportunity to create real mixed use communities. Fairfax didn't."

Private employment in Fairfax County increased from 150,485 in 1980 to 326,458 in 1990. The percentage of workers who commuted to job locations

The Vienna station in Fairfax County, Virginia, sits in the median of Interstate 66. There is little commercial development within a quarter mile. Parking and townhouse development surround this western terminus of Washington, D.C.'s Metrorail system. (Synergy/Photography)

outside the county fell from 62 percent in 1980 to 50 percent in 1990. Despite having several METRO stations and more jobs within the county of residence, Fairfax remained a typical auto-commuting suburb. Besides the usual neighborhood resistance to higher densities near METRO stations, elected local government officials have additional reasons for cautious development policies, because each jurisdiction's formula for financial contributions includes penalties for higher population density and more riders.

Auto Dependence

In 1990, 87 percent of Fairfax workers drove to work, with 71 percent driving alone; the national rate for areas outside a central city is 90.5 percent driving to work, with 78 percent driving alone. On the other hand, 64 percent of Arlington workers and 75 percent of Alexandria workers drove to jobs. Put another way, in Arlington, 50 percent of resident workers arrived at their job sites by means other than driving alone, as did 41 percent of Alexandria's workers. In Fairfax, only 29 percent of resident county workers arrived by means other than driving alone (U.S. Bureau of the Census 1993).

One result for Fairfax County has been a continuation of sprawl development. From 1980 to 1990, the population of Fairfax County increased from 596,901 to 818,584. (By 1995, Fairfax's population reached 887,205, and in

1997, it was estimated at 920,000.) Despite that increase of 221,683 residents in the 1980s, 38 of Fairfax's 141 census tracts actually lost population during the decade. During the same period, 58 other census tracts grew in population by more than 25 percent. Nearly all the population-losing census tracts were inside or close to the I-495 Beltway, while most of the rapidly growing tracts were considerably outside the Beltway. In addition, 46 percent of Fairfax's census tracts declined in median family income relative to the regional median.

Fairfax's public officials recognized that reinvestment was needed. In 1997, the Fairfax County Board of Supervisors recommended that voters approve $487 million in bonds for refurbishing aging public school buildings, including shifting $175 million that otherwise would have been spent on parks, roads, and sidewalks (Lipton and O'Harrow 1997). Later in 1997, the supervisors appointed a new county executive, Robert O'Neill, who declared that older neighborhoods would be a priority, because "we have a stake in making sure these older neighborhoods never get so bad that people start to abandon them" (Lipton 1997). Bonds for investments in declining neighborhood commercial districts had been approved in 1988. Due to ensuing financial shortfalls, expenditures were not made until 1998 for installing street trees and brick sidewalks and placing utilities underground (Pae 1999). In 1999, Fairfax County officials supported a seven-and-a-half-mile, $900 million elevated Metrorail line extending from the Orange Line on the eastern edge of Fairfax County, through the gigantic edge city of Tysons Corner, to Dulles International Airport (Reid and Shear 1999). Despite Fairfax County officials' interest in reinvestment and in expanding fixed-rail mass transit, in 1999 they still had not committed themselves to supporting substantial densities and mixed use near its METRO stations.

Fairfax and Prince William Counties also were experiencing rapid increases in the number of participants in Aid to Dependent Children and food stamp programs. In Fairfax, ADC recipients increased from 4,912 in 1988 to 11,532 in 1994, while the number of food stamp recipients went from 8,254 in 1987 to 24,637 in 1994. In Prince William, the number of ADC recipients went from 1,908 in 1988 to 4,683 in 1994, with food stamp recipients increasing from 2,446 in 1987 to 11,575 in 1994 (Virginia Department of Social Services 1994). When the recession occurred in 1989, the dependent low-income population grew rapidly in both counties. After the recession ended in 1991, ADC and food stamp recipients continued increasing—in contrast with the 1980s, when economic expansion was accompanied by a major reduction in ADC and food stamp recipients.

Stability in Greenbelt amid Rapid Decline Nearby

In Prince George's County, Maryland, every place for which reliable income data were available in 1960 had declined in income relative to the regional median by 1990. Of Prince George's County's 14 jurisdictions in this study, nine

Typical housing in Greenbelt, Maryland. (Synergy/Photography)

declined by more than 20 percent in relative income. Of the 12 jurisdictions in the region in which relative median family income declined faster than in Washington, D.C., 11 were in Maryland and nine were in Prince George's County. Langley Park led with a 42 percent relative income decline. The lowest rate of decline was in Greenbelt, which declined from 90 percent of the region's median family income in 1960 to 86.4 percent in 1990.

Greenbelt's relative stability in a tumult of relative income decline is a puzzle. Greenbelt was not stabilized by being a high-income enclave. In 1960, only two of Prince George's 14 jurisdictions had lower median family incomes. Greenbelt was not a bastion of homeowners with strong attachments. In 1960, 82 percent of Greenbelt's occupied units were owner occupied; by 1990, owner occupancy in Greenbelt had fallen to only 44 percent of occupied housing units, and 65 percent of its residents had moved within the last five years. Nor was Greenbelt dominated by single-family houses. In 1990, only 34 percent of its housing was in single-unit structures, compared with the average in Prince George's County of 62 percent.

Since Greenbelt's housing history was contrary to the norm in affluent suburbs, other factors must be examined in order to solve the puzzle of the community's socioeconomic persistence. Greenbelt's origins, community design, and ownership evolution provide some plausible explanations.

A 1930s New Town

Greenbelt was founded in 1937 as a federally funded new town, built five miles from Washington, D.C. during the administration of President Franklin

Roosevelt. Of the three new towns built under federal control during the Depression, Greenbelt was the one that was guided the most by the planning ideas of Clarence Stein. It was patterned after Stein's 1929 plan for Radburn, New Jersey, with superblocks, cul-de-sacs, walkways, underpasses, a town center, a lake, and a greenbelt. Distances between residences and public and private facilities were geared to walking and bicycling.

Greenbelt was unusual among older suburbs in experiencing substantial post-1960 population growth. Greenbelt's population went from 7,479 in 1960 to 21,096 in 1990, an increase that occurred because of substantial land being available for development. The opportunity to construct housing during different decades, at once including some new housing and remodeling some of the older housing before it reached the vulnerable age of 30 to 50 years, may itself be a significant source of income stability.

In contrast with the introduction of METRO in Arlington and Alexandria, and waterfront and bus system improvements in Alexandria, no special public investments occurred in Greenbelt during the 1980s to enhance its attractiveness to current and prospective residents. The search for explanations of Greenbelt's stability, therefore, led back to the town's origins. The hypothesis with which we began, and with which we ended after investigation, was that the land use plan, the walkable distances between home and a variety of activities, the links to nature, and the feelings of community

The community center in the town of Greenbelt, Maryland. (Synergy/Photography)

attachment have kept Greenbelt attractive to enough middle-income residents and newcomers to maintain its income stability relative to income in the region.

Greenbelt's land use plan has been described (Gillette 1994, 24) as follows:

> ... [T]he designers created a town plan that followed the shape of the landscape—a high, crescent-shaped plateau. ... Houses were built in the area between the curvilinear streets, while the town center filled the bowl of the crescent and a man-made lake extended beyond the center. Cross streets divided the town into superblocks of from fourteen to eighteen acres, each containing approximately 120 houses in rows of two to eight, with the kitchen side—or the service side—having access to the street, the garden side facing within. Walkways wound through the blocks, and underpasses tunneled beneath Crescent Road linking the superblocks to the town center and the lake. ... The town was surrounded by a greenbelt of woods that served as a buffer.

Place and Community

K. C. Parsons (1990, 161) observed that the federal government's ownership of the land and buildings made Greenbelt "one of [President Franklin] Roosevelt's most radical efforts to involve the federal government in urban community development." Continuing later in the article, Parsons (1990, 176) wrote: "After the end of World War II, conservative legislators noted this radical exception to national policy and officially challenged it."

Their challenge resulted in the federal government selling the land and buildings, based on legislation passed by Congress in 1949. But thanks to the efforts of Clarence Stein, on whose Radburn plan Greenbelt had been based, a negotiated sale rather than an auction was conducted. The purchaser was a veterans' cooperative.

To this day, the 1,600 shareholders in a cooperative, Greenbelt Homes, Inc., own about 80 percent of the original planned community. According to Howard Berger (1995), who co-authored an historic district study (Berger and Rivers 1994) about Greenbelt: "The housing cooperative is in charge of maintaining the physical place, both the grounds and utilities, namely those elements shared in common. Building changes are controlled. The Greenbook (of Greenbelt's regulations) governs behavior related to physical places. An ethic about maintaining the physical place is very strong." Parsons (1995) hypothesized that Greenbelt "has more community participation than in other suburban places. The physical and social conditions are reasons for staying and being attracted. Greenbelt is thought to be a good place to live."

Owner-Occupied Housing Values

While residents' income relative to regional income is a valid test of market competition among local jurisdictions, housing value is a more conventional measure of location attractiveness. Housing value at the time of construction is one relevant comparative indicator. For the purposes of this analysis, however, the trend in housing values from decade to decade is a more telling indicator of jurisdictions' competitive attractiveness.

In 1990, the median value of owner-occupied housing was higher in Arlington and Alexandria than the regional median. More surprisingly, by 1990 Arlington and Alexandria housing values had surpassed values in Fairfax County—as well as the previous leader, Montgomery County—for the first time, after trailing in 1970 and 1980 (Table 5.5). This parallel movement of housing values in Arlington and Alexandria, from 116 percent of the regional median in 1980 to 139 and 138 percent in 1990, may have been influenced by the opening of METRO early in the 1980s. The 1990s were a period of generally flat housing values in the region, after actual declines in some areas in the early 1990s. By the late 1990s, values were rising, with Arlington and Alexandria again in the lead. In 1998, for example, housing assessments in Arlington rose 3 percent, with assessments near METRO stations rising the most. Sales prices in Alexandria rose 10 percent. In outlying Fairfax, Loudoun, and Prince William Counties, assessments rose less than 1 percent (Pae and Shields 1999).

The value of location to Arlington and Alexandria may have been observable as well in the relationship of median family income to median owner-occupied housing values. Median family income in Arlington in 1990 was 102 percent of the regional median, whereas in Alexandria it was 94 percent. These ratios were considerably lower than in Fairfax, where median family income in 1990 was 121 percent of the regional median. There was a close correspondence between the median family income ratio and the median owner-occupied housing value in Fairfax (121 to 129) in 1990. In Arlington and Alexandria, however, there were considerable gaps—102 to 139 in Arlington and 94 to 138 in Alexandria. From these substantial gaps between income and housing value, one can infer that many residents of Arlington and Alexandria were willing to pay high proportions of their income for housing, in exchange for the opportunity to live in those jurisdictions. METRO and other amenities related to location may well have contributed to many Arlington and Alexandria residents' enthusiasm about living there.

As for Greenbelt, its median housing value was relatively low in 1990 (Table 5.5). In 1960, however, Greenbelt's median housing value had been by far the lowest of any jurisdiction, large or small, in the Washington, D.C. region. These low values may have reflected the unusual ownership status possessed by participants in a housing cooperative, among other possible influences, including small unit size. Between 1960 and 1990, however, the median housing value in

Table 5.5. Median Owner-Occupied Housing Value for Selected Jurisdictions in the Washington, D.C. Region

	1960		1970		1980		1990	
	Value	(as % of MA)	Value	(as % of MA)	Value	(as % of MA)	Value	(as % of MA)
Washington, D.C.	$15,400	(90.1)	$21,300	(75.5)	$68,800	(86.1)	$123,900	(74.6)
Alexandria	16,500	(96.5)	27,200	(96.5)	93,300	(116.8)	228,600	(137.6)
Arlington County	18,800	(109.9)	29,400	(104.3)	92,900	(116.3)	231,000	(139.1)
Fairfax County	18,700	(109.4)	35,300	(125.2)	95,200	(119.1)	213,800	(128.7)
Prince William County	11,800	(69.0)	23,800	(84.4)	65,000	(81.4)	138,500	(83.4)
Prince George's County	15,100	(88.3)	23,700	(84.0)	63,900	(80.0)	122,600	(73.8)
Greenbelt	5,000	(29.2)	—		37,800	(47.3)	96,000	(57.8)
Montgomery County	19,800	(115.8)	33,700	(116.0)	97,300	(121.8)	200,800	(120.9)
Washington, D.C. MA	17,100		28,200		79,900		166,100	

Source: U.S. Bureau of the Census, Census of Population and Housing

Greenbelt rose faster relative to the regional median than in any other jurisdiction. The sustaining influence of the community design of Greenbelt may be reflected in this increase in housing value.

Planning and Housing Markets

Relative income decline has become common in many suburbs. Older inner suburbs have declined frequently, but some older suburbs have persisted in sustaining or enhancing their earlier status. The examples of Alexandria and Arlington indicate that some suburbs can slow, halt, or reverse decline through the combined influences of location advantages, mass transit investments, higher density, historic preservation, and effective redevelopment planning. Two studies of METRO in Washington, D.C., have found little development impact from heavy-rail transit; but these studies were published in 1983, the same year METRO opened in Alexandria and only four years after the first station opened in Arlington (Gordon and Richardson 1989, 344). On the other hand, Cervero (1994, 90) said that his "results support previous research findings that transit investments—and the ridership and coordinated joint development that they stimulate—encourage dense development." Greenbelt indicates that, as in Alexandria and Arlington, high rates of home ownership and single-family detached housing are not always needed to maintain relative income stability. Ease in walking to diverse activities, whether in the cul-de-sac/pedestrian pathway environment of Greenbelt or in the grid street, mass transit–serviced, through-traffic networks of Alexandria and Arlington, can help sustain communities.

Our findings offer hope for market success for the compact, mixed-use land development and redevelopment elements that many planners consider to be good planning (Calavita and Caves 1994, 489-490; Calthorpe 1993; Cervero 1994; Cervero and Gorham 1995; Newman and Kenworthy 1989; Sasaki Associates et al. 1993). Conversely, these findings challenge the assumptions of those who believe that contemporary markets in land, housing, and employment in the United States will not, and perhaps should not, support mixed-use, relatively high density, mass transit–dependent, and walkable older communities (Audirac, Shermyen, and Smith 1990; Gordon, Richardson, and Jun 1991, 419).

In the instances examined here, the jurisdictions with strong planning traditions—Alexandria, Arlington, and Greenbelt—passed the market test with flying colors. Meanwhile, some neighboring communities with more passive planning traditions were showing signs of strain and decline—sometimes rapid decline.

Planning and markets are sometimes juxtaposed as though they are opposites (Richardson and Gordon 1993). We suggest shifting that emphasis so that planning and policymaking take market contexts into account (Banerjee 1993).

Arlington, Alexandria, and Greenbelt have been implementing some of the redevelopment concepts L. S. Bourne (1992, 512) has described for Toronto and Vancouver: ". . . [T]he plans are intended to encourage substantially more housing construction, . . . in their inner areas. . . . It would also, the planners suggest (perhaps rather too optimistically), maintain and enhance the residential (and commercial) functions of the central city. . . . If successful, . . . the approach could then be extended to the selective redevelopment and intensification of the older, graying inner suburbs and to the design of more diverse, cost-effective, and sustainable suburban communities."

The lesson here is that strong planning by inner suburbs, sustained over decades, can contribute to success in private market competition for residents who are representative of the socioeconomic groups in a metropolitan area. The successes of Arlington, Alexandria, and Greenbelt indicate that redevelopment that emphasizes mass transit, mixed land uses, substantial residential density, and walkable distances between land uses can help some aging communities survive and thrive in competitive housing, labor, and government markets.

Note

Descriptions of events and explanations of influences on development and preservation were based in part on interviews during February and March 1995 with Howard Berger, architectural historian for the Prince George's County Office of the Maryland–National Capital Park and Planning Commission; Anton Gardner, Arlington County Manager; William Hurd, Alexandria Planning Commission chair; Sheldon Lynn, Alexandria planning director; Gretchen Oberdurff, general manager of Greenbelt Homes, Inc.; Thomas Parker, chief of economic development, Arlington; K. C. Parsons, professor of urban planning, Cornell University; and EM Risse, principal, Synergy Planning, Fairfax County.

Chapter 6

Why Cities Succeed
in Some of the 50 States

Strategic planning in metropolitan regions cannot be done well by local governments acting alone. Since few regions have integrated government structures, the federal and state governments also should analyze dangers and opportunities. Dangers can be assessed appropriately if local and regional conditions are interpreted in state and national contexts. State governments are powerful in the United States—powerful enough to be included in the web of responsibility for pervasive city-suburb income disparities. Valid national interpretations of prospects for cities, suburbs, and regions depend on understanding how conditions vary among the 50 states. More effective intervention policies to deal with excessive disparities among jurisdictions, sprawl in suburbia and exurbia, and insufficient reinvestment in established cities and suburbs should emerge from analyzing conditions in the 50 states.

State powers over services, regulations, and taxes that influence community health are numerous and strong. States influence metropolitan conditions to a greater extent, in our view, than the federal government. Environmental scans by local governments and regional agencies about external dangers and opportunities should include effects of state policies. State government officials, for that matter, can evaluate effects of their own policies on local governments and metropolitan regions. The paired concepts discussed in Chapter 3 (area and power, pattern and density, population and neighborhood, and space and place) help illuminate implications of state policies for localities and regions by identifying plausible connections between state powers and local and regional consequences.

States are dominant, for example, in relating area and power. In some instances, states create local government boundaries, and in each instance, they establish procedures by which local government boundaries can be altered. States determine which taxes and charges local governments can levy, which public services they can provide, and the organizational structure with which they can deliver services and regulate activities. States determine procedures by which regions are governed, usually by permitting multijurisdictional special districts for various functions. Spanning local boundaries, these special authorities—for water and sewer, solid waste, airports, mass transit, mental health, health, jails, courts, planning, and the like—constitute disjointed quasi-metropolitan governments, which often are obscured from public view by indirect methods of appointment and limited, often single, functions. State governments also reserve for themselves substantial powers over some functions, including public education, transportation, and health. With their delegated powers and various incentives and disincentives for collaboration among local governments, these reserved powers make states themselves quasi-metropolitan governments. In each of these respects, state governments shape most aspects of complex relationships between area and power.

In addition, states are much stronger than the federal government in the arena of pattern and density. Local governments derive their regulatory powers from states. States decide how to retain some, and delegate other, transportation, sanitation, and public health functions. Their decisions determine which level and type of government will build and finance highways, bridges, public transportation, and airports, and which level and type of government will regulate household waste disposal. Each decision regarding these facilities influences development patterns for decades. Moreover, states authorize land planning powers, primarily delegating them to local governments of varying sizes, including powers concerning zoning, subdivision regulations, site planning review, and appeals of land development regulations. Through these regulatory powers, the tyranny of easy development decisions on the fringe of metropolitan areas takes shape. While easy development decisions are the norm, some variation on this theme occurs. Examples of local and regional efforts to guide land development, emphasizing goals of more redevelopment in existing neighborhoods and less scattered development on the metropolitan fringe, are described in Chapter 9.

Through decisions about policies, services, taxes, and regulations that influence arenas of area and power and pattern and density, states also influence population characteristics in neighborhoods and local government jurisdictions, as well as the relationship between space and place. Inter-local income disparities emerge from interactions among easy development decisions on the metropolitan fringe, numerous local government jurisdictions, and too little reinvestment within middle-aged and local jurisdictions. The framework for these decisions is determined by the direct and delegated authority of state governments. Thus, each state government is implicated in the array of income disparities, easy development decisions, and reinvestment performance that emerges in metropolitan regions.

Analyzing state policies that encourage—or discourage—disparities, sprawl, and disinvestment is an important task. States should undertake such analyses in their own interest. Sprawl and disinvestment, however, are difficult to measure. Discerning policy connections to patterns of sprawl and disinvestment also is difficult.

Income disparities among local government or parts of metropolitan areas, on the other hand, are relatively easy to identify, measure, and compare. Income disparities between cities and suburbs in each state, for example, can be identified and compared. Three questions are examined here:

1. Have city-suburban income disparities varied among the 50 states?
2. Have the disparities been sufficiently varied, and so configured, that state policies may plausibly have influenced the disparity variation?
3. What have been some relationships between growing cities, sizable city-suburb income disparities, and regional economic prosperity?

The answers may help identify some dangers to cities, suburbs, and regions, and may reveal that some state policies actually constitute dangers. Conversely, examining cities that are relatively successful, in terms of disparities, may indicate state policies that have had a positive impact on cities' and suburbs' socioeconomic balance, therefore identifying opportunities.

Federal Policies and States' Influence

Most central cities in the United States have been declining relative to their suburbs since 1960. Although this trend is a less complete clue to metropolitan problems than before the era of suburban decline, it is still a fundamental condition that should influence public policy. It continued to be a prominent trend during the 1970s and 1980s, although some central cities were doing well during this same period. The success of some cities is reason to question whether federal policies have been blamed excessively for central city decline.

Federal housing and transportation policies are commonly blamed for contributing to suburbanization and hence to city decline. Federal tax subsidies for owner-occupied housing (deductions of local property taxes and interest payments from federal income taxes) and 90 percent federal funding of the more-than-40,000-mile interstate highway system are often cited as the federal policies that have most encouraged suburbanization (Ames et al. 1992; Fox 1990; Heilbrun 1987). These federal policies have had suburbanizing effects nationwide. Metropolitan areas where interstate highway capacity is especially large may have experienced more than average suburban sprawl, such as in the Atlanta region. Deductions of local property tax and interest payments from federal income taxes seem less likely to explain variations in city-suburban income disparities. Perhaps other federal policies, such as federal contributions to regional sewage treatment facilities, may have differentially affected sprawl and disparity trends. But given the goal of consistency in federal policies, most city-suburban income disparity differences probably cannot be traced to federal policy differential impacts.

Historical, cultural, geographic, and economic interpretations of suburbanization also are common (Jackson 1985; Marx 1964; Mumford 1961). The vast western frontier, the low cultural value Americans have attributed to places, the ability to feed an expanding population with less land in agriculture, and the marriage of affluence with technical capacity and plentiful infrastructure that made long work commutes palatable—all these forces had some effect on suburbanization trends. But such broad forces seem ill suited to explain variation in city-suburb income disparities among states, especially adjacent proximate states.

Since state governments' policies impact the arenas of area and power, pattern and density, population and neighborhood, and space and place, differences in state policies could influence differences in city-suburban income disparities. State policies may influence residential location decisions and business investment decisions. Residents' location decisions could be influenced by differences in local tax rates, local public service quality, land use regulatory decisions (which may be local or state decisions), the modes and locations of state transportation investments, and allocation formulas of state aid for elementary and secondary public education. Moreover, state policies may influence where public housing for low-income residents is located and whether reinvestment in aging housing is encouraged. Other infrastructure investments, such as whether states invest in water and sewer systems and whether these investments encourage infill, compact development, or sprawling suburban and exurban development, also could influence development patterns and the location decisions encouraged by these development trends.

Our analyses will confirm the presence of large differences in intrametropolitan income disparities, differences in disparities among metropolitan areas grouped by state, and diverse local boundary change and state aid policies that might influence the emergence and persistence of disparities. In this modest but useful beginning, we will include five steps:

1. Describe trends in residents' income from 1960 to 1990 in 147 central cities in relation to residents' income in their metropolitan areas as a whole.
2. Describe the pattern of city-suburb income disparities in 1990, comparing average income disparities in 460 cities and 320 metropolitan areas in all 50 states.
3. Consider whether state policies may impact income relationships between cities and suburbs.
4. Examine several possible causes of city-suburban income patterns in Virginia, Georgia, North Carolina, and West Virginia.
5. Explore whether growing cities promote regional prosperity or, conversely, whether regional growth may exacerbate city-suburb income disparities.

Declining Cities in Metropolitan Areas

A median family income (MFI) ratio of residents will be used to compare each city with its metropolitan area (see Note 6.1). The MFI ratio is derived by dividing the income of city residents by the income of residents in the entire metropolitan area. Every indicator has limitations, but for a limited study, as here, income is the best single indicator (Hill 1974; Logan and Schneider 1982; Lucy and Phillips 1992) because it reflects need for public services, ability to pay taxes, and capacity to choose among location alternatives. The median family income indicator reflects the accumulation of moving decisions that have occurred from decade to decade.

We have examined income relationships between 147 cities and their metropolitan areas for 1960, 1970, 1980, and 1990. These were all the single central city metropolitan areas in existence during those four decades. Avoiding metropolitan areas with two or three central cities permitted clearer comparisons between central cities and their suburbs. City-to-suburb income trends reveal that most cities have declined relative to their outside city areas during the period from 1960 to 1990. Therefore, suburbs and exurbs aggregated have improved. Our findings include:

1. In 1990, only 23 (15 percent) of 147 cities had higher median family income (MFI) than their metropolitan areas. In 1960, 67 cities had higher incomes, declining to 49 in 1970 and 24 in 1980.
2. Eighty-eight percent of cities had declined relative to their suburbs from 1960 to 1990. Only 10 of these 147 cities had improved in median family income by 1 percent or more relative to their suburbs from 1960 to 1990.
3. Only 15 of 147 cities had increased by more than 1 percent in relative MFI by 1990 compared with 1980.
4. Of the declining cities, 10 had declined rapidly in MFI (by 10 percent or more) relative to their metropolitan areas between 1980 and 1990. This was more than the eight rapidly declining cities between 1960 and 1970, but it was considerably less than the 27 rapid decliners between 1970 and 1980 (see Note 6.1).
5. Rapidly improving cities (by 10 percent or more) were scarce in all three decades—two (Newark and Wheeling) between 1980 and 1990, compared with four (Nashville, Macon, Fort Smith, and Knoxville) between 1960 and 1970, and one (Chattanooga) between 1970 and 1980.

In sum, between 1980 and 1990 most cities continued to decline relative to their metropolitan areas, while suburbs and exurbs collectively improved. Decline continued among cities in the West as well as the East, in small cities as well as large cities, and in young cities as well as older cities—relative, in each instance, to their metropolitan areas. Thus, the trend for cities was steadily down, but rather than accelerating as it did between 1970 and 1980, the 1980s trend was more moderate, akin to the 1960–70 period (see Note 6.2). A possible explanation for the apparently moderate pace of city decline in the 1980s may be that suburban decline had spread through enough metropolitan areas to reduce the rate of increase in the city-suburb income gap. But that gap, and growth in it, was still the dominant condition describing metropolitan imbalances and disequilibrium.

City-Suburb Income Pattern Explanations

Explaining why some cities have declined more than others in income relative to their suburbs, and why a few cities have been stable or improved, is another challenge. In a multivariate analysis of income conditions in cities and suburbs in 1960, 1970, and 1980, several conditions were associated with cities faring worse in income relative to their suburbs. Where cities had much lower home ownership rates than suburbs, they tended to have lower median family incomes. Differences in home ownership rates explained more of the income differences than all the other indicators combined (Lucy and Phillips 1992). Other conditions that were relevant in some years were that a large African-American population in cities was associated with lower incomes there (also see Frey 1979; Logan and Schneider 1982), as was a low percentage of total metropolitan population living in cities, and a small amount of annexation of population during previous decades.

These findings were not surprising. The attractiveness of home ownership has long been seen as a prime reason for the rise of suburbia. On average, African-Americans have less income than whites, so low income may be expected to characterize jurisdictions where large numbers of African-Americans live. A larger population share, arrived at partially through annexation, provides a city with more opportunities to capture outward-moving single-family home purchasers who are relatively affluent.

Variations among the 50 States

After expanding the study sample, making it large enough to compare the 50 states, additional clues about the probable importance of state policies emerged. Median family income data for 460 cities and metropolitan areas in 1990 were studied, and MFI ratios were constructed for the cities in relation to their metropolitan areas. Cities that were included in the names of the 320 Metropolitan Areas (MAs) reported by the U.S. Bureau of the Census in 1990 were studied, as were unnamed cities of 100,000 or more. Cities that were named in MA titles but had less than 20,000 residents were excluded, as were counties that were named in MA titles. The regions into which the states have been grouped are shown in Map 6.1.

Our goal here is to infer the relevance of state policies to creating and ame-

Map 6.1. Regions of the United States for City-Suburban Income Study.

liorating city-suburb income disparities. States are compared with each other using the average median family income ratios for their cities and metropolitan areas. This average MFI ratio hides the extremes, of course; in many states whose averages suggested their cities were doing well, one or more cities were doing badly relative to their suburbs. Nonetheless, average MFI ratios are a useful method of ordering and comparing states. In the analysis below, the 50 states have been assigned to four groups. States with generally "Successful Cities" have an average median family income ratio of 1.0 or greater. "Fairly Successful Cities" states had average MFI ratios from .950 to .999. "Struggling Cities" states had average MFI ratios from .850 to .949. "Deteriorated Cities" states had average MFI ratios of .849 or less.

States with Successful Cities

Some of the income patterns in various states were striking. In many states, median family income was much lower in cities than in the balance of their metropolitan areas. But in 10 states, cities on average had higher median family incomes than suburbs, producing an average MFI ratio of 1.0 or greater. We describe these states as being dominated by Successful Cities. These states ranged from Alaska at 1.0 to North Dakota at 1.07 and also included North Carolina, Montana, South Dakota, Arizona, Wyoming, New Mexico, West Virginia, and Arkansas (Table 6.1). In some states with few metropolitan areas (Alaska, Montana, North Dakota, Wyoming), every city had median family income as high as or higher than its suburbs. The 10 states that had average MFI ratios higher than 1.0 contained only 43 of the 460 cities studied. In national policymaking, however, they constituted a substantial force, commanding 20 percent of the votes in the U.S. Senate.

Table 6.1. States with Successful Cities (States Ranked by the Average of Their Cities' Median Family Income Ratios—Ratios of 1.000 or Greater)

	Number of Cities	Average MFI Ratio
North Dakota	3	1.067
Arkansas	6	1.052
West Virginia	4	1.035
New Mexico	3	1.034
Wyoming	2	1.030
Arizona	7	1.028
South Dakota	2	1.023
Montana	2	1.021
North Carolina	13	1.011
Alaska	1	1.000

Another 15 states were bunched with average MFI ratios between .95 and .99. They were Nebraska, Tennessee, Maine, Kansas, Indiana, Florida, Nevada, Iowa, Colorado, Texas, Oregon, Idaho, Oklahoma, Hawaii, and Alabama. These 15 states accounted for another 142 cities, of which 68 were in Florida (31) and Texas (37). These were states characterized by Fairly Successful Cities (Table 6.2). In some of these states, one city or a few cities were not doing well. Still,

Table 6.2. States with Fairly Successful Cities (States Ranked by the Average of Their Cities' Median Family Income Ratios—MFI Ratios from .950 to .999)

	Number of Cities	Average MFI Ratio
Alabama	10	.998
Hawaii	1	.998
Idaho	1	.996
Oklahoma	4	.996
Oregon	5	.995
Texas	37	.990
Colorado	10	.983
Iowa	8	.981
Nevada	2	.976
Florida	31	.966
Indiana	15	.963
Kansas	3	.963
Maine	4	.960
Tennessee	9	.953
Nebraska	2	.952

by and large, it is accurate to say that most cities were fairly successful in attracting and retaining residents with incomes similar to incomes of suburban residents.

These states were doing well enough that many of their state officials and federal representatives probably were not alarmed by city conditions. U.S. senators from the 25 states with average MFI city-suburb ratios of .95 and above were unlikely to be proponents of federal programs to aid cities. The political implication of 25 states in which cities were doing fairly well or better is that serious attention to city problems is more likely to emerge from state than federal action.

States with Deteriorated Cities

States with many troubled cities face the largest challenges. In 13 states, cities were generally severely disadvantaged. These were states dominated by Deteriorated Cities, in which average MFI ratios for the state were below .85 (Table 6.3). New Jersey was the state whose cities were the most disadvantaged relative to their suburbs of all the states studied in 1990, with a MFI ratio of .67 for eight cities (Atlantic City, Elizabeth, Jersey City, Newark, Passaic, Paterson, Trenton, and Vineland), a ratio that would have been lower except for Vineland's 1.02 ratio.

The locations of most of the states characterized by Deteriorated Cities were predictable—the Mideast (New Jersey, Delaware, Maryland, New York, Pennsylvania), New England (Rhode Island, Vermont, Connecticut,

Table 6.3. States with Deteriorated Cities (States Ranked by the Average of Their Cities' Median Family Income Ratios—MFI Ratios of .850 and Below)

	Number of Cities	*Average MFI Ratio*
New Jersey	8	.673
Delaware	1	.716
Georgia	7	.788
Ohio	17	.788
Maryland	3	.804
Michigan	17	.807
New York	15	.813
Rhode Island	4	.815
Vermont	1	.818
Utah	4	.828
Pennsylvania	18	.829
Connecticut	14	.832
Massachusetts	14	.837

Massachusetts), and the Great Lakes region (Ohio, Michigan). Cities in trouble have commonly been associated with the North. Because most southern and western states contained more cities that were doing well than cities doing badly, it was surprising to find one southern state, Georgia, tied with Ohio for the third-lowest MFI ratio, .79, and one western state, Utah, ranked 10th with a MFI ratio of .83. In these states, a few cities had high MFI ratios, even though the state averages were low.

States with Struggling Cities

Another group of 12 states, characterized by Struggling Cities, scored average MFI ratios of between .85 and .949, with South Carolina lowest at .88 and Missouri highest at .94. These states were South Carolina, Virginia, Washington, Louisiana, New Hampshire, Wisconsin, Illinois, Minnesota, California, Kentucky, Mississippi, and Missouri (Table 6.4). Some of their cities were deteriorated, but others were doing well. Diversity among these states contributes ambiguity about the causes and consequences of their cities' problems.

Most states west of the Mississippi River were above .95 in average MFI ratios. Of these states, the only ones in the Deteriorated and Struggling categories were Utah (Deteriorated) and Washington, Louisiana, California, Missouri, and Minnesota (Struggling).

Averaging states' MFI ratios for each region, the Mideast was worst off with a cumulative average MFI ratio of .77, followed by New England .86, Great

Table 6.4. States with Struggling Cities (States Ranked by the Average of Their Cities' Median Family Income Ratios—MFI Ratios from .850 to .949)

	Number of Cities	Average MFI Ratio
South Carolina	7	.883
Virginia	15	.902
Washington	9	.905
Louisiana	8	.911
New Hampshire	5	.916
Wisconsin	14	.924
Illinois	15	.925
Minnesota	5	.928
California	61	.935
Kentucky	3	.939
Mississippi	4	.941
Missouri	6	.943

Lakes .88, Southeast .95, Far West .97, Mountain .97, Plains .98, and Southwest doing best at 1.01.

Regional aggregates of states hide puzzles. In the Southeast, for example, why should North Carolina and West Virginia have average MFI ratios of 1.01 and 1.04, while Georgia was among the states whose cities and suburbs had the largest income disparities, its .79 average MFI ratio tying for third lowest in the nation?

Virginia was the 15th-lowest state in average MFI ratios in 1990. In the 12-state Southeast region, it was the third-lowest state. It was bordered by one state, Maryland, with worse-off cities (.80), and by two states whose cities had higher average MFI ratios, North Carolina and West Virginia. The large differences among these neighboring states add plausibility to the idea that state policies may affect city-suburban income disparities. These puzzles will be explored below.

State Policies and Metropolitan Disparities

One basis for evaluating the effects of state policies should be their contribution to stimulating or preventing large disparities between cities and suburbs within metropolitan areas. A second basis for evaluating state policies should be their contribution to coping with disparities after they exist. A separation or mismatch between public needs and private resources available for taxation is a likely consequence of severe city-suburban disparities (Bahl, Martinez-Vazquez, and Sjoquist 1992; Campbell and Sacks 1967).

Disparities between cities and suburbs are more serious if they are worsening. Pressure is then increased on state governments to increase state aid and also to use state tax revenues to redistribute resources from richer to poorer jurisdictions. Politics in such states may be extremely contentious. The goals of educating a skilled workforce and nurturing a responsible citizenry also are endangered. Low average test scores by U.S. public school students, for example, are primarily attributable to low scores in cities and rural districts (Raspberry 1993). Legal action to force states to redistribute state education aid has become common when disparities are large (Underwood and Verstegen 1990).

Several fundamental conditions, as presented in preceding chapters, will be used for considering possible state policy effects. Nearly all housing in the United States is allocated to occupants based on their ability and willingness to pay market prices, modified by markets' accessibility relative to discrimination. Middle- and upper-income purchasers and renters can consider many housing options. They also can afford housing in many neighborhoods and jurisdictions. With commuting times typically greater than 20 minutes and sometimes more than an hour, and an average of 90 local governments per metropolitan area, residents can usually get to work sites from residences in many neighborhoods and jurisdictions within driving times many commuters consider acceptable.

This financial and technical capacity puts middle- and upper-income people in a powerful position. Most of them can purchase dwellings, and indirectly can purchase neighborhoods and jurisdictions, from an array of alternatives. Disparities among jurisdictions within metropolitan areas, therefore, will be determined mainly by public policies that influence 1) the number, size, and residential exclusivity of local governments, 2) the quality of life within local jurisdictions, including public service quality, 3) the location, timing, and pattern of city, suburban, and exurban development, and 4) residents' location preferences among jurisdictional options.

Which types of state policies influence the attractiveness of city versus suburban location alternatives? Some of the more important include the following:

- rules governing expansion of city boundaries
- distribution of financial responsibility for public services between state and local governments, and among city, town, village, and special district governments
- authorization of, and requirements for, constructing public housing and other subsidized housing, usually in cities and sometimes in suburbs
- regulations affecting construction costs and locations of private market housing
- allocations for mass transit and highways, and decisions about where to locate them
- coordination of economic development policies with transportation and land use policies, determining whether compact and contiguous development will be encouraged or resisted
- financing, locating, regulating, and providing access for public water and sewer services

States have often adopted policies concerning these subjects that have encouraged suburban and exurban sprawl. States with substantial growth policies may be considered partial exceptions to this norm (Brower, Godschalk, and Porter 1989; DeGrove 1984; Porter 1997). In the United States, residential mobility trends make cities vulnerable because of the standard operation of private housing markets (Baer 1991), the trickle-down processes of neighborhood change (Downs 1981), and the feasibility of commuting long distances to work from suburbs and exurbs (Burchell and Schmeidler 1993; Cervero 1986). Sprawl, disinvestment, and disparities have been the typical result.

Boundary Adjustment Policies

Boundary adjustment policies are pertinent to income disparity trends. Every state regulates city boundary expansion, but states have adopted widely varying annexation policies. If cities expand their boundaries as they wish, or if states expand city boundaries as population spillovers occur, then cities in such states could contain large proportions of the metropolitan population, including residents occupying new single-family dwellings on their outskirts. These "elastic cities," as David Rusk (1993) calls them, could retain, and remain attractive to, substantial portions of middle- and upper-income residents by having development opportunities within their expanding borders.

Annexation seemed to influence whether cities were doing well in 1990. In the states characterized by Successful Cities (average MFI ratios of 1.0 or greater), substantial annexations occurred in seven of 10 states between 1980 and 1990. Moreover, substantial annexations by 25 of the total of 43 cities occurred. "Substantial annexations" were defined as annexations of more than 3,000 persons or more than eight square miles. In two states with Successful Cities, previous annexations or consolidations before 1980 produced cities containing about 70 percent (North Dakota) or 100 percent (Anchorage, Alaska) of the metropolitan population.

Of the 13 states dominated by Deteriorated Cities (average MFI ratios below .85), no annexations had occurred in 11 states between 1980 and 1990. Utah, the only western state in this group, experienced no annexations. One annexation had occurred in each of two states, and these two cities (Albany, Georgia, and Battle Creek, Michigan) were doing much better in their MFI ratios than the norm for cities in those states. Only two of 123 cities in these 13 states carried out substantial annexations during the 1980s.

Elasticity and Market-Basket Interpretations

In the following analysis, these elasticity and market-basket approaches will be operationalized as defined below for a few states. Indicators for the elasticity and market-basket approaches will be computed for cities and states; possible connections between these indicators and average median family income ratios by state will then be explored by focusing on Virginia, Georgia, North Carolina, and West Virginia.

Elasticity will be measured partially by cities' share of metropolitan population, as well as by annexation. If city share of metropolitan population helps explain disparities, it will be because that indicator captures the effects of post-1970 low-density single-family housing development within or outside the city limits. Recent low-density single-family housing tends to be purchased by middle- and upper-income people. Therefore, the location of new housing may strongly influence city-suburban income disparities.

The term "market basket" refers to varying combinations of services and taxes in local government jurisdictions that residents may consider in deciding whether they want to remain where they live or move to a jurisdiction with a different set of services and taxes.

Market-basket characteristics will be measured in three ways:

- the state share of total state-local revenues, an indicator that provides information about how much local residents may be able to save on taxes by moving to low tax jurisdictions

- the state share of state-local public education costs, an indicator that is pertinent to residents' interest in avoiding high local taxes for schools
- the ratio of public education expenditures per pupil in the fifth-highest percentile and the 95th-lowest percentile, an indicator that suggests the range of disparities among school districts for state and local combined expenditures per pupil for public education

Interpreting Disparities in Southeastern States

Within the Southeast, disparities between cities and suburbs vary greatly, creating interpretive puzzles. Confronted with the extremes of cities doing badly and well, one may wonder: Why should North Carolina's and West Virginia's average MFI ratios be so high, 1.01 and 1.04, while Georgia's average MFI ratio is so low (.79)?

Georgia cities' low share of metropolitan population invites the belief that it is the dominant influence on city-suburban income patterns. Athens, Atlanta, and Augusta—the cities with a low city population share—had the lowest MFI ratios (Table 6.5). Savannah and Albany, with their higher population shares, did better; and the city with the highest metropolitan population share, Columbus (.74 of metropolitan population), had a MFI ratio of 1.15. Albany annexed 14.5 square miles and about 9,800 people between 1980 and 1990. Columbus, due to earlier annexations, was the 29th-largest city in area in the nation in 1990; it contained 216.3 square miles, while Atlanta contained only 131.8 square miles. Macon, with an MFI ratio of only .78, still had improved between 1960 and 1970 by annexing substantial suburban territory.

On the other hand, the cities' share of metropolitan population in North Carolina was not consistently related to cities' income status. Cities' share of metropolitan population ranged from .20 to .52, with no apparent relationship to city-suburban MFI ratios. In North Carolina, these low city shares of metro-

Table 6.5. Median Family Income Ratios and City Shares of Metropolitan Population in Georgia, 1990

	MFI Ratio	City Share of Metropolitan Population
Albany	.894	.694
Athens	.749	.293
Atlanta	.628	.155
Augusta	.629	.113
Columbus	1.043	.735
Macon	.788	.535
Savannah	.849	.567
STATE MEAN	.797	.442

politan population occurred partially because several metropolitan areas have two or three central cities. With multiple central cities, the metropolitan population share of each city is limited—in contrast to Georgia, which has metropolitan areas with a single central city.

In North Carolina, cities have had significant annexation powers. Those powers have enabled them to be selective as well as frequent in the territory they have annexed, so that they have been able to annex more affluent areas. This selective use of annexation explains part of the relative success of North Carolina cities. In addition, North Carolina's policies concerning state-local revenues, state share of education costs, and local education disparities provide few incentives for better-off residents to avoid living in the same local tax and service jurisdictions as less well-off residents.

Virginia

City share of metropolitan population is a somewhat more useful indicator in interpreting city-suburb income disparities in Virginia, but other indicators are even more helpful. In Virginia, larger city shares of metropolitan population tended to be associated with smaller city-suburban income disparities in 1990, as in Lynchburg (MFI ratio .97 and population share of .47) and Danville (MFI ratio .97 and population share of .49, due partially to Danville's having annexed 27 square miles and about 10,000 people between 1980 and 1990). Charlottesville appeared to be struggling, given its 1990 MFI ratio of .88. That ratio reflected a 21 percent income decline since 1970 relative to Albemarle County, during a period when the city's share of metropolitan population fell from 51 percent to 31 percent. Richmond and Petersburg are examples of Deteriorated Cities relative to the balance of their MAs, Richmond having a MFI ratio of .72 in 1990, while Petersburg's ratio was .68. Richmond had stabilized its MFI ratio between 1960 (.85) and 1970 (.86), a decade when it added 23 square miles to its previous 37 square miles. And Petersburg held its own in its MFI ratio between 1970 (.78) and 1980 (.76) by annexing land that nearly tripled its territory. By 1990, Richmond's share of metropolitan population was 23 percent, and Petersburg's share was only 4 percent (Table 6.6).

The unusual characteristics of the Norfolk–Newport News–Virginia Beach MA are a consequence of state policies and constitute a methodological problem. In the 1950s and 1960s, consolidations of small cities and their counties resulted in the conversion of three counties into cities, an option that prevented adjacent cities from annexing territory and population from the former county. These three "cities"— Chesapeake, Suffolk, and Virginia Beach—would be counties in other states. They have captured much of the suburban growth of the older Norfolk-Portsmouth side of the region. If Chesapeake, Suffolk, and Virginia Beach are eliminated, leaving Virginia with 12 cities in MAs, the state then had an average MFI ratio of .88 in 1990. The Tidewater region of Virginia

Table 6.6. Annexation, City Population Characteristics, and City-MA Median Family Income Ratios in Virginia

Cities	Population		City Share of MA Population in 1990	Annexed 1980–1990			MFI Ratio	
	1980	1990		Square Miles	Population (Estimated)	% 1990 City Population	1980	1990
Alexandria	103,217	111,183	0.028	0	0	0	0.917	0.939
Bristol	19,042	18,426	0.042	0	0	0	1.031	1.087
Charlottesville	39,916	40,341	0.308	0	0	0	0.987	0.878
Chesapeake	114,486	152,175	0.109	0	0	0	1.110	1.380
Danville	45,642	53,056	0.488	27	10,500	19.7	1.036	0.968
Hampton	122,617	133,793	0.096	0	0	0	1.031	0.986
Lynchburg	66,700	66,049	0.465	0	0	0	0.993	0.967
Newport News	144,903	170,045	0.122	0	0	0	0.948	0.896
Norfolk	266,979	261,229	0.187	0	0	0	0.796	0.771
Petersburg	41,055	38,386	0.044	0	0	0	0.760	0.678
Portsmouth	104,577	103,907	0.074	0	0	0	0.902	0.820
Richmond	219,214	203,056	0.234	0	0	0	0.778	0.722
Roanoke	100,220	96,397	0.429	0	0	0	0.866	0.807
Suffolk	47,621	52,141	0.037	0	0	0	0.943	0.902
Virginia Beach	262,199	393,069	0.282	0	0	0	1.181	1.124
Mean	113,226	126,217	0.196	0	0	0	0.952	0.928
Median	103,217	103,907	0.122	0	0	0	0.948	0.902
Mean*							0.910	0.857
Median*							0.948	0.878

*Excluding Bristol, Chesapeake, Suffolk, and Virginia Beach

Source: International City Management Association, *The Municipal Yearbook,* 1993

had older cities—Norfolk (MFI ratio .77), Portsmouth (.82), and Newport News (.90), with MFI ratios more typical of constricted central cities. Each of these cities had low shares of their MA's population (Norfolk 18.7 percent, Portsmouth 7.4 percent, and Newport News 12.2 percent) (Table 6.6).

The prosperity of Chesapeake and Virginia Beach illustrates the inappropriateness of using city share of metropolitan population as an indicator in Virginia. Chesapeake's share of metropolitan population in 1990 was 10.9 percent and Virginia Beach's was 28.2 percent, yet their MFI ratios were 1.38 and 1.12. They were doing well in attracting middle- and upper-income residents because they were capturing single-family, suburban-style development in low-density patterns on the outer fringe of Norfolk and Portsmouth.

When indicators of home ownership, age of housing, and population density are added to city share of metropolitan population, a much clearer and consistent picture emerges, helping to interpret differences within states in city-MA median family income ratios (Table 6.7). In Virginia, Chesapeake and Virginia Beach contained predominantly new housing, with high percentages of owner occupancy, in a low-density pattern. Danville and Lynchburg, which also were doing fairly well on the MFI ratio, had older housing, but they had fairly high percentages of owner occupancy, low density, a substantial proportion of metropolitan population, and slow metropolitan growth. Norfolk and Richmond, at the bottom of the MFI ratio range, scored low on each of these indicators except for density, where they were fairly high. Charlottesville and Roanoke were in a middle range of MFI ratios, consistent with the overall pattern.

Turning to the market-basket indicators of differences between cities and suburbs, Virginia's policies are consistent with the presence of substantial differences in interlocal service quality and tax burdens. Data for the early 1980s were analyzed, because conditions then would be more likely than later conditions to influence residential location decisions before 1990. In 1981, Virginia raised the second-lowest share, 59.9 percent, of total state-local revenue among 13 southeastern states. Stated another way, if all state and local government revenues were combined, the state share in Virginia constituted 59.9 percent of the total. The southeastern mean was 70.7 percent; the national mean was 61.6 percent. In 1982–83, the state of Virginia provided the Southeast's lowest share of total state-local public education cost: 44.5 percent, compared with a southeastern mean of 65.3 percent and a national mean of 55.2 percent. Interlocal education expenditure disparities also were greater in Virginia than the southeastern and national norms (Table 6.8).

The federal government's share of local revenues fell from 11 percent in 1980 to 5 percent in 1990; the state share rose from 30 percent to 32 percent. Central cities in Virginia had much more family poverty, welfare dependency, food stamp recipients, and violent crime than suburban jurisdictions. Analyses by the

Table 6.7. Income, Housing and Population Characteristics in Cities and Metropolitan Areas in Virginia, 1990

	MFI Ratio	Median Housing Age		% Housing Built Pre-1940		% Housing Owner-Occupied		City Share of MA Population	City Population Density per	
		City	MA	City	MA	City	MA		Square Mile	Acre
Alexandria	0.939	1963	1972	10.7	11.4	40.5	60.5	0.028	7,267	11.4
Bristol	1.087	1959	1966	15.9	13.0	63.1	73.7	0.042	1,589	2.5
Charlottesville	0.878	1959	1970	22.2	15.1	42.4	59.4	0.308	3,932	6.1
Chesapeake	1.382	1975	1971	2.3	7.3	73.0	58.9	0.109	446	0.7
Danville	0.968	1957	1964	22.2	17.4	59.4	69.3	0.488	1,232	1.9
Hampton	0.986	1966	1971	8.9	7.3	59.3	58.9	0.096	2,582	4.0
Lynchburg	0.967	1960	1966	21.5	15.4	58.2	68.5	0.465	1,337	2.1
Newport News	0.896	1969	1971	6.0	7.3	50.0	58.9	0.122	2,488	3.9
Norfolk	0.771	1958	1971	14.9	7.3	44.0	58.9	0.187	4,859	7.6
Petersburg	0.678	1962	1969	19.1	12.4	50.9	65.0	0.044	1,678	2.6
Portsmouth	0.820	1958	1971	13.2	7.3	55.9	58.9	0.074	3,135	4.9
Richmond	0.722	1953	1969	30.0	12.4	46.3	65.0	0.235	3,377	5.3
Roanoke	0.807	1956	1964	22.1	15.3	56.6	67.7	0.429	2,247	3.5
Suffolk	0.902	1967	1971	14.4	7.3	67.8	58.9	0.037	130	0.2
Virginia Beach	1.124	1978	1971	1.1	7.3	62.5	58.9	0.282	1,583	2.5
STATE MEAN	0.928	1963	1969	15.0	10.9	55.3	62.8	0.196	2,525	3.9

Source: U.S. Bureau of the Census, Census of Population and Housing, 1993

Table 6.8. City-MA Median Family Income Ratios and State-Local Fiscal Indicators by State

Region and States (Number of MFI Ratios)	Average MFI Ratio, 1990	State Share of Total State-Local Revenue, 1981 (U.S. Rank)	State Share of Total State-Local Public Education Cost, 1982–1983	Within-State Disparities in Core Education Expenditures[1]
New England (42)	.863	54.9	36.5	1.84
Connecticut (14)	.832	55.7 (39)	38.3	1.73
Maine (4)	.960	63.5 (24)	55.2	1.64
Massachusetts (14)	.837	56.1 (38)	41.4	1.96
New Hampshire (5)	.916	36.7 (50)	7.2	1.96
Rhode Island (4)	.815	58.8 (31)	38.8	1.56
Vermont (1)	.818	58.3 (35)	37.8	2.20
Mideast (45)	.767	61.6	50.6	1.77
Delaware (1)	.716	82.3 (2)	76.1	1.64
Maryland (3)	.804	59.5 (30)	42.7	1.61
New Jersey (8)	.673	55.6 (40)	41.5	1.75
New York (15)	.813	48.6 (49)	43.7	1.90
Pennsylvania (18)	.829	62.0 (25)	48.8	1.93
Southeast (117)	.948	70.7	65.3	1.63
Alabama (10)	.998	74.7 (10)	75.4	1.49
Arkansas (6)	1.052	76.6 (8)	62.7	1.88
Florida (31)	.966	64.1 (22)	66.7	1.40
Georgia (7)	.788	64.7 (21)	61.9	2.01
Kentucky (3)	.939	78.9 (5)	79.0	1.51
Louisiana (8)	.911	68.2 (18)	61.7	1.53
Mississippi (4)	.941	77.9 (6)	69.2	1.52
North Carolina (13)	1.013	72.4 (13)	73.3	1.38
South Carolina (7)	.883	75.3 (9)	66.1	1.76
Tennessee (9)	.953	57.7 (37)	54.3	1.89
Virginia (15)	.902	59.9 (28)	44.5	1.82
West Virginia (4)	1.035	77.8 (7)	68.6	1.32
Great Lakes (78)	.881	59.5	45.2	1.79
Illinois (15)	.925	55.0 (44)	41.6	1.91
Indiana (15)	.963	61.9 (26)	62.6	1.64
Michigan (17)	.807	57.8 (36)	39.3	1.74
Ohio (17)	.788	55.6 (40)	42.8	1.95
Wisconsin (14)	.924	67.2 (19)	39.5	1.71
Plains (29)	.980	59.8	43.2	1.56
Iowa (8)	.981	60.6 (27)	45.4	1.29
Kansas (3)	.963	58.7 (32)	46.7	1.64
Minnesota (5)	.928	70.8 (14)	51.3	1.58
Missouri (6)	.943	55.2 (42)	43.1	1.81
Nebraska (2)	.952	52.6 (46)	30.1	1.45
North Dakota (3)	1.067	70.1 (16)	55.6	1.52
South Dakota (2)	1.023	50.7 (47)	30.3	1.61

(continues)

Table 6.8. Continued

Region and States (Number of MFI Ratios)	Average MFI Ratio, 1990	State Share of Total State-Local Revenue, 1981 (U.S. Rank)	State Share of Total State-Local Public Education Cost, 1982–1983	Within-State Disparities in Core Education Expenditures[1]
Southwest (51)	1.012	70.0	65.4	1.54
Arizona (7)	1.028	64.9 (20)	51.6	1.78
New Mexico (3)	1.034	82.3 (2)	86.7	1.38
Oklahoma (4)	.996	73.1 (11)	67.1	1.70
Texas (37)	.990	59.8 (29)	56.3	1.30
Mountain (19)	.972	59.0	50.6	1.67
Colorado (10)	.983	48.8 (47)	39.0	1.67
Idaho (1)	.996	70.3 (15)	67.3	1.56
Montana (2)	1.021	53.7 (45)	51.7	2.18
Utah (4)	.828	63.8 (23)	59.3	1.38
Wyoming (2)	1.030	58.6 (33)	36.1	1.55
Far West (79)	.968	71.1	76.5	1.59
Alaska (1)	1.000	90.2 (1)	83.1	2.80
California (61)	.935	68.7 (17)	90.6	1.48
Hawaii (1)	.998	81.0 (4)	99.6	1.00
Nevada (2)	.976	58.4 (34)	65.6	1.11
Oregon (5)	.995	55.2 (42)	40.4	1.46
Washington (9)	.905	72.9 (12)	79.5	1.69
U.S. MEAN (460)	.927	61.6	55.2	1.67

Sources: U.S. Bureau of the Census, *Census of Population,* 1993; U.S. Advisory Commission on Intergovernmental Relations, *Significant Features of Fiscal Federalism,* Vol. 2, 1992, 188–189; U.S. Advisory Commission on Intergovernmental Relations, *The States and Distressed Communities,* 1985, 158–161
[1] Ratio of expenditures at 95th and 5th percentiles, 1982–1983

Virginia Commission on Local Government (1992) revealed that central cities had somewhat less revenue capacity than their peripheral jurisdictions in 1990. Each central city made a greater revenue-raising effort than urban fringe jurisdictions, sometimes nearly doubling their effort, in using its capacity to meet public service costs. This greater effort was partially attributable to cities' task of serving the public service needs of low-income residents

Based on research findings about why and where people move, these market-basket conditions probably were not prime motivators of location decisions. But these fiscal conditions at least supported the perpetuation of socioeconomic disparities. They did little, if anything, to counteract the effects of interlocal disparities. Thus, they supported the reasoning of middle- and upper-income people who may have chosen suburban and exurban locations for other reasons.

North Carolina

Between 1980 and 1990, the 13 cities in North Carolina for which city-MA median family income ratios were calculated annexed an average of 14.5 square miles containing more than 14,700 persons and constituting 13 percent of their 1990 population (Table 6.9). Ten of the 13 cities annexed more than 10 percent of their 1990 population. The largest city, Charlotte, annexed the most people, 43,900. Other sizable cities also annexed—Durham 25,900, Raleigh 25,400, and Greensboro 18,600. Seven of the 13 North Carolina cities had MFI ratios greater than 1.0 in 1990. Seven of these 13 cities also improved their MFI ratios versus their suburbs between 1980 and 1990. Compared with Virginia cities, North Carolina's cities had a lower percentage of old housing. They also were less dense, creating more opportunities for construction of new single-family housing within city limits (Table 6.10).

The overall result was that most of North Carolina's cities were growing. Their average population increase was 24 percent between 1980 and 1990. None of the 13 largest North Carolina cities lost population (Table 6.9). In contrast, among Virginia's metropolitan areas, seven older core cities (Bristol, Lynchburg, Norfolk, Petersburg, Portsmouth, Richmond, and Roanoke) lost population. Only two older core cities (Charlottesville and Danville) gained population, and Danville's increase was due to an annexation of about 10,500 residents. Whereas seven of North Carolina's 13 cities improved in MFI ratios between 1980 and 1990, only three of Virginia's 15 cities improved (Table 6.6). And these three involved special circumstances. Two of them really were suburbs—Alexandria, a suburb of Washington, D.C., and Chesapeake, a suburb of Norfolk. The third, Bristol, may have been influenced by terrain and a multi-state context in ways similar to cities in West Virginia, as will be discussed below. In contrast, North Carolina's improving cities were older core cities.

In 1980, the median score for median family income ratios among North Carolina's 13 cities was 4 percent higher than the median among Virginia's 15 cities. By 1990, North Carolina's MFI ratio median was 12 percent higher than Virginia's. The gap was even larger if Bristol and Virginia's low-density—suburban, really—cities of Chesapeake, Suffolk, and Virginia Beach were excluded. Then North Carolina's MFI ratio median was 15 percent higher in 1990 than for Virginia's remaining 11 cities. While Virginia's median had declined by 7.4 percent between 1980 and 1990, North Carolina's had improved 2.5 percent. The norm, therefore, was for Virginia's cities to decline moderately while North Carolina's cities improved slightly.

More importantly, Virginia's five worst-off cities, all in the Deteriorated Cities category in 1990 (MFI ratios below .85), declined an average of 7.4 percent between 1980 and 1990 (Norfolk 3.1 percent, Petersburg 10.8 percent, Portsmouth 9.1 percent, Richmond 7.2 percent, and Roanoke 6.8 percent). In

Table 6.9. Annexation, City Population Characteristics, and City-MA Median Family Income Ratios in North Carolina

Cities	Population		City Share Population of MA 1990	Annexed 1980–1990			MFI Ratio	
	1980	1990		Square Miles	Population (Estimated)	% 1990 City Population	1980	1990
Asheville	53,583	61,654	0.381	5.9	10,000	16.2	0.986	0.927
Burlington	37,266	39,368	0.391	3.9	1,500	3.8	1.005	1.011
Charlotte	314,447	396,003	0.341	34.6	43,900	11.1	1.017	1.062
Durham	100,831	136,594	0.186	27.9	25,900	19.0	0.784	0.843
Fayetteville	59,507	75,695	0.276	9.2	15,400	20.3	1.039	1.047
Gastonia	47,333	54,732	0.047	9.3	6,300	11.5	0.866	0.860
Greensboro	155,642	183,521	0.195	19.5	18,600	10.1	1.043	1.044
Hickory	20,757	28,337	0.128	8.5	5,100	18.0	0.968	1.041
High Point	63,380	69,394	0.074	12.0	3,400	4.9	0.899	0.873
Jacksonville	17,056	30,013	0.200	4.9	5,600	18.7	1.241	1.092
Raleigh	150,255	207,951	0.287	34.2	25,400	12.0	1.040	1.015
Wilmington	44,000	55,530	0.462	8.9	8,100	14.6	0.787	0.808
Winston-Salem	131,885	143,485	0.152	9.6	12,500	8.7	0.947	0.968
MEAN	37,378	52,281	0.240	14.5	14,746	13.0	0.971	0.969
MEDIAN	59,507	69,394	0.200	9.3	10,000	12.0	0.986	1.011

Source: International City Management Association, *The Municipal Yearbook*, 1993

Table 6.10. Income, Housing, and Population Characteristics in Cities and Metropolitan Areas in North Carolina, 1990

	MFI Ratio	Median Housing Age		% Housing Built Pre-1940		% Housing Owner-Occupied		City Share of MA Population	City Population Density per	
		City	MA	City	MA	City	MA	Population	Square Mile	Acre
Asheville	0.927	1958	1967	26.1	17.0	56.6	70.3	0.381	1,764	2.8
Burlington	1.011	1960	1965	14.7	13.4	61.7	72.0	0.364	1,937	3.0
Charlotte	1.062	1970	1971	5.9	8.7	55.0	66.9	0.341	2,272	3.6
Durham	0.843	1970	1975	9.6	6.9	44.2	58.9	0.186	1,972	3.1
Fayetteville	1.047	1969	1973	5.3	3.7	54.2	57.7	0.276	1,865	2.9
Gastonia	0.860	1964	1971	13.4	8.7	58.2	66.9	0.047	1,802	2.8
Greensboro	1.044	1967	1969	8.8	9.8	53.7	67.3	0.195	2,300	3.6
Hickory	1.041	1967	1971	12.3	9.1	51.7	74.7	0.128	1,395	2.2
High Point	0.968	1965	1969	11.4	9.8	54.4	67.3	0.074	1,614	2.5
Jacksonville	1.092	1971	1974	1.0	2.6	48.7	53.7	0.200	2,310	3.6
Raleigh	1.015	1974	1975	7.0	6.9	46.9	58.9	0.283	2,359	3.7
Wilmington	0.808	1962	1972	16.3	9.4	47.1	62.7	0.462	1,870	2.9
Winston-Salem	0.873	1964	1969	12.8	9.8	51.9	67.3	0.152	2,017	3.2
State Mean	0.969	1966	1971	11.1	8.9	52.6	65.0	0.237	1,960	3.1

Source: U.S. Bureau of the Census, Census of Population and Housing, 1993

contrast, only two cities in North Carolina had MFI ratios in the Deteriorated category (below .85) in 1990, and they improved an average of 5.1 percent between 1980 and 1990 (Durham 7.5 percent, Wilmington 2.7 percent). Thus, Virginia's worst-off cities continued to decline between 1980 and 1990, while North Carolina's worst-off cities were more successful in attracting affluent residents or annexing them by extending city boundaries.

The key to North Carolina's successful cities probably lies in the state's financial role, the assignment of government functions to local governments, and boundary change legislation. According to Jake Wicker (1999), former director of the North Carolina Institute of Government, the success of North Carolina's cities is related to the fact that the state takes "primary . . . responsibility for financing education and highways, and people services—health, education, and welfare—at the local level are primarily responsibilities of county governments." North Carolina financed nearly 30 percent more than Virginia of the state-local cost of education. Disparities in expenditures between high- and low-spending school districts also were much lower in North Carolina than in Virginia (Table 6.8). In addition, North Carolina's cities were authorized in legislation adopted in 1950 to extend municipal boundaries into unincorporated territory by ordinance of cities' governing body. Because the state limited incorporation of suburban territory, cities retained substantial annexation opportunities on their borders. Cities typically were bordered partially by unincorporated settlements. When it annexed territory, a city was obligated to provide comparable services to its new residents. Annexation was not subject to a voter referendum or rejection by the state legislature. This powerful tool was granted to cities pursuant to the legislature's policy that "sound urban development is essential to the continued economic development of North Carolina" (North Carolina General Statutes 1993, Art. 4, 160A).

West Virginia

The condition of cities in West Virginia seems at odds with an interpretation that city share of metropolitan population and annexation dominate the dimensions of city-suburban MFI ratios. Charleston, Huntington, and Wheeling had MFI ratios ranging from 1.03 to 1.11. But these cities' share of metropolitan population ranged from .22 to .25 (Table 6.11). No major West Virginia city annexed territory or population between 1980 and 1990.

The rugged terrain in West Virginia may have interrupted the typical pattern of suburbanization. Older cities claimed flat and rolling land along water and rail lines. Outlying areas were too hilly and mountainous to permit sizable settlements. Terrain also interfered with providing urban services, such as water, sewer, and fire protection. The portions of West Virginia's MAs that lie outside central cities remained heavily rural in 1990—Charleston 42 percent,

Table 6.11. Annexation, City Population Characteristics, and City-MA Median Family Income Ratios in West Virginia

| Cities | Population | | City Share Population of MA 1990 | Annexed 1980–1990 | | | | MFI Ratio | |
	1980	1990		Square Miles	Population (Estimated)	% 1990 City Population		1980	1990
Charleston	64,968	57,287	0.229	0	0	0		1.037	1.089
Huntington	63,684	54,884	0.175	0	0	0		0.939	0.997
Parkersburg	39,967	33,809	0.227	0	0	0		0.917	0.877
Wheeling	43,070	34,881	0.219	0	0	0		0.957	1.072
MEAN	59,922	45,205	0.213	0	0	0		0.963	1.009
MEDIAN	53,377	44,863	0.223	0	0	0		0.948	1.035

Source: International City Management Association, *The Municipal Yearbook,* 1993

Huntington 68 percent, and Wheeling 54 percent. These areas also had a considerable amount of old housing. Cities had a high percentage of owner-occupied housing compared with the norm in other states (Table 6.12). In addition, some of the population outside the central cities was concentrated in small working-class communities close to factories that emitted large amounts of air and water pollution, making them unattractive to middle- and upper-income people. West Virginia's state policies concerning state-local revenue, state shares of public education costs, and disparities in local education expenditures also provided less incentive, compared to Virginia's and Georgia's policies, for people to choose locations based on public-sector market-basket advantages. In West Virginia, interlocking influences of geography, topography, history, and state fiscal policies seem to have protected cities from decline by avoiding typical suburbanization.

In these four states, circumstances pertinent to each state contributed to understanding the pattern of city-suburb income disparities. In Georgia, the city share of metropolitan population was roughly consistent with variation within the state in city-suburb income disparities, and this fact helped explain why Georgia's cities, on average, were deteriorated. In North Carolina, substantial annexation contributed to cities' relatively high incomes compared with suburbs, despite a low metropolitan population share in most cities. In West Virginia, difficult terrain and rural hinterland obstructed typical paths of suburbanization, sustaining traditional cities. In Virginia, cities were more diverse; some bore city labels but had characteristics more like suburbs. Some cities were still benefiting from previous annexations, but several had deteriorated substantially, having succumbed to the suburban tide years earlier. The net effect was that Virginia, on average, was a state of struggling cities.

Effects of Income Disparities

State policies also may impact central city and metropolitan prosperity. The potential linkage includes state policies affecting disparities and disparities influencing prosperity. But conversely, prosperity may influence disparities. Both of these plausible linkages will be discussed below. Have income disparities between central cities and suburbs contributed to decreased metropolitan economic prosperity relative to other metropolitan areas? This is a very difficult question. Embedded within it, by implication, is this more general question: What have been the major influences on metropolitan economic prosperity, and how important, relative to other conditions, has been the influence of central city-suburban income disparities? The stress here is on regional characteristics, including the role of central cities in their regions. These questions are examined

Table 6.12. Income, Housing, and Population Characteristics in Cities and Metropolitan Areas in West Virginia, 1990

| | MFI Ratio | Median Housing Age | | % Housing Built Pre-1940 | | % Housing Owner-Occupied | | City Share of MA Population | City Population Density per | |
		City	MA	City	MA	City	MA		Square Mile	Acre
Charleston	1.089	1954	1960	30.5	17.6	55.5	71.0	0.229	1,944	3.0
Huntington	0.997	1945	1959	41.5	20.8	57.1	72.0	0.175	3,681	5.8
Parkersburg	0.877	1951	1961	34.9	24.6	63.0	74.1	0.227	3,027	4.7
Wheeling	1.072	1939	1949	55.0	41.3	61.2	72.4	0.219	2,529	4.0
STATE MEAN	1.009	1947	1957	40.5	26.1	59.2	72.4	0.212	2,795	4.4

Source: U.S. Bureau of the Census, Census of Population and Housing, 1993

by analyzing data for 1970, 1980, and 1990 for 59 metropolitan areas in the South.

During the 1970s and 1980s, suburbs matured as employment centers and exurbs intruded into rural areas. The nation's, and the South's, economy was transitioning from an industrial economy to a service, information, finance, and high technology (postindustrial) economy (Benjamin 1984). The spatial spread of metropolitan areas was fueled by affluence, highway extensions, rising automobile usage, and trucked freight. Improved communication facilitated the separation of mass production and back-office information processing from central management headquarters. The internationalization of finance capital, corporate organization, air transportation, electronic communication, and computerization transformed the type and location of U.S. employment (Herschberg 1995; Knight and Gappert 1984). As these transitions unfolded, the economic role of central cities became unstable and uncertain.

City Strengths and Metropolitan Prosperity

Several analysts have claimed that central cities influence metropolitan prosperity. Richard Voith (1992, 25–28) examined central city and suburban population and income growth in 28 metropolitan areas in the northeastern and north central regions of the United States. He found that as city population and income increased, suburban population and income tended to increase: city and suburban growth were complements, growing in tandem rather than one (suburban growth) substituting for the other (city growth). Similar conclusions were reached by William R. Barnes and Larry C. Ledebur (1994, 11) in a study of income change from 1980 to 1990 in the 50 largest metropolitan areas, and by H.V. Savitch et al. (1993, 342–343) in a study of 59 metropolitan areas from 1979 to 1987.

In another study, Ledebur and Barnes (1992, 15) found that in a sample of 85 metropolitan areas, high per capita income disparities between central cities and their suburbs were associated with low metropolitan population growth in the 1980s. In addition, Ledebur and Barnes (1992, 14) found that "metropolitan areas with lower disparities tend to have higher rates of employment change." They argued (Ledebur and Barnes 1995, 7) that the U.S. national economy is a federation of "metropolitan-centered, integrated economies, of which central cities and suburbs are interdependent parts."

This argument was adopted in *A Region At Risk,* a regional plan for the New York region (Yaro and Hiss 1996, 8), as follows: ". . . [R]egions that will thrive [in the 21st century] are regions that have strong centers as well as healthy suburbs. These are the areas in which global businesses feel secure. And that is because a region, economically, is a single job and housing market, which means that suburban wages rise and fall in tandem with the ups and downs of central cities. One reality envelops all: when the inner cities stumble, the suburbs stagger. And when inner cities prosper, suburbs can boom."

David Rusk (1993, 48), using a sample of seven "elastic" and seven "inelastic" paired cities, discovered that the elastic cities that had expanded their boundaries had lower per capita income disparities in 1989 and higher employment growth from 1973 to 1988. Elastic cities had annexed enough territory to have room to grow at the relatively low densities typical of suburbs. In addition, Rusk (1993, 42) found that poverty was greater in central cities that were not growing.

Diverse indicators of economic conditions were used in these studies. Barnes and Ledebur, Savitch, and Voith tracked income change, Rusk tracked employment growth and poverty, and in another study, Barnes and Ledebur examined population and employment growth. They did not use data about earnings per employee, nor did they use income data as reported on tax returns.

Indicators used by Barnes and Ledebur and by Rusk reveal information that is more relevant to quantity planning than quality planning. Growth in population and employment are treated as improvements, even though it is possible that the increased population became poorer and the jobs on average paid less. Income implies more about quality than quantity, but about 36 percent of income comes from sources other than employment. For these reasons, our analysis below emphasized changes in earnings per private employee as a more direct indicator of the quality of economic changes.

In a critique of Rusk's position, Blair, Staley, and Zhang (1996) used a sample of 117 metropolitan areas and data for 1980 and 1990. They found 1) support for Rusk's hypothesis that elastic cities grew in population, employment, and per capita income and declined in poverty concentrations, and 2) no relationship between city elasticity and metropolitan income and poverty changes, although there were mild positive associations between metropolitan population and employment growth.

Blair, Staley, and Zhang argued that increased city prosperity in elastic cities may result from annexation, a claim that Rusk probably would not dispute. They also noted that Rusk's seven elastic cities included five state capitals, compared with two inelastic cities that were state capitals. Conversely, the inelastic cities had higher concentrations of employment in manufacturing. They suggested that better metropolitan economic performance by Rusk's seven elastic cities may have occurred because they included more state capitals and had less employment in the slow-growing manufacturing sector compared with the seven inelastic cities.

The claims of Rusk, Barnes and Ledebur, Savitch, and Voith, and the critique by Blair, Staley, and Zhang, were taken into account in choosing the methodology, including the indicators, time periods, and metropolitan areas, for this study.

Assets and Regions' Prosperity

Many conditions may contribute to regional prosperity. In an analysis of 59 metropolitan areas in the South for 1970, 1980, and 1990, several conditions were often associated with faster than average growth in earnings per private employee. Regions with state capital cities (and the national capital), several radiating interstate highways, a more than average rate of airline flights per resident, and high proportions of college graduates tended to have rapid growth in earnings per private employee. In strategic planning terms, these were strengths. Major seaports and areas with concentrations of military employment tended to be slow growing. Hence, these were weaknesses.

Capital cities, which generally enjoy a sizable population of college graduates, major airports, and effective highway connections, are well attuned to some aspects of the postindustrial, information age economy. In contrast, seaports may be at the end of interstate highways rather than at the intersections of crossing highways, and may have old airports, industrial and wholesaling economies, and public facilities, private buildings, and entrepreneurial habits that are less well suited to contemporary economic opportunities.

Disparities and Other Influences on Economic Prosperity

Populous metropolitan areas grew because of economic strengths during their historical development. Large size should be associated, therefore, with high levels of economic activity and potentially also with prosperity. For this reason, we first took population size and amount of employment into account, discovering that they were correlated significantly with each indicator of economic prosperity (Table 6.13). For a discussion of methodology, see Note 6.3.

Size helps explain relationships between income disparities and prosperity. Cities with low incomes relative to suburbs were in metropolitan areas with high personal income, high earnings, and low family poverty. This finding is contrary to the expectation that low city-suburb income disparities would be associated positively with metropolitan prosperity, as suggested by Ledebur and Barnes (1992) of the National League of Cities and by Yaro and Hiss (1996) in the New York regional plan. Instead, we found the opposite relationship. High-income metropolitan areas tended to have large city-suburb income disparities in 1970. Why?

Higher incomes in populous metropolitan areas made it easier for households to purchase relatively large single-family suburban homes. These residents usually voted to incorporate suburban governments that resisted annexation. Central city boundaries became rigid. Higher proportions of metropolitan middle- and upper-income housing were constructed in suburbs. In other words, the high city-suburb income disparities in 1970 were a result of past metropolitan expansion combined with inelastic city boundaries, which together prevented most low-density, post-1945 development from occurring in central cities (Jackson 1985; Teaford 1979).

Table 6.13. Correlations of City and Metropolitan Conditions with Indicators of Metropolitan Economic Well-Being, 1970

	Personal Income per Capita	Non-Farm Earnings per Capita	Private Earnings per Capita	Private Earnings per Private Employee	Rate of Family Poverty in Metropolitan Area
Population and Employment Size					
Metropolitan Population	0.66	0.64	0.37	0.47	−0.50
City Population	0.48	0.54	0.34	0.41	−0.34
Metropolitan Total Employment	0.66	0.67	0.39	0.43	−0.53
Metropolitan Private Employment	0.66	0.67	0.50	0.48	−0.56
City-Metropolitan Disparity					
City Share of MA Population	−0.40				0.38
City-MA Median Family Income Ratio	−0.47	−0.51	−0.40	−0.40	0.42
City-MA per Capita Income Ratio	−0.45	−0.47	−0.39	−0.37	0.40
Economic Structure					
% Employment in Manufacturing			0.42		
% Employment in Finance, Insurance, and Real Estate	0.67	0.37	0.50		−0.51
% Employment in Service Sector					
% Employment in Military			−0.55	−0.35	
% Employment in State and Local Government					
Labor Force					
Male Participation Rate		0.45			
Female Participation Rate		0.44			−0.40
Demographic					
% African-American Population			−0.31	−0.31	0.50
% over 65 Years of Age	0.34		0.30		
% in College					
% College Graduates	0.29	0.36			−0.34
Crime Rate					
1970 MA Crime Rate	0.53	0.42	0.30		−0.42

Note: A coefficient of +/−.279 was needed for significance at the 5% level.

Low metropolitan personal income per capita (correlation –0.40) and high metropolitan family poverty (+0.38) were associated in 1970 with a high share of metropolitan population in central cities. That finding is consistent with the argument above. Poorer metropolitan areas did not suburbanize as much by 1970 as did richer and larger metropolitan areas. Therefore, higher proportions of metropolitan population were in central cities in these slower-to-suburbanize metropolitan areas.

Similar associations occurred in 1980 and 1990 between metropolitan and city population size, city-metropolitan income ratios, and indicators of metropolitan personal income and earnings per capita. High city scores on the city-metropolitan income ratios were associated with lower metropolitan income and earnings (Tables 6.14 and 6.15).

Table 6.14. Correlations of City and Metropolitan Conditions with Indicators of Metropolitan Economic Well-Being, 1980

	Personal Income per Capita	Non-Farm Earnings per Capita	Private Earnings per Capita	Private Earnings per Private Employee	Rate of Family Poverty in Metropolitan Area
Population and Employment Size					
Metropolitan Population	0.66	0.58	0.35		–0.37
City Population	0.45	0.53	0.35		
Metropolitan Total Employment	0.64	0.63	0.36		–0.39
Metropolitan Private Employment	0.65	0.63	0.43		–0.41
City-Metropolitan Disparity					
City Share of MA Population	–0.35				0.50
City-MA Median Family Income Ratio	–0.43	–0.47	–0.37	–0.34	
City-MA per Capita Income Ratio	–0.40	–0.36	–0.28		
Economic Structure					
% Employment in Manufacturing					
% Employment in Finance, Insurance, and Real Estate	0.66				–0.36
% Employment in Service Sector	0.57	0.33	0.33		
% Employment in Military			–0.61	–0.43	0.35
% Employment in State and Local Government			–0.30		

	Personal Income per Capita	Non-Farm Earnings per Capita	Private Earnings per Capita	Private Earnings per Private Employee	Rate of Family Poverty in Metropolitan Area
Labor Force					
Male Participation Rate		0.40			
Female Participation Rate		0.42		–0.29	–0.28
Demographic					
% African-American Population					0.57
% over 65 Years of Age	0.43				–0.34
% in College					
% College Graduates	0.37	.049			–0.34
Crime Rates					
1980 MA Crime Rate	0.46	0.31			
1980 City Crime Rate	0.52				
1980 MA Violent Crime Rate	0.34				
1980 City Violent Crime Rate	0.43				0.43

Note: A coefficient of +/–.279 was needed for significance at the 5% level.

Divergent Trends in the 1970s

Population and employment grew rapidly in Sunbelt states from 1970 to 1990. The elderly increased substantially in some states. Manufacturing increased in some southern metropolitan areas, including industries relocating from the North. Many inmoving manufacturers paid low wages. They often moved to small metropolitan areas where incomes were lower than in larger MAs, thus contributing to raising incomes in those areas. In these MAs, central cities contained substantial proportions of the metropolitan population. They often had large enough boundaries to facilitate additional city growth. In such instances, economic growth was associated with growing cities, rising incomes, and declining poverty rates in relatively low income metropolitan areas. Data trends were consistent with these interpretations.

Where central cities contained large proportions of the metropolitan population, income and earnings per capita tended to increase (positive correlations from .29 to .40). In addition, there was a strong correlation (.65) between high metropolitan family poverty in 1970 and increases in earnings per private employee from 1970 to 1980. These outcomes may have occurred because low-income metropolitan areas attracted employment and income during the 1970s.

Three distinct trends probably occurred simultaneously in different parts of

	Personal Income per Capita	Non-Farm Earnings per Capita	Private Earnings per Capita	Private Earnings per Private Employee	Metro Family Poverty Rate	Metro Median Family Income	City Median Family Income	City Family Poverty Rate
Size and Growth								
Total Metropolitan Population	0.60	0.59	0.52	0.54	−0.45	0.66		
Total City Population	0.40	0.50	0.45	0.47		0.46		
Change in City Population, 1970–80	−0.33	−0.28		−0.34		−0.41		−0.27
Change in City Population, 1980–90							0.57	−0.55
Change in City Population, 1970–90			−0.32				0.42	−0.44
Total Metropolitan Employment	0.60	0.64	0.55	0.55	−0.47	0.71		
Total Private Employment	0.62	0.63	0.58	0.56	−0.48	0.70		
City-Metropolitan Disparity								
City Share of MA Population	−0.38				0.47	−0.32		
City-MA Median Family Income Ratio	−0.46	−0.45	−0.43	−0.49		−0.45	0.54	−0.58
City-MA per Capita Income Ratio	−0.44	−0.39	−0.36	−0.33		−0.37	0.46	−0.40

	1	2	3	4	5	6	7	8
Economic Structure								
% Employment in Manufacturing	0.70	0.47	0.53	0.38	-0.45	0.52		
% Employment in Finance, Insurance, and Real Estate								
% Employment in Service Sector	0.45	0.32	0.36	0.29		0.38		
% Employment in Military	-0.29		-0.48	-0.35				
% Employment in State and Local Government			-0.33	-0.25				
Labor Force								
Male Participation Rate	0.43	0.62	0.38		-0.45	0.54	0.39	
Female Participation Rate		0.76	0.52		-0.54	0.72	0.46	
Demographic								
% African-American Population					0.44			0.49
% over 65 Years of Age	0.30							
% in College	0.56	0.73	0.44	0.36	-0.48	0.78	0.53	
% College Graduates						0.30	0.35	
Crime Rate								
Violent Crime								0.34

Note: A coefficient of +/-.279 was needed for significance at the 5% level.

the South during the 1970s. Low- and moderate-wage manufacturing continued relocating from the North, affecting primarily the less prosperous parts of the South. The largest average state gains in earnings per private employee occurred in low-wage states like Louisiana and Arkansas, with Alabama, Georgia, and Mississippi also doing well. Earnings gains in Louisiana, an oil-producing and oil-refining state, also were boosted by higher oil prices. Second, many elderly persons moved south, especially to Florida. The elderly, however, needed personal services, which often were not well paid. Average earnings per private employee actually fell in each of Florida's nine metropolitan areas between 1970 and 1980 (Lucy and Phillips 1995a; Luger and Goldstein 1991, 20). Third, high-technology, information processing, and service employment was increasing in some of the larger, more prosperous metropolitan areas (Premus 1984; Warner 1989). This postindustrial trend was associated with different conditions than the other two trends (movement of the elderly and relocation of low- and moderate-wage industry), which scrambled the mix of influences. The net effects of these divergent influences were that correlations among economic indicators in the 59 metropolitan areas were modest to insignificant.

Postindustrial Succession in the 1980s

The 1980s were the decade when the postindustrial era took root, grew, and flowered in the South. The percentage of employment in FIRE (finance, insurance, and real estate) and services in 1990 was positively associated with each of the metropolitan income and earnings indicators; more FIRE and service employment was related to high metropolitan income and earnings (Table 6.15). Strong positive associations also occurred between high percentages of college graduates and high metropolitan and city per capita income and earnings.

Much routine manufacturing had moved offshore or overseas by the 1980s. The manufacturing that was increasing in the United States in the 1980s was more specialized, higher value added, higher capitalized, and higher skill-input manufacturing than the dominant mass-production manufacturing of earlier eras (Blakely 1994; Reich 1991). Increases in manufacturing employment from 1980 to 1990 were positively associated with increases in income and, in particular, earnings during the 1980s (Table 6.16). The fact that these were the strongest correlations between independent variables and changes in economic prosperity indicators from 1980 to 1990 also suggested the prominent role of high-technology, information-era manufacturing employment in increasing earnings. This possibility was consistent with the obverse finding as well, namely that metropolitan areas that lost manufacturing jobs tended to decline in income.

Where private and total employment increased in metropolitan areas between 1980 and 1990, income per capita, earnings per capita, and earnings

Table 6.16. Correlations of City and Metropolitan Conditions with Changes in Indicators of City and Metropolitan Economic Well-Being, 1980–1990

	% Change in Personal Income per Capita 1980–1990	% Change in Non-Farm Earnings per Capita 1980–1990	% Change in Private Earnings per Capita 1980–1990	% Change in Private Earnings per Private Employee 1980–9190	Difference in Family Poverty Rates in Metropolitan Area 1980–9190
Size & Growth					
1980 Metropolitan Population				0.37	
% Change in Metropolitan Population 1980–90	0.34	0.34	0.30	0.38	
% Change in City Population, 1980–90		0.45	0.40	0.39	−0.33
1980 Total Employment				0.40	
% Change in Employment	0.63	0.81	0.76	0.69	−0.68
1980 Private Employment				0.38	
% Change in Private Employment	0.66	0.84	0.83	0.74	−0.73
City-Metropolitan Disparities					
City Share of MA Population, 1980					
City-MA Median Family Income Ratio					
% Change in CC-MA Median Family Income Ratio	−0.28			−0.37	0.28
City-MA per Capita Income Ratio					
% Change in CC-MA per Capita Income Ratio	−0.30				0.33
Economic Structure					
% Employment in Manufacturing, 1980					
% Change in Manufacturing Employment, 1980–90	0.33	0.60	0.65	0.56	−0.47

(continues)

Table 6.16. Continued

	% Change in Personal Income per Capita 1980–1990	% Change in Non-Farm Earnings per Capita 1980–1990	% Change in Private Earnings per Capita 1980–1990	% Change in Private Earnings per Private Employee 1980–1990	Difference in Family Poverty Rates in Metropolitan Area 1980–1990
Economic Structure (continued)					
% Employment in Finance, Insurance, and Real Estate, 1980					
% Employment in Service Sector, 1980					
% Employment in Military, 1980					
% Employment in State and Local Government, 1980					-0.31
Labor Force					
Change in Male Participation Rate, 1980–90	0.61	0.77	0.74	0.70	-0.73
Female Participation Rate, 1980	0.49	0.54	0.53	0.61	-0.35
Change in Female Participation Rate, 1980–90		0.37	0.41	0.31	-0.62
Demographic					
% African-American Population					
% Change in African-American Population		0.29		0.36	
Change in % over 65 Years of Age					
Change in % in College					
Change in % College Graduates	0.61	0.67	0.70	0.68	-0.64

Note: A coefficient of +/−.279 was needed for significance at the 5% level.

per private employee also tended to increase. That was another indication that wage levels in the economy were rising.

Southern metropolitan areas that had adapted to the needs and characteristics of the postindustrial economy by the 1980s were doing particularly well. The strength of these transformations was so impressive that it is surprising that a condition such as capacity for population growth within central cities exercised some influence on rates of increase in regional prosperity.

Disparities in 1980 and 1990

Low incomes in central cities relative to their suburbs were associated in 1990 with high metropolitan personal income and earnings, as in 1970 and 1980. Our interpretation is that economic expansion in prosperous metropolitan areas in the 1950s, 1960s, and 1970s often led to substantial suburbanization and effective opposition to annexation by central cities. These conditions contributed to substantial and increasing city-suburban income disparities, which persisted in 1990.

In contrast, high city incomes relative to suburban incomes were associated with lower metropolitan income in 1990, continuing the pattern found in 1970 and 1980. Although their residents' incomes had often increased in the 1970s and 1980s, these metropolitan areas started from a relatively low wage base and attracted businesses that paid less on average than wages prevailing in more prosperous metropolitan areas.

Most central cities did not increase in population during the 1980s, but some cities did grow. Where the population within cities increased between 1980 and 1990, median family income was relatively high in cities in 1990 (correlation .57) and the city family poverty rate was relatively low (correlation −.55). Cities that had been growing in population, and that had low city-suburban income disparities, had achieved higher incomes and lower family poverty than other cities by 1990. Growing cities that had low income disparities tended to become more prosperous relative to high-disparity cities that were not growing. Thus, income increases in cities between 1980 and 1990 were positively associated with population growth in cities and with low income disparities between cities and suburbs.

Increases in population within central cities also were positively associated with increases between 1980 and 1990 in metropolitan income, earnings per capita, and earnings per employee (correlations from .34 to .45), and with reductions in metropolitan family poverty (−.33). Growing cities, therefore, were associated with increasing prosperity in metropolitan areas, as well as with increasing prosperity within the cities themselves. Conversely, cities that declined in population tended to be in metropolitan areas where economic well-being also was declining. These correlations, while significant, were modest.

Large metropolitan population did not have significant correlations with city median family income and city family poverty, indicating that large size did not consistently produce high income or low poverty in cities. Thus, well-off regions often did not produce well-off cities.

We infer from these relationships that central cities often do not benefit proportionately, compared with suburban and exurban areas, from metropolitan economic growth. Where cities have room to grow, they are more likely to share in the benefits of metropolitan expansion. If cities are locked in inelastic boundaries, they can be prevented from sharing in metropolitan prosperity increases.

Clusters of Metropolitan Areas

Correlations are useful for identifying general tendencies, but they are less useful for describing diversity. Because general tendencies were stronger in the 1980s, correlations were stronger for that period than for the 1970s. During both periods, there was a great deal of diversity in the economies of metropolitan areas in the South. Metropolitan economic prosperity is a complicated matter, with varying bases for prosperity that change as international, national, and sectional economies change (Wallis 1995).

To extend understanding of how metropolitan areas are differentiated from each other, a factor analysis was conducted. The purpose of the factor analysis was to identify city and metropolitan conditions that were associated with each other. Factor analysis combines variables such that associations between factors are low. Clusters of metropolitan areas with similar characteristics were identified. After identifying these clusters, we examined how those factors were correlated with economic prosperity indicators. The results will be summarized here. Details of the factor analysis are available on request.

Fifteen indicators formed five factor clusters for 1970, 1980, and 1990. Although the factors varied somewhat from decade to decade, there was considerable continuity. The five factors in 1970, 1980, and 1990 were clusters with 1) prominent central cities, 2) a well-educated labor force, 3) postindustrial service economies, 4) university communities, and 5) military concentrations.

Prominent Central Cities

The prominent central cities factor was composed of central cities that contained a high proportion of the metropolitan population, where income was relatively high compared with suburban income, population growth was high, and poverty was relatively low compared with the balance of the MA. This factor was negatively correlated, however, with the level of metropolitan income per capita, as well as earnings per capita and per private employee, in 1970, 1980, and 1990. This negative correlation indicated that these metropolitan areas had low incomes and earnings relative to other metropolitan areas. This finding is consistent with the interpretation that in lower-income metropolitan areas, suburbanization and exurbanization were less likely to have occurred early and less likely to have become far advanced during the 1970s and 1980s.

This factor was positively associated between 1970 and 1980 with increases in metropolitan income and earnings, increases in city income, and reductions in metropolitan and city family poverty. It was not significantly associated with per capita income and earnings changes between 1980 and 1990.

Strong cities' insignificant associations with changes between 1980 and 1990 may have been due to the emergence of a strong postindustrial economy. Large, rapidly growing metropolitan areas did better in the postindustrial economy. Those areas varied considerably in central cities' positions in their regions. Some fast-growing metropolitan areas with rising incomes had strong central cities, such as Charlotte, Huntsville, Jacksonville, Lexington, and Raleigh; others had cities with large disparities, lagging behind their suburbs, such as Atlanta, Washington, D.C., Richmond, Baltimore, and Wilmington, Delaware. Other MAs scoring high on this factor were poorer, such as Fort Smith, Arkansas; Lafayette, Louisiana; Columbus, Georgia; and Fayetteville, North Carolina.

The net effect of these divergent conditions was no significant correlation of prominent central cities with metropolitan income and earnings increases. Strong central cities were not an obstacle to metropolitan prosperity, but they were not a necessary condition for achieving it.

Well-Educated Labor Force

The strongest correlations occurred in 1990, and from 1980 to 1990, between economic prosperity in metropolitan areas with a well-educated labor force and growing central cities. In 1990, this factor was composed of high male and female labor participation rates, a low elderly proportion, and a high proportion of college-educated adults, as well as growing central cities. These metropolitan areas were correlated with high levels of metropolitan income and earnings per capita, high city median family income in 1990, and low metropolitan and city family poverty in 1990, and with decreases in family poverty between 1980 and 1990.

A number of the metropolitan areas in this factor had growing cities, such as Huntsville, Alabama, Fayetteville, Raleigh-Durham, Charlotte, and Greensboro, North Carolina; Jacksonville and Orlando, Florida; Charleston, Columbia, and Greenville, South Carolina; Nashville, Tennessee; and Lexington, Kentucky. A few of the metropolitan areas scoring high on this factor did not have growing cities, such as Washington, D.C.; Wilmington, Delaware; Atlanta; and Norfolk, Virginia.

Some metropolitan areas were able to attract a young, well-educated workforce and the businesses that employed them, even though they had distressed central cities. In general, however, the metropolitan areas in this category had strong and growing central cities. Even the relatively distressed cities (Washington, D.C., Wilmington, Atlanta, and Norfolk) contained prosperous neighborhoods with cultural and environmental assets that attracted young, well-educated workers.

Postindustrial Service Economies

The third factor reflected postindustrial service economies. These metropolitan areas had high percentages of employment in services and FIRE and low percentages in manufacturing. In 1970, 1980, and 1990, these postindustrial service economies were positively correlated with high personal income per capita. But they were not significantly associated with high earnings, nor with increases in income or earnings between decades. Because earnings comprised about two-thirds of income, these differences suggest that retirement income influenced these metropolitan areas' economic prosperity. This interpretation is consistent with the prominence of Florida's MAs in this factor.

Other Factors

In addition, there was a military employment concentration factor in 1970, 1980, and 1990. This factor was associated slightly negatively with low income or earnings per capita. MAs scoring high on this factor were Pine Bluff, Arkansas; Fayetteville, North Carolina; Columbus, Georgia; Memphis, Tennessee; New Orleans and Shreveport, Louisiana; Savannah and Macon, Georgia; Jackson, Mississippi; and Norfolk, Virginia. Metropolitan areas with high military employment concentrations generally were not centers of higher education, nor state capitals, nor finance and insurance centers, nor well positioned with interstate highways.

There also was a higher education factor. This factor included a high proportion of the population enrolled in college, high state and local government employment, a high proportion of the population with college degrees, and a low proportion employed in manufacturing. This factor was not significantly correlated with metropolitan or city economic prosperity in 1980 or 1990. Although these metropolitan areas may produce many substantial incomes and high earnings per employee, the per capita averages may be reduced by the presence of large numbers of college students, who often hold only part-time jobs. Examples of MAs scoring high on this factor in 1990 were Charlottesville, Virginia; Raleigh, North Carolina; Baton Rouge and Monroe, Louisiana; Columbia, South Carolina; Jackson, Mississippi; Washington, D.C.; Lexington, Kentucky; and Montgomery and Tuscaloosa, Alabama.

Economic Prosperity, Disparities, and Growing Cities

The question of whether city-suburb income disparities were related to city and metropolitan economic prosperity has been answered in two dimensions. High-disparity MAs continued to be more prosperous overall than low-disparity MAs in 1990, as had been true in 1970 and 1980. Substantial city-suburb income disparities had already emerged in many MAs by 1970, partly because those metropolitan areas had become prosperous earlier. Prosperity had facilitated suburbanization of population, followed by early suburbanization of employment, and subsequently by exurbanization of commuters into rural areas. Substantial city-suburban disparities resulted from rigid city boundaries, as suburbs usually proved immune to significant annexation. Therefore, disparities indicated danger for central cities.

Interstate highway connections, modern airports with room for expansion, state and national capitals, and a highly educated adult population were assets of growing importance in the postindustrial economy of the 1980s. These assets also were conducive to the suburbanization of employment and the exurbanization of population because they eased long-distance commuting and generated employment near airports, which exacerbated the effects of rigid city boundaries.

The influence of such conditions was not outweighed by drag effects, slowing regional growth, from large city-suburban income disparities. Drag effects from income disparities may still have occurred. The presence of drag effects was suggested by high metropolitan crime rates and high city poverty concentrations in some prosperous regions. Income and poverty disparities involve numerous social problems that create policy dilemmas and may eventually limit continued metropolitan prosperity, but no direct evidence on that point emerged from this study.

Growing cities were more prosperous than stagnant or population-losing cities; and, in particular, the metropolitan areas in which central cities were growing also were increasing in prosperity faster than other metropolitan areas. It was not surprising that growing cities tended to improve more in relative income and drop more in relative family poverty than did population-losing cities. The increasing regional prosperity of metropolitan areas with growing cities was more interesting. If the analysis below is correct, then the absence of growing cities is a danger to regions' economic prosperity, a disincentive for reinvestment in neighborhoods, and potentially an inducement to sprawl.

Why might growing cities be assets to their regions? One reason is that growing cities had growing financial strengths, a continuing ability to attract middle- and upper-income residents, areas of newer housing for younger people with school-age children, and a moderately higher proportion of a region's poverty population (rather than an excessively higher proportion). This combination of conditions avoided the worst aspects of poverty concentrations (Downs 1994) while retaining the fiscal capacity to provide satisfactory public education in most parts of the metropolitan areas. Multinational corporations, whose leaders are accustomed to strong central cities on other continents, are likely to be concerned about the capacity of deteriorated cities to meet their needs, especially their need for a good living environment for their employees.

In addition, financially strong cities are positioned to be active participants in metropolitan infrastructure expansion. Growing cities are likely to have the financial strength, development incentives, and political attitudes to participate effectively with county governments in making regional investments. Growing cities are also likely to have the political confidence to consider regional goals in their infrastructure decisions, rather than focusing on playing defense against intrusions into their depleted supply of financial and infrastructure assets.

Conversely, cities that lose population and are disadvantaged in income may have neither resources nor political will to contribute to regional infrastructure investments. High-cost metropolitan living environments that result from suburban and exurban sprawl may also make U.S. metropolitan areas less competitive internationally, as evidenced by the fact that the United States spends 15 percent or more of its gross national product on transportation, compared with 9 percent in Japan (Cisneros 1995). In a sample of U.S. cities, 12.4 percent of the gross regional product was spent on transportation, according to Peter Newman and Jeffrey Kenworthy (1999, 123), compared with 8.1 percent in European cities and 4.8 percent in wealthy Asian cities such as Tokyo.

Henry Cisneros (1995, 15–17) argued that poor cities are not succeeding, and probably cannot succeed, at educating poor children. This education deficiency has negative effects on cities, regions, and the nation. Similarly, intense poverty concentrations in cities have led to higher crime, drug abuse, and isolation from the economic mainstream. Poverty concentrations disrupt the social context so that more economic investments are made outside of cities. In the 1980s, more deteriorating, underfinanced suburbs emerged in many metropolitan areas (Orfield 1997). The combination of large city-suburban disparities and high intrasuburban disparities may restrain regional prosperity in the years ahead.

Policy Prospects and Strategic Planning

Federal policy does not explain much about variation among states in city-suburban income patterns and trends in the United States. The main federal influences on residential location patterns, such as FHA mortgage guarantees, deductions of interest and property taxes from federal income taxes, and interstate highway construction, probably have similar effects on cities in most states. State policies are more likely to contribute to differences in city-suburban income disparities. When disparities occur, state policies could be more important than federal policies in coping with their consequences. Federal aid to localities is small compared with state aid to local governments. State aid to education alone far surpasses the dollar value of all federal intergovernmental payments to local governments. Furthermore, the federal government does not determine, or significantly influence, most important local powers, such as boundary change procedures and responsibility for education. State authority over local government boundaries, land use regulation, education, and transportation contributes to states having greater potential influence on city-suburban income patterns than the federal government.

From a strategic planning perspective, the foregoing analysis describes strengths, weaknesses, dangers, and opportunities in interregional competitive contexts. Several policy responses are plausible. In most states, these policies would require new state legislation. In every state, they would require state political leadership. Greater annexation powers for cities is one plausible policy. North Carolina has followed this policy with positive results in reducing city-suburb income disparities and in promoting metropolitan growth and prosperity. In most states, annexation has become less common, however, and in many states it has not been used for decades.

In city-suburban comparisons, suburban decline is hidden in aggregate data that includes all suburbs and exurban areas as well. As will be discussed in Chapter 7, suburban decline has become a common phenomenon in most large metropolitan areas. State policies also can inhibit suburban decline. In metropolitan areas where suburban decline threatens to become serious, state policies can cope with some of its consequences as well as slow its pace.

Analysis here has focused on income disparities, but income disparities in part result from sprawl and disinvestment. At the same time, when disparities influence the quality of life in neighborhoods and jurisdictions, incentives increase for more sprawl and disinvestment. To counteract these incentives, plausible policies, in addition to annexation, include intrametropolitan revenue sharing, shared services financed on an ability-to-pay basis, service shifts from city to county governments, regional infrastructure financing based on population, income, or poverty, regional growth boundaries, and redeveloped neighborhoods in compact, walkable patterns. Institutions with more capacity to support reinvestment in older cities and suburbs also would have some impact. These policies may compensate deteriorated jurisdictions for current financial deficits and contribute to more assertive regional decision-making. Such policies are described with examples in Chapter 9.

Notes

6.1. The disparity between central cities and each metropolitan area is described by the ratio of their respective median family incomes. Using metropolitan median family income as the divisor, a ratio of less than 1.0 indicates that city residents have lower incomes than residents of their metropolitan areas and suburbs.

To determine whether a city's condition declined or improved between 1980 and 1990, the 1990 MFI ratio was divided by the 1980 MFI ratio. Rapid decline means the MFI ratio declined by 10 percent or more during one decade. Rapid improvement refers to a 10 percent or more increase in the MFI ratio during one decade.

6.2. For an explanation of the trend from 1960 to 1980, see William H. Lucy and David L. Phillips, 1992, *City Competitiveness and Strategic Planning*, Report No. 5, Metropolitan Strategic Public Policies Project.

6.3. From enormous transformations in the national economy and in regional economies, we inferred that influences would vary by decade and by section of the nation, as well as from one metropolitan region to another. These beliefs led to a research strategy to discern differences between the 1970s and 1980s. It also seemed far-fetched that income and population conditions in cities relative to suburbs would be the only, and perhaps not the main, influences on metropolitan economic prosperity. Data were gathered, therefore, with which to evaluate some other possible influences.

We studied the South to limit impacts of divergent national trends. We chose the South rather than the North to examine differences within a growing region. It seemed intuitively that city-suburb income disparities and regional economic stagnation might occur in many northern metropolitan areas. Studies of northern metropolitan areas would limit analysis of rapidly growing metropolitan areas. All 59 metropolitan areas in 14 southern states were analyzed. Delaware, Maryland, West Virginia, and Kentucky made up the northern boundary, and Arkansas and Louisiana were the states farthest to the west. There are large differences, however, among the economies of West Virginia, Alabama, Florida, and North Carolina, and large differences also between Washington, D.C. and Danville, Virginia. Our method limited diverse influences somewhat. Still, recognizing substantial differences between and within state economies is necessary to interpret the findings.

Indicators of economic prosperity rely on metropolitan data reported by the Regional Economic Information Service of the U.S. Bureau of Economic Analysis. Specific indicators of economic prosperity were personal income per capita, nonfarm earnings per capita, private earnings per capita, and earnings per private employee. For central cities, these data were not available; instead, census data for median family income, per capita income, and family poverty were used. Data for 1970, 1980, and 1990 were examined.

Personal income per capita has the virtue of including income from interest, dividends, rent, sole proprietorships, and transfer payments, especially social security, as well as earnings. In 1970, earnings were 70 percent of income; they were only 64 percent by 1990. Nonfarm earnings per capita and private earnings per capita focus on the employment by which most income was obtained. But per capita measures were influenced by an increase in labor force participation by women in the 59 MAs, from 42 percent in 1970 to 57 percent in 1990, reducing these measures' usefulness in this analysis. To get at quality of jobs, an indicator of earnings per private employee was used. Increases in population and employment were not used as indicators of prosperity because they were frequently associated with reductions in earnings per job (Lucy and Phillips 1995a; Warner 1989).

Central city–suburb disparities were measured mainly by income variables. Central city to metropolitan median family or per capita income yielded a median family income ratio and a per capita income ratio. Ratios greater than 1.0 describe areas in which income in cities is higher than income outside cities. Conversely, ratios less than 1.0, which were far more prevalent, describe areas where income in cities is lower than income outside cities.

Correlation analysis and factor analysis were used in this study. Correlation analysis examines the statistical association between different variables, scored from

−1.0 for complete negative association to 1.0 for complete positive association. Statistically significant correlations are presented in the accompanying tables 6.13 to 6.16. Factor analysis is a statistical technique that identifies configurations of variables that are associated with each other. Five patterns of economic conditions that were frequently associated with each other were discovered in the factor analysis. Many of the explanatory variables used in these discussions are correlated with each other. Regression equations incorporating highly intercorrelated variables can give misleadingly high results. Factor analysis recognizes these intercorrelations and constructs a few artificial variables whose components reflect the intercorrelation of the explanatory variables.

Several types of economic conditions are plausible influences on metropolitan prosperity. In the postindustrial era, manufacturing has declined as a proportion of total employment. Some of the manufacturing remaining in the United States has changed. In the past it was common to mass-produce many thousands of the same item, but nowadays production of more specialized items, which requires greater applications of capital, equipment, and skilled labor per item, has become common (Luger and Goldstein 1991; Reich 1991). Thus, some areas that added manufacturing employment may have increased earnings per private employee. Employment in services has increased greatly, as has employment in finance, insurance, and real estate (FIRE). Military employment might impact economic prosperity, because military pay tends to be low.

Labor force characteristics are also related to metropolitan prosperity. The presence of universities and a college-educated workforce has increasingly influenced business location decisions (Blakely 1994; Kasarda 1993a; Premus 1984, 48–49; Warner 1989). In addition, per capita measures of economic prosperity could be influenced by the percentage of females and males in the labor force (especially since women have been increasing their labor force participation, and they on average are paid less than males), the percentage of blacks in the population (because blacks have typically been paid less than whites), and the percentage of elderly in the population (since the elderly are usually not in the labor force and often have considerable income other than earnings).

In addition, location and transportation influences seemed potentially important. In other analyses (Lucy and Phillips 1995b), it was discovered that seaports generally experienced less growth than other metropolitan areas, state and national capitals tended to experience more than average economic growth (Blair, Staley, and Zhang 1996), and metropolitan areas with effective interstate highway systems (Kasarda 1993a), and metropolitan areas with numerous scheduled airline flights tended to perform better than average. These variables could not be formulated efficiently into indicators on which correlation and factor analyses could be performed, so they are not included in this analysis.

Patterns of Suburban Decline

Besides being a significant social phenomenon, suburban decline can help public officials and citizens synthesize the political and conceptual aspects of strategic planning. Because of suburban decline, simplistic interpretations diminish as plausible explanations for central city problems (no longer can the "problems" be attributed solely to "those politicians" or "those people"). Suburban decline means that alliances between central city and suburban elected officials become possible. Geographically wider, more behaviorally interactive, and more socially complex explanations should be sought. The usefulness of governance for, if not by, regions becomes more apparent.

Describing and explaining suburban decline, therefore, becomes important in strategic planning by federal, state, regional, and local public officials. Federal officials need a national picture of suburban decline. State officials need a statewide perspective on it. Regional officials, whether they are responsible for special districts, cooperative regional councils, or, rarely, regional governments, should diagnose their own region. Local officials should interpret the position of their own jurisdiction in the regional network of population, income, fiscal, economic, and environmental transitions. Here we examine suburban decline in 554 suburbs in the 24 most populous urbanized areas as of 1960. Trend data describe conditions in three ensuing decades.

The Era of Suburban Decline

The current era is characterized by suburban decline, outer suburban and exurban sprawl, and scattered revival in some older city and suburban neighborhoods. In short form, we refer to it as the postsuburban era or the era of suburban decline. These phrases, in part, are devices to focus attention on a dramatic shift in metropolitan conditions. They contrast vividly with the concept of an era of suburban dominance bracketed by 1945, the year World War II ended, and 1980, the census year in which a large majority of the metropolitan population lived in suburbs and when incomes in nearly all suburbs were rising more than the incomes of central city residents.

The continuing decline of most, but not all, large central cities in the United States is a grave problem. The decline of cities is widely recognized, although still not sufficiently understood. The emergence of substantial suburban decline in the 1980s helps reveal the forces encouraging, and the obstacles to reducing, decline tendencies. Moreover, suburban decline will create different political conditions in metropolitan areas and states in reaction to altered demographic and fiscal stresses. Different political, economic, and social landscapes, as well as physical landscapes, are emerging. They may dominate metropolitan politics and planning during the next decades.

An image of suburban uniformity is often exaggerated (Jackson 1985). Suburbs created from 1945 to 1980 varied in demographic composition and future prospects. Some were new moderate-income suburbs dominated by modest-quality housing with little business and industry (Gans 1967). Some older communities that had developed around local industries were engulfed by the spread of post–World War II suburbia. These were gritty suburbs. They were more like neighborhoods in central cities, which were suburban only because state laws passed decades earlier prevented annexation by cities (Vance 1990). Where their economic base vanished, these gritty suburbs paid a high price for their independence. In addition, many older railroad and streetcar suburbs were created as commuter villages (Warner 1962). They had meaningful retail, artisan, and professional foundations as well, and sometimes modest industries. These suburbs often had the diversity of small towns, grew slowly, and contained housing of varying size and quality that was built during several eras.

It was the middle class, however, that was primarily associated with the era of suburban dominance. After World War II, the familial middle class chose suburbia in most metropolitan areas. Housing built in the suburbs tended to be what middle-income and wealthier people could afford. It was nurtured with building codes, zoning regulations, and profits for developers, builders, and lenders (Masotti and Hadden 1973). This varied image of types of post–World War II suburbs (moderate-income, gritty, railroad, and middle-income and wealthier) also helps signal the potential for suburban decline that has become prominent since 1980.

Labeling the current era one of suburban decline that began about 1980 is less familiar, and less comfortable, than the prevalent image of suburban dominance. By suburban decline we mean primarily that incomes of residents of some suburbs are declining relative to the median of regional incomes, and sometimes declining faster than the incomes of central city residents. Decline measured this way indicates that some suburbs are not attracting middle-income, or wealthier, residents as they once did. Furthermore, many suburbs have been losing population, a considerable surprise when the news media periodically are filled with tales of large aggregate population increases in suburbia as a whole.

To say merely that suburbia has been declining since 1980 is too abrupt, because many suburbs and exurbs have been growing rapidly in population, income, and business activities (Garreau 1991; Scheer and Petkov 1998), as discussed in Chapters 2, 4, and 5. Many of these still-growing areas are outer suburban and exurban rather than suburban (Nelson 1992). They are being developed either at lower densities than suburbia or with sizable territories between them and suburbs so that they are not contiguous to previous settlement areas.

Theories of Urban Change

Suburban income decline is a little-studied phenomenon. Some suburban decline should be expected. Social science theories, directly or indirectly, assert that in the United States, middle- and upper-income people, especially families with children, tend to choose residences toward the periphery of metropolitan areas. Poorer people have tended to locate in older, smaller, often deteriorating housing, most of which is in central cities and older suburbs.

From these tendencies, the conclusion follows that when jurisdictions contain a majority, or substantial amounts, of older housing, they will be susceptible to income decline. As their housing ages, suburbs are likely to contain growing proportions of low- and moderate-income residents. At some stage, concentrations of low-income residents can become crisis poverty ghettos (Downs 1994), which drain jurisdictions' resources. Such neighborhoods are unlikely to emerge from crisis ghetto conditions without massive government intervention or dramatic shifts in consumer preferences.

These assertions are grounded in theoretical frameworks and empirical descriptions. Neoclassical land economists have claimed that residents' location decisions involve trade-offs between land, housing, and transportation costs. They have claimed that middle- and upper-income people generally prefer more land and housing and can purchase more of it at lower unit costs toward the periphery of cities and metropolitan areas, while affording the transportation costs necessitated by these outer locations. Poorer people, in contrast, are unable to afford the transportation costs or large investments in home ownership that come with more remote locations. Hence they usually occupy smaller, and older, housing that is closer to work sites (Alonso 1964; Luger 1996; Morrill 1991; Muth 1969). Ernest Burgess (1925) predicted that empirical analysis would reveal a concentric zone residential pattern in which lower-income people would locate toward the center and higher-income people would locate toward the edge of metropolitan settlements.

Homer Hoyt (1939) argued that residential income concentrations would also vary by sector within rings. Higher-income sectors would tend to be concentrated on one side of the city, with exceptions occurring because of special circumstances, such as hilltop sites and water views attracting higher-income people to other geographic sectors. The tendency, still, would be for upper- and middle-income people to gravitate over time toward the periphery as the older housing deteriorated with age (Adams 1987).

Theories about trickle-down processes of neighborhood change (Downs 1981) predict results that are consistent with these interpretations by Alonso, Burgess, and Hoyt. In the trickle-down process, most housing is built to middle- and upper-income standards and costs. Low- and moderate-income people cannot afford most new housing. They tend to occupy older housing that is relinquished by middle- and upper-income people as they move to newer housing. Generalizing from this interpretation, older housing, neighborhoods, and jurisdictions will tend to be occupied by poorer people as time passes. Revitalization and gentrification occur in some locations, with middle- and higher-income people reclaiming deteriorated housing. The predominant trend, however, still is from higher-income occupancy to lower-income occupancy as housing ages. Filtering theory (Lowry 1960) and vacancy chain analysis (Hartshorn 1992; Knox 1994) trace housing through a similar evolution. Individuals and families are typically able to move up to better housing as older housing is relinquished by wealthier people. The neighborhood and jurisdiction change effects are similar to those described with trickle-down processes of transition.

Twenty-Four Urbanized Areas and 554 Suburbs: Trends 1960–1990

This inquiry explores whether these expectations are supported by trends in 554 suburbs from 1960 to 1990 in the 24 most populous urbanized areas as of 1960. Metropolitan areas were selected based on the population of the urbanized area (central city and contiguous suburbs) in 1960. The 24 most populous urbanized areas in 1960 are listed in Tables 7.1 through 7.3. Census data are analyzed here for 1960, 1970, 1980, and 1990. Four data points facilitate discovering whether suburban decline is a recent event, whether it is a long-term trend, and whether the trend has been accelerating. Data are reported for the metropolitan areas, central cities, and 554 suburban jurisdictions. Data were available for suburban jurisdictions of 2,500 or more persons. The population threshold used in each metropolitan area was varied sufficiently to obtain enough suburbs to analyze in this study in each MA but not so many as to weight the analysis excessively to the most populous MAs. The number of suburbs analyzed ranged from 10 in the Houston MA, which constitutes all the Houston suburbs for which data were available, to 37 in the New York MA, which is a small proportion of the New York suburbs with available data. In a few instances, a jurisdiction that the Census Bureau officially treats as a second central city is listed here among

Table 7.1. Age of Housing in Suburbs That Declined in Relative Income Faster than Their Central Cities, 1960–90

		Average Percentage of 1990 Housing Built Before 1940			
		Built Before 1940		Built 1980–1990	
Metropolitan Area	*Number of Suburbs Declining Faster than Central City*	*Fast-Declining Suburbs*	*Metropolitan Area*	*Fast-Declining Suburbs*	*Metropolitan Area*
Atlanta	4	6.9%	5.7%	4.4%	37.3%
Boston	2	57.9%	42.8%	12.5%	11.1%
Buffalo	1	45.4%	34.6%	2.4%	7.3%
Chicago	4	33.9%	26.4%	2.2%	11.7%
Cincinnati	8	30.8%	25.2%	4.6%	14.5%
Cleveland	1	41.3%	28.3%	3.6%	8.2%
Dallas	1	42.9%	4.9%	10.0%	34.6%
Denver	4	10.7%	10.5%	11.7%	24.2%
Detroit	1	55.8%	17.6%	3.5%	11.7%
Houston	5	4.1%	4.2%	11.0%	28.6%
Kansas City, Missouri	11	12.3%	16.5%	9.3%	19.9%
Los Angeles	9	9.4%	11.1%	14.0%	17.9%
Miami	2	2.1%	4.9%	22.1%	22.2%
Minneapolis–St. Paul	2	11.4%	20.5%	13.7%	21.8%
New York CMA	1	21.6%	31.1%	2.6%	9.9%
Philadelphia	2	41.1%	31.6%	4.2%	11.8%
Pittsburgh	14	43.0%	34.6%	3.8%	8.8%
San Diego	6	4.7%	5.5%	18.3%	29.5%
San Francisco–Oakland	9	15.8%	23.3%	11.6%	14.4%
Seattle	6	10.7%	15.2%	27.7%	26.0%
St. Louis	7	19.0%	21.3%	4.5%	16.5%
Washington, D.C.	12	10.2%	11.4%	5.3%	23.5%
24 MAs	112	19.8%	19.6%	9.3%	18.7%

Source: U.S. Bureau of the Census, *Census of Population and Housing,* 1990

the suburbs. Examples include Oakland, St. Paul, Long Beach, and Everett. This handful of cases, however, did not alter the findings, except trivially, for the 554 suburban cases. On the other hand, by not treating these jurisdictions as central cities, this method simplified and clarified data about decline in central cities, so that decline conditions in San Francisco, Minneapolis, Los Angeles, and Seattle were not obscured by data for the secondary central cities.

Decline in most instances was measured as relative income decline—that is,

Table 7.2. Range of Suburban Median Family Income Ratios

Metropolitan Area	Number of Suburbs	1960			1990			Mean Change Ratio 1960–90
		High	Low	High-to-Low Ratio	High	Low	High-to-Low Ratio	
Atlanta	12	1.28	.67	1.9	1.47	.57	2.6	.856
Baltimore	14	1.58	.85	1.9	1.39	.75	1.9	.883
Boston	28	1.72	.79	2.2	1.83	.59	3.1	.947
Buffalo	17	1.47	.94	1.6	1.46	.81	1.8	.960
Chicago	30	2.75	.97	2.8	3.24	.62	5.2	.892
Cincinnati	33	1.58	.67	2.4	1.90	.50	3.8	.907
Cleveland	28	2.00	.96	2.1	1.78	.54	3.3	.915
Dallas	14	2.31	.73	3.2	2.13	.74	2.9	.971
Denver	11	1.18	.84	1.4	1.08	.60	1.8	.850
Detroit	29	1.57	.78	2.0	1.72	.40	4.3	.873
Houston	10	1.62	.96	1.7	2.41	.58	4.2	.969
Kansas City	21	1.62	.78	2.1	3.46	.74	4.7	1.030
Los Angeles	32	1.70	.88	1.9	1.99	.62	3.2	.956
Miami	23	1.63	.52	3.1	2.06	.47	4.4	1.036
Milwaukee	18	1.65	.92	1.8	1.83	.81	2.3	1.057
Minneapolis	21	1.77	.92	1.9	1.48	.78	1.9	.910
New York	37	2.07	.94	2.2	1.87	.82	2.3	.994
Philadelphia	36	1.90	.83	2.3	2.01	.45	4.5	.932
Pittsburgh	35	1.87	.75	2.5	1.73	.62	2.8	.916
San Diego	14	1.30	.75	1.7	1.91	.60	3.2	1.075
San Francisco	25	1.81	.86	2.1	2.08	.59	3.5	.943
Seattle	12	1.45	.81	1.8	1.34	.74	1.8	.916
St. Louis	26	1.74	.77	2.3	3.19	.37	8.6	.855
Washington, D.C.	28	1.63	.70	2.3	1.56	.56	2.8	.883
MEANS	554	1.72	.82	2.1	1.96	.62	3.4	.939

Table 7.3. Suburban Decline Percentages by Metropolitan Area, Ordered by Central City Proportion of 1990 MA

	Central City Proportion of 1990 MA Population	Metropolitan Population Growth Rate: 1960–1990	Total Number of Suburbs	Total of Declining Suburbs 1960–1990		Suburbs Declining at Least 20% 1960–1990		Suburbs Declining at Least 30% 1960–1990		Suburbs Declining Faster than Central City: 1960–1990	
				Number	Percentage	Number	Percentage	Number	Percentage	Number	Percentage
Atlanta	13.9%	178.6%	12	10	83%	8	67%	5	42%	4	33%
Minneapolis–St. Paul	14.9%	66.3%	21	17	81%	1	5%	0	0%	2	10%
Washington, D.C.	15.5%	96.0%	28	23	82%	11	39%	2	7%	12	43%
St. Louis	16.2%	18.6%	26	23	88%	13	50%	3	12%	7	27%
Pittsburgh	18.0%	–14.5%	35	26	74%	6	17%	1	3%	14	40%
Miami	18.5%	107.2%	23	11	48%	2	9%	1	4%	2	9%
San Francisco–Oakland	19.6%	32.5%	25	16	64%	3	12%	1	4%	9	36%
Boston	20.0%	10.9%	28	21	75%	1	4%	0	0%	2	7%
Detroit	23.5%	16.5%	29	26	90%	6	21%	2	7%	1	3%
Cincinnati	25.1%	35.6%	33	24	73%	8	24%	0	0%	8	24%
Denver	25.3%	98.9%	11	11	100%	4	36%	1	9%	4	36%
Seattle	26.2%	78.2%	12	10	83%	0	0%	0	0%	6	50%
Buffalo	27.6%	–9.0%	17	12	71%	1	6%	0	0%	1	6%
Cleveland	27.6%	1.9%	28	23	82%	2	7%	1	4%	1	4%
Kansas City, Missouri	27.8%	50.7%	21	14	67%	1	5%	1	5%	11	52%
Baltimore	30.9%	37.9%	14	12	86%	4	29%	0	0%	0	0%
Los Angeles	30.9%	67.2%	32	23	72%	6	19%	3	9%	9	28%
Philadelphia	32.6%	11.8%	36	26	72%	2	6%	1	3%	2	6%
Chicago	38.2%	17.2%	30	27	90%	5	17%	1	3%	4	13%
Dallas	39.4%	135.6%	14	10	71%	1	7%	0	0%	1	7%
New York CMA	40.5%	22.5%	37	21	57%	0	0%	0	0%	1	3%
Milwaukee	43.9%	19.9%	18	8	44%	0	0%	0	0%	0	0%
San Diego	44.5%	141.8%	14	6	43%	4	29%	0	0%	6	43%
Houston	49.4%	165.6%	10	5	50%	5	50%	1	10%	5	50%
TOTAL SUBURBS			554	405	73%	94	17%	24	4%	112	20%

median family income in Suburb A was compared with metropolitan income in a given year, starting with 1960. Median family income in Suburb A, and each other jurisdiction, was expressed as a ratio, greater or less than one, of the metropolitan area's income. That ratio was calculated for 1960, 1970, 1980, and 1990. In that way, the standing of each jurisdiction relative to the metropolitan area, and relative to other jurisdictions, could be tracked from decade to decade. The income decline referred to here, therefore, was decline in any jurisdiction relative to the metropolitan income from decade to decade. An indicator for median family income (sometimes abbreviated as MFI) was used to describe income changes.

While the theories referred to above lead to predictions of central city decline and older suburban decline, they provide few clues about why and where there may be different rates of decline or why one local government or neighborhood might decline faster than another. Useful theories may be stimulated, therefore, by inference from findings about patterns of decline.

Our discovery that many suburbs have declined faster than central cities, in particular, is a finding that the concentric zone, neoclassical, filtering, and trickle-down perspectives would not predict. That discovery, therefore, led to useful speculations about why suburbs sometimes decline faster than central cities. The prospect of making predictions about dangers of neighborhood and jurisdiction decline would be a major step toward greater effectiveness in strategic planning.

Declining Suburbs: Brief Views

Some findings support the dominant expectations. Income levels fell in a majority of these suburbs from 1960 to 1990 relative to each of the 24 metropolitan median family income levels. Population losses also were common and tended to be associated with relative income decline. Racial change also occurred. When the proportion of the suburbs' population that was African-American increased, the relative median family income tended to decline. But minority population percentages also tended to increase in the suburbs with stable and rising income ratios. Family poverty tended to increase in income-declining suburbs relative to metropolitan norms. Values of owner-occupied housing tended to fall in these suburbs relative to metropolitan norms.

As a result of the demographic changes from 1960 to 1990, greater income polarization occurred among the suburbs in our study. Far more suburbs had descended into the low- and moderate-income category by 1990 compared with 1960. In contrast, almost as many suburbs were above the upper-middle- and upper-income threshold in 1990 as in 1960. Over that 30-year period, the number of suburbs with incomes just above and below the metropolitan median income—the middle-income suburbs—declined substantially. Since our study

Table 7.4. Patterns of Suburban Decreases and Increases in Median Family Income Ratios, 1960–1990

Inner Ring Decreases and Outer Ring Increases	Sector Decreases and Increases	Exurban		City Surrounded	
		Decreases	Increases	Decreases	Increases
Atlanta	Baltimore	Minneapolis	Atlanta	Dallas	Dallas
Baltimore	Boston	Philadelphia	Baltimore	Detroit	Houston
Buffalo	Chicago	San Diego	Boston		Los Angeles
Cincinnati	Cincinnati	Seattle	Buffalo		
Cleveland	Cleveland		Cincinnati		
Dallas	Houston		Cleveland		
Denver	Los Angeles		Dallas	*Isolated*	
Detroit	Miami		Denver	Decreases	Increases
Kansas City	Milwaukee		Kansas City		
Milwaukee	Minneapolis		Miami	Dallas	Cincinnati
Minneapolis	New York		Milwaukee	Minneapolis	Dallas
Philadelphia	Philadelphia		Minneapolis	Seattle	Seattle
Pittsburgh	San Diego		Philadelphia		
San Francisco	San Francisco		Seattle		
St. Louis	St. Louis		St. Louis		
	Washington, D.C.		Washington, D.C.		

included the older and not the newer suburbs, our findings may understate the degree of polarization. Many descriptive findings and interpretations from this analysis follow. For additional details, see Tables 7.1 through 7.4.

1. Twenty percent (112) of the suburbs declined faster in median family income ratios than their central cities from 1960 to 1990.

2. Between 1980 and 1990, 32.5 percent (180) of the suburbs declined in income ratios faster than their central cities, reflecting a more rapid rate of suburban decline in the 1980s than earlier.

3. Of those suburbs whose incomes were 110 percent or less of the metropolitan median family income, 43 percent of the suburbs declined faster than their central cities from 1980 to 1990, indicating that moderate- and middle-income suburbs were particularly susceptible to rapid decline in the 1980s.

4. Of the 554 suburbs, 405 declined in income ratios at least slightly between 1960 and 1990.

5. In these 405 declining suburbs, the average income ratio decline rate from 1980 to 1990, 7.4 percent, was more than the average decline in the 24 cen-

tral cities (6 percent), indicating that suburban decline had become pervasive by the 1980s.

6. Suburbs became more polarized. Between 1960 and 1990, the number of suburbs below 80 percent of the metropolitan median family income increased fourfold, from 22 (4 percent) to 90 (16 percent). The number of suburbs above 120 percent of the metropolitan median family income remained similar—148 in 1960 and 142 in 1990. The range from the highest- to the lowest-income suburbs increased from an average ratio of 2.1 to 1 in 1960 to 3.4 to 1 in 1990.

7. Sixty-two suburbs declined by 10 percent or more in the 1960s, while 89 did so in the 1970s, followed by 81 in the 1980s, another indicator of higher suburban decline rates in the 1970s and 1980s than in the 1960s.

8. Suburbs in 11 fast-growing metropolitan areas declined faster relative to their central cities than did suburbs in 11 slow-growing metropolitan areas, indicating that suburbs in fast-growing and prosperous regions may be more vulnerable than suburbs in regions with fewer inmovers.

9. In metropolitan areas with less than 20 percent of their population in central cities, suburban decline was more rapid than in metropolitan areas with larger proportions of population in their central cities, indicating that in the absence of annexation, central cities and inner suburbs both become vulnerable to decline.

10. Of the 554 suburbs, 41.5 percent had fewer residents in 1990 than in 1960.

11. In the 1970s and 1980s, a majority of these suburbs fell in population—63 percent in the 1970s and 56.5 percent in the 1980s, compared with 21 percent in the 1960s.

12. In addition, 28 percent (156) of the suburbs lost 10 percent or more of their residents between 1960 and 1990. Forty-two suburbs (7.6 percent) lost 25 percent or more of their residents.

What are some implications of these relative income decline and population loss trends for strategic planning? How should a more varied mosaic of metropolitan patterns and trends be conceptualized?

Refinements

One refinement of metropolitan models is to recognize that the geographic pattern of suburban income ratio decreases and increases generally conformed to a combination of sector and ring transitions, rather than one or the other. Much of the rapid decline in suburban median family income ratios occurred in inner suburbs, especially those adjacent to central cities. Many of the rapid increases in income ratios occurred in outer suburbs, and sometimes they occurred in exurban settings. These trends conform to expectations in the ring model of metropolitan residential transition. But sector trends were even more prominent. The rapidly increasing and decreasing suburban income ratios tended to be bunched, and often they spanned inner, middle, and outer suburbs. Sometimes the increasing-income sectors were associated with water views, especially ocean and lake views, as Hoyt suggested. Commuter rail and mass transit connections also were prominent in some instances.

Another refinement of traditional models of metropolitan transition is to emphasize that population declines are common in many suburbs even as suburban territories overall continue strong population growth. If suburbs are unable to annex territory, the area of settlement extends far beyond their borders, their residents age, and household size diminishes, then population declines will occur, unless density of housing units increases. Increased density is possible but unusual. Therefore, population losses are common in many suburbs.

Housing Age

The importance of theoretical and empirical refinements is accentuated by a major negative finding. Comparing trends among the sample of 554 suburbs, age of housing was not singularly associated with relative income decline. None of the housing age indicators were significantly associated with the level of median family income or with changes in relative income from decade to decade. In some instances, relative income declined in jurisdictions with more old housing than in other jurisdictions. But about as often, relative income was stable or increased in jurisdictions with higher proportions of old housing. This finding occurred for two measures of jurisdictions' housing age—percentage of occupied housing constructed before 1940 and percentage of occupied housing constructed in 1960 or earlier. In addition, in jurisdictions with substantial proportions of new housing, defined as housing built from 1980 to 1990, relative income was about as likely to decrease as increase. Thus, a major prediction that follows from each version of residential housing and neighborhood transition theory described above was not confirmed in statistical terms among this large set of suburbs, even though decline in aging jurisdictions often occurred.

Analyses described earlier for the Richmond, Virginia, and Washington, D.C. metropolitan areas revealed that neighborhoods with middle-aged (1945–70) housing were most often declining in relative income, while older neighborhoods (pre-1940) were often rising in income. The findings reported here for 554 suburbs in 24 metropolitan areas are consistent with those case studies. The dominant trend is that suburbs that were in existence in 1960 have declined in relative income, often faster than central cities, between 1960 and 1990. But the presence of old housing—pre-1940 and pre-1960 (including pre-1940) housing—was not consistently associated with relative income decline. The likely reason is that it was middle-aged (1945–70) suburbs that were most often declining rapidly. As discussed previously, we hypothesize that the settings of these suburbs, their relative convenience, their planning and design characteristics, their employment circumstances, and their nonprofit institutions played key roles, along with housing characteristics, in influencing their relative stability and decline.

Income Transitions

Income declines in the 554 suburbs were more common than income increases. Four hundred and five (73 percent) of the suburbs declined at least minimally from 1960 to 1990. Substantial decline also occurred frequently, with 238 suburbs (43 percent) declining by 10 percent or more, 94 (17 percent) declining by 20 percent or more, and 24 (4 percent) declining by 30 percent or more. Each of the central cities declined. The most interesting decline rate, however, occurred in the 112 suburbs (20 percent) that declined faster than their central cities from 1960 to 1990, with 180 suburbs (33 percent) declining faster from 1980 to 1990.

Many older, larger cities have been declining, sometimes to severely deteriorated levels, for several decades. In the 24 central cities, income decline occurred in all but three of 72 decade change possibilities from 1960 to 1990. Between 1960 and 1970, Kansas City experienced no change in its relative income ratio, and between 1980 and 1990, Pittsburgh (1.02 change ratio) and Seattle (1.03 change ratio) increased their median family income ratios slightly. The 24 central cities' average median family income ratios were .92 in 1960, .87 in 1970, .79 in 1980, and .74 in 1990. The average rate of median family income decline in the 24 central cities, relative to each metropolitan median, was 5.4 percent from 1960 to 1970, 9.3 percent between 1970 and 1980, and 6.2 percent between 1980 and 1990; it was 19.3 percent from 1960 to 1990.

City Decline

Why did the average decline rate in cities accelerate from the 1960s to the 1970s and then diminish in the 1980s? One reason could be that decline rates will taper off as cities' conditions worsen because they already have achieved a substantial portion of the possible decline. Another reason could be that as many suburbs decline, their decline constitutes a drag on the overall well-being of suburbia, diminishing the rate of increase in the city-suburb income gap. The findings here about suburban decline make this second hypothesis plausible.

Because suburbs are generally newer than cities, they have had a reputation for affluence. The notion of suburbs declining at rapid rates, sometimes faster than cities, is somewhat surprising. Suburbs vary greatly in their age, origin, economic base, and history. Some suburbs, especially older ones, may have had long periods of decline relative to their expanding metropolitan areas. Other suburbs, especially those built primarily as bedroom communities after World War II, may have declined more recently. If income decline is related to aging housing, especially middle-aged housing built between 1945 and 1970, then recent decline in many of these post-1945 suburbs would be common. The number of income-declining suburbs increased after the 1960s, as did the average rate of decline. This decline rate sequence is consistent with an interpretation that middle-aged suburbs were leading the suburban decline parade.

Increase in Suburban Decline

A noteworthy number of suburbs declined at substantial rather than slight rates. From 1960 to 1970, 190 suburbs declined at 5 percent or more; from 1970 to 1980, 214 suburbs did so, followed by 207 suburbs which declined at that rate or more from 1980 to 1990. The number of suburbs that declined in income by 10 percent or more per decade was 62 in the 1960s, 89 in the 1970s, and 81 in the 1980s. Suburbs declining by 20 percent or more per decade also increased from three in the 1960s to 14 in the 1970s and 1980s, and the average rate of decline increased as well. Of those suburbs that declined, the average income decline was 6.2 percent in the 1960s, 7.2 percent in the 1970s, and 7.4 percent in the 1980s. Thus, the average rate of income decline (7.4 percent) from 1980 to 1990 in the 405 declining suburbs was greater than the average decline (6.2 percent) in the 24 central cities. The findings above about income changes are based on 521 cases for 1960–70 and 1970–80, with 554 cases for 1980–90 and 1960–90. Data for 33 cases were not available for 1970. Some rapid suburban decline occurs because of suburbs' small size: cities are composed of neighborhoods (some of which are larger than suburbs) whose sometimes volatile income rises and falls are disguised in citywide data, as was described in Chapters 4 and 5.

Comparing the rates of income decline in suburbs with decline rates in central cities also was useful. One hundred seventy-six suburbs (34 percent) declined faster than their central cities from 1960 to 1970, 109 (21 percent) from 1970 to 1980, and 180 (32.5 percent) from 1980 to 1990. The average rate of decline among these suburbs was 9.0 percent 1960–70, 7.4 percent 1970–80, and 10.1 percent 1980–90. A smaller number of suburbs declined faster than central cities in the 1970s because suburbs declined more slowly, while cities declined faster, than in the other two decades.

High- and Low-Income Suburbs

These numbers of declining suburbs may be misleading, because they include all the suburbs regardless of how high or low they scored in 1960 relative to the metropolitan area's median family income. If suburbs above 110 percent of the metropolitan median are excluded, then the number of suburbs that declined in income at a faster rate than their central city was 94 of 287 in the 1960s, 78 of 322 in the 1970s, and 152 of 357 in the 1980s. In other words, 43 percent of the suburbs with incomes below 110 percent of the metropolitan median declined faster than their central cities in the 1980s compared with 33 percent in the 1960s and 24 percent in the 1970s. These suburbs' average rates of decline were 8.5 percent 1960–70, 7.3 percent 1970–80, and 10.6 percent 1980–90.

These findings deserve additional emphasis. High-income suburbs would be expected to be more stable than other suburbs, more effective at protecting themselves, and more attractive for reinvestment. They have succeeded in the residential marketplace. Using 120 percent of the metropolitan median family income ratio as a measure of higher income, suburban attractiveness in higher-income residential neighborhoods seemed to occur. In 1960, 148 suburbs had 120 percent or more of metropolitan income. In 1990, 142 suburbs were in this higher-income category, although there was considerable turnover as to which suburbs were included in it. These numbers were supported, however, by the rise of a majority of these higher-income suburbs in 1990 from lesser-income status in 1960. Only 37 percent of the higher-income suburbs of 1960 remained in the higher-income category (120 percent or more of metropolitan income) in 1990. Thus, more than 60 percent of the suburbs in the high-income category had fallen from their high-income status by 1990, challenging the notion that suburbs persist in their socioeconomic status against challenges by competitors.

Middle-Income Suburbs

The remaining suburbs, from those with 110 percent of their region's median family income to those with the lowest incomes in 1960 (only six suburbs were below an income ratio of .7), were less successful at attracting middle- and upper-income residents, who have the most choices among location alternatives. Among these 357 suburbs, all of which were relatively typical of the income array in their metropolitan areas, 43 percent declined in relative income faster than their central cities. Most observers would find that a rather remarkable trend.

A larger number of suburbs had income ratios exceeding 1.1 in 1960 than in subsequent decades. In 1960, 267 of 554 suburbs (48.1 percent) had income ratios of 1.1 or more, compared with 199 of 521 (38 percent) in 1970, 197 of 554 (36 percent) in 1980, and 190 of 554 (34 percent) in 1990. The number of suburbs with income ratios between 1.1 and 1.2 declined substantially, from 119 in 1960 to 48 in 1990.

The number of relatively low income suburbs also increased greatly. In 1960, only six suburbs (1.1 percent) had MF income ratios below .7; by 1990 there were 38 (6.9 percent). Only 16 suburbs (2.9 percent) were between .7 and .8 in MFI ratios in 1960; by 1990, there were 52 (9.4 percent). In 1960, 48 suburbs (8.7 percent) were between .8 and .9 MFI ratios; in 1990, there were 92 suburbs (16.6 percent) in this income range. In sum, 70 suburbs (13 percent) were below .9 in MF income ratios in 1960; by 1990, suburbs below a .9 MF income ratio had increased to 182 (33 percent), an increase of two and one half times in 30 years. Between 1960 and 1990, the number of suburbs below .8 in MFI ratios grew from 22 (4 percent) to 90 (16 percent).

More Low-Income Suburbs

Two trends and patterns have emerged. In this older group of suburbs, treating all 554 as old in the sense that they achieved 2,500 or more residents by 1960, many suburbs became relatively low income, with the percentage below a .9 MFI ratio increasing from 13 percent in 1960 to 33 percent in 1990. In contrast, the category of the wealthiest suburbs was replenished by 1990 after it declined earlier, regaining a similar share (26 percent) of the total that was in this category in 1960 (27 percent). Thus, the suburbs were becoming much more polarized. By 1990, one-third of the 554 suburbs were in the moderate- and low-income groups, below .9 MFI ratio, and one-fourth of the suburbs were in the relatively wealthy group. The middle-income suburbs, between .9 and 1.2 income ratios, had diminished from 336 (61 percent) in 1960 to 230 (41.5 percent) in 1990.

Thus, the middle-income suburbs of 1960 experienced difficulty in attracting people of similar relative income standing during the next 30 years. This seems an instance of inadequate reinvestment in middle-income neighborhoods as their housing stock reached middle age. A larger proportion of middle-income households presumably were attracted to newer, and usually larger, housing farther from the metropolitan center where population was increasing. The tyranny of easy development decisions on the metropolitan fringe was reflected in these data.

Suburban Persistence

Did suburbs persist in maintaining their initial socioeconomic status relative to other suburbs? Reynolds Farley (1964) argued that the relative socioeconomic positions of suburban jurisdictions tend to persist for several decades. This concept is consistent with Homer Hoyt's (1939) argument that metropolitan evolution by socioeconomic status occurs spatially in diverse income sectors moving out from the center, rather than in uniform rings of residents grouped by socioeconomic status, as in the Burgess (1925) model. Guest (1978) and Choldin, Hanson, and Bohrer (1980) argued that comparing suburbs only with other suburbs similar in age exaggerated persistence in their socioeconomic standing, because they tended to fall behind newer jurisdictions rather than change positions relative to each other.

In 20 of 24 metropolitan areas in this study, the average median family income ratio among the suburbs declined relative to the metropolitan median family income from 1960 to 1990, as expected from the Guest and Choldin et al. perspective. Among the 20 MAs with negative average suburban change ratios, Denver was the lowest at −15.0 percent. In these 20 metropolitan areas, on average, the older suburbs were declining, not persisting, in their income status relative to newer suburbs. In four metropolitan areas, the older suburbs of our sample were not only persisting but improving, topped by San Diego's average 7.5 percent increase. The other metropolitan areas with income-increasing suburbs were Kansas City, Miami, and Milwaukee. Thus, in 83 percent of the MAs, the average of the median family income ratios for the suburbs in the study declined relative to the metropolitan median family income. The findings in this paragraph seem inconsistent with the findings, reported above, that housing age and income decline were not significantly correlated. Here the finding is that most suburbs in 20 of these metropolitan areas were declining in relative income, regardless of their mix of older and newer housing. In the previous findings above, housing age did not explain rates of decline among the declining suburbs, although relative income decline tended to occur. These relationships would occur if decline was more likely in middle-aged than in older suburbs.

Changing Rank

Another method for analyzing suburban persistence is to measure changes in rank. While movement among narrowly different middle ranks might be considerable, the rich and poor extremes might be more likely to persist in their status. The richer suburbs would be more likely to obtain reinvestment and benefit from peer attractions. The poorer suburbs would be less likely to have the means to enhance their public services or housing quality to attract a higher-income populace.

When the suburban jurisdictions with the three highest and three lowest income ratios were compared in their income ranks relative to each other from 1960 to 1990, there was considerably more persistence in rank in the high-income than in the low-income jurisdictions. Of the 72 suburbs ranked first, second, or third highest in each metropolitan area in 1960, only 10 had fallen out of the top five in income ratios by 1990. Of these 10 high-ranked suburbs, nine fell into ranks from six through 10, while one fell lower, to rank 15. In only two MAs, Atlanta and San Diego (both of which are rapidly growing), did one of the three highest jurisdictions in 1960 fall below the median number of suburbs in income rank by 1990. These findings conform to expectations. High-income suburbs were adept at persisting in their status relative to other older jurisdictions. Those MAs with high population growth rates (Atlanta grew fastest and San Diego third fastest) were more vulnerable to decline in older suburbs, because their geographic territory was moving outward rapidly.

Low Ranks

Of the 72 lowest-ranked suburbs in 1960, 20 rose out of the bottom five by 1990. Of the 20 low-ranked suburbs that rose substantially in their income rank, 11 went into the top 50 percent of their suburbs ranked by median family income ratios. The largest changes were suburbs from the bottom three that rose all the way to positions one and three in the Atlanta MA, positions six and seven out of 21 in the Minneapolis MA, and to position 10 of 28 in the Washington, D.C. MA. In each instance, the jurisdictions that rose fast and far were relatively remote, small villages or outer suburbs that attracted higher-income residents during the exurbanization period that occurred in the 1970s and 1980s. These jurisdictions were Lawrenceville and Roswell, Atlanta MA; Brooklyn Park and Coon Rapids, Minneapolis–St. Paul MA; and Leesburg, Washington, D.C. MA. Consequently, many of the fast-rising suburbs were instances of exurbanization of rural areas rather than examples of older inner suburbs reviving.

Another method of measuring change is to identify the suburbs that moved several ranks during the study period. Of the 554 suburbs, 206 (37 percent) moved four or more ranks from 1960 to 1990. That was about double the rate of suburbs (19 percent) that moved by four or more ranks during any one of the three decades (289 of 1,532 instances for which income data were available for the intervening decades). During the 1980 to 1990 decade, 93 suburbs (17 percent) changed rank by four or more. In comparison, 196 of 978 suburbs (20 percent) changed four or more ranks between 1960–70 and 1970–80 combined (an average of 10 percent per decade), indicating somewhat greater volatility in suburbs' income standing during the 1980s than during the previous two decades. As the geographic scope of metropolitan areas expanded, changes took place in the location attributes that defined older suburbs' reasons for being as they were. As advancing age intersects with changing location advantages, the prospects of suburbs relative to each other can be expected to shift.

More Polarized Suburbs

Greater polarization in income among suburbs is another characteristic of the postsuburban era that emerged in the 1980s. The range from the highest-income to the lowest-income suburbs is one useful measure of income polarization. By 1990, the range of income ratios had grown by more than 50 percent from the range in 1960. In 1960, the average gap between each metropolitan area's richest and poorest suburbs in the study sample was 2.1 to 1. By 1990, the average income ratio gap was 3.4 to 1. The mean of the highest median family income ratios in each MA in 1960 was 1.7, compared with the mean of the lowest ratios in each MA of .8; by 1990, the mean of the highest median family income ratios in each MA was 1.96, with .6 the mean of the 24 lowest ratios. Thus, the mean of the highest ratios had risen by .24 from 1960 to 1990, while the mean of the lowest ratios had fallen from .8 to .6 (Table 7.2).

Income and Race

Income and race are linked in the United States. According to the 1990 census, African-Americans as a group had median family incomes 58 percent of incomes of whites. Increases in African-American shares of suburban populations, therefore, would be expected to be accompanied by relative income declines in many suburbs. Of the 350 suburbs that declined in income between 1960 and 1970, the African-American population increased in 260 (74 percent). Of the 391 suburbs that declined in income between 1970 and 1980, 364 (93 percent) increased their African-American population percentage. Of the 341 suburbs that declined in income between 1980 and 1990, 300 (88 percent) increased their African-American percentage.

The significance of these percentage increases is questionable, however, because African-American increases occurred in nearly all the 554 suburbs. From 1960 to 1970, in fact, the African-American increase in all the suburbs, 88.5 percent, was considerably higher than their increase in the 260 suburbs in which the income ratios declined. While the African-American increases in all suburbs from 1970 to 1980 (88 percent) and 1980 to 1990 (84 percent) were lower than their increase in relative income-declining suburbs, the differences in percentage change were quite small.

On the other hand, where the absolute increase in African-Americans in suburbs per decade was 2,000 or more, MFI ratios in those suburbs almost always fell from 1960 to 1990. Among the 30 suburbs where African-Americans increased by 10 percent or more per decade, MFI ratios declined in 28 (93 percent) from 1960 to 1970, in 54 out of 56 (96 percent) from 1970 to 1980, and in 30 out of 38 (79 percent) from 1980 to 1990.

Tipping-Point Research

Racial change is a plausible explanation of suburban income decline. Income decline in areas with major increases in African-American proportions of the population would seem likely because blacks' incomes on average are much lower than those of whites. Moreover, the "tipping point" hypothesis has claimed that once the African-American percentage in a neighborhood exceeded some threshold, racial change would proceed until the neighborhood was nearly all black. In a review of literature findings about the 1970s and 1980s, however, John R. Ottensmann (1995, 131) found: "Significant numbers of racially mixed neighborhoods exhibited stability during [the 1970s]. Whites were moving into mixed neighborhoods in surprising numbers . . . the tipping-point hypothesis, . . . no longer is adequate for understanding racial change." In a study of census tracts in 58 cities, Lee and Wood (1991) found that 46 percent of racially mixed tracts in 1970 were stable (28 percent) or had significant nonblack increases (18 percent) from 1970 to 1980. Ottensmann (1995) noted that several other studies reported about half of substantially African-American neighborhoods remained racially stable or declined in their black proportion during the 1970 to 1990 period. In our suburban sample, the black percentage increased in about two-thirds of the suburbs, and the white percentage increased in about one-third. An indirect effect of racial transition on property reinvestment, and subsequently on income of residents, may also occur. While race remains relevant to income transitions, it was less likely to dominate explanations of neighborhood decline in the 1970s and 1980s compared with the 1950s and 1960s.

An indirect effect of racial transition on property reinvestment and subsequently on income of residents may also occur. George Galster (1987, 240) has described a sequence of self-fulfilling prophecies that can lead to income transitions through the effects of decreased reinvestment: "There is no evidence that lower-income or black homeowners are less likely to undermaintain their homes' exteriors than are higher-income or white homeowners. . . . Yet, the dynamics of succession and transition can generate expectations . . . that the physical and/or socioeconomic quality of the neighborhood will fail. Neighborhood cohesion may also suffer. As a result, the homeowners originally in the neighborhood reduce their upkeep investments and postpone exterior repairs." As succession proceeds, lower-income people may occupy more of the undermaintained structures.

Income and Family Poverty

The national rate of family poverty fell dramatically between 1960 and 1970 and then rose slightly through 1990. In 1960, the national family poverty rate was 18.1 percent; in 1970 it was 10.1 percent, rising slowly to 10.3 percent in 1980 and 10.7 percent in 1990. Within the 24 MAs in this study, the average of the 24 family poverty rates followed a similar trajectory: 7.4 percent in 1970, 7.9 percent in 1980, and 8.4 percent in 1990. In the 24 central cities, however, the average of the family poverty rates was higher than the MAs' average—11.2 percent in 1970, 14.3 percent in 1980, and 17.2 percent in 1990—while in the suburbs the averages were 5.3 percent in 1970, 5.9 percent in 1980, and 6.5 percent in 1990. Family poverty rates increased in 56 percent of 521 suburbs between 1970 and 1980 and in 54.5 percent of 554 suburbs from 1980 to 1990.

Median family income may decline without poverty increasing, but the opposite is more likely. In the 214 suburbs in which income declined by 5 percent or more from 1970 to 1980, the average family poverty rate increased from 6.1 to 7.9 percent. This relationship continued in the 1980s, when average family poverty rates increased from 7.2 to 9.3 percent in the 207 suburbs where income declined by 5 percent or more.

Averages mask extremes. Four suburbs, for example, exceeded Chicago's 36 percent of preschool children below the poverty line in 1990, and in some suburbs, child poverty grew extremely rapidly—Posen went from 3 to 23 percent and Riverdale, Illinois, increased from 3 to 20 percent in one decade (Orfield 1998, 20).

Population Decreases

Population decreases can be another indicator of decline. In suburbia, in particular, where the popular image has been anticipation of unending expansion, population losses may surprise local residents and public officials. Population decreases occurred in 230 suburbs (41.5 percent) between 1960 and 1990. There were population decreases in 115 suburbs (21 percent) from 1960 to 1970, in 351 (63 percent) from 1970 to 1980, and in 313 (56.5 percent) from 1980 to 1990. Given the image of suburbs, in general, as rapidly expanding settlements during each decade from 1960 to 1990, these proportions of population-losing suburbs seem quite extraordinary. While the suburbs in aggregate have been growing, generally decreasing household size leads to population loss unless jurisdictions are adding residential structures or larger households. Indeed, the large number of small suburbs with rigid boundaries developed in recent decades has apparently led to population losses in a majority of older suburbs. In many instances, large suburban population losses have occurred. From 1960 to 1990, 156 suburbs (28 percent) lost 10 percent or more of their residents, including 42 suburbs (7.6 percent) whose population declined by 25 percent or more.

An increase in the number of population-losing suburbs after the 1960s occurred as expected. The huge increase in the 1970s compared with the 1960s, and then the slight decline in the 1980s, although still with a very large percentage of population-losing suburbs, is somewhat surprising. In this vein, it is also interesting to observe that 189 suburbs (34 percent) lost 10 percent or more of their population in the 1970s, while 54 suburbs (9.7 percent) lost 10 percent or more in the 1980s. Perhaps some suburbs that experienced population declines from aging populations in less dense suburbs in the 1970s replaced some of them with larger but lower-income families in the 1980s.

Population and Income

Where suburbs declined in population, income decline often occurred. Of the 115 suburbs that declined in population between 1960 and 1970, 66 declined in relative median family income by 5 percent or more and 84 by 2 percent or more. Of the 351 suburbs that declined in population between 1970 and 1980, 151 declined in income by 5 percent or more and 235 by 2 percent or more. Of the 313 suburbs that lost population between 1980 and 1990, 120 declined in income by 5 percent or more and 161 by 2 percent or more. Among the population-losing suburbs, 98 of 115 (85.2 percent) declined at least minimally in their MFI ratios from 1960 to 1970, 293 of 351 (83 percent) from 1970 to 1980, and 191 of 313 (61 percent) from 1980 to 1990.

In some instances, population decreases may be associated with income declines. In other instances, population increases and income declines may go together. Population decreases, for example, may occur in old suburbs because some old housing is being converted to other uses and some may be demolished. In addition, household size may be diminishing there, as in most jurisdictions, and if new housing is not being constructed, then population declines will occur. Some long-term residents may be remaining in place, but whereas a particular household may once have been busy with parents and children, perhaps occupancy has been reduced to a surviving widow. Such transitions may be accompanied by income declines as the incomes of some aging residents diminish and people with higher incomes move farther toward the periphery rather than choosing inner suburban locations.

On the other hand, population increases also may be associated with income declines. Poorer families tend to have more children per household, and the average number of children in minority families is also above the national average for children per family. As housing ages, its price tends to decrease; thus, if it becomes more affordable to lower-income people, an influx of larger families may occur. Because these families may include minorities, the minority population also may increase.

The jurisdictions in which income ratios increased despite population losses are more difficult to explain. In general, their income ratios could increase, despite population loss, if outmovers were poorer than inmovers or if stayers were richer than outmovers. Some upgrading of structures may have occurred. High-paying employers within easy commuting ranges could have increased. Transportation improvements could have enhanced commuting from some suburban jurisdictions. Or perhaps family size diminished as children left home, and the middle-aged parents who remained were in their peak earning years.

Jurisdiction Population Size and Income Transitions

On average, about 50 percent of the metropolitan population age 5 and over has moved within five years. That average mobility rate was identified for the 1985 to 1990 period, as well as for the 1975 to 1980 period. The average obscures the highest mobility rates, which sometimes exceed 60 percent. In large jurisdictions, much of this residential mobility occurs within the home jurisdictions. In small jurisdictions, however, residents are less likely to find replacement housing that satisfies their new needs, wants, and capacities. Thus, turnover of residents in small jurisdictions may be greater than in large ones. Among the 554 suburbs in this study, the range of income change variations was much greater in the small than in the large jurisdictions from 1960 to 1990 and from 1980 to 1990.

Because of rapid residential mobility, small jurisdictions are prone to experience more rapid changes in relative income than larger jurisdictions. Land availability, market opportunities, and developers' entrepreneurship may lead to substantial increases in population in some suburban jurisdictions. In small jurisdictions, these population increases may constitute a large proportion of the resulting population. The renter-to-owner ratio also affects potential for rapid income change, because renter mobility rates traditionally have been four times the mobility rates for owners.

Income Decline and Population Change in a Metropolitan Context

The rate of metropolitan and jurisdiction population growth and decline, therefore, also needs study. Faster metropolitan growth could be associated with faster decline of the central city and older suburbs. As the total number of high-, middle-, moderate-, and low-income people increases, the high- and middle-income people are more likely to locate in newer housing toward the perimeter. The larger number of moderate- and low-income people will be left with more of the older housing in cities and older suburbs. Where metropolitan growth is slower, or even negative, the number of low- and moderate-income people will not increase as rapidly, and middle- and upper-income people will have more difficulty selling their residences for prices that they believe are reasonable and that facilitate moving up to more expensive housing, which is often farther out.

Twenty-two of the 24 metropolitan areas increased in population, while two decreased, between 1960 and 1990. Among the growing metropolitan areas, the increase range was from 1.9 percent (Cleveland) to 178.6 percent (Atlanta). For analysis, the growing MAs were divided into two groups, those above and below a 50 percent rate of growth in 30 years.

Central city and suburban sprawl development stretches northwest in this view of Atlanta. High-rise towers mark the stops of the MARTA system heavy-rail, which travels from downtown Atlanta and just north of I-85 to North Atlanta. (Synergy/Photography)

In the 11 fast-growing MAs, there were 198 suburbs. Of these, 43 (22 percent) declined in income by 20 percent or more from 1960 to 1990, 14 (7 percent) declined by 30 percent or more, and 62 (31 percent) declined at faster rates than their central cities. The central cities in these fast-growing MAs averaged 16 percent income ratio declines from 1960 to 1990. That is, in 1990 the central cities' median family income ratios were 84 percent of their ratios in 1960.

Fast and Slow Growth

In the 11 slow-growing MAs, there were 304 suburbs. Of these, 44 (14 percent) declined in income by 20 percent or more from 1960 to 1990, nine (3 percent) declined by 30 percent or more, and 35 (12 percent) declined faster than their central cities. The central cities in these slow-growing MAs averaged 23 percent income ratio declines from 1960 to 1990. Thus, in 1990, their median family income ratios were 77 percent of what they had been in 1960.

Suburban decline occurred at faster rates, therefore, in the rapidly growing MAs than in the slow-growing areas. More rapid suburban decline in the fast-growing metropolitan areas was most evident using the indicator of suburban income decline exceeding the rate of central city income decline.

In the two population-losing MAs, there were 52 suburbs. Of these, seven (13 percent) declined in income by 20 percent or more from 1960 to 1990, one (2 percent) declined by 30 percent or more, and 15 (29 percent) declined faster than their central cities. The central cities in these population-losing MAs averaged 17 percent income ratio declines from 1960 to 1990. The Pittsburgh MA, with 35 suburbs in the sample, dominated this category. The city of Pittsburgh declined less (11.6 percent) than all but four of the 24 central cities in this study. Many of its suburbs were relatively old industrial suburbs with their own local employment centers, many of which were dying out as the steel industry relocated, modernized, or went out of business. This economic phenomenon probably contributed to the Pittsburgh MA having more suburbs declining faster than their central city (14) than any other metropolitan area. This category of population-losing MAs, therefore, is dominated by an unusual case. With only two cases in the category, moreover, no valid generalizations can be drawn from the findings.

Considering the findings for the 22 MAs in the fast- and slow-growing metropolitan areas, the fastest rates of central city income decline were in the 11 slow-growing MAs, and the fastest rates of suburban income decline were in the 11 rapidly growing MAs. This finding has important implications for rapidly growing metropolitan areas. If it is generally applicable, then older suburban jurisdictions in fast-growing metropolitan areas are extremely vulnerable to rapid decline. They often declined faster than their central cities, a phenomenon that occurred in 31 percent, nearly one-third, of the suburbs in the 11 fast-growing MAs in this study. These decline comparisons are consistent with an inter-pretation that central cities, because of diverse resources and attractions as well as liabilities, tend to be better positioned to renew attractions to middle- and upper-income families than many older and middle-aged suburbs, which usu-ally have fewer assets and less diversity. The tyranny of easy development deci-sions that contributes to sprawl may impact middle-aged suburbs with special force.

City Share of Metropolitan Population

The central cities' shares of metropolitan population could also have influenced suburban income decline rates. If so, the influence of cities' population shares would most likely be observed where their share was relatively small or large. In seven metropolitan areas, the central cities' population shares were less than 20 percent of the MAs' population (Table 7.3). The suburbs declined by 20 percent or more in 26 percent of these metropolitan areas (compared with 17 percent for the total sample). Eight percent declined by 30 percent or more (compared with 4 percent for the total sample), and 29 percent declined faster than the cen-tral city (compared with 20 percent for the total sample).

In general, small central city shares of MA population were associated with more rapid suburban decline than the norm. There is irony in this outcome. Small city population shares have occurred because of success by suburban resi-dents and their allies in having prevented annexation by cities. The small size of these suburbs and their inner locations, lacking annexation capacity themselves, contributed to their own income decline during the 1960 to 1990 period. These suburbs often declined at rates faster than the income decline occurring in the central cities from which they may have attempted to separate themselves per-manently by preventing annexation.

Patterns of Income Decline and Revival

Some suburbs declined and then revived in their income ratios. Twenty suburbs declined by 5 percent or more between 1960 and 1970, decreased again by 5 percent or more between 1970 and 1980, and then were stable or increased by 2 percent or more between 1980 and 1990. Sixteen suburbs decreased by 5 per-cent or more between 1960 and 1970, decreased again by 5 percent or more between 1970 and 1980, and then increased by 5 percent or more between 1980 and 1990. Another group of 18 suburbs declined by 5 percent or more between 1960 and 1970 and then increased thereafter without declining again, while 17 suburbs declined by 5 percent or more between 1960 and 1970, declined by 2 percent or more between 1970 and 1980, and then increased in the 1980s.

Thus, fewer suburbs revived in relative income after declining than declined consistently or recently. The relatively unusual trend in these declining and then reviving suburbs indicates they deserve contextual analysis to try to explain why some suburbs stabilize or increase after substantial declines. The role of public policy interventions should be included in these analyses. In addition, the altered position of some suburbs relative to suburban employment concentrations may have given certain "in-between" suburbs a location advantage, especially in two-worker households.

The wealthier suburbs in 1960 were more able to improve their relative standing by 1990 than were the suburbs that were close to each region's median family income in 1960. Of 148 suburbs with a median family income ratio of 1.2 or higher in 1960, 55 (37 percent) had increased their ratio by 1990. In comparison, 28 of 119 suburbs (24 percent) with MF income ratios between 1.1 and 1.2 had increased their ratios by 1990, 24 of 133 (18 percent) between 1.0 and 1.1 had done so, and 18 of 84 (21 percent) between .9 and 1.0 had done so. The diminished rate of income enhancement in the middle-income suburbs, compared with the higher-income suburbs, is noteworthy. Perhaps more surprising, however, is that income improved in only 37 percent of the high-income (1.2 MF income ratio or higher) suburbs from 1960 to 1990.

More of the lower-income suburbs in 1960 had increased their income ratios by 1990: 14 of 48 (29 percent) with MFI ratios between .8 and .9 had increased, as had 8 of 16 (50 percent) between .7 and .8, and 4 of 6 (67 percent) less than .7. The poorer suburbs in 1960 that improved by 1990 were usually geographically remote from the prime areas of pre-1960 suburbanization. They caught later periods of suburbanization and exurbanization by wealthier commuters and experienced income increases. They tended to be outer rather than inner suburbs in 1960. Examples include Leesburg and Manassas Park west of Washington, D.C., Lawrenceville and Roswell north and east of Atlanta, and Leisure City, Naranja, and Perrine south of Miami.

Income and Housing Value

Levels of, and changes in, median family income and median value of owner-occupied housing should be closely associated. Housing value reflects demand. Demand reflects ability to pay. Housing value by jurisdiction may not always be the same as income by jurisdiction, however, because some people may want to live in a jurisdiction and be willing to pay more than the typical portion of their income to live there. When a jurisdiction declines in income or population, its housing values generally should fall relative to housing values in the metropolitan area, reflecting diminished demand for housing. The response of housing values, however, may lag behind changing socioeconomic conditions.

In the suburbs where relative median family income declined substantially, relative median value of owner-occupied housing also usually declined between 1960, 1970, and 1980, but between 1980 and 1990 housing value declines were less frequent. In the 190 suburbs in which median family income declined by 5 percent or more per decade, housing value also declined by 5 percent or more in 124 of them (65 percent) between 1960 and 1970, 147 out of 214 (69 percent) between 1970 and 1980, and 97 out of 207 (47 percent) between 1980 and 1990.

The correlation between 24 MAs' median family income and median value of owner-occupied housing was .68 in 1960, .68 in 1970, .35 in 1980, and .67 in 1990. For 520 suburbs, there was a correlation between income and housing value of .81 in 1960, .80 in 1970, .67 in 1980, and .68 in 1990.

Why have the correlations between median family income and housing value been as low as .67? Some departure from a perfect correlation would occur as long as people have somewhat varying tastes for how much of their disposable income to put into housing. In addition, some people have location preferences that depart from the norm. They may get more housing space and quality but less neighborhood quality, at least as some people see the choices. Housing discrimination by race may cause some discrepancy in these correlations. None of these possibilities, however, suggest why the correlations were lower in 1980 and 1990 than earlier. One possibility is that many suburban homeowners have tended to age in place. Some aging occurs during a life cycle in which residents are earning somewhat more as the years pass, while the housing stock declines in relative value as it ages. Other residents, who were older and retired, may have had incomes fall below the relative value of the housing stock. Perhaps some younger buyers were putting high proportions of their income into housing in order to shift from renting to owning, anticipating being more able to afford their new housing as the years passed. These forces could have operated more strongly in 1980 and 1990 than earlier, but it is not evident why that should have been so.

Another possibility is that certain housing markets have substantially higher housing values relative to incomes than other areas. High-growth areas, such as the three California MAs—Los Angeles, San Diego, and San Francisco—may have run up housing values so that housing values in their suburbs ranked high in the national sample, but their residents' incomes were not comparatively as high. Conversely, in some of the slow-growing or population-losing metropolitan areas, housing values may have slipped relative to the national sample, but the income of their residents may have been high, making housing values a lower multiple of annual family income in those areas than in most faster-growing MAs.

Income and Housing Age

Age of housing, according to most theories, should be related to income. If housing becomes more affordable to low- and moderate-income people as it ages, if new housing is typically affordable only to people above the median family income level, if new housing tends to be built closer to the periphery than to the center of metropolitan areas, and if many people prefer newer, larger housing and more land in more remote areas, as some theories assert, then age of housing in jurisdictions should be associated with current income levels and with future changes in income.

Average life spans of housing vary greatly in the United States (Baer 1991). But the need for greater reinvestment in housing as it ages is clear. Materials wear out, sometimes rather quickly. Roofs on many post-1950 residences, for example, may need to be replaced after 20 years. As the availability of conveniences, such as central air conditioning, has changed, the cost of reinvesting in older housing to bring it to contemporary standards also increases. Age of housing, therefore, provides clues both about quality of housing and about the cost of reinvestment.

In the 24 MAs in this study, 19.9 percent of the 1990 housing had been built before 1940. That was more than the national average, 18.4 percent in 1990. In the 24 central cities, an average of 37.1 percent of the housing was built before 1940. In the 554 suburbs, the average percentage of pre-1940 housing of the total 1990 housing stock was 19.6 percent. The range in these suburbs was quite large, from less than 1 percent in 20 suburbs to more than 60 percent in 15 suburbs.

The youthful end of the housing age spectrum can be measured by the percentage of 1990 housing units built between 1980 and 1990. For the nation, 20.7 percent of 1990 housing units were built during the previous decade. The average in the 24 MAs in this study was 18.3 percent. In the 24 central cities, however, the average was only 8.9 percent. In the 554 suburbs, 11.1 percent of the housing was built from 1980 through 1989, only slightly more recent housing having been built in these suburbs than in their central cities. In the 554 suburbs, the range was from less than 1 percent in 25 northeastern suburbs to more than 45 percent in eight suburbs in the Atlanta, Kansas City, San Diego, and Washington, D.C. MAs.

Plausible hypotheses are that old housing will be highly correlated with low median family income and new housing will be highly correlated with high median family income. In the 554 suburbs, however, there was a correlation of .00 between the percentage of housing built before 1940 and the median family income ratio of each jurisdiction in 1990. This correlation did not vary greatly from decade to decade; it was .03 in 1960, .04 in 1970, and .02 in 1980. For new housing, there was a correlation of .00 between the percentage of housing built in the 1980s and the 554 suburban jurisdictions' median family income ratios in 1990. None of these correlations, of course, were significant.

These correlations indicate the virtual absence of any consistent tendency for old housing and low income ratios to occur together. In addition, there was no tendency for new housing and high income ratios to occur together. That is, there were approximately as many instances of old housing being associated with high income ratios in suburbs, as there were instances of old housing being associated with low income ratios. Thus, old housing sometimes was associated with low income ratios and sometimes not, but the central tendency was no association.

The finding of no correlation between housing age and income ratios is unsettling in the context of several perspectives on urban theory. The absence of a correlation between old housing and income ratios also suggests that the conditions under which old housing is associated with either low or high incomes needs further exploration. The wide variability in income in relation to housing age opens the possibility that public policies, in addition to other conditions, may influence whether a suburb increases, reduces, or remains similar in its income relative to both older and newer suburbs.

Housing Age in Rapidly Declining Suburbs

Of the 112 suburbs where income declined faster than in their central cities from 1960 to 1990, we controlled for the differences in the age of the metropolitan areas by comparing how much age of housing deviated from the average in each metropolitan area. The fast-declining suburbs had higher percentages of 1990 housing built before 1960 than their respective MAs. Eighty-five of the 106 suburbs had more than the mean amount of pre-1960 housing in 1990. Sixty of them were more than 10 percent above the mean percentage of pre-1960 housing.

In another comparison, the percentage of 1990 housing built post-1980 was compared to more rapid relative income decline in suburbs than in central cities from 1960 to 1990. Only 11 of these 112 rapidly declining suburbs had more than the metropolitan area's percentage of post-1980 housing in their 1990 housing stock. These findings suggest that more than a mean share of old housing, and less than a mean share of new housing, makes suburban jurisdictions vulnerable to relative income decline. Yet in both of these circumstances, there was a wide scatter of performance in income change.

In the Atlanta MA, for example, four suburbs declined in income faster than the 30.7 percent income decline of Atlanta from 1960 to 1990. In those four suburbs, the percentage of housing built before 1940 was 6.9 percent, compared with a metropolitan average of 5.7 percent in 1990. A vast difference existed in new housing proportions, however, as only 4.2 percent of all 1990 housing in these four fast-declining Atlanta suburbs was constructed between 1980 and 1990, compared with a metropolitan average of 37.3 percent.

For the suburbs that declined faster than their central city, the average percentage of pre-1940 housing is reported in Table 7.1, along with the metropolitan average. In the same table, the average percentage of housing built during the 1980s is reported for these rapidly declining suburbs, and that is also compared with the metropolitan average in each instance. In most of the metropolitan areas, the rapidly declining suburbs had less new housing than the MA averages. The differences in the amounts of old housing in the rapidly declining suburbs and the MA averages varied greatly, sometimes being higher and sometimes lower. Overall, however, 19.8 percent of the 1990 housing in the 112 rapidly declining suburbs was built before 1940, compared with a 24-MA mean of 19.9 percent. In contrast, only 9.3 percent of their 1990 housing was built in the 1980s, compared with a 24-MA mean of 18.3 percent new housing. This pattern is consistent with an interpretation that large amounts of middle-aged housing (built from 1945 to 1970) and a shortage of post-1980 housing, rather than large amounts of old pre-1940 housing, tend to lead to relative income decline.

Housing Age Groupings

Because housing that is 30 years old typically needs substantial reinvestment to keep it from deteriorating, another age category that may be useful is housing built before 1960. The median age of the national housing stock was 25 years in 1990, meaning that one-half had been built before, and one-half was built after, 1965 (Devaney 1994). In the 24 study MAs, the average percentage of housing built before 1960 was 46 percent; in the central cities, 66 percent; in the 554 suburbs, 56 percent.

In the 94 suburbs where relative median family income decline exceeded 20 percent from 1960 to 1990, an average of 60 percent of the 1990 housing was constructed before 1960. Among the 24 suburbs that declined by 30 percent or more in relative income ratios from 1960 to 1990, the figure was 59 percent—slightly greater than the average of pre-1960 housing in all 554 suburbs studied (56 percent).

Of the 207 suburbs that declined by 5 percent or more between 1980 and 1990, an average of 56 percent of the housing was built before 1960, the same as the average for all 554 suburbs. While these averages hint at hypothesized relations, the variation around these means was large, and overall there was a correlation of only .06 between the percentage of 1990 housing built before 1960 and the change in relative median family income in the 554 suburbs between 1960 and 1990. This correlation was not statistically significant.

In this analysis, we also have tracked suburban jurisdictions by the decade in which construction of their 1990 housing units was concentrated. We considered a jurisdiction to have specialized in a particular decade if more than the metropolitan average proportion of its housing was constructed during that decade. In these 554 suburbs, there was a rising and then diminishing percentage of housing specialization. There were 205 suburbs with more than an average share of pre-1940 housing. Then there were 255 suburbs with more than an average share of 1940s housing, and a greater than average share in more recent decades as follows: 411 in the 1950s, 228 in the 1960s, 202 in the 1970s, and 128 in the 1980s.

Housing construction in most jurisdictions was concentrated in three or fewer decades; no single jurisdiction can be above average in all decades. Many of the 205 suburbs with more than an average proportion of 1990 housing constructed before 1940, for example, also had more than average proportions of housing constructed in the 1940s and 1950s, but few of them exceeded the average proportion of housing constructed in the 1960s, 1970s, and 1980s. In jurisdictions where housing construction was concentrated in the 1940s, it was usually concentrated in the 1950s as well, often with additional concentrations either before 1940 or in the 1960s or both, but rarely with concentrations in the 1970s or 1980s. Jurisdictions with 1950s concentrations often had 1940s and 1960s concentrations as well, but less often had concentrations before or after those decades. Jurisdictions that were substantially built out in a two- or three-decade time period probably were more vulnerable to decline in their income ratios by 1990.

Along with all of the foregoing comments about housing age and income, it is important to bear in mind that no direct information has been obtained or reported about income transitions in specific housing units by age or by any other indicator of housing conditions. Old housing could be attracting middle- and upper-income residents in aging jurisdictions, even though the jurisdictions were declining relative to other jurisdictions. The converse is also possible.

Was Decline Concentrated in Inner Suburbs?

If income, population, and housing value declines, and poverty increases, are related to aging housing, then inner suburbs, which tend to be older, should show more signs of decline than outer suburbs. One also can anticipate variation in status if, as Hoyt (1939) argued, housing quality and cost has varied by sectors as well as in rings of newer housing built on the periphery. But it is an open question whether inner and older suburbs, including higher-status suburbs, have been declining compared with more geographically intermediate and outer older suburbs.

Using maps, we examined the geographic positions of all 554 suburbs in the 24 metropolitan areas. Noting the position of each suburb relative to the central city and with respect to the other suburbs, we observed tendencies for ring and sector patterns of high- and low-income suburbs, and income-decreasing and income-increasing suburbs. In addition, other influences, such as ocean-, bay-, and lakeside locations and river proximity, were noted.

Sectors and Rings

In a majority of metropolitan areas, both sector and ring patterns appeared. In 15 metropolitan areas, inner ring suburbs declined, and outer ring suburbs increased in their median family income ratios, approximating ring patterns of income transition. In 18 metropolitan areas, however, strong inner, midrange, or outer suburban sector income ratio increases occurred. That is, income increases occurred in inner suburbs, as well as in intermediate and outer suburbs, in sectors radiating from the central cities. As in the Washington, D.C. metropolitan area described in Chapter 5, some older inner suburbs (Alexandria and Arlington) were prospering, while in other sectors (Prince George's County, Maryland), the inner suburbs were falling behind rapidly. In 16 metropolitan areas where fairly remote jurisdictions were included, separated sometimes by only a few miles from other suburbs in the sample, sizable increases in median family income ratios occurred. But in four metropolitan areas, remote jurisdictions experienced declines in their income ratios. The metropolitan areas where these ring and sector patterns occurred are listed in Table 7.4.

Interestingly, in four metropolitan areas, central cities surrounded suburbs. In the Detroit MA, Highland Park and Hamtramck were the lowest-income, and also most rapidly declining, jurisdictions in the region. In Dallas, two of the highest-income jurisdictions were surrounded by the city, and one was increasing while the other was decreasing rapidly in its income ratio. In Houston and Los Angeles, suburbs surrounded by the central city were prosperous and increasing in income ratios. Because Dallas, Houston, and Los Angeles have had vigorous annexation programs, these suburbs could have been on the edge of the city at one time, subsequently being encircled by annexed territory and becoming places close to the geographic centers of the main cities. Efforts to avoid annexation through incorporation sometimes seemingly backfire, as in Detroit's surrounded suburbs. In other instances, incorporation may be a successful defensive strategy, as in Houston and Los Angeles, at least for a while.

The most common condition was for both ring and sector patterns to be present. High-income, sometimes improving, inner and midrange sectors interrupted the ring pattern of poorer and declining suburbs near—often adjacent to—the central city. Anomalies sometimes occurred, with low-income suburbs being separated from the central city by several other suburbs. In most instances, these suburbs were on prominent rivers. This low-income river suburb phenomenon was especially prominent in the Philadelphia and Pittsburgh areas. In those instances, older industrial freestanding small cities had been engulfed years ago by the onrushing tide of suburbanization followed by exurbanization. In the Cincinnati area, some inner suburbs on the Ohio River were low income and some were high income. Cincinnati's "river views" are said to constitute a "competitive advantage" (Varady and Raffel 1995, 271) for the central city.

Oceans and Lakes

In the Los Angeles, Miami, San Diego, and San Francisco MAs, many of the wealthy and, in particular, the income-increasing suburbs were on the coasts of the Pacific or Atlantic Ocean, while the suburbs with declining incomes were usually inland. Similar income-enhancing effects related to suburbs with frontage on Lake Michigan appeared in the Chicago and Milwaukee metropolitan areas, and in Seattle with respect to frontage on Puget Sound and Lake Washington. In New York, some of the income-increasing suburbs were on Long Island with Atlantic Ocean frontage, although suburbs elsewhere also increased in income ratios. On the other hand, several of the declining inner suburbs in the Boston area were on the coast of Massachusetts Bay northeast of the city.

In sum, support can be found in the income-increasing and income-declining suburbs of these 24 metropolitan areas for both the sector and ring models of metropolitan evolution, as well as for the influence of coastal and lakefront water as an aesthetic amenity. When these spatial patterns are combined with information about jurisdictions' housing age, tenure, and racial change, and metropolitan scale information about population growth rates and city share of population, then income and population transition results usually seem understandable in specific suburbs.

Speculations about Influences

The postsuburban era is characterized by substantial suburban income and population decline, growing suburban employment proportions, less outcommuting from the main suburban employment counties, rapid population and income increases in exurban rural counties, and rapid farmland loss in exurban rural counties (Lucy and Phillips 1997). A faster rate of income volatility among suburbs compared with each other, in addition to greater disparities emerging among suburbs and more suburbs declining by higher rates, is more common during this postsuburban era.

A number of expectations at the outset of this study were confirmed to some extent by the findings. In general, the older suburbs in this study declined in income and population. Many suburbs declined faster than central cities. In the future, even more suburbs may increase their rates of income and population decline. Housing age was associated with decline when these older jurisdictions were compared with the incomes of the newer parts of 20 of the 24 metropolitan areas. But within the sample of 554 suburbs, housing age was not associated with income decline. Within the middle range of older housing, no statistical associations between housing age and income decline were observed. This outcome would occur if middle-aged housing built between 1945 and 1970, and neighborhoods and jurisdictions dominated by such housing, are the main locations of suburban relative income decline. This influence seems consistent with our findings.

Additional speculations about why this finding occurred should include these possibilities: Does the initial quality of construction enable some jurisdictions to persist in their income standing? Have some middle- and upper-income jurisdictions been more successful than the norm in maintaining safe streets, high-quality public schools, and reinvestment in housing and local businesses? Have

Modest 1950s housing in Chesterfield County, Virginia, is in one of the "declining" suburbs in the Richmond metropolitan region.

certain types of jurisdictions been able to resist the effects of age? To what extent have the multicentered metropolitan area and the multifocused activity patterns of households modified the dynamics of monocentric residential market decisions?

Have some relatively remote villages with substantial old housing been targets of exurban expansion, bringing new blood and higher-income residents to long-established settlements? Have key location features, such as coastal or shore amenities and proximity to commuter rail stations and fixed-rail mass transit, contributed to some jurisdictions' stability, revival, or improvement as their housing has aged? Have planning and design characteristics, such as attractive architecture, grid street patterns, convenient access to employment, shopping, and entertainment, public transportation alternatives, and walkable neighborhoods combined to attract reinvestment and middle- and upper-income residents? Are some of these jurisdictions home to major institutions, such as colleges and universities, which may have employees who prefer short distances to work and other conveniences more strongly than is typical of the general population? Findings in this study increase our belief that some of these conditions have brought about the results described here.

Chapter 8

Housing and Neighborhood Decline: Struggles of Middle Age

In theory and practice, housing age is ambiguously related to neighborhood decline. Aging of housing is associated with transition of dwellings, neighborhoods, and jurisdictions from higher-income to lower-income status in several spatial theories. In practice, materials and systems in dwellings wear out with age, requiring reinvestment to maintain or improve their quality. Findings reported in Chapters 6 and 7 indicated that most cities and many suburbs have declined in relative income over time. Other findings in Chapter 7 revealed little statistical association between housing age and relative income decline in 554 suburbs. Still, the pattern of income decline is consistent with an interpretation that middle-aged (1945 to 1970) housing, rather than older housing, is prominent in declining suburbs. Physical decline will obviously occur without substantial reinvestment. Age of housing, therefore, provides clues about dangers that are relevant for strategic planning. Housing age seems to be one element among several contributors to forces of neighborhood decline.

In this chapter, we discuss the decision-making environment that limits reinvestment in many neighborhoods and jurisdictions. The role of aging housing in neighborhoods and jurisdictions is one crucial aspect of the decision-making environment. Far more is involved in the issue of housing reinvestment, however, than age alone. Some relationships between setting, age, and demand can be inferred from analyses that indicate that reinvestment has occurred in much older housing and in many older neighborhoods in cities and suburbs. We also discuss whether reinvestment in middle-aged suburban (and city) neighborhoods may be as prevalent in the future as in older central city and suburban neighborhoods.

Housing Age and Value

Most theories of housing, neighborhood, and city transitions point toward a similar conclusion: aging is associated with decline in value relative to newer housing and increasing occupancy by lower-income people compared with ear-

197

lier occupants. Whether one considers filtering, vacancy chains, trickle-down neighborhood change, concentric zones, or sector concepts of spatial transitions, the anticipated outcome from these perspectives is that older housing will be occupied by persons of lower relative incomes than those who occupy newly built housing.

Research on residential mobility has revealed that housing characteristics interacting with life cycle (and lifestyle) changes are the most important influences on decisions to move (Goodman 1979; Michelson 1977; Rossi and Shlay 1982; Speare, Goldstein, and Frey 1974). Relatively little destination research, or research on why relocaters choose particular residential locations, has been conducted (Tobin and Judd 1982; Varady and Raffel 1995). But based on research about reasons for moving, as well as destination research, it follows that satisfactory housing influences most movers' destination selections. Other reasons are important for some movers, including convenience, schools, and access to work. Perceived safety (which may not be the same as real safety) is probably important, although there has not been much research about this factor.

Neighborhoods and jurisdictions depend on reinvestment to be sustainable in the long run. In the near term, settlements also need reinvestment to survive longer than the life of basic structural elements. Propensity for reinvestment depends on interactions between buyers' preferences and institutions' decisions about investment opportunities in light of their missions and decision rules. On

Remodeling of suburban homes can include new roofs, air conditioning, garage and room additions, and garden decks and exterior living spaces.

balance, buyers' preferences and institutions' decisions have favored new invest-ment in greenfield settings sufficiently that more new development, usually in a sprawl pattern, has occurred than is compatible with adequate reinvestment to sustain most existing communities in the long run. The loan criteria of the FHA and the VHA, especially from the 1930s through the 1950s, favored new sub-divisions over traditional, usually central city, neighborhoods (Moe and Wilkie 1997). In 1998, remodeling and repair expenditures on existing housing (more than 98 percent of total housing units) were less than spending on new housing (less than 2 percent of total units) (Harvard Joint Center for Housing Studies 1999). Moreover, the longevity of housing has varied by a factor of two among metropolitan areas. For example, in Indianapolis the average life span of hous-ing from construction to demolition has been 100 years, while in Phoenix it has been 40 years (Baer 1991, 327). Housing's longevity is not only a matter of dete-riorating building materials and systems but also a function of owners' willing-ness and ability to reinvest.

These theoretical and historical perspectives indicate that housing reinvest-ment has been limited and that many neighborhoods and jurisdictions will decline with age. They suggest that the public and private environment for housing reinvestment is a serious weakness in many jurisdictions. The environ-ment for housing reinvestment is considerably more varied and complex than these perspectives suggest. In our research, we found that many older neighbor-hoods and jurisdictions have stabilized and revived. Housing age alone is a flawed predictor of trends. Further evidence of the limited usefulness of housing age as a predictor can be gleaned from data that relate age of housing to the value of housing (Tables 8.1 and 8.2).

Housing Age and Value in 44 Metropolitan Areas

Deterioration of housing, and reinvestment in it, should be reflected in hous-ing values. Housing values reflect demand within the available supply. If a sim-ilar array of housing quality and value has been constructed during each decade, then the value of each decade's housing that exists at recent dates should provide clues about how much deterioration and reinvestment have occurred. Such data are available in the American Housing Survey conducted periodically by the U.S. Bureau of the Census. From this source, data for 44 metropolitan areas were available for 1989 through 1995. To test the relation-ship of housing age to the value of owner-occupied housing, the following comparisons were calculated: the time periods when housing had the lowest and highest median values, the number of time periods when housing was val-ued lower than the oldest housing (pre-1920 and 1920–29), the percentage dif-ference between each time period's housing values, and the median value of all owner-occupied housing in each metropolitan area (Table 8.1). Data were reported for the pre-1920 period, by decade from 1920 through 1970, and by

Table 8.1. Median Value of Owner-Occupied Housing Units

Metropolitan Area	Survey Year	Highest Period	Lowest Period	Number of Periods Lower Than		Percentage Difference from Median of All Housing			
				Pre-1920	1920s	Pre-1920	1920-29	1930-39	1940-49
Anaheim–Santa Ana	1994	1990–94	1950–59	No data	No data	—	—	-8.9	+6.7
Atlanta	1991	1985–89	1930–39	4	5	-8.9	-1.4	-30.3	-16.1
Baltimore	1991	1990–94	1920–29	1	0	-29.4	-32.0	-27.3	-27.7
Birmingham	1992	1990–94	Pre-1920	0	3	-31.2	-22.6	-27.9	-25.2
Boston	1989	1980–84	Pre-1920	0	1	-7.8	-6.2	-3.6	+3.0
Buffalo	1994	1990–94	1920–29	1	0	-31.4	-35.3	-20.0	-5.0
Charlotte	1995	1990–94	1940–49	2	7	-18.6	-0.0	-21.9	-27.6
Chicago	1995	1985–89	Pre-1920	0	1	-29.6	-16.2	-14.9	-9.4
Cincinnati	1990	1985–89	1930–39	1	3	-23.4	-12.6	-24.1	-15.2
Cleveland	1992	1990–94	Pre-1920	0	2	-32.1	-28.4	-32.0	-13.2
Columbus	1995	1990–94	1940–49	4	3	-9.3	-14.1	-24.0	-25.5
Dallas	1994	1990–94	1940–49	No data	No data	—	—	-33.1	-36.6
Denver	1995	1990–94	1940–49	2	3	-19.8	-10.4	-7.6	-25.5
Detroit	1995	1990–94	1940–49	2	4	-23.9	-6.8	-30.0	-32.4
Fort Worth	1994	1990–94	1930–39	No data	3	—	-19.9	-49.2	-44.0
Hartford	1991	1980–84	Pre-1920	0	2	-16.6	-10.0	-6.5	-10.7
Houston	1991	1990–94	1940–49	No data	2	—	-18.4	-16.7	-33.1
Indianapolis	1992	1990–94	1930–39	3	1	-22.8	-29.0	-33.6	-25.9
Kansas City	1995	1990–94	1930–39	1	3	-40.0	-25.0	-40.1	-29.1
Los Angeles	1995	1990–94	1980–84	No data	6	—	+1.9	-3.9	+0.5
Memphis	1992	1985–89	1940–49	7	5	+18.3	+4.3	-26.4	-31.0
Milwaukee	1994	1990–94	Pre-1920	0	1	-36.8	-28.1	-27.1	-18.5
Minneapolis–St. Paul	1989	1985–89	Pre-1920	0	2	-20.7	-13.8	-14.2	-12.0
New Orleans	1995	1990–94	1940–49	6	9	+1.9	+7.2	-9.3	-10.2

City									
New York–Nassau–Suffolk	1995	1990–94	Pre-1920	0	4	-3.4	-1.1	-3.3	-0.7
Norfolk–Virginia Beach	1992	1990–94	1930–39	2	3	-19.3	-18.2	-27.7	-20.5
Northern New Jersey	1995	1960–69	Pre-1920	0	5	-19.0	-0.6	-5.7	-4.6
Oklahoma City	1992	1990–94	1930–39	3	2	-30.9	-33.1	-44.0	-35.0
Philadelphia	1995	1985–89	1920–29	1	0	-35.6	-37.0	-31.4	-15.8
Phoenix	1994	1990–94	1950–59	No data	No data	—	—	—	-22.0
Pittsburgh	1995	1990–94	Pre-1920	0	1	-33.7	-32.6	-14.9	-11.5
Portland, Oregon	1995	1990–94	1920–29	3	0	-9.2	-20.8	-13.2	-12.7
Providence	1992	1990–94	1920–29	1	0	-16.0	-20.6	-9.7	-4.1
Riverside–San Bernardino–Ontario	1994	1985–89	1970–74	No data	No data	—	—	-9.7	-10.9
Rochester	1990	1985–89	Pre-1920	0	1	-20.8	-17.7	-16.7	-14.7
Salt Lake City	1992	1990–94	1930–39	3	1	-10.1	-16.5	-23.6	-11.0
San Antonio	1995	1990–94	1930–39	4	2	-21.4	-32.0	-33.6	-33.0
San Diego	1994	1990–94	1930–39	No data	No data	—	—	-17.0	-15.3
San Francisco–Oakland	1993	1990–94	1970–74	4	2	-1.3	-1.7	+6.9	-4.2
San Jose	1993	1990–94 and 1920–29	1970–74	6	9	+9.5	+17.1	+6.5	+13.7
Seattle-Tacoma	1991	1990–94	1970–74	2	4	-7.5	-5.5	-0.2	-8.0
St. Louis	1991	1985–89	1930–39	3	2	-19.3	-23.4	-33.0	-23.6
Tampa–St. Petersburg	1993	1990–94	1970–74	No data	6	—	+1.6	-11.0	-16.2
Washington, D.C.	1993	Pre-1920	1930–39	10	7	+29.2	+1.8	-15.8	-10.4
MEAN				2.1	2.9				
MEDIAN				1.6	2.5				

Sources: U.S. Bureau of the Census, *American Housing Survey* (annual surveys 1990–1996)

Table 8.2. Housing Age Period with
Highest and Lowest Median Value of
Owner-Occupied Housing Units

	Number of Metropolitan Areas	
	Highest Period	*Lowest Period*
Pre-1920	1	11
1920–29	1	5
1930–39	0	12
1940–49	0	8
1950–59	0	2
1960–69	1	0
1970–74	0	5
1975–79	0	0
1980–84	2	1
1985–89	9	0
1990–94	31	0

Source: U.S. Bureau of the Census, *American Housing Survey*
(annual surveys 1990–96)

five-year periods from 1970 through 1994, based on a sample of 5,000 residences in each metropolitan area.

If housing as it ages·is in less demand by higher-income people, who can choose housing in many locations and from many time periods, then the oldest housing would be the lowest valued. Looking at a national sample of housing, this downward slope was the norm. The median oldest housing (pre-1920) was valued at 19 percent below the overall median, while the newest housing (1990–94) was valued at 45 percent more (U.S. Bureau of the Census 1997).

Housing markets operate primarily within metropolitan commuting territories, however, not nationally. Trends within each metropolitan area, therefore, provide more revealing information. From this vantage point, the oldest housing (pre-1920) was valued lowest in only 11 (Birmingham, Boston, Chicago, Cleveland, Hartford, Milwaukee, Minneapolis–St.Paul, New York City–Nassau–Suffolk, Northern New Jersey, Pittsburgh, and Rochester) of the 35 metropolitan areas with such data. In the remaining nine metropolitan areas in the sample, 1920s housing was not the lowest valued in any metropolitan area, and 1930s housing was both oldest and lowest valued in only one of them (San Diego). The oldest housing, therefore, was lowest valued in only 12 of 44 metropolitan areas (27 percent). The significance of this finding in 27 percent of the metropolitan areas is diminished further by the modest difference between the oldest housing and the median value of all housing in some metropolitan areas.

In the New York City–Nassau–Suffolk area, for example, the pre-1920 housing was lowest valued, but it was only 3.3 percent below the median value of all housing. In the Boston MA, the lowest-valued pre-1920 housing was only 7.8 percent below the overall median. It is important to understand this 27 percent of metropolitan areas in which the oldest housing is least valued. The filtering, vacancy chain, trickle-down, concentric, and sector concepts, in some combination, may aid such understanding, but they need support from other concepts in explaining the other 73 percent.

Moreover, the relationship of housing age to median housing value represented a diverse configuration of conditions in the remaining 32 metropolitan areas (Table 8.1). The housing with the lowest median value was constructed in the 1920s in five metropolitan areas (Baltimore; Buffalo; Philadelphia; Portland, Oregon; and Providence), in the 1930s in 11 metropolitan areas (Atlanta, Cincinnati, Fort Worth, Indianapolis, Kansas City, Norfolk–Virginia Beach–Newport News, Oklahoma City, St. Louis, Salt Lake City, San Antonio, and Washington, D.C.), in the 1940s in eight metropolitan areas (Charlotte, Columbus, Dallas, Denver, Detroit, Houston, Memphis, and New Orleans), in the 1950s in two metropolitan areas (Anaheim–Santa Ana and Phoenix), in the 1970–74 period in five metropolitan areas (Riverside–San Bernardino–Ontario, San Francisco–Oakland, San Jose, Seattle-Tacoma, and Tampa–St. Petersburg), and in the 1980–84 period in one metropolitan area (Los Angeles).

In addition, median values in the pre-1950 period showed considerable variation when time periods were compared with each other. Housing built in the 1920s tended to be higher in value than housing built in other periods. Counting only those metropolitan areas where the differences among decades were 1 percent or more, housing built in the 1920s was more valued in 21 of 34 metropolitan areas compared with pre-1920 housing, it was more valued in 23 of 38 metropolitan areas compared with 1930s housing, and it was more valued in 23 of 37 metropolitan areas compared with 1940s housing. Furthermore, there was little difference in the number of metropolitan areas where pre-1920 housing was more, or less, valuable than 1930s or 1940s housing. Pre-1920 housing was more valued than 1930s housing, using the 1 percent or greater difference as above, in 14 of 31 metropolitan areas and in 15 of 33 metropolitan areas compared with 1940s housing. Again, there is little support in these relationships for the belief that housing is usually less valued as it ages.

On the other hand, the belief that new housing tends to have the highest median value was supported by conditions in most of these 44 metropolitan areas. In 31 metropolitan areas, the housing with the highest median value was built from 1990 through 1994, in nine from 1985 through 1989, and in two from 1980 through 1984. The exceptions were Northern New Jersey, where it was built from 1960 through 1969; San Jose, where housing built in the 1920s tied with 1990–94 housing for highest value; and Washington, D.C., where pre-1920 housing was much more valuable than even the most recent housing (Tables 8.1 and 8.2).

The distribution of high- and low-value housing by time periods reveals further puzzles. Why should old housing exceed or tie the value of the new housing in such disparate metropolitan areas as Washington, D.C. and San Jose? And if new housing is usually most valued, why is older housing in these metropolitan areas so varied in value? Perhaps housing that was built in certain decades, such as the 1920s, and that has not been demolished or converted to other uses, had characteristics, such as size, quality of materials, design features, access, and proximity, that helped it hold its value better than housing built in other decades (Gale 1979). George Galster (1987, 226) found the following results in a sample survey of homeowners in Wooster, Ohio (1975), and Minneapolis (1980): "Structural age is associated with progressively higher upkeep expenditures up to a point where expenditures slacken. Compared to a home built since 1969, annual average expenditure on a 1940–1969 vintage home is 70 percent more; on a 1920–39 vintage is 136 percent more; on a pre-1920 vintage is 91 percent more. Such expenditures appear adequate to negate the higher rate of depreciation associated with age completely: older homes are no more likely to evidence exterior defects than others are, all else equal." At a minimum, evidence indicates that housing values are not consistently related to age of housing. Housing values are subject to multiple causation, and potential influences can vary over time (DeGiovanni 1983). Given this modest assessment, policy makers can conclude that a complex environment exists in which to formulate housing reinvestment policies, an environment containing opportunities as well as dangers.

Neighborhood Age and Income Change

As housing ages, most conceptual views of neighborhoods hold that the incomes of neighborhood residents will tend to decline relative to each metropolitan area's median income. On the contrary, a majority of pre-1940 neighborhoods were rising in relative income during the 1980s in three metropolitan areas in Virginia. In contrast, most neighborhoods with prominent 1950s and 1960s housing were declining in relative income. Incomes were rising, as expected, in most (but not all) neighborhoods dominated by 1980s housing.

In the Norfolk–Virginia Beach–Newport News metropolitan area, pre-1940 housing constituted more than 40 percent of total 1990 housing in 17 census tracts distributed as follows: Norfolk 8, Portsmouth 5, Hampton 2, Newport News 1, and Chesapeake 1. Of all 272 census tracts in this MA, median family income increased in 39 percent relative to the change in the metropolitan median income between 1980 and 1990. Median family income increased in 59 percent of the census tracts in which pre-1940 housing was prominent. Moreover, relative income increases exceeding 10 percent occurred in 35 percent of the census tracts dominated by pre-1940 housing, compared with such increases in 17 percent of total tracts. In Norfolk and Portsmouth, incomes in most census tracts (66 percent and 70 percent) were declining in the 1980s. But in most of their pre-1940 census tracts, relative incomes were rising (63 percent of Norfolk's eight tracts, and 60 percent of Portsmouth's five) during the 1980s (Lucy and Phillips 1996a).

In the Richmond–Petersburg, Virginia, metropolitan area, pre-1940 housing was common in the central city. In 24 of Richmond's 67 census tracts, 40 percent or more of the housing was built before 1940. Median family income in Richmond declined citywide in the 1980s relative to metropolitan income. In 72 percent of 43 census tracts where pre-1940 housing was less than 40 percent of total 1990 housing, relative income declined. In contrast, where 40 percent or more of the housing dated from before 1940, the reverse trend occurred, with relative median family income increasing in 63 percent of these 24 tracts. The contrast was more dramatic in terms of relative income increases of 10 percent or more: such increases occurred in 11 of 24 census tracts with prominent old housing (46 percent), but in only three of the remaining 43 census tracts (7 percent) (Lucy and Phillips 1996b).

Similar trends occurred between 1980 and 1990 in the Northern Virginia subregion of the Washington, D.C. metropolitan area. Forty percent or more of the 1990 housing had been built before 1940 in only six census tracts. Median family income increased in each, with increases of 10 percent or more in five of the six tracts. Relative income increases also occurred in 76 percent of the 80 tracts with 5 to 40 percent of their housing built before 1940. In contrast, income increases occurred in only 46 percent of the 193 census tracts where less than 5 percent of the housing was built before 1940 (Lucy and Phillips 1996c). From these much greater propensities for relative incomes to rise in census tracts with only small amounts of pre-1940 housing, we infer that neighborhood characteristics also may have appealed to inmovers. The appeal may have been based on internal neighborhood characteristics or on proximity to work, entertainment, dining, and shopping areas outside these neighborhoods.

Income Decline in Middle-Aged Neighborhoods

Given trends of income increasing in many fairly old neighborhoods and new neighborhoods, many middle-aged neighborhoods must have had less appeal. Hence, they were less likely to increase in relative income between 1980 and 1990. In the Richmond and Northern Virginia regions, we examined income changes in census tracts in relation to the decades when housing was constructed. Average percentages of housing constructed during each decade were identified from 1940 to 1990 and before 1940. Construction averages in each census tract were compared with metropolitan (or subregional in Northern Virginia) averages. Census tracts with more than the metropolitan average constructed during any single time period were said to have specialized in housing of that period—say, 1950s housing or 1980s housing. Consistent with other findings, relative income tended to rise in census tracts that specialized in either pre-1940 housing or 1980s housing.

This analytic method was most useful in revealing changes in neighborhoods dominated by middle-aged (especially 1950s and 1960s) housing. In suburban Henrico County, which wraps around Richmond from northwest to northeast (see Map 4.1 in Chapter 4), about half of the 24 census tracts that specialized in 1980s housing experienced relative income increases during the 1980s. But in the census tracts specializing in the housing of earlier decades, relative income declined in three-fourths of them; the largest number of these tracts specialized in housing built in the 1950s and 1960s. In suburban Chesterfield County to the south and west of Richmond, nearly all of the census tracts where relative income increases occurred had specialized in 1980s housing. In Chesterfield's middle-aged 1950s and 1960s specialized census tracts, relative income declined in 19 of 26 tracts.

In Northern Virginia, relative median family income increased in 56 percent of all census tracts and in 69 percent of tracts that specialized in 1980s housing. Income changes in middle-aged 1950s and 1960s housing specialized tracts were quite different, especially in Fairfax County, where relative income increases occurred in as few as 32 percent of the tracts that specialized in 1960s housing and 40 percent of the tracts specializing in 1950s housing (Table 8.3).

These findings call into question traditional theories about older housing, neighborhoods, and jurisdictions becoming occupied increasingly over time by lower-income people. Something about the settings or the housing that was 50 or more years old in 1990 led to income stability or income increases. Conversely, something about the housing built in the 1940s, 1950s, 1960s, and even 1970s, or their settings, made them less attractive to people who could afford a wide array of housing and location options.

In the suburbs around Richmond (Chesterfield and Henrico Counties), only the census tracts dominated by 1980s housing were as likely to increase as decrease in relative income. Three-fourths of other neighborhoods declined in relative income in these suburban counties. This dependence on new housing for income stability indicated modest to weak attractions of houses and settings in Henrico and Chesterfield. Places had not been created that commanded sufficient loyalty from stayers and attraction for replacement inmovers to sustain relative income levels. Limited attractive power is a strategic planning problem in these counties and may be one in other suburban counties as well.

Table 8.3. Improving Suburban Census Tracts by Housing Age Specialization of 1990 Housing Stock: Northern Virginia

	Older Housing				Middle-Aged Housing				Newer Housing				
	Pre-1940	1940s	Both Pre-1940 and 1940s	One or Both Periods	1950s	1960s	Both 1950s and 1960s	One or Both Periods	1970s	1980s	Both 1970s and 1980s	One or Both Periods	Total
Arlington County													
Increasing Relative Income	17	19	15	21	15	5	3	17	1	3	0	4	21
All Specialized Tracts	29	34	26	37	26	14	8	32	3	5	1	7	39
Percentage	59%	56%	58%	57%	58%	36%	38%	53%	33%	60%	0%	57%	54%
Alexandria City													
Increasing Relative Income	14	15	10	19	11	7	5	13	4	0	0	4	21
All Specialized Tracts	16	17	11	22	15	14	8	21	9	1	1	9	32
Percentage	88%	88%	91%	86%	73%	50%	63%	62%	44%	0%	0%	44%	66%
Fairfax County													
Increasing Relative Income	6	16	2	17	21	21	10	31	39	45	27	57	74
All Specialized Tracts	9	19	4	24	53	66	35	84	73	62	41	94	142
Percentage	67%	84%	50%	71%	40%	32%	29%	37%	53%	73%	66%	61%	52%
Total Northern Virginia													
Increasing Relative Income	50	52	31	71	55	44	24	75	66	75	45	96	
All Specialized Tracts	71	78	46	103	110	118	62	166	123	109	72	160	
Percentage	70%	67%	67%	69%	50%	37%	39%	45%	54%	69%	63%	60%	

Note: The tracts used in the analysis were 1980 census tracts. Where necessary, 1990 data were proportioned into the 1980 tracts to measure the change in relative median family income. Specialization is measured by comparing the percentage of existing 1990 housing units built during a time period with the same figure for the entire metropolitan area. For the purposes of this table, a tract is considered "specialized" if its percentage exceeded the metropolitan percentage.

Why Suburbs May Decline Rapidly

When they were developed, the 1950s and 1960s suburban neighborhoods were said to be causing the downfall of central cities. In light of that history, why they now may be leading sectors of decline is an intriguing question. Following are speculations offering plausible answers.

Sometimes suburban housing was developed to modest standards over wide swaths of land during a short time frame. In these areas, housing aged in unison, creating special pressures on people considering whether to reinvest in maintaining and upgrading their property. After 30 or 40 years, this housing—much of which never was large or grand—needed major maintenance expenditures just to remain habitable. By 1998, the U.S. housing stock's median age was 30 years (Harvard Joint Center for Housing Studies 1999). If outmovement from the city and population growth in the region has expanded the number of home seekers, a lower-income group of buyers and renters is likely to occupy housing of modest quality.

Low- and moderate-income people usually occupy used housing, often past its prime, rather than new or well-maintained, high-quality older housing (Downs 1981). They occupy housing that is relatively affordable. With a rising percentage of the population paying 35 percent or more of their income for housing (Devaney 1994), modest middle-aged and older housing may not be affordable either, but it is the only housing within financial reach. With substantial population expansion, modest-quality middle-aged housing is likely to be occupied by a larger number of low- and moderate-income people.

Roof replacement project.

In suburbs with homogeneous housing age and quality, this occupancy transition process may escalate. Indeed, the conventional wisdom is that substantial reinvestment in such situations is unwise financially. A column in the *Charlottesville Daily Progress* (1998, reprinted from *Popular Mechanics*), summarized this common view as follows: "...if you're [remodeling] as an investment, you want to make sure you don't outprice other houses in your neighborhood. For example, if you own a house worth $90,000 in a neighborhood where the top houses sell for $100,000 and you sink $50,000 into an elaborate renovation, your chances of getting $140,000 at resale are remote at best. People looking for $140,000 houses don't buy houses in a $100,000 neighborhood. A good rule of thumb: Make sure the current market value of your house plus planned improvements doesn't exceed the value of the better houses in your area by 20 percent. That would mean limiting the renovation on a $90,000 house to about $30,000 tops."

Homeowners' and Buyers' Finances

Financial characteristics of owners and buyers of modest-quality, middle-aged housing also illustrate obstacles to major reinvestments. Savings and transitory income increases (tax refunds, bonuses, and credit cards) finance most home improvements, with only 14 percent coming from bank loans (Samadd 1998). Median household savings in the mid-1990s were only $24,000 (Chatterjee 1996). Most homeowners are not likely to invest modest savings in home improvements in risky, marginal neighborhoods. In 1998, homes constituted the largest source of invested wealth for a majority of all homeowners (Harvard Joint Center for Housing Studies 1999). Home equity loans for reinvestment also tend to cost homeowners about 1 percent or more than rates charged on 15-year mortgage loans for purchasing residences, and they have much shorter repayment periods. Moreover, new buyers in such neighborhoods are likely to have committed most of their savings and borrowing capacity to finance the purchase. First-time buyers, even though they are looking ahead to years of occupancy, may not be more likely to expand and upgrade than are current owners who have built up equity. Second-time buyers are more likely to bring equity for upgrading from selling their first dwelling (Harvard Joint Center for Housing Studies 1999).

Suburban separation of land uses, auto dependence, and the absence of nonprofit institutions nearby may accelerate the decline process. Institutions such as government centers, universities, cultural facilities, aesthetic attractions such as interesting architecture, and convenient, walkable mixed-use environments are not present in most suburban neighborhoods. Nonprofit institutions can nurture neighborhood reinvestment when market conditions are questionable. Moreover, major employers formerly located in suburban sites may have moved, leaving a void in some suburbs' attractive capacity. In other suburbs, new job

These older Charlottesville homes have undergone two rounds of reinvestment: first from single-family to student apartments, and more recently from apartments to remodeled single-family homes.

centers may have been created, bringing more traffic, noise, and pollution and disrupting the tranquillity that had inspired many previous residents to move in.

City neighborhoods are more apt to have the advantages of nonprofit institutions, interesting architecture, walkable neighborhoods, and access to mass transit. For the segment of the population that values these qualities, few suburbs will offer attractive alternatives. The attractiveness of substantial portions of cities and inner suburbs to middle- and upper-income people may increase even as other, usually larger, areas of these cities decline, and while some inner suburbs and other suburbs built to modest standards decline also. Gentrification in some city neighborhoods also may displace some longtime renters by leading to higher rents as well as higher purchase prices (Henig 1980; Wald 1987).

Dangers in Suburbs

Dangers faced by many suburbs have captured the news media's attention. Richmond's newspaper, for instance, has featured many articles about crises in suburbia, including one with the banner headline "Saving the Suburbs" that left doubt about suburbs' prospects (Smith 1996). A commentary in the *Chicago Tribune* (McCarron 1998) argued that the central city was coming back. While acknowledging that downtown's revival had not improved most neighborhoods, the author went on to emphasize "the far more dangerous, longer-term situation that is developing elsewhere on the metropolitan map. Consider Harvey, a south suburb that, along with 13 others in Cook County, has a higher crime rate than Chicago. It's a place where the tax base is so depleted that the owners of a house worth $100,000 must pay about $5,500 a year in taxes, or three times what they'd pay in Barrington Hills. . . . The Harveys . . . have no lakefront, no cultural treasures, no sophisticated urban cachet around which to stage a comeback. They have no rich part of town—no Gold Coast, where rising property values may one day fund the kind of school reform and community policing initiatives that are starting to show results in Chicago." A *USA Today* front-page article (Nasser 1999) was headlined "Soaring Housing Costs Are Culprit in Suburban Poverty," and set the suburban scene as follows: ". . . [I]n growing numbers, poor people are living unnoticed next to middle-class families, and the suburbs are beginning to face the same problems cities have struggled with since the flight to the suburbs began in the 1950s."

The Harveys, and hundreds of similar suburbs, do not attract the concern or loyalty of economic and political elites. Whereas some will say the vitality of Chicago is crucial to the health of the Chicago metropolitan area, few would say that about Harvey or even about a substantial collection of Harveys. Given such suburbs' independent endangered school systems, and few if any meaningful cultural resources, which inside or outside political and economic forces can be expected to make turning around the Harveys a concern or a cause?

Reinvestment Challenges: Neighborhoods, Size, and Age

The processes of housing and neighborhood deterioration and decline present difficult strategic planning challenges. As suburbs reach middle age, they may be no more successful, or even less successful, than central cities in coping with deterioration. Here we will consider three dimensions of this challenge—neighborhood effects, size of dwelling problems, and physical deterioration with age.

With each of these dimensions, a crucial hurdle is to secure reinvestment in existing structures and facilities. Reinvestment depends on whether the holders of capital, and those who can gain access to it, are sufficiently motivated to reinvest in existing settlements versus investing in new settlements. Neighborhood effects come into play— that is, reinvestment decisions are not based solely on the condition or attractiveness of structures; the nearby, intermediate, and commuting dimension of settings also influences whether the quality of living in a given structure will be reinforced by the quality of living in the environs of that structure. In addition, reinvestment in structures is related to expectations about a neighborhood's future. Galster (1987, 229) found in Wooster and Minneapolis that "pessimistic expectations about qualitative neighborhood changes are associated with less home reinvestment. Compared to the most optimistic homeowners, the most pessimistic ones are likely to spend 61 percent less annually on their homes. . . . If homeowners perceive the quality of their areas as improving, they will flow with the trend and intensify their own reinvestment behaviors. . . . The upshot is that homeowner responses reinforce the qualitative changes the homeowners originally foresaw: the self-fulfilling prophecy." Neighborhoods pose a multitude of reinvestment challenges, some of which flow from the character of the structures and others that are related to the physical and social character of the environs. Three illustrations will enrich this observation.

Old Neighborhood

These neighborhoods are dominated by pre-1940, and much pre-1920, housing. Some have been gentrified; some never declined markedly, because of characteristics of their structures and proximity—close enough to be convenient for residents, not close enough to be business sites for an expanding central business district. Some have experienced modest and intermittent reinvestment. Some have decayed, particularly those close to 19th-century manufacturing factories. Many buildings in decayed versions of these neighborhoods have been demolished and not replaced.

Neighborhoods of this vintage have often been described as experiencing stages of decline and sometimes revival. Middle- to upper-income people first occupy new dwellings. Three forces, separately or together, may reduce the attractiveness of the neighborhood—deterioration through age, requiring repair and replacement; more appealing housing built elsewhere; and intrusions by business activity, traffic, or social problems into the neighborhood. Some replacement residents have less money to invest in upkeep. Some structures are not maintained. Some properties convert from owner to renter status. Some landlords disinvest, limiting repair and replacement as they calculate business costs and benefits. Such processes may be accelerated by institutional practices (redlining or foreclosures by lenders, racially inspired blockbusting by Realtors and speculators, dual market discrimination against minorities in some neighborhoods, rental property depreciation rules for federal income taxes) (Lauria 1998; Varady 1986, 6-10).

Stages of revitalization also have been described. First, young couples, including professionals and designers, move in to stay, investing their savings and "sweat equity." They are followed by other young professionals who are more sensitive to risk but who have been encouraged by improvements made by the preceding pioneers. Prices rise. Some displacement occurs. Then more affluent residents move in, and some investors speculate on rapid gains well in excess of improvements. Displacement increases. The population has changed greatly. Property values and taxes are high (Clay 1979; DeGiovanni 1983; Gale 1980). Analysts disagree about the sequence and combinations of events and give varying weights to the influences on decline and revival (DeGiovanni 1983, 32–35; Varady 1986, 9–19). When a neighborhood has declined but is not devastated, it has necessarily received some reinvestment. In many neighborhoods, therefore, the circumstances are ambiguous, subject to several interpretations, with changes occurring slowly.

Imagine a particular neighborhood that is in the modest and intermittent reinvestment category. Questions among public officials, private institution managers, businesses, and residents concern prospects for reinvestment in structures of an age, size, and architectural character that, in other neighborhoods, have sometimes been revived and sometimes demolished. What will determine the direction of such neighborhoods? The influences range from the pace of regional expansion and development on the fringe, the strength of employment in the central business district or in other nearby employment concentrations, the presence of one or more institutions whose leaders and constituents nurture reinvestment, the quality of political, governmental, and civic leadership, the interest of lenders and developers, the architectural character of buildings and the ambiance of streets, perceptions of safety and public school quality, the preferences of current and potential residents among the range of neighborhood settings afforded by metropolitan areas, and the quality of public services and regulations.

These neighborhoods are likely to suffer liabilities from crime and troubled public schools, but their proximity to work and recreation is a strength. Walking and public transportation are often alternatives to cars. And perhaps most important, the housing may be of a size and quality that makes it adaptable to contemporary spacious ambitions. These neighborhoods are prime candidates for attention by public officials and actors in private markets because of neighborhood strengths, the importance for the jurisdiction that some neighborhoods revive, and the prospect that many middle-aged (1945–70) neighborhoods will decline.

Middle-Aged Neighborhood

These neighborhoods are dominated by single-family houses of a size (800 to 1,300 square feet) and construction quality typical of the 1950s. In one particular area under consideration, the entire neighborhood was constructed within 10 years. The elementary school, now closed, was built during the 1950s. Cul-de-sacs dominate the interior street skeleton. Once they kept out some strangers and through traffic; now some types of people formerly excluded are living on the cul-de-sacs. Strip shopping on a major traffic artery is nearby, but it can be accessed only from a few streets. The population has aged. Some younger people have moved in. The trees have matured, as has the housing (although maturity wears better on the trees than on the houses). Little expansion of houses is apparent. Most seem adequately kept up, but there are numerous exceptions. Cars and light trucks are also middle aged. The neighborhood does not look poor, but it looks vulnerable. The jurisdiction in which it is located has been losing population and falling behind neighboring jurisdictions toward the metropolitan fringe in income of residents. Reinvestment is needed; without it, aging housing will deteriorate rapidly. The search for plausible reinvestment strategies is puzzling; the need for reinvestment in this neighborhood, compared with other neighborhoods, is a matter of disagreement among public policy makers.

In the year 2000 housing market and beyond, these may be starter homes for first-time buyers, but the neighborhood—lacking many children and a school—has some liabilities for young families. Even for childless couples, small unit size makes space for a home office problematic. Since these structures are 40 or more years old, many building elements and operating systems are worn out. They need to be replaced, or they already have been replaced once or twice and are ready for a new replacement round. While the location is not as inconvenient as those of many other neighborhoods, this neighborhood was built at densities low enough that public transportation is not available, shopping is not within walking distance, commuting to work requires a car, and no major institutions are nearby. The architectural quality is mundane or worse. Except for mature trees, aesthetic attributes are scarce.

Neighborhood obstacles to housing reinvestment in such 1950s settings are substantial; characteristics of the housing itself are greater obstacles. Size may be the biggest problem. The typical suburban house built at Levittown in the late 1940s was 800 square feet. The average new single-family house built in 1954 was 1,140 square feet (U.S. Bureau of the Census 1956, 774). By 1971 the median size had increased to 1,375 square feet. By 1995 the median-size new house was more than 1,900 square feet, and the average was nearly 2,100 square feet. In 1995, only 10 percent of the new single-family houses constructed were 1,200 square feet or less, indicating a modest market for small detached houses. Other differences also indicate market problems for many pre-1970 houses. In 1995, 80 percent of new houses had central air conditioning, compared with 36 percent in 1971 and far less in the 1950s. In 1995, 48 percent of new single-family houses had at least two and a half bathrooms, compared with 15 percent in 1971. In addition, two-story houses had become much more common, con-stituting 48 percent of new houses in 1995 compared with only 17 percent in 1971 (National Association of Home Builders 1997). During the 1990s, nine-foot ceilings became the norm in new housing in some metropolitan areas, suc-ceeding several decades in which eight-foot ceilings were typical in new con-struction (Haggerty 1999). These size, air conditioning, bathroom, and style characteristics suggest that even if typical 1950s houses were available in mint condition, the market for them might be quite limited (Table 8.4).

But 1950s houses are not in mint condition. Often they are worn out. Usually they need some major repairs. Average life expectancies of materials, according to a 1993 survey by the National Association of Home Builders (1997, 9–11) were as follows: kitchen countertops 10 to 15 years, kitchen cab-inets 15 to 20 years, fiberglass bathtub and shower 10 to 15 years, sinks 10 to

Table 8.4. Characteristics of New Single-Family Homes, 1971–1995

	1971	1975	1980	1985	1990	1995
Total Completed (in Thousands)	1,014	875	957	1,073	966	1,065
Characteristics (Percentage)						
Central Air Conditioning	36%	46%	63%	70%	76%	80%
2 1/2 or More Bathrooms	15	20	25	29	45	48
2 or More Stories	17	23	31	42	49	48
1,200 Square Feet or Less	36	25	21	20	11	10
2,400 Square Feet or More	9	11	15	17	29	28
AVERAGE SQUARE FEET	1,520	1,645	1,740	1,785	2,080	2,095
MEDIAN SQUARE FEET	1,375	1,535	1,595	1,605	1,905	1,920

Source: National Association of Home Builders, 1997

30 years, carpeting 11 years, furnace 18 years, heat exchanger 24 years, asphalt shingle roofing 15 to 30 years, and window casements 10 to 50 years. In each instance, a reservation notes "depends on quality." In many instances, the quality of these houses is modest. More rapid than average deterioration will occur in some instances.

Making these houses as attractive today to the income groups for whom they were initially built will take upgrades (air conditioning and modern kitchen) and often expansion (one or two more bedrooms/offices, family room, additional bathroom, deck), but neighborhood conditions usually do not encourage such upgrades and expansions. According to the National Association of Home Builders (1997, 34), an average additional bathroom would cost $11,645 in 1997, a minor kitchen remodeling $8,507, conversion of an attic to a bedroom with bath $22,840, adding a family room $31,846, and adding a deck $6,172. These additions and upgrades could easily equal the value of a preremodeling 1950s house.

Consider the decision-making problem of owners or purchasers who contemplate major upgrades and additions in these settings. Assuming they have the financial means to proceed with these investments, at least four problems arise. First, remodeling may make the house the most expensive one on the street or block, perhaps by a large margin. Will the first such upgrader-expander, in particular, be willing to risk a large reinvestment? What will they estimate their potential will be for regaining their investment at the time of sale? The Home Building & Remodeling Network (1999) estimated a national average payback of 83 percent of reinvestment on 12 common remodeling projects, but the variation among metropolitan areas was large, and the estimates were based on average rather than below-average neighborhoods. Second, will local banks be confident of such reinvestments? What will the estimated appraised value be? If they are willing to make mortgage loans, will they insist on large down payments for protection? Will such demands reduce the interest, and the feasibility, of the reinvestor proceeding? Third, will a proposed house expansion conflict with set-back requirements in zoning ordinances? Fourth, will builders add a large "fudge factor" to protect themselves against unforeseeable problems associated with rehabilitation, sending the per-square-foot cost above the cost of new construction?

What incentives would incline owners and prospective purchasers toward reinvesting rather than investing the same or less in a house that already meets their preferences? Given the decision rules of contemporary institutions, and the preferences of owners and prospective purchasers, it seems unlikely that rein-vestment will be the dominant choice in such circumstances. The logic of this decision-making analysis leads to the same conclusion as did the findings of income decline in suburbs with prominent 1950s and 1960s housing: it is less likely that people of similar or higher incomes will reinvest than that they will buy newer, larger housing or perhaps purchase larger, older housing in neigh-borhoods with greater charm and accessibility. This conclusion indicates why many suburbs face declines in income and housing value that have been, or will be, more precipitous than decline in many central cities.

University Neighborhood

These neighborhoods are dominated by one- and two-family dwellings built from 1920 through 1960. They have been steadily converted from single-fam-ily home ownership to multifamily rentals; there is still some residual home ownership, but it is diminishing. The renters are students, low-income single people, and a few families with children. The most apparent reinvestment has occurred in dividing dwellings into multiple units and erecting rear and side exterior stairways. Landscaping has become tattered. When plantings deteriorate or die, they are rarely replaced. Crime has increased. Nearby is a university; near some of its borders, it has been an anchor for stable housing, walking to work by faculty and staff, and much reinvestment.

In this type of situation, some forces described above are in play, as are some different elements. Neighborhood trends are flowing against the probability of an increase in single-family home ownership, and against maintaining current amounts of home ownership, but there is substantial demand for housing. Although the steady, even rising, demand is from people (mainly students) with lower household income than the previous occupants, they are often willing to pay more per dwelling unit, trading less space (doubling, tripling, and quadru-pling up) for closer proximity to classes, library, friends, and entertainment. In addition, a major employer (the university) is committed to its location, which attracts users (students) who are not employees but are willing to pay more for proximity. The university's location commitment means that at any moment, its leaders may increase their neighborhood investment priorities. Thus, the university can become a major source of capital, managerial energy, and political support for a housing reinvestment strategy.

The best interests of the neighborhood and jurisdiction are not self-evident. On one hand, transitions in housing use are occurring because of demand. Besides the students who are benefiting, lower-income nonstudents (including some families) have been moving in, although they may be subject to overcrowding in order to afford the location. Property owners are also making a profit, and paying ample property taxes, without overburdening public schools.

On the other hand, residents' income has been declining in the jurisdiction relative to its suburbs, crime has increased, and more schools are troubled. Neighborhoods with the potential for revival—including a return to higher levels of home ownership, rising family incomes, and more middle-class children in the public schools—are likely to be both vitally important to the jurisdiction and in short supply. University neighborhoods are prime prospects for revival due to inherent strengths, including employees who value proximity to work. In addition, many graduate students have small children who can contribute to a solid learning environment in public schools. Thus, a built-in clientele for housing reinvestment may contribute to reducing crime and enhancing the public schools—a rare combination.

The strategic problem for the university and city, however, is potential excess demand rather than too little demand. The demand for rental space may have bid up the price of existing units above what most families will pay. Although many families may be willing to pay more if conditions change for the better (improved schools, less crime, and fewer students, for instance), the process of changing conditions requires that more such families be willing to pay more *before* conditions have improved. This market dynamic indicates a potential role for the university. It can enter the market, buying rental properties to convert them to single-family or condominium ownership, or it can buy properties to keep them from shifting from owner to renter, reoffering them for sale for owner occupancy. These actions run some risk of losing money—the difference between purchase, fix-up, and sales prices—at least in the short run. The university needs incentives to risk losing money in the short run in order to stabilize the neighborhood and the jurisdiction in the long run. Provided that university leaders take a long view, those incentives do exist: in particular, a safe and sound neighborhood and jurisdictional environment in which students, faculty, and administrators can complement productive work settings with constructive residential settings.

These three illustrations describe complex decision situations in which characteristics of structures and settings intertwine. They also reveal challenges in the path of adequate housing reinvestment. Neighborhoods and jurisdictions tend toward decline because of the combination of deteriorating materials and development opportunities in greenfield settings. These decision situations are not immune to intervention. Institutions, policies, and procedures can be designed to increase housing reinvestment. Strengths and opportunities can be drawn upon, if the political will and social desire are strong enough.

How Much Reinvestment Is Enough?

In many interpretations of urban problems in the United States, one common theme has been that reinvestment in housing is often viewed as limited and the means of increasing reinvestment are problematic. Interpretations vary about the seriousness of this tendency (Solomon and Vandell 1982). From one perspective, deterioration of housing with age makes it available to lower-income households who cannot afford new housing, so such a process may benefit lower-income households. Provided that supply exceeds demand over time, and new housing is built to higher standards than older housing, then lower-income households stand to improve their housing quality gradually through filtering processes. From this perspective, reinvestment may not be deficient. But this perspective devalues the quality of places, as though the quality of people's lives can be contained atomistically within dwellings rather than being partially dependent on the quality of larger settings.

The answer to the question of how much reinvestment is enough depends partly on one's vantage point. A minimal notion of "enough reinvestment," for example, from an owner's perspective concerns whether a sales price exceeds the remaining mortgage amount. Reinvestment that produces more mortgage than sales price would be too much reinvestment from this perspective.

Middle-income homeowners may see a major need for reinvestment in their neighborhoods to protect their housing equity and their quality of life. Homeowners may also count on reinvestment to appreciate their property's value, building equity to assist in their next housing purchase. Low-income renters may see reinvestment as leading to higher rents that may push them from the neighborhood, but if they remain, they may like other changes that reinvestment brings.

As for investors, current institutional investors may fear overexposure if the neighborhood is declining. They also may fear what will happen if they, and other investor institutions, stop reinvesting or do not invest enough in the neighborhood. Need, in this instance, is defined as enough reinvestment to protect existing investments without adding excessively to investors' exposure.

For local governments, several perspectives are likely. A significant perspective for public policy makers could be that assessed value changes should maintain a neighborhood's standing relative to its jurisdiction's and metropolitan area's assessed values. Public officials in poor jurisdictions will often be conflicted. On one hand, reinvestment to retain and attract middle- and upper-income residents is an obvious need. On the other hand, constituents may not appreciate "favored" treatment for more prosperous neighbors, and this attitude can cause political tensions. Public officials also will be uncertain about the equity of such policies. As David Varady (1986, 142) observed: ". . . [H]ousing rehabilitation would have greater spillover effects, as long as it was sufficiently concentrated [in white ethnic communities]. On the other hand, equity criteria would favor ethnically changing and predominantly black communities, since the social needs would be greater. . . ." Public officials in well-off jurisdictions may understand that their modest housing offers prospects for more affordable housing and a more diverse population in the future, but their constituents may fear deterioration in their quality of life and investments. Hence, the politics of well-off jurisdictions are often not hospitable to increasing affordable housing through new low-cost housing, housing vouchers, or housing deterioration.

In most jurisdictions, public officials may see their settings lodged between rich and poor poles, with a diverse array of current neighborhood conditions and future reinvestment prospects. Difficult questions concern which neighborhoods most "deserve" reinvestment. Where is reinvestment likely to have secondary positive effects? Where can governments expect positive impacts on reinvestment or other problem conditions? Answers to these questions also may vary with jurisdiction size. Public officials in small jurisdictions may fear that changes in their housing stock and population signal rapid transitions. Small jurisdictions can decline rapidly, with slim prospects for recovering, if a downward slide becomes strong.

Anticipating Housing and School Trends

Focusing on housing problems of low-income households is a tradition in many local governments, especially where low-income households are numerous. That emphasis is warranted because the private sector is not oriented to meeting low-income housing needs. On the other hand, such a policy bias may inhibit local governments from conducting realistic environmental scans that reveal housing-related dangers to neighborhoods and their jurisdiction. Charlottesville, Virginia, is a community where this has occurred. Charlottesville's officials expanded attention to housing reinvestment and to insufficient housing opportunities for middle-income people within city limits, based partially on the following analysis. A policy bias against local government addressing middle-income housing needs is more likely to occur in cities than suburbs. When suburban decline becomes severe, however, similar challenges confront suburban officials. Both city and suburban public officials face serious diagnostic and policy obstacles to being effective in combating sprawl and enhancing reinvestment.

Charlottesville had a Comprehensive Plan (1996), a Strategic Economic Development Plan (1994), and a Public Education Strategic Plan (1995). With three so-called strategic plans and comprehensive plans in place, population trends and conditions, problems and challenges in the public schools, tax base characteristics, and relationships between housing conditions and other community characteristics could have been noted and analyzed, with relevant proposals made concerning them. Actually, none of these plans identified population trends as problems. Nor did they relate population trends to concepts of community well-being. Nor did they treat population, poverty, income, free-lunch eligibility, or housing conditions as leading indicators that provided clues about the future. No predictions about the future, in fact, were made. These plans were actually neither strategic nor comprehensive; they were like work plans (economic development and schools) or general descriptions of conditions with proposals only vaguely related to those conditions (comprehensive plan).

A Declining City

Charlottesville is an excellent example of a rapidly changing city for which census data provide a relevant but meager picture of dangers. Between 1980 and 1990, the family poverty gap between Charlottesville and its surrounding county, Albemarle, grew noticeably. In 1980, family poverty in Charlottesville was 7.5 percent; in Albemarle it was 7.1 percent. By 1990, the family poverty gap had grown to a 2 to 1 ratio—10 percent in Charlottesville and 4.8 percent in Albemarle. Among families with children less than age 18, poverty rates were higher: 21.2 percent in Charlottesville and 9.4 percent in Albemarle. Median

Substantial middle-income ranch-style housing of the late 1960s in Charlottesville has been well maintained but has an uncertain future in the dynamics of the metropolitan area.

family income trends confirmed that Charlottesville was becoming poorer, while Albemarle was growing richer. In 1980, median family income in Charlottesville was $19,115, 93 percent of Albemarle's $20,554. By 1990, Charlottesville's median family income was $33,729, 79 percent of Albemarle's $42,661.

The search for leading indicators of weaknesses and dangers should include housing characteristics, because housing, more than any other issue, affects location decisions. In Charlottesville, about 50 percent of the total housing stock was constructed between 1945 and 1970, as was 60 percent of the owner-occupied housing. Elementary schools that have experienced the most rapid increase in free-lunch eligibility compared with other elementary schools are surrounded by neighborhoods dominated by small houses, many of which were built in the 25 years after World War II. Free-lunch data give credence to the connection between small, middle-aged housing and income decline. Careful analysis of the relationship between housing age and income decline would be a useful investment in time and funds in Charlottesville and in many cities (see Appendix 8.1 for a discussion of housing and income change analysis methods).

Free-Lunch Eligibles' Test Scores

Post-1990 free-lunch trends revealed additional dangers. In 1990, 33 percent of the students in Charlottesville's public schools were eligible for the federal government's free-lunch program. By 1997, Charlottesville students' free-lunch eligibility had grown to 51 percent. The increase in free-lunch-eligible students was a problem, in particular because of their levels of learning readiness and performance. In standardized test scores, the differences between free-lunch- and non-free-lunch-eligible students were alarming. Among fourth-graders in 1995, free-lunch-eligible students' reading average was in the 32nd percentile nationally and their mathematics average was in the 34th percentile, while non-free-lunch-eligible fourth-graders averaged in the 59th percentile on the reading test and in the 62nd percentile in math. The differences were even more striking when examined by deciles. Forty percent of the free-lunch-eligible fourth-graders scored in the bottom 20 percent nationally in reading and math; only 4 percent were in the top 20 percent in reading, and only 6 percent were in this top category in math. Among the non-free-lunch-eligible fourth-graders, 29 percent scored in the top 20 percent nationally in reading, and 38 percent did so in math. Similar patterns and relationships for the free-lunch- and non-free-lunch-eligible students occurred in 8th grade and 11th grade in 1995.

During the rapid increase in free-lunch eligibility among public school students from 1990 to 1994 (from 33 to 47 percent), Charlottesville's city government experienced fiscal problems influenced by the national recession, state cutbacks, suburbanization of retailing, and federal mandates affecting landfills. In response, the city government reduced the nonschool city workforce by 11 percent, implemented a trash collection fee and upgraded recycling, and adopted a cigarette tax. Taxable retail sales declined: in 1990, 52 percent of combined Charlottesville/Albemarle receipts were collected in Charlottesville, versus only 43 percent in 1995. A citizens group conducted a petition drive during 1995 and 1996 to start an official process, guided by a state agency, to have Charlottesville revert to being a town in Albemarle County. In Virginia, this change in form of government would have the effect of shifting responsibility for financing and administering public education from the city to the county, because cities are governmentally separate from countries but towns are part of counties. In December 1999, Charlottesville's city councilors finally decided not to seriously consider the town reversion option.

Charlottesville faced a formidable educational and fiscal challenge. The city needed resources to provide quality education to the low, middle, and high achievers in a student population that was substantially flat but that had somewhat more low and high than middle achievers. The city needed to retain the current proportion of non-free-lunch-eligible children in the schools. But a more detailed analysis by grade in school suggested that the free-lunch percentage would increase.

School free-lunch eligibility data are useful, in addition, because they are available by grade in school. One can determine whether cohorts of students in the early grades have higher proportions of free-lunch eligibility than do the upper-grade cohorts. In high school, 30 percent of the students were free-lunch eligible in the fall of 1996, compared with 48 percent in the entire school system. In seventh and eighth grades, 51 percent were eligible for free lunches, as were 52 percent in fifth and sixth grades, 56 percent in kindergarten through fourth grade, and 65 percent in kindergarten alone. Ironically, in 1990, when the rapid increase in free-lunch eligibility began, 47 percent of kindergartners were eligible for free lunches, virtually the same as the percentage that emerged for the entire school system six years later. Thus, if history repeated itself in another six years or so, free-lunch eligibility in the Charlottesville public schools would approximate 60 percent. Drawing inferences from free-lunch eligibility by grade in school, the future of the Charlottesville schools appeared ominous.

Speculating from past trends (increasing family poverty from 1980 to 1990, increasing free-lunch eligibility from 1990 to 1997, and higher rates of free-lunch eligibility in elementary grades and kindergarten in areas dominated by small single-family detached housing units built between 1945 and 1970), it seemed reasonable to expect the following to be true of Charlottesville:

- It would face a continuing increase in its rate of family poverty, especially among families with children.
- It would probably experience an exodus of some middle-class families from public schools.

- It might have stagnant residential real estate values in many middle-aged neighborhoods.
- It would experience a tighter squeeze between demands and needs for public services and local financial resources.

This Charlottesville example illustrates how public school free-lunch and test score data can provide clues as leading indicators of future transitions, and how school data can reinforce environmental scans of housing conditions in anticipating dangers. The utility of free-lunch data in diagnosing neighborhood transitions will depend in part on whether attendance zones are contiguous to schools, which may in turn be affected by how much busing occurs to achieve racial balance and how much choice among public schools is available to families.

Balance, Equilibrium, and Sustainable Communities

Equilibrium and balance are concepts that can help guide judgments. A metropolitan area is composed of a wide array of housing types and quality. The population is diverse. If specific jurisdictions contain a similarly diverse array of housing and population, they are in balance with the region. The same can be said of neighborhoods, or of any partial territory within the region. Since jurisdictions, neighborhoods, and housing units themselves change over time, equilibrium is achieved if they gravitate toward balance from high or low levels over time. Everything is in flux. But the flux need not inevitably diverge toward polarized conditions; instead, it may pull subparts of the metropolitan area toward middle-range conditions of housing value and income distribution. This flux around middle-range conditions can be measured and tracked. The minimum tracking necessary for strategic planning for jurisdictions and regions is to measure disparities, reinvestment, and sprawl. Simple but incomplete methods of measuring disparities, reinvestment, and sprawl are described below; more thorough methods are described in Appendix 8.1.

Minimum Indicators of Disparities, Reinvestment, and Sprawl

Indicators of income disparities, housing reinvestment, and suburban/exurban sprawl should be compared to norms. For some indicators, national and state metropolitan census data can be used. Even without comparisons with other metropolitan areas, however, understanding of conditions and trends can be enhanced by comparing conditions and trends in central city and suburban jurisdictions with metropolitan median and mean conditions and trends.

Income disparities. Use national median family (and household and per capita) income data for central cities, outside central cities, and metropolitan areas. Compute ratios of central city income to these other categories.

Income data for some suburban jurisdictions will be available, and these same ratios should be calculated. Trends for three or, preferably, more decades should be calculated. The outside central city category, or perhaps an urban balance category, will be useful for comparative purposes, because this will be closer to the normal suburban condition than will central city and individual suburban and exurban conditions.

Housing reinvestment. Additional indicators of disparities can be used, such as owner-occupied housing value, but housing value might better be considered an indicator of reinvestment. Housing in which reinvestment has been vigorous should hold its value. Strong housing reinvestment indicates substantial demand for residences. For metropolitan areas for which annual housing survey data are available, housing value will measure reinvestment by age of housing, but only for each metropolitan area as a whole, not for the central city and suburban jurisdictions. If possible, a census tract analysis should be conducted to determine change in income and housing value. This analysis should be supplemented by relating income and value changes to size of housing (number of bedrooms and number of rooms) and to the decades in which a greater than average share of the regions' new housing was constructed in each census tract.

Suburban/exurban sprawl. A number of indicators can be used from census data, as described in Chapter 4. Relevant data include percentage of employees working outside the county of residence, commuting times to work, farmland loss, population density changes in fringe counties, and addition of counties to metropolitan areas. At least one indicator each of population, employment, and farmland should be used, because these are three distinct dimensions of sprawl.

Central cities, counties, and some smaller jurisdictions can be compared with each other, and with the metropolitan region, in terms of these indicators of disparities, reinvestment, and sprawl. They will help local, regional, state, and federal officials evaluate some important strengths, weaknesses, dangers, and opportunities.

Equilibrium

The equilibrium concept is much different from the traditional models of metropolitan evolution (concentric zone, sector, filtering, vacancy chain, trickle-down neighborhood change), each of which embodies an assumption that dwellings (hence neighborhoods and jurisdictions) will be occupied by lower-income people as they age, and, in time, nearly all aged housing will be demolished. One consequence of the traditional models of metropolitan evolution is that it is not evident that any dwelling or neighborhood needs reinvestment, since every house and neighborhood will deteriorate with age and eventually be demolished. Reinvestment serves only to stave off the inevitable. No amount of reinvestment is enough, since demolition is the predicted end result. These implications derive from the descriptive rather than prescriptive intentions of the theories. Our focus here, on the other hand, is to posit stability or renewal as goals and ask whether institutions, processes, and policies are organized to achieve these goals.

Given the goals of balance and equilibrium, reinvestment helps maintain the position of jurisdictions in the array of housing quality and income levels of a metropolitan area. Neighborhoods will rise and fall, but enough should rise through reinvestment, while others fall, that overall jurisdiction vitality will be maintained. Continuity over time, one of the essential characteristics of sustainable communities, is inherent in balance and equilibrium.

Large territories and many jurisdictions should be included in strategic planning analyses, because the prospects of houses, neighborhoods, jurisdictions, and metropolitan regions are intertwined. If the population of a metropolitan area is growing, for example, and all income segments also are increasing, then where will the additional lower-income people live? If they are concentrated in a few neighborhoods or a few jurisdictions, then reinvestment in those neighborhoods or jurisdictions will be difficult, because income for rent and mortgage payments will decline compared with income of the previous occupants who have moved elsewhere for better investments and quality of life. The need for reinvestment will increase, but the risks for reinvestors will also increase. Scenarios can be constructed to aid analysis of plausible consequences for jurisdictions from regional changes, such as increases or decreases in population and employment, or from public policies, such as changes in federal or state housing policies.

Scenarios as Aids to Analysis and Predictions

Reasoning from scenarios to facilitate analysis and predictions is illustrated below. Two scenarios concerning population, employment, and housing will be used to illustrate dangers and opportunities.

SCENARIO 1: CITY AND SUBURBAN INCOME DISPARITY TRANSITIONS IN A REGION GROWING BY 50 PERCENT IN 20 YEARS AND ADDING EMPLOYMENT AT A STILL FASTER RATE

When a metropolitan region's population increases and the central city's boundary remains fixed, what happens to the central city–outside central city income ratio, and what happens to the income disparity range among suburbs?

Assume, for example, that the metropolitan area had 200,000 residents 20 years ago, of which 100,000 lived in the central city. Today the metropolitan population is 300,000, and the central city's population is still 100,000. Twenty years ago, median family income among central city residents was 90 percent of the metropolitan area's median, and the outside central city median family income ratio was 110 percent. Among the additional 100,000 residents who now live in the metropolitan area, the same income distribution prevails as occurred 20 years ago among 200,000 residents. Hypothetically, there are 35 percent low- and moderate-income households, 50 percent middle-income households, and 15 percent upper-middle- and upper-income households in the additional population and in the population of 20 years earlier. While some new jobs were added in the central city, most new employment was outside it. Living in the central city did not become less convenient in terms of job access, but living outside the central city became more convenient for some residents despite more traffic congestion in some areas.

Given these conditions, what probably happened to the income ratio between the central city and its suburban/exurban area? Was the city richer, poorer, or no different in relation to the outside central city area?

Discussion: The central city probably was poorer. This outcome depends on other probabilities. Most of the new housing probably was built outside the central city. Given a fixed central city boundary and no population increase, the median and mean size of central city housing probably diminished relative to new suburban/exurban housing, because the median size of new housing increased from 1,350 square feet in 1970 to 1,905 square feet in 1990 (National Association of Home Builders 1997). Of the 100,000 new residents, 35,000 were low and moderate income. Although some of these lower-income people may live on the fringe, perhaps in manufactured housing, few new units for sale are affordable to persons below 110 percent of median income. Consequently, most of the additional lower-income people moved into existing housing that had been vacated by others. People vacating housing often moved to larger or more expensive units, some of which were new housing. More often than not, these larger, new, and more expensive units were outside the central city.

On the other hand, some older central city housing may seem more attractive due to effects of sprawl and greater inconvenience for people living on parts of the fringe. With relatively few large, high-quality housing units available for the larger middle- and upper-income population, some of these high-quality units and their neighborhoods were bid up in price through greater demand. This trend mitigated some of the potential widening of the central city–suburban income disparity, but it was accompanied by somewhat greater income polarization within the central city as the number of low- and moderate-income people increased in other parts of the central city.

In addition, greater polarization probably occurred among suburban jurisdictions. The national average is about 90 local governments per metropolitan area. In a modest-size metropolitan area with 300,000 residents, perhaps there were 20 local government jurisdictions. With 20 jurisdictions, perhaps there were 16 suburbs, other than the central city and three suburban/exurban counties. The average-size suburb, given some population in unincorporated territory, would probably be less than 10,000 residents with perhaps 3,000 to 4,500 housing units. With housing for about 100,000 residents in place 20 or more years ago, a considerable amount of the currently available housing would be small and somewhat isolated, inconvenient, and at least moderately deteriorating. Some of these suburbs would be declining, with perhaps a few severely declining. With considerable new housing having been built, much of it in unincorporated territory or in relatively affluent suburbs with good schools, a considerable number of previous residents would have moved up to larger and higher-quality housing; such areas would likely have attracted many new residents as well. With 50 percent of households moving every five years, considerable change within a decade in some suburbs was likely. As a consequence of these conditions, income disparities among suburbs may have increased considerably, even though the outside central city area in aggregate was wealthier than 20 years earlier in relation to the central city.

Such trends are predictable, based on the theories, concepts, analyses, and findings in this and previous chapters. The dangers to many jurisdictions inherent in these trends are apparent. Affluent jurisdictions, some new areas, and perhaps a few old neighborhoods also may see opportunities in these trends; however, these opportunities may mean additional benefits for themselves and their small areas at the expense of deterioration elsewhere. Incentives for more sprawl, some disincentives for reinvestment, and increasing income disparities seem inherent in these trends. The main opportunity, one might say, is to organize governance (federal, state, regional, and local) to cope with these conditions to reduce sprawl, increase reinvestment, and limit disparities. Examples of policies and governance structures with such aims are described in Chapters 9 and 10.

SCENARIO 2: CITY AND SUBURBAN INCOME DISPARITY TRANSITIONS IN A
METROPOLITAN AREA LOSING POPULATION AND GAINING SOME EMPLOYMENT

Although this metropolitan area gained some employment in the past 20 years, population in the region declined. With more women in the workforce, the employment gains were not sufficient to provide jobs for the same number of families. Because household size decreased, there was a slight increase in demand for housing units. The region's population declined 5 percent, but the central city's population fell 15 percent as the city's boundary remained fixed and new construction of housing in the city was insufficient to replace abandoned housing. The region's income distribution (e.g., the proportion of the population that was categorized as low/moderate, middle, and upper middle/high income) remained the same as 20 years earlier.

This metropolitan area had 800,000 residents 20 years ago, of whom 200,000 lived in the central city. Today the region's population is 760,000, with 170,000 residents in the central city. As is typical of an old industrial region, suburbanization occurred early in the 20th century. Small suburbs accumulated along commuter rail stops, and more small suburbs incorporated during the automobile era, especially during the 20 years after World War II. The region has 110 local governments, of which five are counties, plus one central city. The average population in the nonoverlapping local governments (some governments overlap—villages in townships, for example—and several special districts overlap counties and townships) is 7,000 residents. The income ratios 20 years ago were as follows: central city income 85 percent of the regional median, outside central city income 110 percent of the regional median.

Under these circumstances, would the income gap between the central city and outside central city areas, and the income disparity range among suburban jurisdictions, be likely to increase, decrease, or remain the same?

Discussion: The income gap increased moderately, and the range of disparities among suburbs increased substantially. Why? A higher percentage of residents moved from the central city than from the region. Central city outmovers to suburbs had higher incomes than residents who remained in the central city. Many moved up to larger and more costly residences or transitioned from renter to owner status. As middle-income people (often families) moved out, other moving opportunities were created. Smaller households, which became more numerous, occupied some of the vacated housing. Some housing was abandoned, lacking buyers and renters. In such neighborhoods, push factors (negative neighborhood influences) increased. Some moderate-income outmovers relocated in middle-aged suburbs. They had lower incomes than the suburban median income. These moderate-income movers restrained the increase in the income gap. The mobility rate was also restrained by difficulties in selling and renting properties (in this metropolitan area 35 percent of households moved in five years, compared with a national norm of about 50 percent), which occurred because of population decline and modest demand for replacement housing. In addition, some low-income people moved from the region in search of work, and more of them moved from the central city than from the suburbs, again restraining the rate of increase in the city–outside city income gap.

Disparities among suburbs increased. More suburbs passed into middle age. In most instances, they declined in income relative to the region and to other suburbs. Although the region lost population, real per capita income rose slightly, and per household income rose more as the mean number of workers in two-adult households increased. Thus, demand for larger housing units increased. This demand was reflected in gentrification in some central city neighborhoods, but more often it led to construction of larger homes in unincorporated areas or in two favored older suburbs with room for development. Effective demand from middle-income residents fell, therefore, in many suburbs. Where suburbs had been developed within a few years at modest standards, which today are regarded as below current standards, relative income of residents fell considerably faster than in the central city. As a consequence, the income disparity gap among the lowest- and highest-income suburbs increased faster than the central city–outside central city income gap.

USING SCENARIOS IN STRATEGIC PLANNING

Scenarios 1 and 2 are written as plausible explanations of trends for which data are available from 20 years ago to a recent date. Similar reasoning can be applied to predictions 10 and 20 years into the future. Key variables to consider are the size, age, and quality of housing, and the role of anchor employers in downtowns (like banks, government offices, and information and technology businesses) and elsewhere (such as universities and hospitals, which are often surrounded by neighborhoods separated from the downtown area). High rates of regional growth increase the vulnerability of neighborhoods and jurisdictions by increasing the rate of change and increasing the number of low- and moderate-income people who tend to live in housing constructed more than 20 years earlier. Proximity to employment, other aspects of convenience, and quality of structures, including aesthetic and atmospheric appeal, may enable some neighborhoods to stabilize or revive, especially if they gain additional transportation advantages, such as proximity to heavy- or light-rail transit. Negative neighborhood social effects may mitigate against the effectiveness of such characteristics, especially if they have eroded the quality of neighborhood schools. Small-scale analysis, therefore, should supplement central city, outside central city, and regional trend descriptions and predictions.

Insufficient Reinvestment

Reinvestment in housing through contemporary institutions, policies, and preferences has not been adequate. Insufficient reinvestment is partially a problem of housing size and internal characteristics in relation to affluence and location options. Affluence has brought larger dwellings and more costly mechanical and electrical systems. Automobiles have increased middle-income residents' location options. To attract middle-income buyers, housing must at least meet minimum criteria. But contemporary buyers' preferences are for houses larger than the typical housing built 30 to 50 years ago. Therefore, reinvestment to upgrade and expand considerable existing housing should increase in some places to augment the attractiveness of the housing to middle-income home buyers. Otherwise the danger is that 50 percent mobility rates every five years will raise socioeconomic status and housing values in newer jurisdictions and neighborhoods while lowering them in middle-aged and older jurisdictions and neighborhoods.

Some may object that because renters move more often than owners do, the 50 percent mobility rate overstates dangers to neighborhoods with high owner occupancy. But it is not much comfort to know that the median homeowner stays in place for only eight years; this still means that 50 percent of homeowners move in eight years or less, and many neighborhoods and metropolitan areas will have more rapid homeowner turnover rates. These homeowner mobility rates reveal substantial potential for neighborhood change.

Appendix 8.1

Indicators for Analyzing Dangers in Neighborhood and Jurisdiction Trends

Strategic planning efforts to discern dangers should use indicators that address housing reinvestment needs and risks. Housing indicators must be included in such a system. Other neighborhood, jurisdiction, and region indicators also are needed because of the reciprocal relationships between reinvestment in housing and the quality of its context, but the minimum indicators required are for housing value and income of residents. These indicators describe the attractiveness of a particular territory over time relative to other territories within a commuting region. Indicators should be for small areas, at least as small as block groups, and for areas of increasing size, including census tracts, jurisdictions, and regions, and probably some part of the suburban territory proximate to the central city area or older suburban area of greatest program interest. Data for at least two, and preferably several, points in time are needed to track trends between conditions in small areas, like census tracts, and also in jurisdictions and metropolitan regions.

It would be useful to measure transitions toward and away from the region's medians, rather than measuring them only as increasing or decreasing from their own previous levels. Each approach—measuring movement toward a median and movement up or down from a starting point—is useful. Sometimes high-income areas, for example, decline and do not stabilize near the median, instead descending to a low level. Thus, timely reinvestment may not occur even in wealthy neighborhoods, so that decline from a high level, if it persists, may be a sign of a reinvestment problem.

If a territory that is below the median housing values and household incomes is rising toward the region's medians, this would be an indication that reinvestment, new investment, or both may be satisfactory, or that other factors are present to keep the area attractive. If a territory is below the region's medians in housing value and incomes and is stable or falling further behind the region's medians, that would be an indication that reinvestment and new investment are probably not adequate.

Concerning risk of and need for reinvestment, what indicators would be particularly relevant? These would be indicators of below-median housing value and household incomes, less owner occupancy (and perhaps less single-family housing, either detached, attached, or condominium), fewer bedrooms and fewer rooms, and more substandard units (lacking complete plumbing). If these conditions are trending further below (or above with substandard conditions) the regional median from 1980 to 1990 to 2000, then the need for, and risk of, reinvestment would be greater.

The notion that housing values and median incomes in specific territories should be measured to determine whether they are moving toward or away from the regional medians can be extended to other indicators to determine, for example, whether a subarea is moving toward or away from:

- the regional distribution between single-family and multifamily housing (a mixed-use indicator and a social balance indicator)
- the region's median rate of owner occupancy
- the median number of rooms or bedrooms (an indicator of value and accommodation of preferences of middle- and upper-income households)
- indicators of substandard conditions, such as the presence of complete plumbing

An owner-occupancy rate also is needed. If increase in owner occupancy is a goal, then data about its rate is necessary to estimate its potential expansion. In addition, since owner occupancy is a goal for most middle- and upper-income households, a reduction in owner occupancy may signal that an area is becoming less attractive to such households.

More direct indicators of reinvestment could be obtained from assessors' data or building inspection records or perhaps, if these have been added to a data bank, planning department computer files. Pertinent indicators would include data about adding rooms and adding air conditioning. In low- and moderate-income neighborhoods, data about below-market-rate rehabilitation loans for major plumbing or electrical upgrades or donations of new furnaces, roofs, or other basic replacements would also help identify reinvestment needs and risks. These data, in most instances, would be more difficult to access than would census data.

These indicators may also make policy dilemmas explicit. It is one thing for a lender to react to the capacity of a particular borrower to pay off a loan, whatever the value of the given property or its surrounding properties. It is another thing to determine that the territory as a whole is risky and that lending policy should reflect that. Of course, such a determination could lead to opposite tendencies. A lender might decide not to make new loans for rehabilitation or new construction because of high risk. On the other hand, a lender might decide to make additional loans to buttress investments it had already made in that area, or it could make additional loans, alone or with other lenders, as part of a civic policy to strengthen areas that are below par in their current attractiveness.

Population density may also change, but this may not necessarily signify greater or less attractiveness. Population may decline, for example, because an area's housing is aging, as are its longtime residents. If the residents do not move out at a normal rate, they cannot be replaced by traditional movers, who tend to be younger than the average person who stays in place. As residents age, their households often shrink in number of occupants of existing housing. Population loss, therefore, is unevenly related to housing value and income increases and decreases. The same can be said of population increase. In subdivisions, higher-end housing is sometimes built before townhouses are built to round out a development. In other instances, sites with more amenities are developed first. Leftover sites may not command the same size and quality of housing as the sites developed earlier. In addition, new buyers may stretch borrowing to their financial limits, while departing higher-income owners may move to smaller quarters due to reductions in household size, even though their incomes were more than ample to support the housing they were vacating.

Indicators for General Knowledge Systems and Project-Focused Systems

Two sets of indicators can be suggested for an environmental scan of small-scale dangers. The first set will be indicators that are fully available from census data or other readily available standard sources. These can be used to create a general knowledge system. A second set of indicators can be added that are available from other public sources, with degrees of difficulty for incorporating them that will vary among jurisdictions. These indicators will be in less standardized formats. They may be qualitative rather than quantitative. They may be available for some subareas but not for others. These supplementary indicators can create project-focused systems that are more complicated than the general knowledge system.

A wide range of influences on neighborhood reinvestment needs and risks are plausible. Converting these influences into indicators is challenging; data availability varies greatly, as do data precision and data relevance. In deciding which indicators to include in an analysis, attention also must be paid to the potential users and the extent to which comparable data and methodology should be used for each region, jurisdiction, and neighborhood.

Some indicators and methods are useful for expanding the state of knowledge about conditions sufficient to make general policy decisions, while other indicators and methods may be relevant to local agencies making neighborhood and project investment decisions. The ensuing analysis will address, first, indicators and methods of general applicability, and, second, judgment enhancers using indicators that will be available inconsistently for local initiatives. For simplicity, we will refer below to these alternative goals and uses as a general knowledge system and a project-focused system.

The indicators discussed here serve several goals of understanding and take varied numerical form. The goals of understanding involve reinvestment needs and risks, potential for increasing home ownership, and the relationship of sustaining neighborhood characteristics to housing value and median income transitions. One result of the varied numerical forms is that the indicators are not in additive form consistently, so they cannot be collapsed into a single index. Instead, the indicators take more of the form of a checklist of important information to aid judgment. In specifying indicators, an effort should be made to be consistent in formulating them so one indicator can be more easily compared with another.

A list of indicators for a general knowledge system from U.S. census sources, for small and large units, for two or more decades follows: income, housing age, housing value, owner occupancy, number of bedrooms, number of rooms, housing units lacking some plumbing, number of housing units, percentage of housing units that are single-family detached/attached/multifamily/condominium, affordability (housing value or rent divided by median income), family poverty, race, population, age (children, elderly, median), and rate of regional population growth.

For a project-focused system, these general knowledge system indicators are useful, but they have the disadvantage of being available only after each decennial census is taken. For some purposes, the data are out of date as soon as they are compiled and reported. Additional data from local sources will be needed to analyze dangers during intermittent periods, due, in particular, to high residential mobility rates that can erode neighborhood vitality in a few years. Additional project-focused system indicators include the following: remodeling (expansions and upgrades), violent crime, burglaries, free-lunch eligibility by school, test scores by school, public housing units, fixed-rail stations, and magnet employers, especially nonprofit employers. These indicators are discussed in the following section.

Plausible Influences on Neighborhood and Jurisdiction Dangers

Spatial pattern indicators illustrate housing's context. Many plausible indicators embody elements of mixed use, accessibility, walkability, and lower household costs associated with these conditions, to take one set of plausible influences on a neighborhood's appeal. These conditions also connect to characteristics of individual structures with sustaining tendencies (attached dwellings, multistory buildings). There are interesting methods for mapping the connectivity of streets, distances from transit stations, distances from grocery stores, distances from employment and retail concentrations, distances from parks, and the like.

But these methods have the deficiency of requiring mapping, ambiguous data scaling, and, frequently, on-site observations and inquiries. Thus, these methods are costly and uncertain; interpreting and weighting the findings will be based on insufficient knowledge. Simpler methods are needed if spatial pattern information is to be incorporated into a general knowledge system rather than being available only for a project-focused system.

With the goal of simplicity in mind, a numerical indicator from census data is worth considering. The most general influence on spatial pattern comes from the number of single-family detached, attached, condominium, duplex, and apartment dwelling characteristics. It is likely, but not certain (how certain is a question), that dominance of attached single-family dwellings, condominiums, and apartments, especially in central cities, is associated with relatively high degrees of connected streets, short blocks, and moderate distances to grocery stores, schools, playgrounds, other retail, some employment, and public transportation. These dwelling characteristics were available for census tracts in 1980 and down to block groups in 1990, as well as for central cities, other jurisdictions, and metropolitan areas.

In some newer suburban areas, and even exurban areas and some central city areas, these relationships may not apply strongly. Many townhouse and apartment developments, for example, in large metropolitan areas in new suburban and exurban areas rarely have any of the general tendencies listed above, except for easy access to a playground and perhaps some retail. Neighborhoods that score high on this indicator, conversely, are usually in older (especially pre-1940) rather than middle-aged (1945–70) or newer (post-1970) areas. Since they are older, these neighborhoods are also those that need reinvestment and that will be at some risk if it is not forthcoming. Consequently, this type of indicator can serve as a proxy for an accessible, sustainable neighborhood that probably needs substantial reinvestment. A sustainable neighborhood, in most instances, is compact and accessible, meaning that it has mixed land uses to which many nearby residents can walk, as well as walking, bicycling, or public transportation access to employment.

A problem with this indicator, especially if it stands alone, is that pre-1940 neighborhoods tended to rise in relative median family income during the 1980s, while neighborhoods in which housing was built between 1950 and 1970 tended to decline in relative income standing. These neighborhoods are usually dominated by single-family detached housing. They need reinvestment because of their age and, in some instances, their construction quality. These areas are also more accessible than many newer neighborhoods farther out, but they may score low on indicators like connected streets and proximity to public transportation. To be attractive to the middle class, which has the capacity to reinvest, these neighborhoods may need expansion and upgrading of housing stock, in addition to maintenance and replacement of key worn-out housing elements.

An indicator of the need for reinvestment in these neighborhoods would be the percentage of housing built during the 1950s. More often than not, this housing would be smaller than the sizes preferred by contemporary tastes and pocketbooks. It would often have a style, configuration, and equipment that would be outmoded by current standards. Thus, if this housing is not the subject of substantial reinvestment, it may deteriorate excessively. Deterioration of neighborhoods could be pronounced, because large tracts of such housing were often developed within a few years. In consequence, large areas of middle-aged housing exist with little old or new housing or anchor attractions to leaven the norm. Without major reinvestment, some of these neighborhoods will deteriorate rapidly.

As for specific indicators, block groups, census tracts, central cities, and other jurisdictions could be compared with metropolitan norms in terms of the percentage of total housing in single-family attached and in multifamily units (compact neighborhood) or the percentage of total housing built in the 1950s and 1960s (middle-aged neighborhood).

Ratio scores above 1.0 (the ratio of the census tract, for example, to the metropolitan area) would suggest increasing degrees of need for reinvestment as the score rises. In terms of sustaining characteristics, however, these conditions point in opposite directions. The compact neighborhood characteristics tend to be sustaining and to stimulate, as well as indicate need for, reinvestment. The middle-aged neighborhoods need reinvestment but tend not to stimulate it.

Finance Indicators

Demand and supply of housing and other community buildings, facilities, and services influence neighborhood conditions and trends. Indicators should provide clues about both supply and demand, since they are intertwined. Demand involves interactions among preferences, capacities, and consideration of available options.

Finance mediates among these aspects of conditions and choices. If financial instruments are not available to fund certain preferences, then some options are foreclosed, except for those with strong independent financial capacities. Finance affects both demand and supply. Finance has the potential to be a leading influence on which choices are available and who has the practical capacity to consider these choices. One important choice-shaping role concerns whether finance is appropriately available for reinvestment (including maintenance, replacement, upgrading, and expansion), for new construction, and for purchases of housing.

Specifying useful indicators is challenging. Availability of funds for reinvestment seems crucial. But how can that be identified? One approach would be to infer availability from performance if such data are available—that is, the actual number and dollar amount of reinvestment loans could be identified for neighborhoods (census tracts) over some time period. Supplementary data could be identified by age of dwelling to determine how many dwellings in various age categories had been the subject of reinvestment. The total number and values of loans could then be calculated as percentages of total housing units reinvested in, and the relationship between the value of loans and the value (assessed? census data?) of the dwellings could be identified. But what would these amounts and total numbers be compared to? How much is enough?

Another approach would be to compare the dollar volume of reinvestment loans to purchase loans and, perhaps, to new housing construction loans. Such information could be mapped and associated with income and income change data, and with housing value and housing value change data. This analysis could lead to insights, but it is not evident what a meaningful indicator would be like or how it would be used.

Perhaps more useful data could come from assessors' files. Data could be obtained about assessed value increases from expansions. But would upgrades (kitchen remodeling, new air conditioning) be discernible? Probably not. Nor would simple maintenance and replacements be identifiable. Data on expansions could be revealing, however, especially if they could be related to age and size of housing units.

Another approach might be to infer reinvestments from increases in housing value in established areas in excess of the median increase in the median values per owner-occupied housing unit in the region. This indicator would be simple, but it would not reveal anything directly about finance, except that finance was sufficiently available by some means to support, or not prevent, median housing value increases.

None of these approaches speak directly to whether finance was available. Finance could be available but unused due to low demand or low eligibility. Finance could be available in terms of the secondary mortgage market, but front-line lenders might resist making loans.

Loan terms also would be relevant. For example, comparisons between interest rates on housing expansions, upgrades, equipment replacement, and maintenance versus new construction and housing purchases would be interesting. Are most home improvements financed with home equity loans? How do these interest rates compare with purchase rates? Why should home equity loans that are actually used to reinvest in housing be assigned higher rates by lenders than longer-term loans on housing purchases? What are the rates on explicit home improvement loans relative to housing purchase loans? This is relevant policy information, although how such information would be formulated into an indicator is not evident. Perhaps the interest rate difference between home improvement/home equity loans and home purchase loans could be used to indicate a negative or positive effect on reinvestment in established neighborhoods compared with other neighborhoods.

Other Housing Indicators

Some other housing indicators can help elaborate on the attractiveness of neighborhoods and jurisdictions. For example, housing units are entering and departing from the scene in most territories during a decade. An indicator of new construction illustrates whether much investment of that type has been occurring relative to other territories as a percentage of the total housing in each territory. If it is possible to discern the value of new housing (information that is probably not available from census data), then a glimpse of investors' interpretations of market forces can be discerned as well. As for departures, housing demolished or converted to other uses can be revealed by comparing the number of units built during each decade that still existed in 1980 and determining how many fewer there were in 1990. In this way, it can be ascertained how much older, middle-aged, and newer housing may be demolished or converted to nonhousing uses. It should be noted, however, that new housing may be of lower value and quality than the norms for a specific territory and for a region. The presence of new housing does not always signify expensive housing or greater attractiveness compared to other areas. Nor does disappearance of housing necessarily signify abandonment and demolition; it may indicate conversion to nonhousing uses and thus may increase mixed use.

A housing affordability indicator will be useful. This indicator can be framed to facilitate comparisons among regions, as well as to compare parts of regions. The indicator should be the median value of housing divided by median (family or household) income. This ratio should be derived for the region. Similar relationships for jurisdictions, census tracts, and block groups will indicate whether each subarea is more or less affordable for its residents than the median housing for the region. Whether the median value housing for the region is affordable can be ascertained by dividing it by the median (family and household) income for jurisdictions, census tracts, and block groups.

The number of public housing units and other lesser degrees of public-subsidized units would be pertinent to reinvestment needs. These units would be correlated, usually, with low incomes of households and families and with high poverty rates. The age of these units would also indicate reinvestment needs. A reasonable hypothesis would be that the higher the proportion of subsidized housing, the greater the need for reinvestment. Some of these data are available by census tract, but not for all forms of housing subsidy.

Crime Indicators

The relevance of crime and safety to neighborhood viability is one of those things that "everyone knows." But this subject is one for which there is a large gap between what everyone knows and what can be constructed in an indicator.

One question concerns the relationship between beliefs and reality. Presumably it is beliefs that affect decisions to move in, move out, or stay put, but information about beliefs is rarely available, beliefs change, and information about beliefs is disconnected from information about location decisions. Crime data based on reports to police are not necessarily correlated with beliefs about safety, nor are they good indicators of the occurrence of crime, if victimization surveys are a guide to actual occurrence of crime. If reported crime data are to be used, which ones? Violent crimes or property crimes? Certain violent crimes? Reported crime data for homicides are rather accurate, but data for rape are not. Beliefs about danger of crime may be general rather than specific—that is, new-comers may believe that cities are more dangerous than suburbs. With little time to consider location options, many newcomers may write off the central city without having any information about crime in different parts of the city. Moreover, location decisions may be influenced by certain types of safety, such as safety in schools, for which there may be no crime data.

In most respects, however, these problems are not relevant for general knowl-edge system indicators, because crime data are not available for the units (census tracts and block groups) for which indicators are being constructed. On the other hand, local police data may be available, as may surveys of citizens, that can be used for project-focused systems in some cities. Police data, however, are more likely to be available for police precincts rather than for census tracts.

School Indicators

Schools are fundamental considerations to some people when deciding where to move or stay where they are, although this populace does not make up a large percentage of the moving population, since far less than half the population has children of school age. For most families with children, there are a number of acceptable school districts in any given metropolitan area. On the other hand, for many middle- and upper-income families, there are also many unacceptable school districts. Some of these families may choose a neighborhood despite this problem, and then enroll their children in private schools. Still, the reputations and performance of schools affect housing markets.

Census data are not useful for constructing indicators, however, because they do not measure school conditions that are relevant to residential location deci-sions. From census data, one can learn the number of children in school and the percentage of residents who have attained varying numbers of years of educa-tion, but the data relevant to location decisions would pertain more to perfor-mance of students or characteristics of students. Scores on standard tests, for example, are used as clues about schools' quality; test scores also are correlated with race and poverty. Free-lunch eligibility is an indicator of income available for each school. Parents' evaluation of schools may involve several dimensions, such as student performance, school programs, peer characteristics, school safety, and quality of physical facilities. Data about most of these conditions will not be available. If available, the data are not easily arrayed on a standard scale.

Further, they will not be available for census tracts, only for school attendance zones—which may be ambiguous because of gerrymandering, leapfrogging, and busing in pursuit of racial integration goals. For these reasons, school indicators may not be useful for a general knowledge system, but they may be of some use for a project-focused system.

On the other hand, one possible indicator available in census data is percentage of children by race in public schools. High percentages of minorities are usually associated with low test scores and high free-lunch eligibility. Thus, race and ethnicity may be proxies for test scores and income, factors that may affect location decisions of middle- and upper-income families. These data also are available for census tracts. Thus, race and ethnicity of public school children may be the closest available practical indicator of school conditions routinely available for census tracts.

Poverty Indicators

Poverty is an income indicator. In contrast with median family income, which measures a central point in the array of incomes, poverty measures the percentage of the population that is below a specified income level. This quality makes poverty an indicator of need in a way that measures of central tendency are not. It also measures limited capacities, in some respects, such as limited capacity to qualify for a mortgage loan. Thus, poverty indicators can identify a target population that may not be reachable by a goal of increasing home ownership rates.

In addition, poverty is related to other social phenomena. Neighborhoods with high poverty also tend to have higher than average crime rates. These neighborhoods tend to have more free-lunch-eligible schoolchildren, and their schools' test scores tend to be lower than test scores in schools with fewer free-lunch-eligible students. Poverty data are included in the census. They are available at census tract and block group scales. They can be used in constructing indicators for a general knowledge system, therefore, where crime and school data cannot.

Poverty data deserve to be included because they measure a low-income segment of the population that has difficulty qualifying for mortgage loans. This population also tends to live in neighborhoods where housing quality, or housing values at least, are lower than the median. Poverty data, then, indicate need for reinvestment indirectly. In addition, because of their association with high crime and low test scores, they partially compensate for the absence of useful crime and school data for national or other comparative purposes.

Family poverty data are more useful than data on poverty of individuals. In some jurisdictions and neighborhoods with large numbers of college and university students, poverty rates may be very high because students are often treated as being below the poverty level. Schoolchildren's test scores, of course, are more influenced by family poverty than by poverty of unrelated individuals.

Thus, either a family poverty indicator or, perhaps, an indicator of poverty in families with children should be used in a general knowledge system. Because of the multiple purposes that poverty data can serve (since they substitute for unavailable data), extra weight for this indicator should be considered.

Race and Ethnicity Indicators

Race is a consequential subject for an indicator for two reasons. First, the minority rate of home ownership is lower than the national average. If minorities are a target group for increasing home ownership, it is essential to know the potential for increasing their home ownership in each region and in each subarea within regions. Second, the presence of minorities may influence location decisions. It is common knowledge that some people want to avoid minorities; thus, minority presence is sometimes treated as an avoidance factor. On the other hand, in a sample of census tracts with large percentages of African-Americans in 24 metropolitan areas, it was found that the minority percentage decreased in one-third of them from 1970 to 1990. Thus, it cannot be assumed that as a minority share grows large, it will inevitably grow larger. The diversity of racial change trends suggests that the notion of "tipping points" leading inevitably to 100 percent minority neighborhoods, an idea that became common in the 1950s and 1960s, needs to be amended based on trends in the 1970s and 1980s.

These recent trends contribute ambiguity to constructing indicators of race as well as to weighting them. Perhaps comparing the percentage of African-Americans who are homeowners with the percentage of whites who are homeowners would yield a sense of reinvestment need and potential for increase in home ownership. A similar indicator for home ownership among Hispanics will be needed as well. In a number of metropolitan areas in the West, Southwest, and South, Hispanics are more numerous than African-Americans, and in a few places they are more numerous than whites. Nationally, the increase in Hispanic population has been rapid; forecasts estimate that Hispanics will come to outnumber African-Americans early in the 21st century.

Because of the potential location influence of racial and ethnic minority presence, indicators of the African-American and the Hispanic population also will be needed. The percentages of the total population in block groups, census tracts, jurisdictions, and regions that are African-American or Hispanic may be the best indicator. These percentages can be expected to range from 0 to 100 percent.

Regional Growth Indicator

Regional growth should be included in the indicator array, because high regional growth tends to be associated with outward movement of middle- and upper-income residents. A companion tendency is that low-income residents, who become a larger group under high-growth trends, also become more numerous in old and middle-aged neighborhoods. Most new housing is too costly for people below a region's median income. Therefore, rapid regional growth usually includes outer suburban and exurban population growth and income increases. At the same time, median income (and sometimes population) go down in the central city, some inner suburbs, and perhaps one or more sectors.

An indicator of central city (and census tract and block group) vulnerability is needed. It could involve a ratio of city to regional population growth, but if the city, or census tract or block group is losing population, appropriate mathematical representation of this relationship becomes problematic. A simpler and probably more appropriate approach would be to use an indicator based on the rate of regional population growth. The appropriateness of this indicator will be compromised for growing central cities, which will tend to capture more middle- and upper-income population growth than will cities that are stable or losing population. For a general knowledge system, however, a simple percentage rate of regional population growth in the most recent census decade is probably best. For a project-focused system, complementary information about city growth and census tract growth can be added, since the project-focused system will be more complex and have less mathematical consistency.

Employment Indicators

Employment should be included in the indicator array, because it is related to convenience. Many urban economists and geographers have argued that location decisions can be understood as trade-offs between housing and transportation costs. The main transportation cost in these estimates is the journey to work.

Unfortunately, it is nearly impossible to obtain accurate employment data for small areas. National sources provide partial employment data for counties, excluding public employment (U.S. Bureau of the Census, County Business Patterns), or for metropolitan areas (U.S. Department of Commerce Bureau of Economic Analysis). State employment services may have data, but it will typically exclude the self-employed (a growing sector) and public employees, and it will often be difficult to relate to census tracts.

Consequently, it is not practical to include employment data in a general knowledge system. To some extent, employment data can be included in a project-focused system. These data may not be quantified accurately by census tract; it will be apparent to local observers, however, that there is a great deal of employment in some census tracts and little in others.

The potential location influence of anchor employers will come into play in project-focused systems. Anchor employers can be public or private. Most employment is private, but most private employers have location options; even private employers who are tied to a specific metropolitan area will usually have location options within it. Some public employers and private nonprofit institutions, on the other hand, have massive investments in fixed locations that cannot be moved. Universities are the most numerous and largest examples. Hospitals and museums are often are in the same category. Not only are universities the largest employers in this category, but they also have the most clients (students) who live nearby and probably have the largest number of employees who are attracted to having short distances between home and work. Thus, anchor employers such as universities can have enormous importance in the plans of strategists using project-focused systems. Anchor employers, in fact, may be one of the significant reasons why pre-1940 neighborhoods have shown signs of resurgence in the 1980s. The presence of anchor employers should be considered in explaining why some old neighborhoods have been attractive and others have not.

Postindustrial transformations in regional economies may help explain region, jurisdiction, and neighborhood trends in employment. These in turn may help explain population and income transitions. While information and analysis of these trends may enhance understanding of transitions for project-focused systems, we do not have proposals for how to make them useful for a general knowledge system in understanding neighborhood reinvestment needs, risks, and sustainable characteristics.

Transportation Accessibility Indicators

We will hypothesize that proximity to bus routes is not a significant influence on location decisions. Bus routes may, however, indicate need for reinvestment—that is, they may pass through older, denser neighborhoods and through middle-aged, less diverse residential areas. Reinvestment may be needed in both types of areas.

Fixed-rail mass transit (heavy and light rail), including commuter rail, is more likely to influence location decisions because fixed rail has more appeal to middle- and upper-income residents, as well as to families. Fixed rail may be a better indicator of areas that will attract reinvestment, as well as areas where new investment may occur. Greater density will often occur near transit stops, but this investment may lead to a decrease rather than an increase in per capita and median family income. Smaller units may not appeal to families of means. We hypothesize that the main income gains will occur outside the typical area of greatest accessibility. Income gains, under this hypothesis, would be likely in areas within one-half mile to two miles of transit stations. In this area, disadvantages of traffic and intruders would be outweighed by advantages of optional short trips to transit stations and nearby commercial goods and services.

If these observations are accurate, it is not clear how they lead to an indicator of accessibility, reinvestment, or location influences for a general knowledge system. They can be used for project-focused systems, however.

Summary

Many useful indicators can be constructed from U.S. census data. Even though they are available only every 10 years, conditions and trends in these data can reveal income decline, need for reinvestment, and sprawl on the metropolitan fringe. These data alone, when converted into trend information about neighborhoods and suburbs, can reveal dangers that are usually ignored in strategic planning, comprehensive planning, and other types of policy planning. Data for indicators discussed here for general knowledge systems and project-focused systems can provide rich interpretations of dangers. Modest predictions about future trends, and policy judgments about the severity of local conditions, are possible. Strategic planning can be a powerful tool for making policy and choosing priorities if relevant information about population, income, housing, and related variables is emphasized rather than, as happens too often, ignored.

Chapter 9

Regional Governance of
the New Metropolitan Mosaic

Cities, suburbs, and rural areas suffer from consequences of excessive sprawl, insufficient reinvestment, and severe income disparities. These problems result in imbalances and disequilibrium. Excessive sprawl and disparities and too little reinvestment can be coped with separately; however, mitigating these problems will be more probable if their interactive effects are reflected in public policies and private actions. Based on environmental scans that reveal dangers and opportunities, strategic planning processes should aim, if possible, at synthetic policy approaches. But synthetic policies are difficult to formulate and implement. Eight examples of approaches to sprawl, reinvestment, and disparity problems that reflect synthetic thinking are discussed here, along with a proposal to supplement such examples with a Sustainable Region Incentive Fund.

Emergence of crisis ghetto conditions can be anticipated, as can decline of cities and suburbs when greenfield development on the fringe of metropolitan areas is emphasized over reinvestment and infill in established neighborhoods. Wide income disparities among jurisdictions within a metropolitan area signal inequity and ineffectiveness in some public services. Large income disparities are a sign of political, economic, and social stress.

Policies affecting metropolitan areas more often pursue quantity than quality goals. Achieving long-range quantity, as well as quality, goals has become increasingly dependent on environmental quality. The tyranny of easy development decisions reduces the quality of the living environment. Mutual adjustments among diverse public- and private-sector actors involve conflicts between security-motivated behavior by households and businesses versus more abstract public interest goals.

Public interest goals should include a semblance of balance and a search for equilibrium. Balance is not uniformity, and equilibrium is not immobility. Each implies that avoiding extremes is desirable. Extreme inequalities and spatial concentrations of poor people and minorities, for example, should be avoided. Extreme rates of change, especially declines, in neighborhoods and jurisdictions are destabilizing. Balance implies that the territorial, including jurisdiction and neighborhood, parts of a metropolitan region should not deviate too far from social and economic conditions that represent regional conditions.

Characteristics of balance are appropriate subjects for debate, whether by income, race, density, pattern, finance, transportation, education, housing, the range within which equilibrium is sought (ratios of social conditions not greater than 10 to 1, 5 to 1, 2 to 1, or some lesser ratio), or the territories that are relevant (jurisdictions, neighborhoods, school catchment areas, commuter sheds). Extremes should be coped with, compensated for, and limited.

Regions generally lack governance systems explicitly focused on promoting their good health. As Richard Briffault (1996, 1164) has argued: "The traditional model of decentralization of authority to local governments with broad regulatory, revenue-raising, and service-provision powers within their boundaries but minimal responsibilities to people and localities outside those boundaries is in tension with the basic economic and social structure of contemporary metropolitan areas." Most regional governance addresses isolated functions—water, sewer, highways, public transportation, airports, jails, public health, and welfare. Due to the United States' wealth, large internal market, insulation from ravages of war, vital economy, and penalties for extreme violations of public health and safety, the infrastructure of metropolitan areas has adapted gradually to serious stresses. Few believe, however, that the results are effective. They do not compare well with results achieved in less wealthy developed nations (Newman and Kenworthy 1999). Ineffective results follow from insufficient attention to considering influences of area and power, pattern and density, population and neighborhood, and space and place.

Here we will examine eight approaches to settlement patterns, disparities, and more sustainable communities and regions, each of which holds promise, each of which involves uncertain effectiveness. Concluding this chapter, we will offer a modest proposal for an additional method by which regional perspectives on reduced disparities, settlement patterns with less sprawl, increased reinvestment, and regenerating equilibrium might be enhanced.

Eight Attempts to Cope with the Postsuburban Metropolis

Identifying the following approaches to metropolitan governance as instances of coping with postsuburban conditions may be overreaching. The actors probably have not referred to postsuburbia. Still, they know the conditions used here to identify the postsuburban era—farmland loss, low-density fringe development, rising fringe incomes, substantial suburban income decline, suburban job increases, overall city decline, and volatile improvement and decline in city neighborhoods.

Two of these approaches to metropolitan governance—Minneapolis–St. Paul and Portland, Oregon—started in the 1960s and 1970s. Three approaches—

Virginia, Maryland, and Tennessee—began in 1996, 1997, and 1999. A sixth approach is the New Urbanism, a movement that gained considerable force during the 1990s. The seventh is the Third Regional Plan for New York of 1996. As we explain later, some of the small- and large-scale principles of the New Urbanists are consistent with the regional concepts of the New York Regional Plan Association. The eighth concerns prospects for knitting together the post-suburban metropolis with public transit. A ninth conceptual approach is our proposal for a Sustainable Region Incentive Fund, which is intended to overcome some obstacles to success of the systems in Portland, the Twin Cities, Virginia, Maryland, and Tennessee.

Minneapolis–St. Paul

The Minneapolis–St. Paul Metropolitan Council was created as a planning agency by the state legislature in 1967. The governor appointed its 16 members. For 27 years the Metropolitan Council held some supervisory powers over the Metropolitan Transit Commission, the Regional Transit Board, and the Metropolitan Waste Commission, plus review power regarding capital projects over $5 million at the Minneapolis–St. Paul International Airport. In 1994, the Metropolitan Council assumed control over transit and waste operations and their respective commissions and boards were abolished, giving the council direct responsibility for a $300 million budget. The Metropolitan Council also collected revenues and dispensed payments to jurisdictions pursuant to the seven-county growth-sharing policy. Since 1971, 40 percent of real property tax revenue from new industrial and commercial development has gone into a central account, with the host jurisdiction retaining 60 percent of the revenue. The growth-sharing revenues were distributed annually based on the inverse of each jurisdiction's commercial revenue capacity. By the mid-1990s, this growth-sharing fund totaled $367 million, about 20 percent of the region's commercial and industrial real property tax base. Sharing this growth fund has reduced interjurisdictional tax base disparities from 50 to 1 to a 12 to 1 ratio (Orfield 1997, 87).

Myron Orfield (1997, 87), a leader of efforts in the Minnesota legislature to reform metropolitan governance, has observed: "This system makes regional competition marginally fairer, but actual disparities remain high and fiscal zoning and competition for tax base intense. . . . Two other distributional inequities can arise. Cities with a higher than average commercial base, but with low-valued homes and increasing social need, contribute tax base. At the same time, cities with mainly high-valued homes and large per household tax bases that have eschewed commercial development receive money from the system."

Minneapolis and St. Paul have sometimes been net contributors to this growth-sharing system. On the other hand, effects of tax base disparities among suburbs have been mitigated. Public service and property tax rate differences also have been lessened. Limiting differences in tax and service capacity could have restrained tendencies for residents to move where their taxes would be lower and public service quality would be higher. Income disparities increased less from 1960 to 1990 in the Minneapolis–St. Paul suburbs compared with 23 other metropolitan areas that were studied (Lucy 1994b).

Planning, Growth, and Sprawl

Upon its creation in 1967, the Metropolitan Council developed a comprehensive plan to guide regional growth. The ensuing *Metropolitan Development Guide* had a housing chapter whose goals included increasing affordable housing and broadening its geographic distribution. The suburban share of subsidized housing increased from 10 percent in 1971 to 41 percent in 1983. Thereafter, the Metropolitan Council stopped enforcing this policy, according to Orfield (1997, 175), because there were insufficient federal housing funds to warrant continuing it.

Although the Metropolitan Council was created, in part, to guide development and, some hoped, to reduce sprawl, pricing policies for sewage collection and treatment have had the opposite effect. During the 1960s, the price of sewer connections rose with greater distance from the central treatment plant. This policy captured the higher cost of serving more remote locations. Hence, it was an inducement to compact development. In the 1970s, however, the suburbs succeeded in changing the policy to average-cost pricing, so that remote locations paid the same connection fees as central and intermediate locations. In 1987, the Minnesota legislature fully regionalized the average cost of both capital and operating expenditures, reducing residual obstacles to sprawl (Orfield 1997, 176). With costs equalized, the tyranny of easy development decisions was operating to encourage more sprawl in the Minneapolis–St. Paul region. The Metropolitan Council had established a growth boundary, in effect, by providing sewer connections inside, but not outside, a service boundary. But metropolitan planners acknowledge (Porter 1997, 67) that most development within the service boundary "could be characterized as urban sprawl."

Decline and Revival

Myron Orfield (1997, 178 and 180), summarized the decline of the Metropolitan Council in the 1980s, and its incipient revival in the mid-1990s, as follows:

> Despite the regional authority embodied in the council and the existence of a superstructure for tackling the problems of the city and older suburbs, few problems have been solved. Instead, the Met Council has become part of the problem of regional economic polarization, helping exclusive, economical-

ly powerful communities to grow at the expense of the region. The council has neither promoted economic stability and equity nor provided consistent leadership to deal with regional conflict.

In the mid-1990s, the advent of a newly reinvigorated regional agenda and a legislative power base in the central cities and inner and low-tax-base suburbs helped to revitalize the Met Council. It was forced to consider issues such as housing, land use, and transportation in the context of what is happening at the region's core. Its progress, though unspectacular, has been a major improvement. After more than a decade of dormancy, the council helped spearhead the Livable Communities Act, improved language in the Regional Blueprint on affordable housing, put forth legislation to repeal the uniform sewer pricing policy, and is beginning to tentatively discuss denser land use patterns. An elected council would provide the needed impetus and regional leadership to bring about real progress on these and other issues.

Reform

From 1993 through 1998, a series of metropolitan governance reform measures were promoted by a coalition of elected officials representing Minneapolis, St. Paul, and suburbs with a low tax base (especially those north of the Twin Cities) and by a growing consensus of public interest groups, churches, and newspapers. These measures would have reduced barriers to affordable housing in suburbs with high housing values, reintroduced marginal pricing of sewer connections to assign the real cost of sewer extensions to the growing outer suburbs, given preference to transportation investments to assist older cities and suburbs, altered metropolitan tax-base sharing to give more revenue to jurisdictions with low housing values and increased the pool of revenue to be shared, and switched from an appointed to an elected Metropolitan Council. Bills were passed by the Minnesota legislature on these subjects, often by wide and increasing margins. Nearly all of them were vetoed by Governor Arne Carlson (Orfield 1997, 104–105).

The Minneapolis–St. Paul experience demonstrates that a formal regional structure for governance is no guarantee of results. The terms of legislation that guide the regional structure matter. The mode of selecting members of the regional governing body matters. The interaction between local jurisdictions, the metropolitan governance structure, and the state legislature and the governor matter most of all. Local governments are creatures of the state. Meaningful metropolitan reform needs ongoing state support, as well as local and metropolitan support.

Portland

The Portland metropolitan area is better known than any other region in the United States for making aggressive use of a growth boundary to influence development patterns. The growth pattern in the Portland metropolitan area has changed. Presumably much of the change is traceable to the growth boundary, although other policies and conditions may have influenced development trends. The boundary must include enough land for 20 years of growth. Estimates identify 95 percent of population growth as having occurred within Portland's growth boundary (Nelson and Moore 1996). Investments in light-rail transit (which contributed to 33 to 43 percent of downtown commuters arriving by transit in 1990) (Corbett 1994), a downtown river park, and major urban design projects have helped slow movement of middle-income families to the suburbs. One ambiguity in ascertaining the causes of development patterns is that other cities and towns in Oregon are required to designate growth boundaries, but other Oregon cities have had less success than Portland in guiding growth.

In addition, the Metropolitan Portland Housing Rule requires that local governments permit housing developments such that 50 percent or more of new units will be in attached single-family or multifamily structures. The Home Builders Association of Metropolitan Portland and 1000 Friends of Oregon, a land-use and environmental organization, concluded in 1991 that suburban development included more multifamily and attached single-family units than before the Rule went into effect, and it was constructed in more compact patterns that conserved land (Beatley and Manning 1997, 44). The reasons for this relative success need additional explanation in light of other findings that more development occurred outside the growth boundaries of three other Oregon metropolitan areas than occurred in the Portland region. This could be because of greater undeveloped subdivided land in the other three metropolitan areas than in Portland (Nelson and Moore 1996). Perhaps lower densities within the growth boundaries occurred because other metropolitan areas lacked the Portland requirement that housing development occur at greater than minimum allowable densities rather than at less than some designated maximum density. This requirement, that development occur at no less than 4 to 10 units per acre in different zones, "is unique among American metropolitan regions" (Porter 1997, 215).

Support for Growth Boundary

Land development regulations are often unpopular, but this tendency does not seem to afflict the Portland growth boundary concept. The Portland region has an elected council that adopts regulations. Since 1979 voters have elected representatives directly to the Metropolitan Council rather than electing municipal and county councils that, in turn, could appoint members to serve on the Metropolitan Council. If voters are angered, they can turn the regulating body's members out of office promptly. In a growth boundary referendum in 1993, voters chose the policy option that would restrict development by the year 2040 to the existing Urban Growth Boundary rather than allow it within an expanded UGB. Implementing this preference will prove challenging if projections of a population increase of 720,000 (a 65 percent increase) by 2040 actually occur. The policy preference for infill and density in corridors and around transit stations was favored over expanding the growth boundary and developing in the newly encompassed fringe or pursuing a combination of infill, development near transit, and some fringe development within an expanded UGB (Beatley and Manning 1997, 206). The 2040 framework envisions 25 town centers with shops and services within easy walks of residences, plus nine regional centers of more intense development, mainly around light-rail links (Claiborne 1997).

In 1997 the Portland Metropolitan Council set aside 19,000 acres outside the UGB as a 30-year reserve for future development. The council also was debating alternative proposals to open 3,000 to 10,000 acres of land for immediate development. Agitation to expand the UGB was occurring partly due to rapid growth in the 1990s, which may have occurred because of quality of life achievements in which the UGB played a part. High-tech companies, including Intel, invested $13 billion in new plants inside the UGB. In 1999, Intel's expansion by as many as 1,000 additional jobs, for a total of 5,000 employees, was encouraged with property tax breaks by Washington County officials, but with the proviso that Intel would pay the county $1,000 per worker per year if expansion rose above 5,000 total employees (Verhovek 1999). The average new development lot size shrank from 13,000 square feet (three units per acre) in 1979 to 7,400 square feet (six units per acre) in 1997. Due to rapid growth in the 1990s, the median price of a single-family home had risen from $64,000 in 1989 to $139,900 in 1996 (Claiborne 1997). That rise, though rapid, brought the median price only a little above the national median in 1998 ("Real Estate Notes" 1998). The rise in housing prices was significant, since during the 1970s and 1980s Portland's housing prices were 72 percent or less of the national median price. Analyzing housing prices from 1976 through 1990, Gerrit Knapp and Arthur Nelson (1992, 86–87) concluded: "Changes in relative price [in Portland]—which fell throughout the 1980s—offer little evidence of constrained housing supply. . . . [D]emand-side variables, which stem largely from regional economic performance, appear to dominate movements in housing price and starts." Demand for housing picked up during the 1990s due to the popularity of Oregon and Portland as places to live and work. Higher demand may have influenced housing price changes more than land use regulation influenced supply.

Growth Boundary and Housing Values

The Portland area's attractiveness does not demonstrate problems with the UGB. If anything, Portland's attractiveness is partially attributable to the UGB. Trends in Portland demonstrate that success in managing development brings a new variation on development pressure flowing from greater attractiveness in competition with the sprawling disintegration typical of most metropolitan areas in the United States.

Portland's regional development pattern causes some concerns. The southwest suburban quarter has dominated regional employment growth. Fiscal capacity has increased there, while its social needs are fewer than elsewhere. The suburbs with a high tax base had a median household income (1990) and median housing value (1993) that was about 50 percent higher than in the central city and the suburbs with a low tax base (Orfield 1997, 157–158). These disparities in the Portland area were smaller than in other regions studied by Myron Orfield, where the household incomes and housing values in suburbs with a high tax base were double those in the central city and suburbs with a low tax base, as in the Chicago or (even larger) Philadelphia region (Orfield 1997, 161 and 165).

Elected or Appointed Councils

In influencing development patterns, the elected Portland Metropolitan Council has arguably been more effective than the appointed Minneapolis–St. Paul Metropolitan Council. Myron Orfield (1997, 101–102) described different results in defending growth boundaries in both regions and then offered an explanation:

> Oregon and Minnesota both have strong land use laws with growth boundaries. . . . In twenty years, [Portland] Oregon has permitted 2,000 acres of exceptions to its boundary. In Minnesota, the Twin Cities Met Council, with its weak derivative power, has avoided confrontation and has never brought a lawsuit to enforce its land planning act. Between 1987 and 1991, the Twin Cities allowed seventy-eight exceptions to the boundary, and 18,000 acres of forest and farmland were added.
>
> In Portland, Oregon, politicians win and lose major elections on growth management issues. Most voters in the Twin Cities and most other parts of the nation are completely unaware of the vital importance of these issues to their daily lives. . . . An

elected official's power derives from voters. . . . Elected officials tend to test the limits of their authority vis-à-vis other units of government. Similarly, because elected officials defend their prerogatives, competing governments are less likely to usurp power from elected bodies than from appointed bodies. . . . Oregon's regional government has been more willing than the Twin Cities' appointed Metropolitan Council to exercise its powers vis-à-vis competing authorities.

Orfield's opinion became the dominant view among state legislators. In 1997 the Minnesota legislature attempted to enact legislation specifying that Metropolitan Council members should be elected by the voters, not appointed by the governor, but Governor Carlson vetoed it (Claiborne 1997).

Maryland and Virginia

Maryland and Virginia border each other and Washington, D.C. Their governance policies contrast vividly, although each has strong counties, few cities, no townships, and fewer towns and villages than most states. Maryland has traditionally granted substantial development authority to local governments, authorizing them to adopt annual growth caps, adequate public facilities ordinances, and transferable development rights. Montgomery County, north of Washington, D.C., for example, adopted an Adequate Public Facilities Ordinance in 1973, an Annual Growth Policy in 1979, and Transfer of Development Rights in 1980. With these tools, local governments can prioritize capital investments, deny some development permissions based on public facilities being inadequate and low priority, and shift some development to higher-priority locations. Virginia, in contrast, does not permit this type of local government influence. Maryland provides significant funding to localities for building roads and financing public transportation from a state gasoline tax. In Virginia, the state is responsible for building and maintaining all roads outside of cities, although it will permit exceptions. Maryland shares the cost of building local public schools as well as the capital costs of water supply and sewage treatment. Virginia provides no state funds for water and sewer. In 1998 the Virginia General Assembly authorized the first state general funds since the 1950s to help local governments build public schools. These policies constitute important background conditions for major initiatives adopted by the state governments of Maryland in 1997 and Virginia in 1996.

Smart Growth

In Maryland, Democratic Governor Parris Glendening promoted the Smart Growth Areas Act. Smart growth meant influencing where, when, and how development occurred. It did not necessarily imply slowing growth; growth could perhaps even be accelerated. In a summary, the Maryland Office of Planning (Kreitner 1997) described smart growth this way:

> This legislation directs State spending to "Priority Funding Areas." . . . Focusing State spending in these areas will provide the most efficient and effective use of taxpayer dollars, avoid higher taxes which would be necessary to fund infrastructure for sprawl development, and encourage development there and, thus, reduce the pressure for sprawl.
>
> Beginning October 1, 1998, the State must direct funding for "growth related" projects to Priority Funding Areas. "Growth related" projects defined in the legislation include most State programs which encourage or support growth and development such as highways, sewer and water construction, economic development assistance, and State leases or construction of new office facilities.
>
> State funding in communities with only water service (without a sewer system) and in rural villages is restricted to projects which maintain the character of the community. The projects must not increase the growth capacity of the village or community except for limited peripheral and in-fill development.
>
> Prior to funding a growth related project, State agencies must obtain a written statement from the local government that the proposal is in a Priority Funding Area. In addition, local governments must demonstrate a commitment to these growth areas by insuring that non-State funding for planned water and sewer systems moves forward in advance of, or concurrent with, State funding for growth related projects.
>
> The legislation formalizes a State school construction funding policy that facilities in established neighborhoods should be of equal quality to new schools. The legislation also requires coordination and cooperation between counties and their municipalities for school facility planning to avoid overcrowding and to help defray the cost of school construction required to serve new residential development.

State-Local Interplay

A potential problem is embedded in the method of designating Priority Funding Areas with maps developed by county officials. Initial maps were submitted in the fall of 1998 to the Maryland Office of Planning: ". . . [T]hey range widely, from narrow and carefully targeted plans for growth to . . . plans that essentially declare the entire county open for growth," as Allegany County did (Gurwitt 1999, 20).

The rationale of the Maryland Smart Growth Areas Act follows from the previous state role of providing some funding assistance to local governments for a variety of public facilities that adapted to growth but also encouraged growth. Having placed itself in that facilitating role, the state government was vulnerable to being pulled along excessively by local development decisions, regardless of the cumulative results, as well as to having state costs escalate while exercising little control over decisions.

Instead, Governor Glendening and the state legislature attempted to improve development results at less cost to the state. The potential to achieve this combination is hinted at in Montgomery County's description (1997) of its growth planning, in which it claims: "By channeling development into areas best served by roads and transit, Montgomery County is able to support almost 150,000 additional jobs and almost 70,000 more housing units without overburdening its existing transportation network." Since the 1970s, Montgomery County has integrated low- and moderate-income housing in subdivisions of 50 or more dwellings. In exchange for requiring that 12 to 15 percent of units be set aside for low- and moderate-income households, developers have been given density bonuses. The outcome is more dispersal of low- and moderate-income households than is typical of affluent suburban counties (Orfield 1998, 37).

Virginia

The rationale for Virginia's Regional Competitiveness Act of 1996 follows from its tradition of state infrastructure finance and network of local and regional roles concerning land development. In Virginia, state government has not assisted localities with water and sewer construction or, until 1998, with school building construction and refurbishment from general revenues. The state builds and maintains highways inside and outside cities and lesser roads outside cities. Local governments have not been given regulatory tools such as growth boundaries, annual growth caps, adequate public facilities ordinances, and transferable development rights. On the other hand, there are relatively few local governments, counties perform functions exercised by townships and villages in some states, the state is blanketed by regional planning agencies, cities are geographically separate from counties (Virginia is the only state in which city-county separation is a statewide norm), and there are strong, relatively independent community colleges and state universities.

In this milieu, state government has relatively few capital facilities partnerships with local governments that drag them into higher expenditures in response to local decisions, in contrast with Maryland. There are relatively few local governments, and these are more autonomous than in many states. Given these structural and financial traditions, the Regional Competitiveness Act (RCA) of 1996 can be viewed as an attempt to extend traditions rather than as a bold innovation.

The Regional Competitiveness Act

The main features of the RCA are the following:

- Financial incentives are provided for localities to participate in regional activities, with points being assigned for current regional cooperation and agreements for additional multijurisdictional cooperation.
- Regional policy-making partnerships are required, with partnership members including chief executives of local governments, major businesses, public schools, community colleges, and universities.
- The regional partnerships must develop strategic economic development plans that take into account their region's strengths and weaknesses relative to their main regional competitors in other states.

Points are assigned to determine eligibility, in addition to evaluating the features above, with 50 percent of the points based on economic development plans. In the first round of 17 submissions by June 30, 1997, seven were deemed eligible, and the $6 million fund was divided among them based on regional population. The main regional activity that was proposed in the successful strategic plans was workforce development—an ironic outcome in light of the origins of the RCA, as discussed below.

The Urban Partnership

The RCA grew out of a two-year organizing, research, policy development, and lobbying effort by the Partnership for Urban Virginia, a coalition of most of the larger cities and a number of large businesses represented by the Virginia Chamber of Commerce. Their main theme was that strong regions require strong central cities. Virginia's regions were viewed as growing more slowly than some competitor regions, especially the Charlotte and Raleigh-Durham areas in North Carolina. Growing income disparities between Virginia's cities and suburbs, and growing poverty concentrations in the central cities, were viewed as dangers that diminished the economic competitiveness of Virginia's regions. One important goal of the Urban Partnership, therefore, was to promote policies that would reduce income disparities between central cities and suburbs and that would cope with the existing disparities.

In the draft legislation that emerged from the Urban Partnership's deliberations, the point system did not include economic development proposals. Instead, it emphasized public programs that distributed burdens based on ability to pay (regional revenue sharing, development tax-base sharing, regional finance of public education) and distribution of low-income residents more evenly throughout metropolitan areas (fair-share housing programs). To broaden legislative support and gain the support of Republican Governor George Allen, the Urban Partnership and its legislative allies accepted economic development projects, plus the original regional finance measures, as the highest priority. Because the point system recognized prior cooperative agreements among local governments, adding economic development to the eligible project list eliminated the need for any additional cooperation on public services, sharing of revenues, or financial burdens in order to qualify (Richman and Oliver 1997).

Economic Development Wins

As the regional partnerships recognized this situation, the winning proposals in 1997 emphasized economic development projects. Most proposed projects were not geographically specific. By emphasizing workforce training, the strategic plans accomplished four decision-making objectives. They addressed an aspect of interregional economic competition that was genuine in a high-technology, information-based business era. They provided a role for the education and business organizations that had been brought to the negotiating table as regional partnership members. They avoided strain on their emerging regional coalitions by not choosing any specific location at which to concentrate investment. And they picked a subject on which some progress could occur with the available low funding level.

What began as a major effort to redefine intergovernmental relations within Virginia's metropolitan areas evolved into another in a 35-year series of workforce training programs that began with the federal Manpower Training Act of 1962. Would greater funding shift attention to other projects? The biennial budget adopted for the 1998–2000 fiscal years allocated only $16.5 million to the RCA. This slight increase was accompanied by allocation of at least a minimum amount of funding for workforce training to each region in the state. Economic development projects remained sufficient to qualify for larger funding. Thus, reform of metropolitan governance or policies to cope with poverty and income disparities are not likely to occur within the 1999 framework of the RCA.

Tennessee

In 1998, the Tennessee General Assembly adopted and Governor Don Sundquist signed Public Act 1101 on Growth Policy, Annexation, and Incorporation, also known as the Tennessee Growth Policy Act of 1998. Effective January 1, 1999, each metropolitan area in Tennessee was required to create and adopt a comprehensive growth policy plan, including a boundary for 20 years of growth, by July 1, 2001, and was then prohibited from amending it for three years. Territory not within an urban growth boundary (UGB) or a planned growth area was to be "preserved for agriculture, recreation, forest, wildlife, and uses other than high-density commercial or residential development." In addition, a city "may use any statutory method to annex territory within its UGB, including annexation by ordinance and referendum." If the annexation is by ordinance, a county can challenge it. The case will be heard by a judge trained in mediation, and "the burden of proof is on the petitioner to show that the annexation is unreasonable." If it annexes, a city must formulate a plan for providing public services. Any county (and municipalities within it) with an approved growth plan by July 1, 2000, would become eligible for a 5 percent addition to its score in being evaluated to receive a variety of state grants for industrial infrastructure, water and wastewater treatment, and housing and community development funds. In addition, any county lacking an approved growth plan by July 1, 2001, would lose its eligibility for some of these grants, as well as for federal funds authorized under the Community Development Block Grant and the Intermodal Surface Transportation Efficiency Act (ISTEA) (Institute for Public Service 1998).

Potential Growth Boundary and Annexation Effects

This legislation makes Tennessee the first state to mandate a statewide system of growth boundaries with annexation rights by city council ordinance within those boundaries. The intent of the act includes reducing sprawl, preserving agriculture and natural uses of land, and encouraging higher-density development. Measures of high density are not described, but one can infer that annexation by cities, combined with the growth boundary, is expected to result in less sprawl outside the boundary and more compact development within it. Lower income disparities and more reinvestment in cities also would be likely. The requirement that the annexing city provide services comparable to those delivered in the balance of its jurisdiction creates an incentive for the city to require compact development that is less expensive to service than low-density development. Whether the process works as intended will depend on whether the deadline for adopting growth policies is enforced, whether cities will annex and achieve compact development, whether counties will achieve compact development in the absence of city annexation, and whether exceptions to rural preservation designations will be permitted. Subsequent state legislation could rescind or amend these provisions, in addition to implementation being inconsistent perhaps with the initial goals.

Although the Tennessee state government's intention seems consistent with the Smart Growth goals of Maryland, in Tennessee the state role is relatively passive once the growth boundaries have been approved. On the other hand, it is assertive in insisting that growth boundaries be established. The state is flexible in leaving the location of growth boundaries to local deliberations within state guidelines. Annexation is also at local option, and service agreements are generated locally. Furthermore, the act does not contain substantive standards against which to measure whether development has been sufficiently compact and whether sprawl has been adequately reduced. In the absence of standards, there are no state incentives to reward good performance or penalties to punish unsatisfactory results. The act seems aimed at enhancing quality of life goals and restraining quantity of growth, but it does not identify characteristics of the quality of life sought, nor does it identify standards or indicators by which public officials and citizens can determine whether progress is occurring.

The New Urbanism

The New Urbanism emphasizes community design principles. Its practitioners advocate augmenting public civic spaces, stress pedestrian convenience, and criticize physical isolation of neighborhoods. Although these issues require small-scale plans, the New Urbanists seek large impacts via creating compelling physical examples that stimulate imitators. The New Urbanism is most identified with practitioners Andres Duany and Elizabeth Plater-Zyberk, based in Miami, and Peter Calthorpe in California.

Duany and Plater-Zyberk's first well-known project was a Florida resort called Seaside, an 80-acre community started in 1981. It was a freestanding small town designed with narrow connecting streets (most of them 18 feet wide), a town center, mixed land uses, interspersed public spaces, front porches, pre–World War II building materials, and building styles that generally predated modernism in architecture. It has been praised, as in James Howard Kunstler's *Home from Nowhere* (1996), and parodied, as in the movie *The Truman Show,* which starred Jim Carrey.

Walkway in Kentlands, a New Urbanism development in Gaithersburg, Maryland. (Synergy/Photography)

As the New Urbanists hoped, publicity about Seaside contributed to the spread of their design principles. By 1994 Duany and Plater-Zyberk had been hired to design 70 sizable projects in several states, such as Kentlands in Montgomery County, Maryland, and Belmont Forest in Loudoun County, Virginia (Langdon 1994). Calthorpe has advocated similar design principles, but he has worked most prominently in transit-oriented development, advocating relatively dense mixed-use developments near train and transit stations (Kelbaugh 1989). His early prominent projects were primarily on the West Coast (Sacramento, San Jose, San Diego, San Mateo, and Portland) (Calthorpe 1993).

The New Urbanism and Tyranny Effects

Duany has been criticized for catering to the wealthy in Seaside, designing projects on the metropolitan fringe that contributed to suburban sprawl, and promoting building designs that lend an antiquated quality to his communities. Other New Urbanism projects, such as John Clark's widely publicized and long-gestated Haymount community near Fredericksburg, Virginia, have been criticized for similar alleged sins. It should not be surprising that some New Urbanism projects tend to be located where other large-scale development projects are sited. The same market conditions that define the tyranny of easy development decisions influence New Urbanism project locations.

Wherever they are located, Philip Langdon (1994, 123) argues that New Urbanist developments are most typified by six types of connections:

> First, they try to connect the streets into a network so that people can readily reach other sections of their neighborhood or town. Second, they try to connect residents to shops and services by encouraging retail and institutional development within walking distance of where people live. Third, they try to connect individuals to one another by insisting that walkways be sociable—usually running alongside narrow streets, rows of trees, picket fences, and front porches, balconies, terraces, or other inviting exterior elements of houses. Fourth, they try to bridge the divide of age, household size, and economic status by mixing together houses and apartments of assorted sizes and prices. Fifth, they try to connect new developments to mass transit. Sixth, they try to connect individuals to civic ideals and public responsibilities.

These principles can be implemented most readily where intricate street networks and multimodal transportation facilities are in place. Downtowns in cities large and small usually have these characteristics, but the mixed-use character of downtowns is often deficient, with housing being in short supply, antiquated, or

Belmont Forest is a New Urbanism–style neighborhood with short walkable streets and public spaces, isolated from suburban development in Loudoun County, Virginia. (Synergy/Photography)

derelict. New Urbanism principles applied in downtowns may add housing, substitute streetfront retailing for ground-level office building uses and parking lots, and add civic spaces and pedestrian amenities. Duany and Plater-Zyberk also have entered the downtown planning arena, as in Gaithersburg, Maryland, where Kentlands is located.

Ahwahnee Principles

Whereas most developers of disconnected metropolitan fringe projects defend them as responses to market demands and oppose limitations as restrictions on property rights, the New Urbanists, including Duany and Calthorpe, have proposed community design principles that emphasize connections between a network of compact communities. At the regional scale, these communities would be linked by public transit, bounded by greenbelts, and integrated with nature in terms reminiscent of Ebenezer Howard's *Garden Cities of Tomorrow* (1965). These design principles were synthesized in the Ahwahnee Principles, presented in 1991 at a conference in Yosemite National Park by Calthorpe, Duany, Plater-Zyberk, Michael Corbett, Elizabeth Moule, and Stefanos Polyzoides. The regional component of the Ahwahnee Principles follows:

1. The regional land use planning structure should be integrated with a larger transportation network built around transit rather than freeways.

2. Regions should be bounded by and provide a continuous system of green-belt/wildlife corridors to be determined by natural conditions.
3. Regional institutions and services (government, stadiums, museums) should be located in the urban core.
4. Materials and methods of construction should be specific to the region, exhibiting continuity of history and culture and compatibility with the climate to encourage the development of local character and community identity.

New Urbanism principles lead to a new twist on an old problem. When is development on the metropolitan fringe better than most other development, and perhaps the best that is achievable under contemporary policies that encourage the tyranny of easy development decisions? These questions were generated by a proposed development of 2,900 houses, one million square feet of office space, and a town center that would look like Old Town Alexandria. It would be located in Spotsylvania County, Virginia, four miles south of Fredericksburg and 60 miles south of Washington, D.C., and half of its residents might work there as well (Blum 1999). In the town center, buildings would have stores on the first floor, offices on the second, and apartments on the third. There would be a retirement community, apartments, and townhouses as well as single-family detached houses, along with a civic center and an outdoor amphitheater. To county planners it was a major step toward compact development for Spotsylvania County, where population had increased 45 percent since 1990. But to a citizen group called the Coalition for Smarter Growth, it was too far from traditional job centers and lacked sufficient roads or schools.

A Livability Agenda

Whatever the outcome of this development case in Spotsylvania County, the New Urbanism has captured the attention of people who matter—planners, architects, mayors, governors, state legislators, members of Congress, developers, citizens, and Vice President Al Gore. Describing a three-day conference on the New Urbanism at Harvard University, Benjamin Forgey wrote (1999):

> . . . [I]n recent years the movement has blossomed into a full-fledged assault on America's most pervasive pattern of growth—the wasteful, continuing outward expansion known as sprawl, and the concomitant, equally wasteful abandonment of center cities and older suburbs. . . . More than 170 state and local initiatives having to do with land use, open space and the environment were adopted in elections last fall. Vice President Gore began testing a "livability agenda" as a possible theme for his presidential election campaign next year. "We've seen more

activity on such issues in the last 25 weeks than in the last 25 years," observed Rep. Earl Blumenauer (D-Ore.), a smart-growth advocate. . . . "The interesting thing is that this movement is being driven from the grass roots up."

Grass-roots support is essential for both incipient and sustained political success. Strategic planning is a political activity, among other things. It cannot be put to effective use over time unless it is grounded in policies that significant segments of the public will support actively or at least accept.

The Third Regional Plan of New York

With a population of nearly 20 million in three states in 1990, as well as about 1,600 cities, counties, towns, and villages and 13,000 square miles, the New York metropolitan area constitutes a unique governance problem. One response to this problem by civic (especially business) leaders was the creation of the Regional Plan Association (RPA), which produced its first regional plan in 1929. The RPA may be the most ambitious, long-surviving, and effective private regional civic planning organization in the United States. In 1996, the RPA issued its Third Regional Plan, *A Region at Risk* (Yaro and Hiss 1996, 2), which builds proposals around analyses of what it calls the Three E's—economy, equity, and environment: "Our economy faces new pressures from technology and global competition. Communities are threatened by sweeping economic and demographic changes as concerns once associated with inner-city communities spread to a wider range of established suburbs. Our last remaining intact ecological systems are finally caught in the shadow of development as we expand to new areas instead of addressing these issues where they occur."

The RPA describes its plan as an "early warning system" for other regions, noting that "[t]his region, as the first to begin growing out of its 20th century infrastructure systems, is facing these problems a little bit sooner than anyone else." Lamenting slow growth, and the loss of 300,000 jobs in urban centers as the suburban ring gained 2 million jobs from 1970 to 1995, the RPA notes that while population grew by 13 percent, land consumption increased by 60 percent (1996, 7).

The RPA (1996, 19–20) observed that current settlement patterns replicate the popular vision, and its many deficiencies, described by Anthony Downs in *New Visions for Metropolitan America* (1994): ". . . [F]or the last 50 years we got precisely what we asked for: good highways to travel fast and frequently; spread-out homes with equally big lots for those who could afford them; well-stocked, bright, air-conditioned 'one-stop' shopping malls, close to home; and office buildings nearby that resembled home, set back on large lawns and nestled under the tree line."

Greensward, Centers, Mobility, Workforce, and Governance

Below is a summary of the main recommendations in the Third Regional Plan (1996, 88, 119, 159, 185, 201), which reveals many proposals aimed at reducing sprawl, reinvesting in the regions' multiple centers, and coping with and compensating for income disparities.

The greensward theme was described by the RPA as 11 regional reserves constituting "a no sprawl zone that encompasses all of the major natural areas that are still intact." Because of significant reductions in the scale of natural areas since the previous regional plan, the RPA emphasized that the "region should develop, and redevelop, around its natural systems, instead of at their expense. . . ." These natural areas and the region's cities also should be connected in a network of hiking paths, bicycle routes, and natural corridors.

Preservation of the greensward, the RPA said, will require "tremendous job growth in the region's existing centers over the next 25 years—with more than a million new jobs distributed across the Central Business District; among 11 regional downtowns . . . [and] a constellation of compact, smaller, centered towns that are rail-served, walkable communities built around a main street or a mini-downtown." In the suburban edge cities, where most job growth in recent decades had occurred, another million new jobs were projected. The RPA said these edge cities should "take on the characteristics of true centers and become vibrant, 24-hour-a-day communities."

Turning to transportation, the RPA observed that "by building only a handful of miles of new rail lines, along with a second handful of miles of new highways," the entire region could be put within reach of nearly everyone. The seven subregional railways and subways should be linked with a few new miles of track, producing a region-spanning, and in some places a high-speed, rail line.

The importance of workforce connections to new jobs, new skills, and new employment locations was emphasized by the RPA "to make the region's workforce more competitive in a global economy" and to connect citizens and communities to a growing job market. Lifelong learning opportunities and better transportation links between communities and jobs were recommended.

Numerous governance proposals were made to implement the Third Regional Plan. State growth management systems, the RPA said, should create incentives for community plans and regulations needed to promote development in centers, create effective urban growth boundaries, and protect the greensward reserves. Education financing should provide greater equity among school systems, including removing incentives for fiscal zoning. A new Regional Transportation Authority and a Tri-State Infrastructure Bank were proposed to finance priority capital projects with dedicated taxes. Principles of sustainable economics were recommended for capital budgeting and tax and regulatory systems, as well as multiple uses of infrastructure and alternatives to end-of-the-pipe waste treatment to benefit the economy and environment.

The Role of Housing

These proposals embody a comprehensive agenda reflecting a judgment that contemporary information-based businesses are attracted and retained by productive employees operating in an environment with a high quality of life. Hence, economic prosperity, environmental conservation, and equitable governance are viewed as mutually reinforcing. Housing is treated in a conventional manner, however, in that the plan considers the increase in housing unit size as an obstacle to affordability (1996, 136) rather than recognizing that small size contributes to city and suburban decline and, therefore, to sprawl. The emphasis on affordability is warranted, to be certain; housing prices rose at double the rate of income increases during the 1980s (1996, 56), and housing increases are generally regarded as an essential aspect of reconstituting viable urban centers. The plan does not deal significantly with deficiencies in institutional housing reinvestment capacity. Enhancing the mass transit and rail systems may contribute considerably to achieving that recentering goal, but housing is examined too little as a cause of city and suburban decline and as a potential resource for strengthening centers.

Public Transit for the Postsuburban Era

Few people commute to work in the United States by public transportation. Even fewer use public transit for noncommuting purposes. And these already low percentages have been falling. In 1995, 3.5 percent of commuting trips were by transit, down from 4.5 percent in 1983; all person trips had fallen to 1.8 percent in 1995 from 2.2 percent in 1983 (Cervero 1998, 2). Such numbers augur poorly for a significant role for public transit in the postsuburban era.

The research and arguments of Robert Cervero in *The Transit Metropolis* (1998) suggest that it is still possible for public transit to play an important role. Observing that "good quality designs (like transit-oriented development and the New Urbanism) are without question absolutely essential to creating places that are physically conducive to transit riding," Cervero (1998, 4) added, ". . . islands of TOD in a sea of freeway-oriented suburbs will do little to change fundamental travel behavior or the sum quality of regional living."

Four Classes of Transit Metropolises

Some cities—New York, London, Paris, Hong Kong, Moscow, and Toronto—have had successful transit systems through most of the 20th century. Cervero (1998, 5) set out to demonstrate that other cities have made progress in "co-planning and co-development of transit systems and cityscapes . . . under largely free-market conditions during the past half-century of rapid automobile growth and ascendancy." Cervero (1998, 5-6) analyzes 12 cases on five continents in four classes of transit metropolises.

Downtown Toronto has been attracting mixed-use development in the vicinity of its subway stations. (Synergy/Photography)

Adaptive cities (Copenhagen, Singapore, Stockholm, and Tokyo). These are transit-oriented metropolises that have invested in rail systems to guide urban growth for purposes of achieving larger societal objectives, such as preserving open space and producing affordable housing in rail-served communities. All feature compact, mixed-use suburban communities and new towns concentrated around rail nodes.

Adaptive transit (Adelaide, Karlsruhe, and Mexico City). These are places that have largely accepted spread-out, low-density patterns of growth and have sought to appropriately adapt transit services and new technologies to best serve these environs.

Strong-core cities (Melbourne and Zurich). Two of the cases have successfully integrated transit and urban development within a more confined central city context. They have done so by providing integrated transit services centered around mixed-traffic tram and light-rail systems.

Hybrids: adaptive cities and adaptive transit (Curitiba, Munich, and Ottawa). Three of the cases have struck a workable balance between concentrating development along mainline transit corridors and adapting transit to efficiently serve their spread-out suburbs and exurbs.

Transportation and Land Use Connections

Experience in some of these cities contradicts the myth (Cervero 1998, 413) that "[i]n modern societies, the link between transportation and land use is too weak to matter. . . . It is a view framed in part by studying experiences in countries like the United States where perverse price signals and other market distortions, such as exclusionary zoning, stack the odds heavily in favor of car travel." Using the four classes of transit cities above, Cervero (1998, 415) is optimistic that Portland shows signs of being an adaptive city "whose built forms are highly conducive to transit riding," with San Diego and St. Louis emerging as hybrid transit metropolises, and Houston standing "the best chance of mounting world-class adaptive transit services. . . ."

While transit usage in these cities increased during the 1980s or 1990s, the evidence supporting claims of transit gains is modest. Cervero (1998, 440) concluded that "Stockholm and Copenhagen began investing in high-capacity transit systems a good half-century ago. In these places, too, it took time for the benefits of these investments to accrue. . . . Today's residents of East Coast cities such as Boston and New York owe a considerable debt of gratitude to their forefathers and foremothers for having had the foresight to invest in regional metros. Indeed, intergenerational transfer of benefits captures the very essence of what is meant by sustainability."

Sustainable Region Incentive Fund

Lobbying in Virginia for passage of the Regional Competitiveness Act (RCA) of 1996 began as an effort to increase the rate of growth by enhancing the equity and quality of governance within metropolitan areas. In its adopted form, the RCA emphasized increasing the rate of growth by increasing assets of direct benefit to growth businesses, namely workforce training. Quality of life and equity in governance goals faded into the background.

Here we introduce a regional organizing concept, a Sustainable Region Incentive Fund (SRIF) that puts quality of life and equity in the forefront. Moreover, it argues for taking a long view, hence the term "sustainable." Our concept differs from the Portland, Minneapolis–St. Paul, Maryland, Virginia, and Tennessee approaches by addressing results explicitly, rewarding the achievement of measurable goals, and providing funds from outside individual jurisdictions as incentives for achieving goals. The goals sought are essentially those proposed by the New Urbanists, the Third Regional Plan for New York, and Robert Cervero in *The Transit Metropolis*. Our concept also differs in trying to encourage certain political forces to be more persistent and successful. It respects current jurisdictional arrangements and does not impose either a superjurisdictional government structure or an extrajurisdictional regulatory authority. In these ways, it embodies elements that are politically feasible, while having other characteristics—namely the focus on rewarding measurable results—which are more difficult to put into practice.

Multicentered Governance

Our proposal was initially conceived to cope with the complex governance situation in the Washington, D.C. region. Having a central city independent of its suburbs in two different states, with the central city subject to control directly by the federal government, is unique in the United States. This governance system is not necessarily more complex in all respects than that of other large multistate metropolitan areas, but it has certain aspects of complex governance that are not shared by other regions. The SRIF attempts to respond to this Washington, D.C. regional context by retaining a laissez-faire relationship among local governments and avoiding superjurisdictional structure and regulatory authority. The SRIF would be relevant in other metropolitan areas where the obstacles to reorganization of governance also are overwhelming.

In addition, our proposal was designed for a region, such as Washington, D.C., where the growth rate has been strong and where there is controversy about how to cope with a projected fast growth rate. The Metropolitan Washington Council of Governments (1995), for example, projected population growth of 1.7 million people (42 percent) between 1990 and 2020.

In this metropolitan Washington, D.C. context, the dangers faced by the region are driven mainly by how a large quantity of growth can diminish the quality of life, making the rate of growth and the current quality of life unsustainable. While rapid expansion brings up many large-scale infrastructure investment issues, enough major investments have occurred, such as expansion in 1997 of the two largest airports, Dulles International and Reagan National, that a high quantity of growth seems likely.

Reinvestment in Places

The dangers, therefore, are more subtle. They call for a complicated and decentralized set of policies: not only revitalizing the central city but also creating numerous neighborhoods characterized by walking, bicycling, mass transit use, and short auto trips, as proposed in the Portland plan for the year 2040. These transportation results require redevelopment, infill, reinvestment, and, occasionally, greenfield development—policies designed by local governments and supported by federal, state, and regional governance systems, as well as supported and implemented partially by private institutions. Reinvestment in established communities, from large cities to small neighborhoods, is the action necessary to cope with a central city in crisis, many declining middle-aged suburbs, and exurban sprawl that is straining fiscal resources all the while debilitating the natural environment.

Many local government officials, nonprofit organizations, private businesses, and households are animated by goals that are focused on, or are compatible with, creating more sustainable communities. But they are challenged, and more often than not defeated temporarily, by forces of inertia that keep moving development farther toward the fringe at lower aggregate densities.

The forces that are focused on enhancing the quality of life within and across jurisdictions need to be strengthened. One way of strengthening them would be to establish a Sustainable Region Incentive Fund, as follows:

1. Create a fund with which to encourage reinvestment and enhance neighborhood quality or lighten local financial burdens, at local option.
2. Make eligibility for sharing these funds a function of achieving measurable progress toward policy goals.
3. Assign responsibility for achieving results to local and state governments subject to meeting technical standards.
4. Reward results that make the region and its constituent parts more sustainable in the long run and more competitive in the short run by becoming more efficient, effective, and equitable.

Rewards for Results

If results are to be rewarded, then the key questions involve which results to reward and what the effects will be of achieving them. Specifying these results, therefore, becomes the central policy problem.

To encourage community and regional sustainability, result indicators should encourage resource conservation, efficient transportation, lower business and government costs, less sprawl, and greater redevelopment of aging cities and suburbs. The number of indicators should be limited to make them comprehensible, since they should be understood by public officials and citizens in order to enhance civic participation. They should be limited so that calculations for a revenue-sharing formula are feasible.

It is also crucial that the indicators concern results that can be influenced substantially by local governments and by regional multigovernment actions. Results also must be easily measurable. Some subjects, such as energy consumption, seem necessary elements of sustainability indicators (Newman and Kenworthy 1999, 18), but energy in aggregate is not amenable to either local government action or routine measurement. Air pollution is another likely candidate for a sustainability indicator, but air pollution data vary based on local climate conditions from year to year, obscuring the effects of public policies. Therefore, energy consumption and air pollution are best accessed through other indicators, such as mass transit and train ridership and density, especially near public transit stations.

As a first cut at result indicators for sustainable communities and regions, the following are our suggestions:

1. Increase in median age of housing is rewarded, but a decrease is not penalized. This indicator encourages reinvestment in housing and is consistent with rewarding new housing that increases compact patterns (see 2 and 3).
2. Increases in residents, sales, and employment within one-half mile of fixed-

rail mass transit and commuter rail stations are rewarded. This indicator encourages compact development, while also encouraging construction of rail lines and stations.

3. Increases in public transit (including buses), carpooling, and train ridership are rewarded. This indicator encourages compact development, day care facilities near mass transit stations, and feeder lines to express bus and fixed-rail mass transit.

4. Farmland losses are penalized and farmland increases are rewarded. This indicator encourages favored tax treatment for farming. If fruit and vegetable farming is encouraged, more money will be retained within the region and long-distance truck travel will be reduced.

5. Increases in fourth-grade reading and math test scores, reductions in test score disparities between the high- and low-scoring schools within a jurisdiction, and combining high and low free-lunch eligibility schools within and across jurisdiction lines are rewarded. This indicator encourages improved student and school performance as well as socioeconomic mixing, rather than segregation and high income disparities, within and between school districts.

These indicators would measure changes whose effects would reduce disparities, limit sprawl, and encourage reinvestment. Because performance would be rewarded, indicators would also become incentives for better performance and disincentives for worse performance. Better and worse performance would be defined by weights assigned to scores for each indicator in a grant formula.

Benefits of the SRIF

Why should local government officials and their constituents support using these result indicators to distribute Sustainable Region Incentive Funds? They reward conservation of resources, compact development and redevelopment, reduction in air pollution, conservation of productive open space, reinvestment in existing housing, and improved school and student performance. These are results that improve the quality of lives of most individuals. They also reduce many costs of governments. They help stabilize jurisdictions in relation to each other, reducing the likelihood of income and financial polarization among jurisdictions. They increase the economic competitiveness of the region. They reduce resource consumption, enhancing sustainability.

These indicators of sustainable communities and regions also are balanced. They encourage growth limits (housing and farm indicators), but they do not preclude growth. If growth occurs in compact patterns (mass transit, train ridership, carpooling, walking), more funds may be obtained to cope with growth. High-quality governance, irrespective of growth, is also rewarded (housing reinvestment and fourth-grade test scores). By rewarding greater density, these result indicators may facilitate greater profits for some developers. By reducing current living costs and improving workforce education, business competitiveness versus other regions will be enhanced. These indicators also tend to be feasible to apply annually (ridership, test scores) or over a few years (housing age and farmland), if not annually, at little or no additional administrative cost.

The biggest differences between this proposal for a Sustainable Region Incentive Fund and Virginia's Regional Competitiveness Act are the following:

- Under the RCA, subjects were identified on which regions could be rewarded for cooperating without specifying any measurable results that qualified them for receiving state revenues.
- Under the RCA, economic development projects became the most important elements used to determine eligibility to receive state funds.

In contrast, our SRIF proposal specifies the following:

- Eligibility for payments would flow from achieving measurable results.
- Economic development projects would not qualify unless they contributed to the measurable results.

Finance, Politics, and Focus

It would be possible to finance this proposal from private funds such as contributions from foundations. Public funding from national, state, or regional sources could be more generous. New tax revenues, perhaps from a one-time surtax, could be used, or, in periods of strong economic performance, a large annual reserve in federal or state (or perhaps regional) revenues could be set aside, which would earn interest if not spent and would carry over from year to year, contributing to the next year's reserve.

Such an incentive fund to reward local governments for contributing to better regional performance has not been used to our knowledge. Some of the principles embedded in this concept, however, are familiar. In the private sector, chief executives, and often other employees, are rewarded with bonuses and profit sharing based on company performance. In government, it has become common to give rewards to construction contractors who finish a job before the target date for completion (and also to impose penalties for tardy completion). State governments routinely establish incentives to encourage regional collaboration by local governments. Regional provision of health, jail, solid waste, and other services may be rewarded by state contributions to construction and operating costs above the amounts paid for similar services provided by smaller units of local government. The federal government provides funds for regional planning for various services, sometimes requiring regional planning as a condition of eligibility for other federal funds. In our proposal, traditional incentives of these types are married with regional performance goals. Individual governments can make useful contributions acting alone or together to achieve these goals. They are rewarded for doing so to increase the odds that effective collaboration will occur, when it is useful, and that individual local governments will perform more effectively also.

The prospect of rewards for achieving results may be intriguing, but local governments are more likely to collaborate if funds are provided for organizing, planning, and communicating to improve performance. In addition, funds to encourage persistence, such as for staffing and small construction or equipment grants, will be useful. Larger benefits, however, should be available for achieving measurable results. Participation in planning and collaboration in implementation are necessary but not sufficient. Results are the goal.

This proposal is intended to increase the strength of the political forces that currently aspire to achieve these goals. Too often they lose focus, do not maintain continuity, or miss connections that should occur between divergent policies. Having a fund as an incentive, and having indicators that emphasize connections among land use, housing, transportation, environment, finance, education, and economic development, can augment the politics of sustainability. The Virginia Regional Competitiveness Act experience has demonstrated that a small annual amount of funds ($6 million in the first year and $8 million in the second year) can capture the attention of leaders of major local government, education, and business organizations who previously saw little reason to talk to each other.

From this experience, one can infer that a substantial amount of money would capture attention for more difficult subjects. The SRIF answers the question that busy people must ask: Why should I devote my scarce time to this subject rather than to other subjects? The SRIF provides three answers: because success is worth pursuing and the SRIF improves prospects for success, because your jurisdiction or organization may gain a windfall, and because you may be embarrassed if others gain a windfall and you do not.

Recalling Concepts and Looking Ahead

Although no single government can conduct strategic planning for regions, there are many governments—state, special district, local large and small, and federal—that can use concepts effectively to pursue quality of life goals. Quantity goals too often dominate what passes for strategic planning. The tyranny of easy development decisions, however, will nearly always subvert the intentions of government officials and citizens who pursue more quantity as their primary goal. Paired concepts such as the relationships between area and power, pattern and density, population and neighborhood, and space and place can help government officials and citizens understand why quality of life goals are essential.

The search for balance and equilibrium should counteract extremes, encouraging public officials to compensate for severe imbalances in the short run and correct for them in time. Governance of regions can be reformed without constructing unitary governments. Plausible paths toward improvements are suggested by the experiences of Portland, Minneapolis–St. Paul, Maryland, Virginia, and Tennessee, as well as by the proposals of the New Urbanism, the Third Regional Plan of New York, and transit metropolises. Their variety is striking. Acting through a directly elected regional government with limited powers, Portland used a growth boundary, encouragement of higher density, and public transit infrastructure to alter settlement patterns, thus reducing sprawl and enhancing the central city. Through a board appointed by the governor, Minneapolis–St. Paul combined regional planning, limited revenue sharing from commercial and industrial growth, and some regional infrastructure management. Numerous policies concerning housing, infrastructure, and revenue-sharing formulas have been proposed that would address some of the deficiencies in the Twin Cities governance system.

Maryland tightened coordination between state and local governments to reduce sprawl, promote infill and reinvestment, and control escalating state government costs through state and local planning and capital investment coordination. Virginia promoted public-private cooperative planning to enhance regional economic development, after setting aside, at least temporarily, its consideration of using an incentive fund to nurture intraregional revenue sharing and reallocation of service and cost burdens. Tennessee mandated creation by local officials and civic leaders of 20-year development growth boundaries, with annexation by cities permitted within the growth boundaries, judicial processes for settling disputes about growth boundary locations, and withholding of state and significant pass-through federal funds for failure to meet deadlines in moving toward adoption of growth boundaries. Each of these approaches uses administrative and financial means in hopes of altering future events.

In contrast, our concept of a Sustainable Region Incentive Fund focuses on results, promising payments retroactively for achieving goals related to compact development, use of mass transit, and walking. The concept of rewarding results could be combined with other policies that require planning, strengthen regulations, invest infrastructure funds to encourage compact development, and compensate for existing income and resource disparities. Because it is retrospective, an SRIF could be combined with other systems that focus on plans, investments, and regulations.

These diverse experiences and options also indicate that reforms face imposing obstacles. Formal arrangements that seem promising may disguise regression in practice. The success of any path depends on politics, which is an open system with many possibilities. Focused politics requires understanding, and understanding requires concepts supported by facts and arguments. The concepts presented here can help with each of these dimensions of politics.

Policies and Plans to Reduce Sprawl, Increase Reinvestment, and Limit Disparities

The era of suburban decline has seen rapid changes. Central cities in the 24 most populous urbanized areas declined 19 percent in median family income relative to their metropolitan areas from 1960 to 1990, and 33 percent of suburbs declined faster than their central cities from 1980 to 1990. In some instances suburban income fell below city income. The average range of median family income differences among suburbs in these metropolitan areas grew from a 2 to 1 ratio to a 3 to 1 ratio during these 30 years. Because of the poor prospects of many suburbs, with little to recommend them for reinvestment and revival, greater income disparities in the future are likely.

With disparities severe and growing, balance among jurisdictions and equilibrium in jurisdictional prospects over time are useful but difficult goals. The size of disparities that society should tolerate is not evident, although we believe that disparities are now much too large and that their large size has numerous destructive effects on social well-being and environmental sustainability. Conditions that lead to, and exacerbate, disparities can be articulated.

People, Places, and the Four Paired Concepts

The four paired concepts discussed in previous chapters—area and power, population and neighborhood, patterns and density, and space and place—reveal some dimensions of balance and equilibrium. Each pair of concepts can be framed as a typology. One pole of the typology supports public and private decisions in markets that reduce sprawl, encourage reinvestment, and limit disparities. The other pole supports decisions that stimulate sprawl, reduce reinvestment, and encourage extreme disparities between neighborhoods and jurisdictions. Some policies structure markets to encourage balance. They strengthen places in which to nurture healthy people (Carmon 1997; Ladd

1994; Lucy 1994a). Other policies structure markets to encourage disequilibrium—tendencies toward disparities that are self-reinforcing in moving toward extremes.

Area and Power

Area and power, for example, can be organized to minimize the number of governments within a commuting territory, assign state government substantial regional responsibilities, and overlay a significant regional government on existing local governments. In conceiving a regional governance structure, Richard Briffault (1996, 1165–1166) suggests following the rule of subsidiary, meaning that "only those functions necessary for metropolitan governance should be shifted to regional institutions. . . . The optimal metropolitan area government needs three crucial powers: to determine land use questions of regional significance; to collect and distribute revenues in order to promote greater equalization of local fiscal capacity and local service quality; and to provide regionwide physical infrastructure." On the other hand, area and power can be structured with many small local government units within a commuting territory, with very little state responsibility for the region, and with little if any significant regional governance to oversee local government taxation and service delivery performance. Such arrangements encourage self-promoting location decisions that reward isolation of advantaged persons from those with few resources.

Population and Neighborhood

Population and neighborhood relationships can range from heterogeneous to homogeneous along many dimensions (income, race, ethnicity, age, family structure, religion). Heterogeneity in every neighborhood reduces potential for disparities among neighborhoods and jurisdictions anywhere. Homogeneity in every neighborhood, by definition, guarantees severe disparities among neighborhoods. Typical policies that use private markets to allocate land and housing, and facilitate access to disparate jurisdictions and schools through location choices, may exacerbate tendencies to create homogeneous neighborhoods. Many people pursue personal safety, secure housing investments, and quality public schools through location opportunities promoted by the tyranny of easy development decisions. The spatial result is excessive sprawl, too little reinvestment, and growing income disparities.

Pattern and Density

Pattern and density can be organized to emphasize mixed land uses, sufficient density to provide many walkable distances between activity types, and multimodal pedestrian and vehicular connections to disparate routine public and private daily and weekly needs. Pattern and density can also be designed for auto dependence, separating land uses widely and providing only circuitous connec-

The pedestrian plaza and bridge over a parking structure and ring road of Freiburg, Germany, is also served by light-rail transit. Careful planning can serve both the local and regional traveler. (Synergy/Photography)

Light-rail transit serving Freiburg, Germany. (Synergy/Photography)

tions between them. Auto dependence helps cause sizable disparities in income and race between neighborhoods and jurisdictions. It imposes location obstacles for the poor and opens wide territories for homogenous settlements, including gated subdivisions.

Space and Place

Space and place concepts direct attention to territories, structures, and activities. Places are created from spaces by attachments based on activities and duration of living in a neighborhood. Long commitments to property, family, friends, institutions, voluntary associations, and activities pertinent to each of these commitments enhance feelings of attachment to places. Conversely, temporary lodging without meaningful associations and activities interferes with attachments so that spaces remain only as vital as the immediate functions served.

Creative methods for moving materials needed for residential rehabilitation in Tourrette-sur-Loup, France, have evolved over the centuries. (Synergy/Photography)

Place attachments help residents and, by extension, neighborhoods cope with changes. They also may slow the pace of change, making it more comprehensible and manageable. Place attachments do not necessarily reduce disparities, but they make them easier to cope with. In addition, if place attachments are not valued, exurban sprawl becomes more likely. Paradoxically, strong small-scale place attachments may be expressed through the NIMBY (Not in My Back Yard) syndrome, in which residents may oppose nearby development even if it adds value indirectly to their residences, leading to greater strength in the tyranny of easy development decisions on the metropolitan fringe. And more sprawl leads to less reinvestment. Hence, weak place attachments (and sometimes strong place attachments), though not amenable to easy measurement, may have important effects on sprawl, reinvestment, and disparities.

Public Policy Alternatives

The four paired concepts—area and power, population and neighborhood, patterns and density, and space and place—help reveal the implications of three public policy approaches to settlement problems. They aid understanding about what can be done to avert formation of crisis poverty ghettoes and substantial middle-aged suburban decline and to reduce sprawl, increase reinvestment, and limit disparities. Three principal policy options exist: gilding poverty ghettoes, balancing cities and suburbs socially and economically, and containing social ills spatially.

Gilding Poverty Ghettoes

Gilding poverty ghettoes means concentrating investments and public services in poverty areas. Investments can be in businesses, physical infrastructure, housing, education, social services, and criminal justice. One goal is to assist, empower, and perhaps rehabilitate the people who live there. A second goal is to make economic and social activities and the physical appearance of poverty areas more attractive so that some middle- and upper-income people will move in and so that current residents who succeed financially will stay.

The United States flirted with these goals in the 1960s era of urban renewal, war on poverty, and model cities programs, but they were never combined with policies for regional balance between cities and suburbs. Failure to seek socioeconomic and fiscal balance within entire metropolitan regions is one reason that spatial disparities of wealth and poverty, and ever larger poverty ghettoes, have increased (Jargowsky 1997). The 1960s policies were a holding action. The growth of poverty ghettoes could not be restrained without relocating some of the poor to the suburbs and slowing growth on the periphery, but relocation of the poor to suburbia (by means of housing subsidies) was not entertained because it was political dynamite. It would have called for a strong federal, state, or regional governance role that no state or region was motivated to pursue effectively. Private-market relocations of the poor via housing deterioration in the suburbs were not then widespread. State policies to slow suburban sprawl did not receive significant attention until the 1970s, and then they were sporadic and proved generally ineffective through the 1980s and 1990s.

Gilding the Ghetto Is Vulnerable to Mobility

Gilding the ghetto is enormously expensive and not very effective in isolation. Successful businesses with expensive equipment and highly skilled employees need major inducements to move to high-risk areas. Few will do so no matter how great the targeted incentives. Engineers and scientists in high-tech research and development enterprises do not want to work there; they fear for their safety. Banks prefer to lend where arson is less likely.

Marginal manufacturing and service firms that benefit from very low rents are prospects. Local retail services owned by entrepreneurs, such as Korean immigrants, who pool their resources to provide their own capital are the most likely investors (Pan and Pae 1999). These businesses cannot provide many middle-income jobs for local residents, however.

Michael Porter (1995) has argued that there are significant economic opportunities in inner cities. In some instances they have been realized, especially where a large neglected market has been identified, as in Harlem in New York City (Grunwald 1999). In Harlem, an "empowerment zone" financed by the federal government has contributed to an economic revival. Harlem also has dwellings and streets with some architectural and accessibility characteristics that have attracted more affluent inmovers than old neighborhoods in other parts of New York City. In most low-income neighborhoods, however, economic development has not been achieved (Kantor and Savitch 1993). Research about results of empowerment zones and enterprise zones has not revealed any success stories, defined as significant increases in per capita income compared with other neighborhoods, according to David Rusk (Orfield 1998).

Gilding the ghetto will benefit some residents living in poverty, but most people who succeed economically will still decide to leave (Ladd 1994; Lemann 1994). During the 1970s, 1980s, and 1990s, the departure of the black middle class from poor neighborhoods became about as likely as the exodus by white middle-class emigrants from declining neighborhoods. Indeed, the exodus of the black middle class, which was facilitated by a reduction in housing discrimination, has been blamed for an increase in social problems in many ghetto areas (Wilson 1987). In brief, the policy of gilding poverty ghettoes can succeed in most instances only if it is combined with the second policy option—greater regional social and economic balance.

Balance

The second policy option is to balance cities and suburbs socially and economically within politically connected regions. This policy is typically pursued indirectly through investments in housing, employment, transportation, and education, while providing some compensatory payments to poor individuals and poverty areas. The key is to have nodes, neighborhoods, or districts throughout metropolitan areas in which people have the potential to walk to work or take mass transit, and where people of diverse socioeconomic groups, including the poor, are not far from each other.

Social and economic balance has been among the policy goals emphasized in Canada and the nations of western Europe (Goldberg and Mercer 1986; Norton 1984; Zielinski 1983). While some spatial disparities will always occur by income and race, poverty groupings in these nations are smaller in size, less remote from public resources, and less noticeable, even though incomes are generally lower than in the United States (Heidenheimer, Heclo, and Adams 1983). Several public policies have led to these results. Housing, transportation, land use, education, and public finance policies influence balance. Balance occurs when sprawl and disparities are mitigated and reinvestment is sufficient. Balance among neighborhoods and jurisdictions in metropolitan areas is evident in Europe and Canada compared with the United States. Below are some examples of how typical policy elements, interacting with individuals' and businesses' location decisions, have achieved better balance:

1. Substantial amounts of low-income, moderate-income, and other subsidized housing have been built in suburbs (Coppa 1976; Goldfield 1979; Rubenstein 1978).

2. In many western European metropolitan areas, public transit facilitates home-to-work travel in cities and suburbs by several times as many commuters as in U.S. metropolitan areas (Newman and Kenworthy 1999, 82–83).

3. Many suburbs include high-density affordable housing close to sources of work. Four times more people in western European than in U.S. metropolitan areas walk or bicycle to work (Newman and Kenworthy 1999, 82–83).

4. Fringe development is limited by many methods, including encouraging infill and high densities in urban areas, greenbelts, development prohibitions, tax advantages for farming, and public acquisitions at use value rather than development potential value, so that clear distinctions between urban development and rural uses are common (Alterman 1997; Beatley 1999; Hall 1988).

5. Public education is financed mainly at the national, state, or regional scale, with very small (if any) local financial responsibility and with smaller differences in resources among school districts than in the United States (Noah and Sherman 1979).

6. Most public services, especially social services, education, and major infrastructure investments, are financed from national, state, or regional tax sources. In contrast, the United States is the nation with the most local governments and the largest share of taxes raised by local rather than national,

Reinvestment and rehabilitation in central Stockholm takes place just west of the Slussen stop of the Tunnelbane, or subway. (Synergy/Photography)

Light rail in Toronto serving high-density lakefront residential and mixed-use development.
(Synergy/Photography)

state, or regional governments (U.S. Advisory Commission on Intergovernmental Relations 1994).

A Governance Structure That Adapts to Expansion

Although a considerable variety of policies and results occurs, a common effect of these six public policies is to encourage more social and economic balance within metropolitan regions in Canada and western Europe compared with the United States. Neither cities nor suburbs are typically remote from work centers. While commuting distances have increased in western Europe, they have increased considerably more in the United States. As a result, they remained shorter in western Europe, and the difference between commuting distances in western Europe and the United States increased between 1980 and 1995 (Cervero 1998, 32).

Both cities and suburbs are often parts of effective regional governance systems in Canada and western Europe. Regions there are more likely to tackle finance and administration on an appropriate scale for many government functions. Rather than increasing the number of local governments as metropolitan areas expand, some European nations centrally determine the number and size of local governments (Alterman 1997), even periodically reducing their number to make regional governance more effective. In addition, "most European planning systems have a formal structure that reflects a hierarchical approach, allowing national policies to be superimposed on regional and local ones. . . .

[G]reater emphasis on strategic planning has followed [in the 1990s] . . . from the difficult challenge of combining objectives of economic development and environmental sustainability" (Healey 1997, 9 and 13). Moreover, as Europe moves toward greater integration, even more ambitious regional policies are being promoted. Political aims adopted in the Maastricht Treaty state, in essence (Van Der Meer 1998, 10): "Regional disparities should be narrowed, solidarity between regions and social groups should emerge, policies should be geared towards sustainable developments, and at the same time Europe's economy should be made more competitive vis-à-vis the United States and Japan."

The general consequence is that residential escapism is discouraged; less abandonment of poor areas occurs. There is less reason, and less opportunity, to move to this or that insulated enclave to concentrate community advantages and to keep out "dangerous others." Each of the four paired concepts—area and power, population and neighborhood, pattern and density, and space and place—is managed so that disparities and sprawl are limited and reinvestment and equilibrium are encouraged.

Containment

The third set of policy alternatives is spatial containment of social ills (Downs 1994; Katz 1998). High percentages of low-income and minority people tend to live close to each other and segregated from middle- and upper-income people (Jargowsky 1997). These patterns result from housing market processes, location choice limitations, and government policies. Government policies have direct and indirect effects; spatial containment of social ills describes the effects, including the unintended effects, of these policies. The United States has emphasized spatial containment policies throughout the 20th century, increasingly so from the 1970s to the present. What are the main elements of these policies?

1. The United States provides more than 98 percent of housing privately, allocates it to the highest bidder, and encourages home ownership for middle- and moderate-income households with federal income tax deductions of local property taxes and mortgage interest.
2. The United States has made most of its transportation investment in highways that connect, and encircle, most metropolitan areas and that also facilitate metropolitan fringe development. When the federal government has invested in mass transit, local governments' zoning typically has maintained low density near transit stations.
3. Governments in the United States rarely regulate business and residential locations to facilitate home and work being close together and linked by public transportation.
4. Development on the metropolitan fringe is relatively easy due to zoning

powers delegated by states to local governments, interlocal competition for development, strong private property development rights, generally weak public regulatory power, and public acquisition of land priced according to its development potential rather than its current use value.

5. Public housing is underfunded by federal and state governments, and it is excluded by most suburban governments.

6. Between 40 and 50 percent of public education costs have been funded with local taxes, usually property taxes levied in small local districts. This is the national average; in some states, the local tax share is higher.

Small Governments and Unintended Consequences

The latent function of this set of six policies to contain low-income areas is supported by most residents of small jurisdictions, although they may not be fully aware of that effect of the policies. Small jurisdiction size and freedom from strong regional governance are often exalted as special trophies of citizen democracy. Small jurisdictions are thought to strengthen citizen control of government (Syed 1966), and they do—within limits. But the limits are crucial to diagnosing the problem of democratic virtue run amok.

Containment policy is consistent with U.S. traditions of providing freedom of choice in housing locations for those who can afford choices, idealizing home ownership, and preferring small local governments. Each of these traditions is valuable in some respects, is strongly supported, and in isolation does not seem to be part of a containment policy.

Outward movement of the middle class has been eroding city strength for decades, but the pace of erosion has quickened. In the 1970s, the black middle class joined the exodus that was previously called "white flight." Between 1970 and 1990, 87 percent of cities declined in income of residents relative to their suburbs, up from 78 percent between 1960 and 1970, and the rate of decline in these cities also increased. Ironically, many suburbs have been declining, with some sinking into poverty ghetto conditions. The pace of suburban decline will continue to quicken as small, moderate-quality 1940s, 1950s, and 1960s housing suffers disinvestment.

Few citizens have understood how public policies have been producing frightening consequences in crisis poverty ghettoes as well as causing the problems of suburban decline that have recently become more noticeable. Confusion was the dominant cause suggested by citizens for riot-prone conditions in south-central Los Angeles. That confusion was captured in an opinion survey in which a majority of citizens said the biggest problem was "a lack of knowledge and understanding about how to solve the problems" (Toner 1992). A common confusion is the usually mistaken belief that problems manifested in a specific government jurisdiction can be solved by appropriate actions taken within that jurisdiction alone.

Six Policies for Healthy Communities and Regions

Given the goals of reducing sprawl, nurturing reinvestment, constraining spatial income disparities, and promoting quality environments, the following six policies are necessary. A variety of policy forms, combinations, and nuances are possible and desirable to fit diverse circumstances, but effective interactions among these six policies are essential.

1. *Reinvestment.* Enhance reinvestment capacity in existing housing and infill in neighborhoods to retain or increase middle-class presence through such methods as greater purchasing of remodeling mortgages on the secondary mortgage market; below-market interest rates for repair, refurbishment, replacement, upgrading and expansion; governments or other institutions paying the difference between upgrade costs and sales prices; tax abatement or tax credits for substantial upgrading and expansion; greater capacity for planning, architectural rendering, and reconstruction facilitation; and greater incentives for local elected officials to cope with neighborhood opposition to infill and some expansion of existing housing.

2. *Transportation.* Emphasize transportation that facilitates access for all ages and income groups, providing alternatives rather than auto-only modes, rewarding tight networks of streets and land uses, and encouraging mixed uses and significant density wherever fixed-rail transportation is provided.

Lakefront high-rise residential condominiums bracket a hotel in Toronto. (Synergy/Photography)

3. *Places.* Design and reinforce places to which residents feel attracted, including such community design techniques as mixed uses, viable institutions, good-quality public services, historic preservation, walkable neighborhoods, public spaces, small parks, connected streets, short blocks, continuous street frontage, on-street parking, low speed limits, aligned street trees, and compatible signage.

4. *Compact regional development.* Constrain fringe growth. Many techniques may help, but few have achieved cumulative success. Growth boundaries are most explicit. Greenbelt investments, farm and forest acquisitions, conservation easements, property taxation based on use rather than development potential, density minimums instead of density maximums, fair-share housing programs, affordable and multiunit housing, smart-growth channeling of infrastructure and education investments to compact locations, and transferable development rights are some of the means possible. The sum of these and other devices must be meaningful constraints on fringe development; otherwise the tyranny of easy development decisions will dominate settlement patterns.

5. *Education.* Create and maintain school facilities and instructional resources in low- to moderate-income and aging neighborhoods that are at least as effective as those in higher-income and new neighborhoods. In some instances, shifts in attendance zones, new development, and reinvestment strategies can reduce socioeconomic disparities among schools and school districts so that peer associations and test score performance do not polarize and create severe obstacles to stabilizing old and middle-aged neighborhoods.

6. *Revenue sharing.* Develop a system among local jurisdictions that shares revenue from commercial and industrial development, so that efficient location choices are encouraged that take advantage of infrastructure and do not excessively reward sprawl and interlocal competition. Structure revenue-sharing formulas so that current low- and moderate-income jurisdictions are compensated. Allocate state and federal aid to compensate poor jurisdictions for tax resource, income, and poverty disparities and to support the five preceding policies.

Effects on Sprawl, Reinvestment, and Disparities

These six policies, with variations, are necessary to reduce sprawl, increase reinvestment, and limit income disparities. By so doing, a semblance of balance and equilibrium in the parts of metropolitan areas and, therefore, in regions in their entirety may be achieved. By balance and equilibrium, we mean significant ongoing spatial and temporal capacity for reinvestment to occur in neighborhoods and jurisdictions sufficient to mitigate rapid or excessive decline and to support social, economic, physical, and political renewal. Balance and equilibrium may seem modest goals. Within the context of urban history in the United States, however, they are ambitious. These six policies are similar in intent, although they vary some in specifics, to proposals by Rachel Alterman (1997), Peter Calthorpe (1993), Naomi Carmon (1997), Robert Cervero (1998), Anthony Downs (1994), Bruce Katz (1998), Peter Newman and Jeffrey Kenworthy (1999), Myron Orfield (1998), Neal Peirce (1993), David Rusk (1993), and David Varady and Jeffrey Raffel (1995).

Strategic policies deftly applied at key moments seem more practical and persuasive than heavy regulation. The arenas in which the policies must be crafted can be inferred from the previous discussion of four paired concepts. The disjunction between area and power calls for organizational means of coping with large metropolitan regions. The governance and policy system that has emerged in the Portland region is promising, and the emerging Maryland system may have prospects. The growth boundary and annexation policies implemented in Tennessee in 1999 are thus far the most ambitious policies in the United States aimed at restraining sprawl and curbing interjurisdictional income and finance disparities. Some elements of the Minneapolis–St. Paul and Virginia systems may prove fruitful, although in their present form they seem unlikely to produce good results. Goals of the New Urbanism, the Third Regional Plan of New York, and transit metropolises are worth pursuing.

Extreme population disparities among neighborhoods and jurisdictions call for enhanced institutional reinvestment capacity in housing and business. Investments in multimodal transportation infrastructure and sufficient density to make it efficient can nurture the location advantages that old settlements have had during each stage of their evolution and that many continue to have today, as the revival of many city neighborhoods attests. Suburbs also can benefit from investments that reinforce patterns and add density, as the experiences of Alexandria and Arlington, Virginia, indicate. Attachments to places can be nurtured by these policies as well. Modifying single-use suburban districts to include more activities within walking distances of residences may help reduce the pace of suburban decline.

Opportunities

Strategic planning, whether by planners, other public officials, or citizens, should take into account characteristics of the postsuburban era. In our view, the combination of relative income decline in many middle-aged neighborhoods and relative income increases in many older neighborhoods provides insights into probable future conditions. These trends do not foreshadow a general central city revival or uniform suburban decline, but they signal complex conditions and trends in cities and suburbs. Many outcomes are possible, and opportunities are numerous. Public action can make a difference. Changes in government structures and planning processes matter. Private initiatives and alterations in market incentives and regulations influence outcomes. State policies, and perhaps federal policies also, change prospects.

To achieve greater balance and equilibrium among the parts of metropolitan areas, with more stability and sustainability included, greater reinvestment in old and middle-aged housing is essential. Reducing the force of the tyranny of easy development decisions is a necessary companion of a significant increase in housing reinvestment. As Rachel Alterman (1997, 238) observed, some environmentalists should broaden their perspectives: "Decisionmakers and 'green' constituencies in most states are used to focusing on issues such as soil quality and agricultural production capabilities, rather than on urban densities, infill, urban-countryside balance, and regional planning." Clues to combinations of public policies that will lead to greater reinvestment and sustainability can be discerned in western Europe and, to some extent, in Canada. In evaluating the net effect of public policies, the concepts of area and power, population and neighborhood, pattern and density, and space and place can help policymakers predict whether policies will tend toward increasing suburban-exurban sprawl and interjurisdictional disparities or whether they will restrain both sprawl and disparities, leading to more reinvestment and balance.

We expect that better results will occur if public officials, citizens, businesses, and interest groups in cities, suburbs, and exurbs agree on the problems, their causes, the direction of desirable changes, and how those changes can be

The rural hamlet of Häuslingen in Bavaria, Germany, concentrates residential development to preserve farmland productivity. (Synergy/Photography)

Town amenities and streetscape give the farm hamlet of Häuslingen, Bavaria, Germany, an urban feel in the midst of the rural landscape. (Synergy/Photography)

New and rehabilitated residential development near the Potomac waterfront at the end of the block in Alexandria, Virginia.

achieved. If they are correct, as well as in agreement, of course, prospects for success will improve. Disagreement, however, is certain. Taking a positive course of action will require political struggle as well as overcoming conceptual and analytical ambiguities.

A Few Essentials

Reducing the conceptual ambiguities to a few essentials, as we have here, may be both comforting and intimidating. Concluding that goals should focus on reducing sprawl, increasing reinvestment, and restraining spatial income disparities has the virtue, provided it is accurate, of simplicity. These three goals cut to the core of public- and private-sector interactions. They require decisions in central cities, suburbs, and exurbs. Hoping for serious and effective action may seem unrealistically utopian. Each of these goals, however, can be addressed incrementally, within a single jurisdiction, and by federal and state governments without inclusive, coordinated, or otherwise grand schemes within any government's political grasp. The possibility that the federal government might again become engaged with metropolitan problems was foreshadowed in 1999 by candidates for president of the United States testing ideas for coping with suburban sprawl as never before (Mitchell 1999). And as we have seen, in recent years some states have displayed more signs of seeing connections among these problems.

It is essential to remember, however, that the actions required are not by government alone, or even primarily by government, although government action is important and often indispensable. Postsuburban conditions have been achieved through decentralized action dominated by the private sector through business and household decisions. Remedies, if they occur, will evolve through a similar diversity of decentralized decisions.

Decentralized decisions expressed in distorted markets have led to the current briar patch of postsuburban problems. The current era rarely produces new desirable living environments. A great many older neighborhoods, developed during simpler times, have been reviving because more residents have been recognizing the value of these older areas. This greater awareness means that some surprising revivals of old government jurisdictions also may occur. In some instances these will be old central cities; in others they will be old suburbs. These revivals will be savored for the irony of the near dead having been restored to renewed strength. But even in these situations, which are unlikely to represent a majority of old jurisdictions, another outcome is likely to be growing income disparities, to the disadvantage and sometimes despair of middle-aged suburbs. Because of the immense variety of circumstances, the next decades will be filled with danger. But these dangers will be matched with many opportunities.

References

Adams, John S. 1987. *Housing America in the 1980s*. New York: Russell Sage Foundation.

Alonso, William. 1964. The Historic and the Structural Theories of Urban Form: Their Implications for Urban Renewal. *Land Economics* 40: 227–231.

Alterman, Rachel. 1997. The Challenge of Farmland Preservation: Lessons from a Six-Nation Comparison. *Journal of the American Planning Association* 63, 2: 220–243.

Ames, David L., Nevin C. Brown, Mary Helen Callahan, Scott B. Cummings, Sue Marx Smock, and Jerome M. Ziegler. 1992. Rethinking American Urban Policy. *Journal of Urban Affairs* 14, 3/4: 197–216.

Angwin, Julia. 1993. Sometimes, It's a Matter of Size: In Remodeling, Bigger Isn't Always Better. *Washington Post,* March 13.

Argetsinger, Amy. 1999. Beating Poverty in the Classroom. *Washington Post,* May 16.

Audirac, Ivonne, Anne H. Shermyen, and Marc T. Smith. 1990. Ideal Urban Form and Visions of the Good Life: Florida's Growth Management Dilemma. *Journal of the American Planning Association* 56, 4: 470–482.

Baade, Robert A. 1996. Professional Sports as Catalysts for Metropolitan Economic Development. *Journal of Urban Affairs* 18, 1: 1–18.

Baer, William C. 1991. Housing Obsolescence and Depreciation. *Journal of Planning Literature* 5, 4: 323–332.

Bahl, Roy, Jorge Martinez-Vazquez, and David L. Sjoquist. 1992. Central City-Suburban Fiscal Disparities. *Public Finance Quarterly* 20, 4: 420–432.

Banerjee, Tridib. 1993. Market Planning, Market Planners, and Planned Markets. *Journal of the American Planning Association* 59, 3: 353–360.

Banfield, Edward C. 1961. *Political Influence*. Glencoe, IL: Free Press.

———. 1974. *The Unheavenly City Revisited*. Boston: Little, Brown.

Barnes, William R., and Larry C. Ledebur. 1994. *Local Economies: The U.S. Common Market of Local Economic Regions*. Washington, DC: National League of Cities.

———. 1995. Local Economies: The U.S. Common Market of Local Economic Regions. *The Regionalist* 1, 2: 7–32.

Beatley, Timothy. 2000. *Green Urbanism*. Washington, DC: Island Press.

Beatley, Timothy, and Kristy Manning. 1997. *The Ecology of Place: Planning for Environment, Economy, and Community*. Washington, DC: Island Press.

Beatley, Timothy, David J. Brower, and William H. Lucy. 1994. Representation in Comprehensive Planning: An Analysis of the Austinplan Process. *Journal of the American Planning Association* 60, 2: 185–196.

Benjamin, Robert L. Cook 1984. From Waterways to Waterfronts: Public Investment for Cities, 1815–1980, in Richard D. Bingham and John P. Blair, eds., *Urban Economic Development*. Beverly Hills, CA: Sage Publications.

Bentley, Arthur F. 1908. *The Process of Government*. Chicago: University of Chicago Press.

Berger, Howard S., and Robert D. Rivers. 1994. *Greenbelt Historic District Study*. Upper Marlboro, MD: Maryland–National Capital Park and Planning Commission.

Bish, Robert. 1971. *The Public Economy of Metropolitan Areas*. Chicago: Markham.

Blair, John P., Samuel R. Staley, and Zhongcai Zhang. 1996. The Central City Elasticity Hypothesis: A Critical Appraisal of Rusk's Theory of Urban Development. *Journal of the American Planning Association* 62, 3: 345–353.

Blakely, Edward J. 1994. *Planning Local Economic Development*, 2nd ed. Thousand Oaks, CA: Sage Publications.

Blum, Justin. 1998. Loudoun Rethinks Business Growth. *Washington Post*, June 14.

———. 1999. Spotsylvania Plan Stirs Concerns about Sprawl. *Washington Post*, March 6.

Boarnet, Marlon, and Randall Crane. 1997. L.A. Story: A Reality Check for Transit-Based Housing. *Journal of the American Planning Association* 63, 2: 189–204.

Bourne, L. S. 1992. Self-Fulfilling Prophecies? Decentralization, Inner City Decline, and the Quality of Urban Life. *Journal of the American Planning Association* 58, 4: 509–513.

Bradbury, Katharine L., Anthony Downs, and Kenneth A. Small. 1982. *Urban Decline and the Future of American Cities*. Washington, DC: Brookings Institution.

Briffault, Richard. 1996. The Local Government Boundary Problem in Metropolitan Areas. *Stanford Law Review* May: 1115–1171.

Brookings Institution. 1998. *The Future of the Washington, D.C. Metropolitan Area: Reducing the Growing Polarization in the Region*. Washington, DC.

Brower, David J., David R. Godschalk, and Douglas R. Porter, eds. 1989. *Understanding Growth Management: Critical Issues and a Research Agenda*. Washington, DC: Urban Land Institute.

Bryson, John M. 1995. *Strategic Planning for Public and Nonprofit Organizations*. San Francisco: Jossey-Bass.

Bryson, John, and Barbara Crosby. 1992. *Leadership in the Common Good: Tackling Public Problems in a Shared Power World*. San Francisco: Jossey-Bass.

Bryson, John M. and Robert C. Einsweiler, eds. 1988. *Strategic Planning: Threats and Opportunities for Planners*. Chicago: Planners Press.

Bryson, John M. and William D. Roering. 1987. Applying Private-Sector Strategic Planning in the Public Sector. *Journal of the American Planning Association* 53, 2: 9–22.

———. 1988. Initiation of Strategic Planning by Governments. *Public Administration Review* 48: 995–1004.

Burchell, Robert W., and Emilie Schmeidler. 1993. *The Demographic and Social Differences between Central Cities and Suburbs as They Relate to the Job Fulfillment of Urban Residents*. New Brunswick, NJ: Rutgers University, Center for Urban Policy Research.

Burgess, Ernest W. 1925. The Growth of the City, in Robert E. Park, Ernest W. Burgess, and Roderick McKenzie, eds., *The City*. Chicago: University of Chicago Press.

Burnell, James D., and George Galster. 1992. Quality-of-Life Measurements and Urban Size: An Empirical Note. *Urban Studies* 29, 5: 727–735.

Calavita, Nico, and Roger Caves. 1994. Planners' Attitudes Toward Growth: A Comparative Case Study. *Journal of the American Planning Association* 60, 4: 483–500.

Calthorpe, Peter. 1993. *The Next American Metropolis: Ecology, Community, and the American Dream.* New York: Princeton Architectural Press.

Campbell, Alan K., and Seymour Sacks. 1967. *Metropolitan America: Fiscal Patterns and Governmental Systems.* New York: Free Press.

Carmon, Naomi. 1997. Neighborhood Regeneration: The State of the Art. *Journal of Planning Education and Research* 17, 2: 131–144.

Caulfield, Ian, and John Schultz. 1989. *Planning for Change: Strategic Planning in Local Government.* London: Longman.

Cervero, Robert. 1986. *Suburban Gridlock.* New Brunswick, NJ: Rutgers University, Center for Urban Policy Research.

———. 1989. *America's Suburban Centers: The Land-Use Transportation Link.* Boston: Unwin Hyman.

———. 1994. Rail Transit and Joint Development: Land Market Impacts in Washington, D.C. and Atlanta. *Journal of the American Planning Association* 60, 1: 83–94.

———. 1998. *The Transit Metropolis: A Global Inquiry.* Washington, DC: Island Press.

Cervero, Robert, and Roger Gorham. 1995. Commuting in Transit Versus Automobile Neighborhoods. *Journal of the American Planning Association* 61, 2: 210–225.

Charlottesville Department of Community Development. 1996. *Comprehensive Plan.* Charlottesville, VA: Office of the City Manager.

Charlottesville Office of Economic Development. 1994. *Strategic Economic Development Plan.* Charlottesville, VA: Office of the City Manager.

Charlottesville Superintendent of Schools. 1995. *Public Education Strategic Plan.* Charlottesville, VA: Board of Education

Chatterjee, Satyajit. 1996. Taxes, Homeownership, and the Allocation of Residential Real Estate Risks. *Business Review* (Federal Reserve Bank of Philadelphia), September/October.

Chesterfield County Planning Department. 1995. *Aging Neighborhoods: Trends and Response.* February 28.

Choldin, Harvey M., Claudine Hanson, and Robert Bohrer. 1980. Suburban Status Instability. *American Sociological Review* 45, December: 972–983.

Cisneros, Henry G. 1995. *Urban Entrepreneurialism and National Economic Growth.* Washington, DC: U.S. Department of Housing and Urban Development.

Claiborne, William. 1997. Cracks in Portland's 'Great Wall.' *Washington Post,* September 29.

Clark, W. A. V., and James E. Burt. 1980. The Impact of Workplace on Residential Relocation. *Annals of the Association of American Geographers* 70, 1, March: 59–67.

Clay, Philip. 1979. *Neighborhood Renewal: Middle Class Resettlement and Incumbent Upgrading in American Neighborhoods.* Lexington, MA: D.C. Heath.

Coppa, Frank J. 1976. Cities and Suburbs in Europe and the United States, in Phillip C. Dolce, ed., *Suburbia.* New York: Anchor Press.

Corbett, Judith. 1994. *Portland's Livable Downtown: From Auto-Dependence to Pedestrian Independence*. Washington, DC: Surface Transportation Policy Project.

Daniels, Tom. 1999. *When City and Country Collide: Managing Growth in the Metropolitan Fringe*. Washington, DC: Island Press.

Davis, Judy S., Arthur C. Nelson, and Kenneth J. Dueker. 1994. The New 'Burbs': The Exurbs and Their Implications for Planning Policy. *Journal of the American Planning Association* 60, 1: 45–59.

Deane, Daniela. 1999. Sellers See Red after Finishing Out of the Money. *Washington Post*, May 22.

DeGiovanni, Frank F. 1983. Patterns of Change in Housing Market Activity in Revitalizing Neighborhoods. *Journal of the American Planning Association* 49, 1: 22–39.

DeGrove, John M. 1984. *Land, Growth, and Politics*. Chicago: Planners Press.

Devaney, F. John. 1994. *Tracking the American Dream: 50 Years of Housing History from the Census Bureau, 1940 to 1990*. Washington, DC: U.S. Department of Commerce.

Dionne, Jr., E. J. 1999. Daley's Obsession. *Washington Post*, May 18.

Dodge, William R. and Kim Montgomery. 1995. *Shaping a Region's Future: A Guide to Strategic Decision Making for Regions*. Washington, DC: National League of Cities.

Douglass Commission. 1969. *Building the American City*. Washington, DC: U.S. Government Printing Office.

Downs, Anthony. 1973. *Opening Up the Suburbs*. New Haven, CT: Yale University Press.

———. 1981. *Neighborhoods and Urban Development*. Washington, DC: Brookings Institution.

———. 1994. *New Visions for Metropolitan America*. Washington, DC: Brookings Institution.

Drucker, Peter F. 1992. *Managing for the Future: The 1990s and Beyond*. New York: Dutton.

Duarte City Council. 1988. *Duarte Resurgence: Concept to Reality*. City of Duarte, CA.

Eadie, D. C. 1983. Putting a Practical Tool to Powerful Use: The Application of Strategic Planning in the Public Sector. *Public Administration Review* 43: 447–452.

Eagan, Dan, and Ann O'Hanlon. 1999. Inner Suburb Residents Rallying for Slow Growth. *Washington Post*, November 23.

Ehrenhalt, Alan. 1998. Lessons of a Suburban Comeback. *Governing*, December.

Farley, Reynolds. 1964. Suburban Persistence. *American Sociological Review* 29, February: 38–47.

Fladeland, Michael. 1991. Strategic Planning in Communities of Selected North Central States. *Economic Development Review* 9: 76–78.

Forgey, Benjamin. 1999. A Breath of That Old Town Atmosphere. *Washington Post*, March 13.

Fox, Kenneth. 1990. *Metropolitan America: Urban Life and Urban Policy in the United States, 1940 to 1980*. New Brunswick, NJ: Rutgers University Press.

Frey, William H. 1979. Central City White Flight: Racial and Nonracial Causes. *American Sociological Review* 44, June: 425–448.

Gabris, Gerald T. 1992. Strategic Planning in Municipal Government: A Tool for Expanding Cooperative Decision Making between Elected and Appointed Officials. *Public Productivity and Management Review* 16: 77–93.

Gale, Dennis E. 1979. Middle Class Resettlement in Older Urban Neighborhoods: The

Evidence and Implications. *Journal of the American Planning Association* 45, 3: 293–304.

———. 1980. Neighborhood Resettlement: Washington, D.C., in Shirley Laska and Daphne Spain, eds., *Back to the City: Issues in Neighborhood Renovation*. New York: Pergamon Press.

Galster, George C. 1987. *Homeowners and Neighborhood Reinvestment.* Durham, NC: Duke University Press.

Galster, George C., and Sean P. Killen. 1995. The Geography of Metropolitan Opportunity: A Reconnaissance and Conceptual Framework. *Housing Policy Debate* 6, 1: 7–43.

Galster, George C., and Ronald B. Mincy. 1993. Understanding the Changing Fortunes of Metropolitan Neighborhoods: 1980 to 1990. *Housing Policy Debate* 4, 3: 303–352.

Gans, Herbert J. 1961. The Balanced Community: Homogeneity or Heterogeneity in Residential Areas. *Journal of the American Institute of Planners* 27, 3: 176–184.

———. 1967. *The Levittowners: Ways of Life and Politics in a New Suburban Community.* New York: Pantheon Books.

Garcia, Joseph E., David E. Merrifield, and Stephen V. Senge. 1991. Coordinating Strategic Planning for Community Economic Development. *Public Administration Quarterly* 15: 83–105.

Garrah, Michael. 1992. Strategic Planning for Small Communities. *Public Management* 74: 7–9.

Garreau, Joel. 1991. *Edge City: Life on the New Frontier.* New York: Doubleday.

Giddens, Anthony. 1979. *General Problems in Social Theory: Action, Structure, and Contradiction in Social Analysis.* London: Macmillan Press.

Gillette, Jane Brown. 1994. Back to the Future: Utopian Housing Survives in Greenbelt, Maryland. *Historic Preservation,* September/October.

Glastris, Paul. 1992. A Tale of Two Suburbias. *U.S. News & World Report,* November 9.

Goldberg, Michael A., and John Mercer. 1986. *The Myth of the North American City.* Vancouver: University of British Columbia Press.

Goldfield, David. 1979. Suburban Development in Stockholm and the United States: A Comparison of Form and Function, in Ingrid Hammerstrom and Thomas Hall, eds., *Growth and Transformation in the Modern City.* Stockholm: Swedish Council for Building Research.

Goodman, John L. Jr. 1978. *Urban Residential Mobility: Places, People, and Policy.* Washington, DC: Urban Institute.

———. 1979. Reasons for Moves out of and into Large Cities. *Journal of the American Planning Association* 45, 4: 407–416.

Goodman, Peter S. 1998. Glendening vs. Suburban Sprawl. *Washington Post,* October 6.

Gordon, Gerald. 1993. *Strategic Planning for Local Government.* Washington, D.C.: International City/County Management Association.

Gordon, Peter, and Harry W. Richardson. 1989. Gasoline Consumption and Cities: A Reply. *Journal of the American Planning Association* 55, 3: 342–346.

Gordon, Peter, Harry W. Richardson, and Myung-Jin Jun. 1991. The Commuting Paradox: Evidence from the Top Twenty. *Journal of the American Planning Association* 57, 4: 416–420.

Gottdiener, Mark. 1985. *The Social Production of Urban Space.* Austin: University of Texas Press.

Grunwald, Michael. 1999. Harlem Finally Rides the Economy's 'A' Train: As Crime Falls, a Retail Boom Arrives. *Washington Post,* May 5.

Guest, Avery M. 1978. Suburban Social Status: Persistence or Evolution. *American Sociological Review* 43: 251–264.

Guest, Avery M. and George H. Nelson. 1978. Central City/Suburban Status Differences: Fifty Years of Change. *Sociological Quarterly* 19, Winter: 7–23.

Gurwitt, Rob. 1999. The State vs. Sprawl. *Governing,* January.

Guterbock, Thomas M., William H. Lucy, and Joanne Cohoon. 1996. *Location Preferences of Lynchburg Area Homebuyers.* Charlottesville, VA: University of Virginia Center for Survey Research.

Haggerty, Maryann. 1999. Things Are Looking Up. *Washington Post,* February 13.

Halachmi, Arie, ed. 1993. Strategic Planning: From a Concept to Application. *Public Administration Quarterly* 17: 127–200.

Hall, Peter. 1988. *Cities of Tomorrow: An Intellectual History of Urban Planning in the Twentieth Century.* New York: Basil Blackwell.

Hartshorn, Truman A. 1992. *Interpreting the City: An Urban Geography.* New York: John Wiley and Sons.

Hartshorn, Truman A., and Peter O. Muller. 1989. Suburban Downtowns and the Transformation of Metropolitan Atlanta's Business Landscape. *Urban Geography* 10: 375–395.

Harvard Joint Center for Housing Studies. 1999. *The State of the Nation's Housing 1998.* Cambridge: Harvard University.

Harvey, David. 1989. *The Urban Experience.* Baltimore: Johns Hopkins University Press.

Havemann, Judith. 1998. Public Housing's Upscale Idea. *Washington Post,* April 18.

Healey, Patsy. 1996. Planning Through Debate: The Communicative Turn in Planning Theory, in Scott Campbell and Susan Fainstein, eds., *Readings in Planning Theory.* Cambridge, MA: Blackwell Publishers.

———. 1997. The Revival of Strategic Spatial Planning in Europe, in Patsy Healey, Abdul Khakee, Alain Motte, and Barrie Needham, eds., *Making Strategic Spatial Plans: Innovation in Europe.* London: UCL Press.

Heidenheimer, Arnold J., Hugh Heclo, and Carolyn Adams. 1983. *Comparative Public Policy: The Politics of Social Choice in Europe and America.* New York: St. Martin's Press.

Heilbrun, James. 1987. *Urban Economics and Public Policy,* 3rd ed. New York: St. Martin's Press.

Henig, Jeffrey R. 1980. Gentrification and Displacement within Cities: A Comparative Analysis. *Social Science Quarterly* 61, 3: 638–653.

Hennepin County Office of Planning and Development. 1983. *Strategic Planning Manual.* Hennepin County, MN.

Herschberg, Theodore. 1995. The Case for Regional Cooperation. *The Regionalist* 1, 3: 13–32.

Hill, David R. 1992. America's Disorganized Organicists. *Journal of Planning Literature* 7, 1: 3–21.

Hill, Richard Child. 1974. Separate and Unequal: Governmental Inequality in the Metropolis. *American Political Science Review* 68: 1557–1568.

Hogan, Dennis P., and Evelyn M. Kitagawa. 1985. The Impact of Social Status, Family

Structure, and Neighborhood on the Fertility of Black Adolescents. *American Journal of Sociology* 90, 4: 825–855.

Home Building & Remodeling Network. 1999. The 1996–97 Cost vs. Value Report. http://www.remodeling.hw.net/consumer/1997/costval/intro2.sl.

Howard, Ebenezer. 1965. *Garden Cities of Tomorrow.* Cambridge: MIT Press.

Hoyt, Homer. 1939. *The Structure and Growth of Residential Neighborhoods in American Cities.* Washington, DC: Federal Housing Administration.

Innes, Judith E. 1992. Group Processes and the Social Construction of Growth Management. *Journal of the American Planning Association* 58, 4: 440–453.

Institute for Public Service and Advisory Commission on Intergovernmental Relations. 1998. *Growth Policy, Annexation, and Incorporation under Public Act 1101 of 1998: A Guide for Community Leaders.* Knoxville: University of Tennessee.

Jackson, Kenneth T. 1985. *Crabgrass Frontier: The Suburbanization of the United States.* New York: Oxford University Press.

Jargowsky, Paul A. 1997. *Poverty and Place: Ghettos, Barrios, and the American City.* New York: Russell Sage Foundation.

Jenne, Kurt. 1986. Strategic Planning: Taking Charge of the Future. *Popular Government* Spring: 36–43.

Kantor, Paul, and H.V. Savitch. 1993. Can Politicians Bargain with Business: A Theoretical and Comparative Perspective on Urban Development. *Urban Affairs Quarterly* 29, 2: 230–255.

Kasarda, John D. 1993a. Economics and Technology, in *Land Use in Transition: Emerging Forces and Issues Shaping the Real Estate Environment.* Washington, DC: Urban Land Institute.

———. 1993b. Inner-City Concentrated Poverty and Neighborhood Distress: 1970–1990. *Housing Policy Debate* 4, 3: 253–302.

Katz, Bruce. 1998. *Reviving Cities: Think Metropolitan.* Washington, DC: Brookings Institution.

Kaufman, Jerome, and Harvey Jacobs. 1987. A Public Planning Perspective on Strategic Planning. *Journal of the American Planning Association* 53(1): 23–33.

Kelbaugh, Doug, ed. 1989. *The Pedestrian Pocket Book: A New Suburban Design Strategy.* New York: Princeton Architectural Press.

Kemp, Roger L. 1992. *Strategic Planning for Local Governments.* Chicago: Planners Press.

Kling, Rob, Spencer Olin, and Mark Poster, eds. 1991. *Postsuburban California: The Transformation of Orange County Since World War II.* Berkeley: University of California Press.

Knapp, Gerrit, and Arthur C. Nelson. 1992. *The Regulated Landscape: Lessons on State Land Use Planning from Oregon.* Cambridge, Mass.: Lincoln Institute of Land Policy.

Knight, Richard V., and Gary Gappert. 1984. Cities and the Challenges of the Global Economy, in Richard D. Bingham and John P. Blair, eds., *Urban Economic Development.* Beverly Hills, CA: Sage Publications.

Knox, Paul L. 1994. *Urbanization: An Introduction to Urban Geography.* Englewood Cliffs, NJ: Prentice-Hall.

Kreitner, Ronald M. 1997. *Smart Growth Areas Act: An Overview.* Annapolis, MD: Maryland Office of Planning.

Kunstler, James Howard. 1996. *Home from Nowhere.* New York: Simon & Schuster.

Ladd, Helen. 1994. Spatially Targeted Economic Development Strategies: Do They Work? *Cityscape* 1, 1: 193–219.

Lamb, Richard F. 1983. The Extent and Form of Exurban Sprawl. *Growth and Change* 14, 1, January: 40–47.

Langdon, Philip. 1994. *A Better Place to Live: Reshaping the American Suburb.* Amherst: University of Massachusetts Press.

Lauria, Mickey. 1998. A New Model of Neighborhood Change: Reconsidering the Role of White Flight. *Housing Policy Debate* 9, 2: 395–424.

Ledebur, Larry C., and William R. Barnes. 1992. *City Distress, Metropolitan Disparities and Economic Growth.* Washington, DC: National League of Cities.

Lee, Barrett A., and Peter B. Wood. 1991. Is Neighborhood Racial Succession Place-Specific? *Demography* 28, 1: 21–40.

Leinberger, Christopher B. 1995. The Changing Location of Development and Investment Opportunities. *Urban Land,* May: 31–34.

Lemann, Nicholas. 1994. The Myth of Community Development. *New York Times Sunday Magazine,* January 2.

Leven, Charles. 1979. Economic Maturity and the Metropolis' Evolving Physical Form, in Gary A. Tobin, ed., *The Changing Structure of the City.* Beverly Hills, CA: Sage Publications.

Levin, Charles, and Jonathan H. Mark. 1977. Revealed Preferences for Neighborhood Characteristics. *Urban Studies* 14: 147–159.

Levinson, David M., and Ajay Kumar. 1994. The Rational Locator: Why Travel Times Have Remained Stable. *Journal of the American Planning Association* 60, 3: 319–332.

Lindblom, Charles E. 1965. *The Intelligence of Democracy: Decision Making Through Mutual Adjustment.* New York: The Free Press.

Lipton, Eric. 1997. Fairfax's Older Neighborhoods Gain an Ally. *Washington Post,* August 31.

Lipton, Eric, and Robert O'Harrow, Jr. 1997. Fairfax Board Backs Half-Billion-Dollar Rebuilding of Schools. *Washington Post,* April 9.

Logan, John R. 1976. Industrialization and the Stratification of Cities in Suburban Regions. *American Journal of Sociology* 82, 2: 333–348.

Logan, John R., and Mark Schneider. 1982. Governmental Organization and City/Suburb Income Inequality, 1960–1970. *Urban Affairs Quarterly* 17, 3: 303–318.

Long, Larry H., and Celia G. Boertlein. 1976. *The Geographical Mobility of Americans: An International Comparison.* Washington, DC: U.S. Government Printing Office.

Long, Norton. 1959. The Local Community as an Ecology of Games. *American Journal of Sociology* 65, 2: 251–261.

Lowi, Theodore J. 1979. *The End of Liberalism,* 2nd ed. New York: W.W. Norton.

Lowry, Ira. 1960. Filtering and Housing Standards: A Conceptual Analysis. *Land Economics* 36: 362–379.

Lucy, William H. 1975. Metropolitan Dynamics: A Cross-National Framework for Analyzing Public Policy Effects in Metropolitan Areas. *Urban Affairs Quarterly* 11, 2: 155–185.

———. 1988. *Close to Power: Setting Priorities with Elected Officials.* Chicago: Planners Press.

———. 1992. Recognizing Reality Is the First Step Toward a Solution. *Planning,* July.

———. 1994a. If Planning Includes Too Much, Maybe It Should Include More. *Journal of the American Planning Association* 60, 3: 305–318.

———. 1994b. *Report on Suburban Income Disparities in 24 Large Metropolitan Areas.* Charlottesville, VA: University of Virginia, Department of Urban and Environmental Planning, School of Architecture.

———. 1994c. *Richmond: Social Decline Despite Economic Vitality.* Charlottesville, VA: University of Virginia, Department of Urban and Environmental Planning, School of Architecture.

Lucy, William H., and David L. Phillips. 1992. *Declining Cities: Patterns and Trends in 150 Metropolitan Areas, 1960 to 1980.* Charlottesville, Va.: University of Virginia, Department of Urban and Environmental Planning, School of Architecture, Metropolitan Strategic Public Policies Project.

———. 1994. *Metropolitan Sprawl in the Richmond-Petersburg Region: City Decline, Suburban Transition, and Farmland Loss.* Richmond, Va.: Report to the Virginia Commission on Population Growth and Development.

———. 1995a. *The Economic Competitiveness of Virginia's Metropolitan Areas.* Richmond, Va.: Report to the Center for Urban Development, Virginia Commonwealth University.

———. 1995b. *Assets, Liabilities, and Economic Performance in Metropolitan Areas in the South, 1970 to 1990.* Richmond, Va.: Report to the Center for Urban Development, Virginia Commonwealth University.

———. 1996a. *The Post-Suburban Era in the Hampton Roads Region: City Decline, Suburban Transition, and Farmland Loss.* Richmond, Va.: Report to the Center for Urban Development at Virginia Commonwealth University.

———. 1996b. *The Post-Suburban Era in the Richmond-Petersburg Region: City Decline, Suburban Transition, and Farmland Loss.* Richmond, Va: Report to the Center for Urban Development at Virginia Commonwealth University.

———. 1996c. *The Post-Suburban Era in the Northern Virginia Region: City Decline, Suburban Transition, and Farmland Loss.* Richmond, Va.: Report to the Center for Urban Development at Virginia Commonwealth University.

———. 1997. The Post-Suburban Era Comes to Richmond: City Decline, Suburban Transition, and Exurban Growth. *Landscape and Urban Planning* 36, Jan/Feb: 259–275.

Luger, Michael I. 1996. Quality-of-Life Differences and Urban and Regional Outcomes: A Review. *Housing Policy Debate* 7, 4: 749–771.

Luger, Michael I., and Harvey A. Goldstein. 1991. *Technology in the Garden: Research Parks and Regional Economic Development.* Chapel Hill: University of North Carolina Press.

Maclaren, Virginia W. 1996. Urban Sustainability Reporting. *Journal of the American Planning Association* 62, 2: 184–202.

Marx, Leo. 1964. *The Machine in the Garden.* New York: Oxford University Press.

Masotti, Louis H., and Jeffrey K. Hadden, eds. 1973. *The Urbanization of the Suburbs.* Beverly Hills, CA: Sage Publications.

Massey, Douglas S., and Nancy A. Denton. 1993. *American Apartheid: Segregation and the Making of the Underclass.* Cambridge: Harvard University Press.

Mayer, Susan E. 1991. How Much Does a High School's Racial and Socioeconomic Mix Affect Graduation and Teenage Fertility Rates, in Christopher Jencks and Paul Peterson, eds., *The Urban Underclass.* Washington, DC: Brookings Institution.

McCarron, John. 1998. Tip of the Iceberg: Only a Matter of Time before Some Suburbs Come Tumbling Down. *Chicago Tribune,* April 27.

McConnell, Grant. 1966. *Private Power and American Democracy.* New York: Alfred A. Knopf.

McLean, Mary L., and Kenneth P. Voytek. 1992. *Understanding Your Economy: Using Analysis to Guide Local Strategic Planning.* Chicago: Planners Press.

McQuilken, Jeffrey. 1998. Sustainability in Alexandria, Virginia. Unpublished paper. Charlottesville, VA: University of Virginia, Department of Urban and Environmental Planning.

Metropolitan Washington Council of Governments. 1995. *Analysis of Households and Jobs per Acre 1990 and 2020.* Round 5.2 Cooperative Forecasts. Washington, DC: Metropolitan Washington Council of Governments, December 4.

Michelson, William. 1977. *Environmental Choice, Human Behavior, and Residential Satisfaction.* New York: Oxford University Press.

Milwaukee Strategic Planning Team. 1996. *City of Milwaukee Strategic Plan, Working Draft #1.* Milwaukee, WI.

Mitchell, Alison. 1999. 2 Parties Seek to Exploit Nonstop Suburban Boom. *New York Times,* May 4.

Moe, Richard, and Carter Wilkie. 1997. *Changing Places: Rebuilding Community in the Age of Sprawl.* New York: Henry Holt.

Molotch, Harvey, and John Logan. 1987. *Urban Outcomes.* Berkeley: University of California Press.

Montgomery County Department of Park and Planning. 1997. *Planning for Growth in Montgomery County, Maryland.* Silver Spring, MD: Maryland–National Capital Park and Planning Commission.

Morrill, Richard L. 1991. Myths about Metropolis, in John F. Hart, ed., *Our Changing Cities.* Baltimore: Johns Hopkins University Press.

Mumford, Lewis. 1961. *The City in History.* New York: Harcourt, Brace & World.

Muth, Richard F. 1969. *Cities and Housing.* Chicago: University of Chicago Press.

Nasser, Haya El. 1999. Soaring Housing Costs Are Culprit in Suburban Poverty. *USA Today,* April 28.

National Association of Home Builders. 1997. *Housing Facts, Figures and Trends.* Washington, DC: National Association of Home Builders.

Nelson, Arthur C. 1992. Characterizing Exurbia. *Journal of Planning Literature* 6, 4, May: 350–368.

Nelson, Arthur C., and Terry Moore. 1996. Assessing Growth Management Policy Implementation: Case Study of the United States' Leading Growth Management State. *Land Use Policy* 13, 4: 241–259.

Newman, Peter, and Jeffrey R. Kenworthy. 1989. Gasoline Consumption and Cities: A Comparison of U.S. Cities and a Global Survey. *Journal of the American Planning Association* 55, 1: 24–37.

———. 1999. *Sustainability and Cities: Overcoming Automobile Dependence.* Washington, DC: Island Press.

Noah, Harold J., and Joel D. Sherman. 1979. *Educational Financing and Policy Goals for Primary Schools*. Organization for Economic Co-operation and Development: Centre for Educational Research and Innovation.

Norquist, John, and Bret Schundler. 1999. Saving Main Street. *Washington Post,* June 5.

North Carolina General Statutes 1987 (1993 Supplements). Article 4, Corporate Limits, Section 160A.

Norton, Phillip. 1984. *The British Polity.* London: Longman Publishing.

Nunn, Samuel, and Mark S. Rosentraub. 1997. Dimensions of Interjurisdictional Cooperation. *Journal of the American Planning Association* 63, 2: 205–219.

Nyden, Philip, John Lukehart, Michael T. Maly, and William Peterman. 1998. Neighborhood Racial and Ethnic Diversity in U.S. Cities. *Cityscape* 4, 2: 1–19.

Orfield, Gary, and Susan E. Eaton. 1996. *Dismantling Desegregation: The Quiet Reversal of* Brown v. Board of Education. New York: New Press.

Orfield, Myron. 1997. *Metropolitics*. Washington, DC: Brookings Institution.

———. 1998. *Chicago Metropolitics: A Regional Agenda for Members of the U.S. Congress.* Washington, DC: Brookings Institution.

Ostrom, Vincent, Charles M. Tiebout, and Robert Warren. 1961. The Organization of Government in Metropolitan Areas: A Theoretical Inquiry. *American Political Science Review* LV, December: 831–842.

Ottensmann, John R. 1995. Requiem for the Tipping-Point Hypothesis. *Journal of Planning Literature* 10, 2, November: 131–141.

Ozawa, Connie. 1991. *Recasting Science: Consensual Procedures in Public Policymaking.* Boulder, CO: Westview Press.

Pae, Peter. 1999. Annandale's First Step to a Fresh Look. *Washington Post,* January 14.

Pae, Peter, and Todd Shields. 1999. Rising Home Values Mirror Demand for Close-In Addresses. *Washington Post,* March 9.

Pan, Philip P., and Peter Pae. 1999. Welcome to Koreatown: Immigrant Community Flourishing in Annandale. *Washington Post,* May 16.

Parsons, K. C. 1990. Clarence Stein and the Greenbelt Towns: Settling for Less. *Journal of the American Planning Association* 56 (1): 161–183.

Peirce, Neal. 1993. *Citistates: How Urban America Can Prosper in a Competitive World.* Washington, DC: Seven Locks Press.

Peterson, Paul E. 1981. *City Limits*. Chicago: University of Chicago Press.

Phillips, David L., and William H. Lucy. 1996. *Suburban Decline Described and Interpreted, 1960 to 1990: 554 Suburbs in 24 Largest Urbanized Areas.* Richmond, Va.: Report to the Center for Urban Development, Virginia Commonwealth University.

Plugge, Patricia. 1993. Self-Help Strategic Planning for Small Communities. *Economic Development Review* 11: 14–17.

Popkin, Susan J., James E. Rosenbaum, and Patricia M. Meaden. 1993. Labor Market Experiences of Low-Income Black Women in Middle-Class Suburbs: Evidence from a Survey of Gautreaux Program Participants. *Journal of Policy Analysis and Management* 12, 3: 556–573.

Popular Mechanics. "Renovating Your Home: A Worthwhile Investment." Reprinted in *Charlottesville Daily Progress,* May 24.

Porter, Douglas R. 1997. *Managing Growth in America's Communities.* Washington, DC: Island Press.

Porter, Michael E. 1995. The Competitive Advantage of the Inner City. *Harvard Business Review,* May/June: 55–71.

Premus, Robert. 1984. Urban Growth and Technological Innovation, in Richard D. Bingham and John P. Blair, eds., *Urban Economic Development.* Beverly Hills, CA: Sage Publications.

President's Council of Economic Advisors. 1996. *President's Annual Economic Report, 1949–1996.* Washington, DC: U.S. Council of Economic Advisors.

Raspberry, William. 1993. The Brighter Side of American Schools. *Washington Post,* October 8.

"Real Estate Notes." 1998. Existing Homes Sales Up, Maintain Record Pace. *Washington Post,* June 27.

Reich, Robert B. 1991. *The Work of Nations.* New York: Alfred A. Knopf.

Reid, Alice, and Michael D. Shear. 1999. Tysons Loop, 7 Stations in Metro Expansion Plan. *Washington Post,* January 23.

Richardson, Harry W., and Peter Gordon. 1993. Market Planning: Oxymoron or Common Sense? *Journal of the American Planning Association* 59, 3: 347–352.

Richman, Roger, and James B. Oliver. 1997. The Urban Partnership and the Development of Virginia's New Regional Competitiveness Act. *The Regionalist* 2,1: 3–19.

Risse, EM. 1998a. *The Shape of Loudoun's Future.* Fairfax, VA: Synergy/Planning.

———. 1998b. *Testimony before the Joint Subcommittee on Land-Development Patterns and Ways to Address Demands for Increased Services and Infrastructure Resulting from Residential Growth.* Fairfax, VA: Synergy/Planning, September 24.

———. 1999. *It Is Time to Fundamentally Rethink METRO and Mobility in the National Capital Region.* Fairfax, VA: Synergy/Planning, January 25.

Robinson, W. S. 1950. Ecological Correlations and the Behavior of Individuals. *American Sociological Review* 15, 3: 351–357.

Rosen, Sherwin. 1979. Wage-Based Indices of Urban Quality of Life, in Mahlon R. Straszheim and Peter M. Mieszkowski, eds., *Current Issues in Urban Economics.* Baltimore: Johns Hopkins University Press.

Rosenbaum, James E. 1995. Changing the Geography of Opportunity by Expanding Residential Choice: Lessons from the Gautreaux Program. *Housing Policy Debate* 6, 1: 231–270.

Rosenbaum, James E., Marilyn J. Kulieke, and Leonard S. Rubinowitz. 1988. White Suburban Schools' Responses to Low-Income Black Children: Sources of Successes and Problems. *Urban Review* 20, 1: 28–41.

Rossi, Peter H., and Anne B. Shlay. 1982. Residential Mobility and Public Policy Issues: 'Why Families Move' Revisited. *Journal of Social Issues* 38, 3: 21–34.

Rubenstein, James M. 1978. *The French New Towns.* Baltimore: Johns Hopkins University Press.

Rusk, David. 1993. *Cities without Suburbs.* Baltimore: Johns Hopkins University Press.

Samadd, Michelle, 1998. More Homeowners Tapping Savings for Springtime Fix-Ups. *Bank Rate Monitor.* http://www.Bankrate.com

Santa Barbara Board of Supervisors. 1996. *Strategic Plan for the County of Santa Barbara.* Santa Barbara, CA.

Sasaki Associates, Peter Breitling, JHK Associates, White Mountain Survey, and ZHA

Associates. 1993. *Transit and Pedestrian Oriented Neighborhoods Design Study, Part II: Reports of the Consultants.* Silver Spring, MD: Maryland–National Capital Park and Planning Commission.

Savitch, H. V., David Collins, Daniel Sanders, and John P. Markham. 1993. Ties That Bind: Central Cities, Suburbs, and the New Metropolitan Region. *Economic Development Quarterly* 7, November: 341–355.

Sawicki, David S., and Patrice Flynn. 1996. Neighborhood Indicators: A Review of the Literature and an Assessment of Conceptual and Methodological Issues. *Journal of the American Planning Association* 62, 2: 165–183.

Schattschneider, E. E. 1960. *The Semi-Sovereign People.* New York: Holt, Rinehart and Winston.

Scheer, Brenda C., and Mintcho Petkov. 1998. Edge City Morphology: A Comparison of Commercial Centers. *Journal of the American Planning Association* 64, 3: 298–310.

Schelling, Thomas. 1963. *The Strategy of Conflict.* New York: Oxford University Press.

Schnore, Leo F. 1972. *Class and Race in Cities and Suburbs.* Chicago: Markham.

Schubert, Glendon A. 1960. *The Public Interest: A Critique of the Theory of a Political Concept.* Glencoe, IL: Free Press.

Simon, Herbert A. 1997. *Administrative Behavior: A Study of Decision-Making in Administrative Organizations,* 4th ed. New York: Free Press.

Sipress, Alan. 1999. Changes Near Beltway, Not on It. *Washington Post,* May 27.

Smith, Randolph. 1996. Saving the Suburbs. *Richmond Times-Dispatch,* January 14.

So, Frank. 1984. Strategic Planning: Reinventing the Wheel? *Planning* 50: 16–21.

Solomon, Arthur P., and Kerry D. Vandell. 1982. Alternative Perspectives on Neighborhood Decline. *Journal of the American Planning Association* 48(1): 81–98.

Spain, Daphne. 1980. Black-to-White Successions in Central City Housing: Limited Evidence of Central City Revitalization. *Urban Affairs Quarterly* 15, June: 381–396.

———. 1989. Why Higher Income Households Move to Central Cities. *Journal of Urban Affairs* 11, 3: 283–299.

Speare, Alden, Jr., Sidney Goldstein, and William H. Frey. 1974. *Residential Mobility, Migration and Metropolitan Change.* Cambridge, Mass.: Ballinger.

Spinner, Jackie. 1999. Upping the Ante in Enterprise Zones. *Washington Post,* March 14.

Stover, Mark E., and Charles Leven. 1992. Methodological Issues in the Determination of Quality of Life in Urban Areas. *Urban Studies* 29, 5: 737–754.

Streib, Gregory, and Theodore H. Poister. 1990. Strategic Planning in U.S. Cities: Patterns of Use, Perceptions of Effectiveness and an Assessment of Strategic Capacity. *American Review of Public Administration* 20: 29–44.

Syed, Anwar. 1966. *The Political Theory of American Local Government.* New York: Random House.

Teaford, Jon C. 1979. *City and Suburb: The Political Fragmentation of Metropolitan America, 1850–1970.* Baltimore: Johns Hopkins University Press.

Temkin, Kenneth, and William Rohe. 1996. Neighborhood Change and Urban Policy. *Journal of Planning Education and Research* 15, 3: 159–170.

Tiebout, Charles M. 1956. A Pure Theory of Local Expenditures. *Journal of Political Economy* 64: 416–424.

Tobin, Gary A., and Dennis R. Judd. 1982. Moving the Suburbs to the City: Neighborhood Revitalization and the 'Amenities Bundle.' *Social Science Quarterly* 63, 4: 771–778.

Toner, Robin. 1992. Los Angeles Area Warning, Americans Fear. *New York Times,* May 11.

Truman, David B. 1951. *The Governmental Process.* New York: Alfred A. Knopf.

U.S. Advisory Commision on Intergovernmental Relations. 1987. *The Organization of Local Public Economies.* Washington, D.C.: U.S. Government Printing Office.

U.S. Bureau of the Census. 1956. *Statistical Abstract of the U.S. 1956.* Washington, DC: U.S. Government Printing Office.

———. 1962 (and 1992). *County Business Patterns 1990, Virginia.* Washington, DC: U.S. Government Printing Office.

———. 1992. *1990 Census of Population, General Population Characteristics United States.* Washington, DC: U.S. Government Printing Office.

———. 1993. *Census of Population and Housing 1990.* Washington, DC: U.S. Government Printing Office.

———. 1996. *USA Counties.* CD-ROM.

———. 1997a. (and 1990 through 1996). *American Housing Survey.* Washington, DC: U.S. Government Printing Office.

———. 1997b. *County Business Patterns 1995.* Washington, DC: U.S. Government Printing Office.

U.S. Bureau of Economic Analysis. 1994. *Regional Economic Information Service.* Washington, DC: U.S. Government Printing Office.

Underwood, Julie K., and Deborah A. Verstegen, eds. 1990. *The Impacts of Litigation and Legislation on Public School Finance.* New York: Harper & Row.

Van Der Meer, Leo. 1998. Red Octopus, in Wolfgang Blaas, ed., *A New Perspective for European Spatial Development Policies.* Aldershot, Great Britain: Ashgate Publishing.

Vance, Jr., James E. 1990. *The Continuing City: Urban Morphology in Western Civilization.* Baltimore: Johns Hopkins University Press.

Vandell, Kerry D. 1995. Market Forces Affecting Spatial Heterogeneity among Urban Neighborhoods. *Housing Policy Debate* 6, 1: 103–140.

Varady, David P. 1986. *Neighborhood Upgrading: A Realistic Assessment.* Albany: State University of New York Press.

Varady, David P., and Jeffrey A. Raffel. 1995. *Selling Cities: Attracting Homebuyers through Schools and Housing Programs.* Albany: State University of New York Press.

Verhovek, Sam Howe. 1999. Fighting Sprawl, A County Gets Intel to Limit Jobs. *New York Times,* June 9.

Virginia Commission on Local Government. 1992. *Report on the Comparative Revenue Capacity, Revenue Effort, and Fiscal Stress of Virginia's Cities and Counties, 1989/90,* Richmond, Va.:June.

Virginia Department of Social Services. 1994 (and 1988). *Social Welfare Statistics.* Richmond, VA.

Voith, Richard. 1992. City and Suburban Growth: Substitutes or Complements? *Business Review* (Federal Reserve Bank of Philadelphia), September/October.

Wald, Matthew L. 1987. Managing Gentrification: A Challenge to the Cities. *New York Times,* September 13.

Wallis, Allan. 1995. Regional Governance and the Post-Industrial Economy. *The Regionalist* 1, 3: 1–11.

Warner, Paul D. 1989. Alternative Strategies for Economic Development: Evidence from Southern Metropolitan Areas. *Urban Affairs Quarterly* 24, 3: 389–411.

Warner, Sam Bass. 1962. *Street Car Suburbs: The Process of Growth in Boston, 1870–1900.* Cambridge: Harvard University Press.

West Hartford Town Council. 1994. *A Plan for the Future: Recommendations of Public Actions for the 21st Century.* West Hartford, CT.

Wicker, Jake. 1999. *Characteristics of the North Carolina System of Government,* at the Commission on the Condition and Future of Virginia Cities-Summit II, June 7.

Wilson, William Julius. 1987. *The Truly Disadvantaged.* Chicago: University of Chicago Press.

Yaro, Robert, and Tony Hiss. 1996. *A Region at Risk: The Third Regional Plan for the New York–New Jersey–Connecticut Metropolitan Area.* Washington, DC: Island Press.

Zielinski, Heinz. 1983. Regional Development and Urban Policy in the Federal Republic of Germany. *International Journal of Urban and Regional Research* 7, March: 72–89.

Zuiches, James J. 1981. Residential Preferences in the United States, in Amos H. Hawley and Sara Mills Mazie, eds., *Nonmetropolitan America in Transition.* Chapel Hill: University of North Carolina Press.

Index

About the Authors

William H. Lucy is professor and David L. Phillips is associate professor in the Department of Urban and Environmental Planning at the University of Virginia. They have collaborated on numerous studies of metropolitan sprawl, city-suburb income disparities, and decline in middle-aged city and suburban neighborhoods. Professor Lucy is the author of *Close to Power: Setting Priorities with Elected Officials* (Planners Press).

Island Press Board of Directors

Susan E. Sechler, *Chair*
Vice President, Aspen Institute

Henry Reath, *Vice-Chair*
President, Collector's Reprints, Inc.

Drummond Pike, *Secretary*
President, The Tides Foundation

Robert E. Baensch, *Treasurer*
Professor of Publishing, New York University

Catherine M. Conover

Gene E. Likens
Director, The Institute of Ecosystem Studies

Dane Nichols
Chairman, The Natural Step, U.S.

Charles C. Savitt
President, Center for Resource Economics/Island Press

Victor M. Sher
Environmental Lawyer

Peter R. Stein
Managing Partner, Lyme Timber Company

Richard Trudell
Executive Director, American Indian Resources Institute

Wren Wirth President, The Winslow Foundation